TEXAS IN THE MIDDLE EIGHTEENTH CENTURY

STUDIES IN SPANISH COLONIAL HISTORY AND ADMINISTRATION

BY

HERBERT EUGENE BOLTON

PUBLISHED IN COOPERATION WITH

THE TEXAS STATE HISTORICAL ASSOCIATION

UNIVERSITY OF TEXAS PRESS, AUSTIN & LONDON

Standard Book Number 292-70034-2
Library of Congress Catalog Card No. 62-15151
Originally published in 1915 as Volume 3 of
The University of California Publications in History
Texas History Paperback, 1970
Printed in the United States of America

PREFACE

In the middle eighteenth century Texas occupied an important position on the northeastern frontier of New Spain. Down to 1762 it was the buffer province between France and Spain in their contest for empire on this continent. After that date it reflected in a most interesting way the fundamental changes effected by the Louisiana cession. The keynote to the period following the transfer was reorganization.

In spite of its importance, the history of Texas after 1731 has been little known, and has been regarded as more or less barren. As a matter of fact, the province in that period experienced much activity, and its history offers many and varied interests. The interval between 1731 and 1745 was one of testing the original establishments rather than of founding new ones. The period from 1745 to 1762 was one of numerous expansion projects looking to the occupation of new frontiers and to the provision of new elements of defence. The next quarter century was characterized by an interesting series of readjustments occasioned by Spain's acquisition of Louisiana.

The present volume is not a history; it is, rather, a collection of special studies, closely related in time and subject-matter, and designed to throw light upon a neglected period in the history of one of the most important of Spain's northern provinces. The *raison d'être* of the volume is to be sought especially in Parts II-V. Since these studies are detached, however, it has seemed necessary to preface them by a general sketch of the history of Texas during the half-century within which they fall. Such a procedure has seemed the more appropriate because there is available no satisfactory general account of the period. This method has resulted unavoidably in some repetition, since some portions of the general sketch are mainly summaries of the special studies which follow.

While the papers here published are historical in their treatment, they contain much that should be of interest to the ethnologist and to the student of actual government in the Spanish provinces. It is only through a detailed study of such episodes as those which are treated here that we shall be able to determine the true character of Spanish colonial government. This consideration has led the writer to give full space to administrative as well as to narrative history. In the same way, since most of the subjects treated are to a large extent questions of Indian policy, due attention has been given to matters of importance regarding the Indian situation.

The special studies here presented are based almost exclusively upon manuscript sources, chiefly in the archives of Mexico, Spain, and Texas, and for the most part hitherto unknown and unused. The assembling of these materials, during a period of thirteen years, has been the greater part of my task. My quest has been as romantic as the search for the Golden Fleece. I have burrowed in the dust of the archives of Church and State in Mexico City, in a dozen Mexican state capitals, in Natchitoches, Louisiana, and in numerous places in Texas. The distance travelled in my pursuit of documents would carry me around the globe. I have lived with the *padres* in ruinous old monasteries in out of the way villages in the mountains of Mexico. I count among the treasures of my personal archive the letters of introduction from ambassadors, secretaries of state, and governors; cardinals, archbishops, bishops, friars, and parish priests, who have smoothed my way.

My researches have taken me not only into foreign archives in quest of records, but also over hundreds of miles of old trails in Texas, Louisiana, and other parts of the Southwest, in search of topographical and archaeological data, for light on the historical tale. I have ridden by team long distances over the Old San Antonio Road, where no railroads run, and on horseback in mud fetlock deep, over the historic trail from Natchitoches, the old French outpost of Louisiana, to Los Adaes (now Robeline), the Spanish outpost of Texas. In a successful search for the lost San Sabá mine, I have ridden and tramped in the hills of the Llano and the Colorado. To examine the ruins and map out the sites of the forgotten missions near Rockdale, I have several times driven and tramped back and forth, up and down the valley of the San Gabriel. But in the discovery of lost sites, I count as my cardinal joy the identification of the location of La Salle's fort, on the Garcitas River, near the shores of Lavaca Bay.

Transcripts of the major portion of the documents cited are contained in my own collection. For most of the work of gathering in Spain and for much of it in Mexico, I am greatly indebted to Mr. W. E. Dunn, of the University of Texas. For collecting in Spain I am also under obligations to Professor Chas. E. Chapman and Dr. Wm. Lytle Schurz, of the University of California. Extensive portions of the volume have been published from time to time in the Texas State Historical Association *Quarterly* and *The Southwestern Historical Quarterly*. The permission of the editors to reprint them here, with revision, is highly appreciated.

ERRATA

Page 2, line 5 from bottom, *for* Nadaco *read* Natsoos.

Page 21, line 9, *for* missions *read* mission.

Page 28, at end of line 1, *for* period *read* comma; and, in line 2, *for* In *read* in.

Page 32, line 5, *for* settlements *read* missionaries.

Page 89, line 7 from bottom, *for* Tlescaltecos *read* Tlascaltecos.

CONTENTS

ix

I.   A GENERAL SURVEY
(1731-1788)

INTRODUCTION

TEXAS, A BUFFER PROVINCE

1. *The extent of the province.*—Geographically considered, Texas in the eighteenth century was a somewhat indefinite and changing entity. The original Texas was the territory of the Hasinai (Texas) Indians, between the Trinity and the Red rivers, and included much of what is now Louisiana. Early in the eighteenth century the boundaries were extended westward to include the settlements on the San Antonio River and Matagorda Bay. With the founding of the province of Nuevo Santander, in 1746, the western boundary of Texas was officially fixed at the lower Medina River, but toward the interior limits were indefinite, and a question frequently debated in the middle of the century was whether the San Sabá district belonged to Texas, Coahuila, or New Mexico. Later in the century the Nueces River, in part of its extent, came to be regarded as the boundary.

Before the middle of the century one point of the eastern boundary was tentatively fixed a little west of the Red River, at Arroyo Hondo and Gran Montaña. On the coast Spain fortified and held the mouth of the Trinity as another point on the French border, though claiming territory further eastward. After the acquisition of Louisiana by Spain, a long but indecisive discussion was held by Spanish officials looking toward the moving of the eastern boundary westward to the Sabine River.[1] On the north, Texas was generally regarded by Spain as extending to the Red River, but before the Louisiana cession most of

---

[1] This matter is discussed in *Expediente sobre Comercio entre las Prov^as. de la Luisiana y Texas* (MS in the Archivo General y Público, Mexico, Provincias Internas, vol. 182).

what is now northeastern Texas was under French rather than Spanish influence, and even after that event it was for a time controlled by Spain through Louisiana rather than through Texas agencies. During all of this period the country west of the upper Nueces and of the San Sabá district and now included in Texas was connected historically with Coahuila, Nueva Vizcaya, and New Mexico rather than with Texas. Generally speaking, then, Texas in the middle eighteenth century comprised the eastern half of the present State of Texas and a part of western Louisiana.

2. *The Indians.*[2]—The history of Texas in the eighteenth century was determined in no small part by the distribution and interrelations of its native tribes. The province was inhabited by several well-marked groups of Indians. In northeastern Texas lived two confederacies of the great Caddoan linguistic stock, the Hasinai and the Caddo proper. The Hasinai lived on the Angelina and upper Neches rivers, and comprised some ten or more tribes, of which the best known were the Hainai, Nacogdoche, Nabedache, Nasoni, and Nadaco. They were a settled people, who had been living in the same region certainly ever since the time of La Salle, and probably long before. They dwelt in scattered villages, practiced agriculture to a considerable extent, and hunted buffalo on the western prairies. The Caddo, whose culture was similar, lived northeast of the Hasinai, along the Red River, between Natchitoches and the region of Texarkana. Of this group the best known tribes were the Adaes, Natchitoches, Yatasí, Petit Cado, Cadodacho, Nassonite, and Nadaco. It was in the midst of these two confederacies, particularly of the Hasinai, that the Spanish establishments of eastern Texas had been planted.

South of the Hasinai, on the lower Trinity, Neches, and

<hr />

[2] For this section, see Bolton, *De Mézières*, I, 18–28, and map, frontispiece; Hodge, F. W., *Handbook of American Indians* (Washington, 1907–1910), under the names of the different tribes.

Sabine rivers, were the Bidai, Orcoquiza, Deadose, and Attacapa, members of the Attacapan family. They had little agriculture, and lived mainly by hunting and fishing. Along the coast, between the Trinity and Nueces rivers, dwelt a large group of Karankawan tribes, including the Coco, Cujane; Karankawa, Coapite and Copane. They were without agriculture, lived by fishing and hunting, were fierce cannibals, and were extremely warlike. It was in their midst that the mission and presidio of La Bahía had been established at first. Inland from the Karankawan tribes and west of the Hasinai and Bidai roamed several Tonkawan bands, of which the Tonkawa, Mayeye, and Yojuane were the best known.

Farther down the coast lived numerous unclassified tribes, who may or may not have been of the Karankawan stock. By 1731 they were little known, but in the course of the middle half of the eighteenth century they became an object of attention to the missionaries of Texas, Coahuila, and Nuevo Santander. Inland from the last-mentioned tribes, along the Camino Real between San Antonio and the Rio Grande, roamed numerous weak, unsettled bands, many of whom spoke a common language, which was recorded in 1760 by Father Bartolomé García, of the mission of San Francisco de la Espada, and has become known as the Coahuiltecan. It was from these last tribes that the missions at San Antonio and San Juan Bautista principally drew in the early days.

At the opening of the eighteenth century the greater portion of western Texas had been the home of the Apache, a people who lived mainly by following the buffalo. Early in the century the Comanche, likewise followers of the buffalo, began to drive them southward, and they in turn to crowd the Coahuiltecan and other tribes toward the coast. The easternmost division of the Apache family, the Lipan, in the middle of the century had their central haunts on the Llano, San Sabá, and upper Colorado rivers. By this time the Witchita, another group of southward-moving tribes, had entered Texas, and had settled on the upper Red, Brazos, Trinity and Sabine rivers. The Witchita were a semi-agricultural people of the Caddoan stock. The principal divisions known in Texas were the Taovayas, Tawakoni, Kichai, and Yscanis. As distinguished from the Apache and the coast tribes, the Indians of northern and eastern Texas were collectively spoken of as the "Norteños," or Nations of the North.

The foregoing native groups were of concern to the Spaniards mainly for one or more of three reasons. All were objects of solicitude to the missionaries. The tribes of eastern and northern Texas were exposed to French influence, which must be counteracted. The Apache, Comanche, Witchita, and Karankawa were powerful, warlike, and hostile tribes, to be feared by the settlements. All played most interesting rôles in the history of the province. Perhaps the most significant feature of the entire Indian situation was the implacable hatred for the Apache felt by the Nations of the North. On this hostility turned much of the history of Texas for several decades.

3. *The settlements in 1731.*—At the close of the first third of the eighteenth century Texas was distinctly a buffer province. The two principal factors which made it worth while at the time to occupy the district were its French neighbors and its native inhabitants. By 1731 Spanish claims to most of the region had been vindicated and the outlines of the province drawn, but little more than this had been accomplished. The points of occupation at that time fell into two distinct groups, one lying between the Neches and the Red rivers—the original Texas; another on the San Antonio and Guadalupe rivers. On the Rio Grande at San Juan Bautista there was a third group, which, although within the province of Coahuila, was intimately connected with the development of the region between the Rio Grande and the San Antonio rivers.

The capital of the province was Los Adaes, a military post fifteen miles west of the Red River and facing the French settlement of Natchitoches. Half a league away was the mission of Los Adaes; to the westward, near the Angelina River, the mission of Nacogdoches; between the two, on Ayish Bayou, that of Los Ais. These missions were administered by Franciscan friars of the College of Guadalupe de Zacatecas. Until 1730 another presidio had been maintained on the Angelina River, and near by there had been three other missions, administered by the College of Santa Cruz de Querétaro, but in the year named the presidio had been suppressed and the missions removed to the San Antonio River.

The center and defence of the western settlements was the presidio of San Antonio de Béxar, founded in 1718. By its side stood the mission of San Antonio de Valero (later known as the Alamo), established in the same year. Within a stretch of twelve miles down the river there were four other missions, named Concepción, San José, San Juan Capistrano, and San Francisco de la Espada, and located in the order here given. The second, founded in 1720, was administered by the College of Guadalupe de Zacatecas. The other three were the missions removed in 1730 from eastern Texas and re-established in March, 1731, on the San Antonio. They and the mission of San Antonio de Valero were in charge of the College of Santa Cruz de Querétaro. Near the presidio and the last-named mission was the villa of San Fernando de Béxar, founded in 1731 of Canary Islanders and a nucleus of other settlers already on the ground.

On the Guadalupe River, near the site of the present city of Victoria, were the presidio of Nuestra Señora de Loreto, or La Bahía, and the mission of Espíritu Santo de Zúñiga. These establishments had been founded some nine years before on the Garcitas River, near Lavaca Bay, and in 1726 had been moved inland. The mission was under the Zacatecan College of Guadalupe. Round about San Antonio and between there and La Bahía cattle ranches were springing into existence.

On the Rio Grande, below modern Eagle Pass, stood the presidio of San Juan Bautista and the missions of San Juan Bautista and San Bernardo, all of which had been established at the close of the seventeenth or the opening of the eighteenth century. These two missions were administered by the College of Santa Cruz de Querétaro.

As yet the Texas establishments proper had scarcely had an opportunity to acquire economic independence, and with one or two exceptions they depended largely upon supplies brought from the outside. From Mexico, Saltillo, and San Juan Bautista, therefore, came pack-trains loaded with provisions for missions, garrisons, and settlers. Saltillo was the principal market in which food articles were procured. For the eastern establishments many of the supplies were obtained from the neighboring French of Natchitoches, and others from the agricultural Indians of the surrounding country. The roads were beset by hostile Indians, and travellers, pack-trains, and mail carriers usually went under military escort.

4. *The secular administration.*[3]—As an administrative unit, Texas was a part of the Kingdom of New Spain. In civil and military affairs the province was subject directly to the viceroy and to the Audiencia of Mexico, and in ecclesiastical matters to the archbishop of Guadalajara. The government of Texas, apart from the missions, was almost wholly military. The villa of San Fernando de Béxar, the only civil community in the province, had its own cabildo and a modicum of self-government.[4] The official head of the province was the governor. He held his office

---

[3] This section is based mainly upon the materials used in the course of the detailed studies in Parts II–V. Only the barest summary is attempted here, hence detailed references are unnecessary.

[4] Austin, Mattie Alice, ''The Municipal Government of San Fernando de Béxar, 1730–1800,'' in Texas State Historical Association *Quarterly*, VIII, 277–352; Jones, O. Garfield, ''Local Government in the Spanish Col-

by royal appointment; *ad interim* governors might be appointed by the viceroy. The governor was *gobernador* and *capitan general* of his province and captain of the presidio of Los Adaes, the capital. In these capacities, he exercised both civil and military authority. In the course of the period under survey, one of the governors at least, Pedro del Barrio, had a much more comprehensive title, for he was, in addition, *comandante* of the *gobiernos* of Coahuila and Pensacola.

All important matters of administration, such as the founding of new missions, new presidios, and new colonies, or the making of military campaigns, were referred directly to the viceroy. He in turn customarily sought the advice of the fiscal of the Royal Audiencia and of the *auditor de guerra.* In case these two functionaries disagreed, or in matters of unusual moment, a *junta de guerra y hacienda,* composed of leading officials of the different branches of the administration, was called. In all matters of importance the decisions of the viceroy were made subject to royal approval, but it frequently happened that the act for which approval was asked had already been performed. In ordinary affairs of provincial administration the fiscal and the *auditor de guerra* really controlled the government, for the viceroy usually despatched such business with his *"Como dice el señor fiscal"* ("As the fiscal says"). Men like Dr. Andreu, fiscal of the Audiencia, and the Marqués de Altamira, *auditor de guerra,* really had more to do with the actual administration of Texas than the viceroys under whom they served.

Checks upon the governors were provided through *visitas,* or inspections, and through the *residencia,* or investigation, at the end of the governor's term. As a rule the *residencia* was formal, but sometimes, as in the cases of Sandoval and Barrios, investigations were serious matters.

---

onies as Provided by the Recopilación de Leyes de las Indias,'' in *Southwestern Historical Quarterly,* XIX, 65–90; Blackmar, F. W., *Spanish Institutions of the Southwest,* Chapter VIII.

In the half-century between 1731 and 1780 Texas had thirteen governors and governors *ad interim*.[5]   The average term of
office was about four years, but it varied from a few months in
the case of Boneo y Morales to about eight years in the cases of
Barrios y Jáuregui, Martos y Navarrete, and Ripperdá.   As a
rule the governors were professional soldiers.   Orobio Bazterra
had been a merchant at Saltillo; Winthuisen and García Larios
seem also to have been civilians.   Martos y Navarrete had been
a naval officer with the rank of *teniente de navío*.   The rest were
soldiers.   Two of them, Bustillo and Sandoval, came to Texas
with the rank of captain.   Of the others, two were lieutenant-
colonels, four were colonels, and one a general.   Some of the
men were of high social rank.   Boneo y Morales was a Knight
of the Order of Santiago.   Barrio was *alcalde provincial* of the
Santa Hermandad of all New Spain, and Ripperdá was a baron.
On the whole, judging by its occupants, the office of governor
increased in importance, and its military character was emphasized as time went on.

Not only were the men professional soldiers, but they belonged also to what might be termed a class of professional office-
holders.   In several cases they came from governorships and were
sent to others after serving in Texas.   Bustillo was promoted to

---

[5] A useful sketch of the governors of Texas down to 1772 is given in
Antonio Bonilla's "Brief Compendium of the Events which have Occurred in the Province of Texas" (written in 1772; translated by Elizabeth Howard West in the Texas State Historical Association *Quarterly*,
VIII, 9–72).   The following is a list of governors during the period, with
their dates, based on the list in Bolton, *Guide to Materials for the History
of the United States in the Principal Archives of Mexico* (Washington,
1913), 478–479: Juan Antonio de Bustillo y Zevallos (1730–1734); Manuel
de Sandoval (1734–1736); Carlos Benites Franquis de Lugo (1736–1737);
Fernández de Jáuregui y Urrutia, governor of Nuevo León, governor
extraordinary and *visitador* of Texas (1737); Prudencio de Orobio Bazterra, *ad interim* (1737–1740); Tomas Felipe Winthuisen (1741–1743);
Justo Boneo y Morales (1743–1744); Francisco García Larios, *ad interim*
(1744–1748); Pedro del Barrio Junco y Espriella (1748–1750); Jacinto
de Barrios y Jáuregui (1751–1759); Angel de Martos y Navarrete (1759–
1767); Hugo Oconor, *ad interim* (1767–1770); The Baron de Ripperdá
(1770–1778); Domingo Cabello (1778–1786); Rafael Martínez Pacheco
(1787–1790).

the office from the captaincy of the presidio of La Bahía. Sandoval and Martos had been governors of Coahuila, and Barrio
of Nuevo León; Franquis held the office while waiting for the
governorship of Tlascala. After leaving Texas Barrio returned
to the governorship of Nuevo León; Barrios went to that of
Coahuila, and Ripperdá became governor of Comayagua in Central America. Oconor became *comandante inspector* of the
Interior Provinces. Probably none of the governors were great
men, but, being placed on a military frontier with slender forces,
they had little opportunity to distinguish themselves in the only
field where distinction was possible. Their contemporary renown
depended much upon the views of partisan writers.

The administration of Texas, as of the other provinces, was
corrupt with "graft." The positions of governor and presidial
commander were made attractive largely by the opportunity
which they afforded for making money in addition to the fixed
salaries. The pay of soldiers was made chiefly in food, clothing,
and equipment, purchased by the governor and commanders, and
charged to the presidial soldiers at enormous profits. Thus the
post of governor or captain was scarcely less that of merchant
than of soldier. To give a single example, it was charged that in
the eight years of his incumbency Governor Martos y Navarrete
made over $80,000 in profits on the goods which he sold his
company at Los Adaes, not to mention his gains from trade with
Indians, missions, and French neighbors and from his private
stock ranch, all conducted, without private expense, through the
labor of his soldiers.[6]

The government of New Spain was highly centralized in
theory, but the effects of the centralization were greatly lessened
by the fact of distance. Through the right of petition, which
was freely exercised, the local leaders in the frontier province of

---

[6] *Cargos, que en Vistta de las Declaraziones Juradas, rezividas a la
Compañia del Presidio de los Adaes*, etc., September 23, 1767, and related
documents pertaining to the inspection made by the Marqués de Rubí.

Texas often exerted a high degree of initiative in government, and, on the other hand, through protest and delay they could and frequently did defeat mandates of the higher authorities.

5. *The mission system.*—The missions, like the presidios, were characteristically and designedly frontier institutions. From the standpoint of the Church the principal work of the missionaries was to spread the Faith, first, last, and always. But the missions were agencies of the State as well as of the Church, and were supported by the State to serve the State's purposes. As viewed by the government, the work of the missionaries was to assist in extending, holding, Christianizing, and civilizing the frontiers. By going among the outlying tribes they were often most useful explorers and diplomatic agents. By gaining an influence over their neophytes, they counteracted foreign influence among them, deterred them from invading the interior settlements, and secured their aid in holding back more distant tribes. But the Spanish policy looked to the civilizing of the Indian as well as to the holding of the frontier, and it saw in the mission the best possible agency for bringing this about. Since Christianity was the basic element of European civilization, and since it was the acknowledged duty of the State to extend the Faith, the first task of the missionary was to convert the heathen. But neither the State nor the Church in Spanish dominions considered the work of the missionary as ending here. If the Indian were to become either a worthy Christian or a desirable subject he must be disciplined in the rudiments of civilized life. This task likewise was turned over to the missionary. Hence the missions were designed not only as Christian seminaries, but also as so many industrial and agricultural schools.

The central feature of every successful Spanish mission was the Indian pueblo, or village. If he were to be disciplined, the Indian must be kept in a definite spot where discipline could be imposed upon him. The settled Indians, such as the Pueblo Indians of New Mexico, could be instructed in their native towns, but the wandering or scattered tribes must be assembled and established in pueblos, and kept there by force if necessary. To make the Indians self-supporting as soon as possible, and to afford them the means of discipline, the missions were provided with communal lands for gardens, farms, and ranches, and with workshops in which to practice the crafts.

Religious instruction and industrial training were imparted by a definite routine of tasks, prescribed by the superior authorities but administered with much practical sense and regard for local circumstances.[7] To aid the missionaries in keeping good order, and, indeed, to give the Indians training in civic life, the mission villages were organized into communities with limited self-government, modelled in form on the Spanish town, but closely supervised, of course, by the Spaniards. As a symbol of force, and to afford protection for the missionaries and mission Indians, as well as to hold the frontier, presidios, or garrisons, were established near by; and to assist the missionaries in their work of disciplining and instructing the neophytes each mission was usually provided with a guard of two or three soldiers.[8]

---

[7] By the Laws of the Indies the missionaries were enjoined to instruct the Indians in their native languages, and in the colleges professorships were established to teach them. But, in the first place, the native languages usually lacked terms in which properly to convey the meaning of the Christian doctrine. In the second place, on some frontiers there were so many dialects that it was impossible for the friars to learn them. This was eminently true in the region between the Rio Grande and San Antonio, where there were more than twenty dialects or languages regularly spoken. As a rule, all mission Indians except those adult upon arrival, soon spoke Spanish. Hence instruction was given in Spanish, reliance being placed when necessary upon native interpreters. In 1760 Father Bartolomé García published a *Manual* for religious instruction in the Coahuiltecan language which served for about twenty tribes represented at the missions on the San Antonio and lower Rio Grande. The form outlined for the confessional in this book reflects the horrible moral conditions with which the missionaries had to contend in their work of civilization.

[8] Lamar Papers, Nos. 33 and 37. The toil and care necessary to discipline the barbarian Indians is reflected in a memorial by the guardian

Designed as frontier institutions, the missions were intended to be temporary. As soon as his work was done on one frontier, the missionary was expected to pass on to another. In the theory of the law, within ten years each mission was to be turned over to the secular clergy and the common lands distributed among the Indians. But this law was based upon experience with the civilized natives of central Mexico and of Peru; on the northern frontier, among the barbarian tribes, a longer period of tutelage was always found necessary.

The missions of Texas were conducted by two Franciscan missionary colleges *de Propaganda Fide,* of Querétaro and Zacatecas, excepting the Apache missions, where part of the work was done by friars from the sister college of San Fernando de México. The colleges, in turn, were supervised by a *comisario general* of the Franciscan Order, exercising authority in all New Spain. The government of each college was in the hands of a guardian and a *discretorio,* composed of several members of the house. The missions were grouped into presidencies. Thus the Zacatecan missions in eastern Texas and those on the San Antonio constituted separate presidencies, as did the Querétaran missions on the San Antonio and those on the Rio Grande. Each college sent out an occasional *visitador,* or inspector. In their local affairs the missionaries were subject to their president, who

---

of the College of Santa Cruz to the viceroy, November 12, 1729: "All the Indians of those missions which are in the care of the presidio of the Rio Grande del Norte and San Antonio de Vejar are at present most barbarous, since some are recently converted Indians and others under catechism to receive holy baptism. At present, as is notorious, they are incapable of governing themselves. It is necessary that the missionary religious take them out to the work of planting, and that he go about with them in planting and in harvesting, and that he take care that they guard the stock, that he count them, that he go with them to work on the buildings, and in fine, in all temporal occupations; for experience shows that if the religious does not go about in this work and leaves it in their care, everything is lost and they go at once to the forest. Of the truth of this the soldiers of those parts will testify. Every day it is necessary to give rations to each Indian, for if the food is left to their disposition in two days it is exhausted."

freely conferred with his subordinates but was not responsible to them.

As a rule the annual stipends (*sínodos*) of the missionaries, $450 each, were paid by the royal government, which bore also the initial expense of founding a mission (*ayuda de costa*). A marked exception to this rule was the munificent gift of Don Pedro de Terreros in 1757 for the support of missions among the Apache. The stipends were spent by the *síndicos* of the respective colleges for annual mission supplies (*avíos*), which were sent to the frontier by mule trains in charge of lay brothers, acting in the capacity of conductors of supplies.[9]

Quarrels between the missionaries and the secular authorities were almost constant, in Texas as elsewhere. It is difficult to determine whether the seat of the trouble was the imperfect definition and distribution of authority provided by the administrative system, or the pride, "headiness," and insubordination in the Spanish character. Whatever the cause, wrangling was a chronic and disastrous malady in all the frontier Spanish provinces.

---

[9] Excellent chapters on the mission system, especially as exemplified in California, will be found in the learned work by Fray Zephyrin Engelhardt, *The Missions and Missionaries of California* (San Francisco, 1908–1915). The view presented above, however, has been arrived at entirely independently.

CHAPTER I

THE PROVINCE ON TRIAL
(1731-1745)

1. *The Work of the Missionaries.*[1]—The decade and a half which elapsed after 1731 was not for Texas a period of multiplication of new settlements; it was, instead, a period in which the original establishments were on trial. It was, however, a period of no small interest, as exhibiting the conditions of a Spanish buffer colony planted on the French border and on a difficult Indian frontier.

The most conspicuous work of the period was that done by the missionaries. No new missions were founded in the interval, but the missionaries in charge of the missions already established instructed their neophytes with commendable zeal, improved the material plants of their missions, and sought new recruits among many new bands constantly more removed from the mission centers. During the fifteen years a score or more priests, not to mention the lay brothers, labored at the San Antonio missions alone. The central figure among them was Fray Benito Fernández de Santa Ana, who arrived in 1731 and most of the time thereafter until 1750 was president of the four Querétaran missions. After living three years at Mission San Antonio de Valero, he made his headquarters at Concepción. Scarcely less conspicuous was Father Francisco Mariano de los Dolores y Viana, who arrived in 1733 and remained until 1763,

---

[1] The best printed account of the missionary work in Texas down to 1746 is that contained in Espinosa, *Chrónica Apostólica y Seráfica de Todos los Colegios de Propaganda Fide de Esta Nueva-España* (Mexico, 1746); at this point, however, the work is very brief and general. A manuscript account is contained in Fray Juan Agustín de Morfi, *Memorias para la Historia de Texas* (ca. 1781). Most of the data for this period, however, still lie buried in unpublished records.

succeeding Father Santa Ana as president. His residence was at Mission San Antonio de Valero. Among the missionaries of this period were two who later became martyrs. These were Fathers José Ganzábal and Alonso Giraldo de Terreros, one of whom was killed on the San Gabriel River in 1752, the other on the San Sabá in 1758. None did a more valuable service for history than diligent Fray Martín García, of Mission San Antonio, who wrote a long disquisition concerning the management of Indians, and copied in his own handwriting many of the older records of the missions to preserve them from destruction. The painstaking reports and correspondence of the missionaries as a whole will always stand as a monument to their training and intelligence, and, though as yet little known, will constitute a priceless treasury of history and ethnology.[2]

Notable among the efforts with the outlying bands were those of Father Mariano de los Dolores, who after 1733 made frequent visits to the Tonkawan tribes near the middle Brazos River. In 1739 a general epidemic swept through the missions at San Antonio, after which there was renewed activity among the distant tribes. In the year named the Tacame, after having deserted Mission San Francisco, were taken to that of San Antonio de Valero. About 1745 Father Juan Mariano de Molina visited the Cujane, Karankawa, Manos de Perro, and Piguique, tribes living in the main down the coast to the southwest of the Guadalupe River. In the year last named the missionaries of San Juan

---

[2] A partial list of the missionary priests at San Antonio is given in Schmitt, E. J. P., *A List of Franciscan Missionaries in Texas, 1528–1859* (Austin, 1901). It contains some evident errors in transcribing and confuses Spanish and English forms. Those named for the years 1731–1745 are the following: Alonso Giraldo de Terreros, Benito Fernández de Santa Ana, Juan Hurtado de Jesus María, Ignacio Antonio Cyprian, Joseph Gonzales, Saluad de Amaya, Gabriel de Vergara, Francisco Joseph de Frías, Henrique Arquellos (*sic*) de la Concepción, Phelipe Miguel Suarez Espinosa, Joseph Hurtado de Jesus María, Joseph Guadalupe Prado, Joachim Camargo de Santa Anna, Diego Martín García, Lud. (elsewhere Juan) Maria Ano de Molina, Joseph Francisco de Ganzábal, Juan de los Angeles.

Bautista and San Bernardo prepared an expedition to the natives of the lower Rio Grande, but it was prevented by a revolt at Lampazos in which the coast tribes joined.[3] The foregoing are only a few of the recorded missionary expeditions made during the period. Besides these there must have been numerous other journeys equally notable. This is clearly shown by the data contained in the mission records. At Mission San Antonio de Valero alone no less than forty different bands or tribes were represented by the baptisms between 1731 and 1745. In general they included people living between the middle Colorado and the Rio Grande, the San Antonio Road and the Gulf coast. The original tribes at the mission of Concepción were three—the Pajalat, Siquipil, and Tilpacopal—but by 1745 members of at least fifteen others had been attracted thither.[4] The tribes taken to the three new missions—that is, those transferred to San Antonio in 1731—during this period were mainly from the coastwise district rather than from the interior.

These facts suggest long and weary journeys by the missionaries, not only to attract new heathen, but also to recover fugitives. On this point President Santa Ana wrote in 1740: ''The conversions are not difficult, but they are vexatious, for it is necessary to deal with them like a mother instructing a child. Until after five, or six, or seven years they are unable to enter into a

---

3 Fray Fernández de Santa Ana, *Descripción de las Misiones del Colegio de la Santa Cruz en el Rio de San Antonio, Año de 1740*, MS in *Memorias de Nueva España*, XXVIII, 200–207.

4 The list of tribes at Mission San Antonio includes the Apion, Chulujan, Chaguantapam, Censoc, Caguas, Cocomeioje, Charro, Emet, Juamaca, Juncatas, Mesquite, Merhuan, Mecocoma, Pacha, Payaya, Peana, Pachaug, Patagua, Papanac, Pazac, Pamaya, Paxcaz, Patou, Pacuache, Pojosay, Quepana, Quinso, Secmoco, Siaguan, Sijame, Timamar, Tuu, Tacame, Tena, Tetzino, Ujuiap, Zacpo, Zerquan, Zana (MS baptismal records of the Mission of San Antonio de Valero. For a description of these records see Bolton, H. E., in the Texas State Historical Association *Quarterly*, X, 1–11). See also Bolton, in Hodge, *Handbook of American Indians*, II, 424–426. At Mission Concepción there were Patumaca, Pachalaque, Patalca, Tiloja, Xarame, Pamache, Cujan, Pacoa, Guapica, Pausana, Payaya, Pastia, Tacame, Orejon, and Chayopin (MS marriage records of Mission Concepción, *Testimonio de Asiento de Misiones, 1731*).

perfect understanding; and thus it is rare that one does not flee to the forests twice or three times, and so far that they sometimes go inland as many as a hundred leagues. But we have the patience to seek them, and as soon as they see the father they come like lambs. This is one of the worst vexations which the ministers suffer, for, without course or path, guided only by an Indian of the mission, they journey sometimes one hundred, sometimes two hundred leagues, suffering accidents and danger from the enemy, who kill only to eat.'"⁵

That Father Santa Ana did not exaggerate is shown by actual instances of runaways which here and there come to light during the period between 1731 and 1737.⁶ It is clear that the fugitives did not always ''submit like lambs'' to the soldiers, small escorts of whom usually accompanied the missionaries, and that they sometimes fought, and even committed suicide by drowning or jumping over cliffs, rather than return to the flogging which they feared they would receive as punishment for their flight. Troubles over desertions were especially bad in 1737. In June all of the one hundred and thirty-seven neophytes of Mission San Francisco de la Espada absconded in a body. In June and August most of those of San Juan fled, with some from Con-

---

⁵ Santa Ana, *Descripción*, 202.

⁶ We learn, for example, that the Pampopas fled and were pursued to their rancherías near the ''Old Ford'' of the Medina, where a few were recovered. The Tiopanes escaped to their haunts below the Guadalupe crossing, and none could be retaken. More than two hundred Tacames from Mission Espada returned to their ranchería on the Colorado where a few were secured by Father Ysasmendi and the soldiers; the rest escaped by swimming across the river. The Pastías fled to their homes at the Atascoso spring, and when pursued took asylum in a marsh, where many were recaptured. At another time the Tiopanes and Pastías fled to Rio Blanco in the hill country north of San Antonio, and took refuge on a high cliff which their pursuers could not ascend. In the winter of 1735–36 most of the two hundred or more neophytes of Mission San José deserted. Part of them were recovered, but again they fled, this time to Ranchería Grande, near the Brazos. In August, 1737, there remained in the mission only about fifteen men, besides women and children. In 1736 a part of the Pampopas, from Mission San José, were fugitives on the Rio Frío. (Correspondence concerning pursuit of fugitives in Lamar Papers nos. 33 and 37; investigation of complaints of neophytes, in A. G. M., Misiones, vol. 21).

cepción. After several unsuccessful attempts had been made to recover them, Father Ysasmendi, of San Juan, escorted by ten soldiers, made an expedition lasting twenty-one days, by which he regained most of his charges. Similarly, by means of a journey lasting nearly a month, most of the fugitives from San Francisco were recovered by Father Mariano de los Dolores and a military escort.[7]

In spite of all these tribulations, the missions in the vicinity of San Antonio and on the Rio Grande made a good showing. At Mission San Antonio de Valero, during the first decade after its establishment in 1718, there had been about two hundred and fifty baptisms; by 1740 there had been eight hundred and thirty-seven. At the same time two hundred and fifty persons had been baptized at Concepción, four hundred and thirty-one at San José, two hundred and seventy-eight at San Juan, and two hundred and thirty-three at San Francisco. There were then living at these five missions two hundred and sixty-one, one hundred and twenty, ninety-five, two hundred and eighteen, and one hundred and twenty, respectively, or a population of more than eight hundred Indians, most of whom had been baptized.[8]

Five years later nine hundred and eighty-one persons had been baptized at Mission San Antonio, five hundred and eighteen at Concepción, five hundred and fifteen at San Juan, and four hundred and twenty-seven at San Francisco. Thus the four Querétaran missions had baptized nearly seven hundred neophytes in the past five years. By this time the older missions of San Juan Bautista and San Bernardo had baptized more than a thousand Indians each, many of whom came from north of the Rio Grande. For this period statistics of the Mission of Espíritu Santo are not available. There were now living (1745) at the four Querétaran missions at San Antonio eight hundred

---

[7] Lamar Papers, nos. 33 and 37.

[8] Fray Gabriel de Vergara, *Padron de Baptismo*, 1734; Santa Ana, *Descripión*, 1740.

and eighty-five Indians, of whom one hundred and thirty-five were still unbaptized; in the two missions on the Rio Grande there were resident nine hundred and forty Indians, of whom three hundred and eighty-nine were still unbaptized. The unbaptized neophytes were mainly newcomers, and their number is an indication of the current activity among the outlying tribes. The discrepancies between the total numbers baptized and the numbers remaining at the missions is explained partly by runaways, but chiefly by deaths, for the majority of the adult baptisms were made at the deathbed, while disease at all times made sad havoc among the children.

At the same time, the missions on the San Antonio, the Guadalupe, and the Rio Grande were able to give a good account of themselves on the side of temporalities. It must be remembered in this connection, as well as in considering the spiritual work, that most of what was accomplished with these untamed savages at each mission was the work of one or two missionaries, assisted by two or three soldiers of indifferent qualities and zeal.

By 1745 all of the missions at San Antonio had good irrigating ditches and raised maize, beans, melons, calabashes, sweet potatoes, and other vegetables in abundance, often having a surplus to sell to the garrison. The maize crop of the four Querétaran missions in 1745 was eight thousand bushels. Cotton was raised regularly at Mission San Antonio and sometimes at San Francisco. On the ranches of the four missions combined, over nine thousand head of horses, sheep, and goats were pastured. At Mission San Antonio, at least, there were shops for spinning and weaving cotton and woolen fabrics. In all these respects the two missions on the Rio Grande, being older, were much in advance of those at San Antonio. At the mission of Espíritu Santo several years had been spent, after the transfer to the Guadalupe River, in an attempt to build a dam across that stream as a preliminary to irrigation. Meanwhile the missionary had supported his charges on provisions purchased with his annual stipend. But this did not suffice, and during the greater part of the year the Indians sought their own food on the prairies and in the forests. In 1736, however, the attempt to build the dam was abandoned, and agriculture without irrigation was at once successfully established. Thereafter the Indians raised, by their own labor, plentiful maize and vegetables, and cared for large herds of stock.

The buildings of the missions had not yet taken their permanent form, and yet substantial beginnings had been made. In 1740 President Santa Ana wrote that the mission of San Antonio de Valero was better able to withstand an invasion by the enemy than any of the three presidios of the province. This, of course, was only a relative excellence. At this mission the cornerstone of a stone and mortar church was laid on May 8, 1744. Meanwhile another building was being occupied temporarily. According to a report of the next year, the Indian pueblo consisted of houses, some of adobe, some of thatch, ranged in two rows separated by a water ditch, and surrounded by a wall. The missionaries lived in a small monastery containing in the upper story three cells and a *vivienda,* or suite of living-rooms. There were also a weaving room where the women and old men worked, a granary, offices, and various other apartments. In the weaving room *sayal, mantas* and *terlinga* were manufactured from wool and cotton. The buildings of the other Querétaran missions were quite similar to those just described.[9] Concerning Mission

---

[9] Santa Ana to Fray Pedro del Barco, March 26, 1740; *Carta del P. Muñoz* [*Santa Ana*] *Del estado de las cosas de adentro,* 1740; Fray Francisco Xavier Ortiz, *Visita de las Misiones hecha de orden de N. M. R. P. Comm⁰. Gral. Fr. Juan Fogueras . . . 1745.* At Concepción, in 1745, a stone church was about half completed. For the time being an adobe building was used in its place. The Indian pueblo was composed of thatched huts, but was enclosed by a wall of stone and mortar. There were three stone houses for the soldiers, and a stone granary. The missionaries lived in a stone building of two stories, the living rooms and cells being above and the offices below. At San Juan both the church and the houses of the Indian pueblo were of thatch. The missionaries

San José, the most substantial of all the missions on the San Antonio, we have no data for precisely this period. The missions on the Rio Grande were still more advanced than those at San Antonio. At both of these missions fine stone churches had been completed, and manufactures had been well established.

In contrast with the missions about San Antonio, those of eastern Texas were already confessed failures. It was on this premise that three of them had been moved to San Antonio in 1730. In the Spanish system the essence of the missions was the discipline, religious and industrial, which it afforded. This discipline could not be imposed upon the Indians unless they could be made to congregate in mission pueblos and to submit to instruction and toil. The Caddoan tribes of eastern Texas were powerful, had a regular food-supply, and enjoyed the favor of the French. Hence, though peaceable and friendly from the outset, they had steadily refused to settle in mission pueblos, and without more soldiers than were available it was impossible to coerce them. Accordingly, the missionaries in eastern Texas had to content themselves with going among the scattered Indian settlements, ministering to the sick, preaching, and baptizing *in articulo mortis.*[10]

2. *Discords at San Antonio.*—The routine of daily life at San Antonio was broken by Indians raids, the arrival of packtrains

---

lived in a stone building containing two cells; besides, there were a room serving as an office and a storeroom for maize. At San Francisco a stone church had been begun, the sacristy being completed and serving temporarily as the church. The houses of the Indians and the soldiers were of thatch. The missionaries lived in a stone building having two cells above and two offices below. There was also a stone granary.

[10] Fray Simón Hierro, *Informe de las Misiones de Texas,* January 8, 1762. A fundamental misapprehension regarding the history of early Texas is revealed in Coman's *Economic Beginnings of the Far West* (New York, 1912), in the description, on pp. 99–100, of the mission régime among the "Tejas and the Cenis." The description given would fit the situation on the San Antonio, three hundred miles away, fairly well, but it is a patent fact that the Tejas (Cenis) never consented to live in pueblos or to submit to mission discipline. Hence, so far as eastern Texas is concerned, the whole passage is incorrect and beside the point. This misapplication of an interesting passage is due in part to an inadequate study of the Indian situation.

from the interior, expeditions against the Apache or to recover absconding neophytes, periodical buffalo hunts and cattle-killings on the prairies, and disputes between the missionaries and their secular neighbors. The principal quarrels arose over questions relating to the mission guards, the control of the labor of the mission Indians, the ownership and use of lands, the killing of mission cattle, and the sale of agricultural products in the local market. Inevitably the disputes sometimes degenerated into personalities. What was more deplorable, they greatly impaired the prosperity of the province.

One form of discord arose over the mission guards. The missionaries needed and always demanded a few soldiers to protect them on their missionary journeys, to aid them in supervising the work of the neophytes, and to assist in the manual labor of the missions. For their expeditions to recover fugitives special escorts were usually granted. Recognizing the need of a guard, the king required the presidios to furnish a specified number of soldiers for the purpose. But it was sometimes charged that these orders were disobeyed, or were indifferently carried out. In 1737, for example, when the neophytes deserted the mission of San Francisco de la Espada, the reason assigned by the missionaries was that Governor Franquis had taken away the guard of three soldiers, leaving the mission without a man.[11]

---

[11] Fray Pedro de Ysasmendi to Governor Orobio Bazterra, November 24, 1737, in Lamar Papers, no. 33. The impression is sometimes given that the missionaries objected to the presence of soldiers at the missions. As a rule the case was quite the contrary. What they objected to was unsuitable soldiers and outside interference with their control of the guards. Concerning the necessity of soldiers to aid in the missionary work the materials are voluminous. See *Transsumpto de vn. Memorial que por parte de este collegio se remitio al Rey en el Consejo Real de Indias estaño de 1729* (A. C. S., K. leg. 3, no. 3); *Escrito del P. Sevillano pidiendo dos soldados en cada mision; despacho en que se concede uno. Yt. una carta del assumpto, 1730* (ibid., K, leg. 19, no. 20); *Tanto del Despacho del Exmo. Señor Virrey Marq^s. de Casafuerte, mandando se ponga en cada miss^on. del Rio grande, y Sn. Antonio Vn. soldado. Fecha 23 de Febrero de 1730* (ibid., K, leg. 3, no. 4); *Oficio, para que el Governador de la Provincia de Texas observe y execute la Real Cédula inserta conforme á lo resuelto por su Majestad, y ultimamente determinado por Vex^a. en razon de la pretención del P^e. Fray Miguel Sevillano de Paredes, sobre q. se le asista con la escolta de soldados.* Feb. 15, 1734 (Lamar Papers, no. 42).

By a superior order the presidio of La Bahía was required to furnish three soldiers for each of three missions at San Antonio. But in 1740 the president, Father Santa Ana, complained to Captain Urrutia, at San Antonio, that Captain Gabriel Costales, of La Bahía, had sent soldiers unfit for service, and demanded that two such at Mission Concepción be replaced by more suitable men. At the same time he complained that Urrutia had failed in his duty of inspecting the mission squads to see that they were of suitable character and properly equipped. Father Santa Ana threatened, in case of non-compliance, to complain to the viceroy, and Captain Urrutia yielded. But this compliance did not prevent the matter from going to the viceroy, and by a decree issued in December, 1740, Costales was ordered to provide suitable and well-armed men, and not to remove them except at the request of the religious.[12]

Between the missionaries and Joaquín de Orobio Bazterra, the successor of Costales at La Bahía, the quarrel took a different form. The missionaries had been in the habit of compensating the guards not only with provisions but also with clothing. In consequence the soldiers were relieved of the necessity of purchasing supplies from the captain's store. Orobio, offended at this, removed the guard, but the missionaries again protested, and in 1743 secured an order from the viceroy that Orobio should restore the soldiers and see to it that they assisted the missionaries in the instruction of the Indians in agriculture, care of the cattle, and other civilized pursuits.[13]

One of the most bitter wrangles of the period was that between Governor Franquis and the missionaries. Franquis took office in September, 1736. All the evidence forthcoming seems to indicate that he was a violent man. The Marqués de Altamira

---

[12] Fray Fernández de Santa Ana to Captain Urrutia, May 31, 1740, and related documents, in A. C. S., K, leg. 19, no. 37; Morfi, *Memorias*, Bk. VIII, paragraph 8.

[13] Morfi, *Memorias*, Bk. VIII, paragraph 14.

wrote[14] that "he at once manifested his tempestuous, petulant, and hasty nature, whereupon followed complaints of disgraceful and insulting temerities with which he treated those missionary religious." It was charged that soon after he arrived at San Antonio he took the Indians from their missions and compelled them to work without compensation, and that to escape this burden they deserted from the missions, while heathen Indians were deterred from entering them. The missionaries protested to the viceroy, whereupon Franquis made a personal attack upon the complainants, banishing them, intercepting their letters, impeding their exercise of authority, and using insulting language. In May, 1737, the viceroy ordered Franquis, under a heavy penalty, to desist from removing the neophytes from their missions, to leave them wholly in charge of the missionaries, and to cease his abuses.[15]

But the matter did not end here. In the same year, while Franquis was at Adaes arresting his predecessor, Sandoval, occurred the wholesale desertion of the missions related elsewhere. On his return in August other mission Indians went to him in a body and complained of ill-treatment at the hands of the missionaries. In the inquiry which Franquis now instituted testimony was given to show that, since Father Santa Ana had been president, the Indians had been overworked, underfed, and mercilessly flogged; that this was the cause of the desertions; and that during Sandoval's term the greatest cruelties had been practiced in recovering runaways.[16] Since this testimony was partisan, it cannot be too seriously considered.

---

[14] El Marqués de Altamira, *Testimonio de un Parecer, Año de 1744*, in Yoakum, *History of Texas*, Appendix No. 1, p. 398.

[15] *Ibid.*, 398; Morfi, *Memorias*, Bk. VII, paragraphs 76–78. For a statement concerning involuntary service by the mission Indians see *Despacho librado pr. el Virrey Marqués de Casa fuerte pa. que no se obliguen á los Yndios de la frontera de N. S. de Guadalupe á servicios involuntarios. Año de 1732.*

[16] Investigation of complaints of neophytes, MS in Archivo General y Público, Mexico, Misiones, vol. 21.

The missionaries came into conflict with another element of the population, namely, the citizens of the adjacent Villa of San Fernando de Béxar. The quarrel over Indian labor which had taken place with Governor Franquis was renewed with the citizens of the villa. The Canary Islanders desired to utilize the labor of the mission Indians, on condition of paying them wages. To get authority for doing so, about 1740 they sent two men named Travieso and Leal to Mexico to ask permission to take Indians from the missions to work on their lands. Failing in their design, in 1743 they renewed the attempt, sending another deputation to Mexico. The agents this time convinced the viceroy of the justice of their cause, and secured an order directing the missionaries to furnish the Indians asked for, and commanding them to abstain from trading in farm produce and from extending their agricultural operations. The same order provided that the presidial captains should purchase their provisions from citizens of San Fernando and not from the missions. The missionaries, thus charged with unseemly conduct—for there were strict regulations regarding trade by missionaries—were aroused, and appealed through their prelate for justice.[17] A long investigation followed, with the result that the viceroy was convinced of the falsity of the charges. Accordingly, in January, 1745, he rescinded the previous order, as based on false information, expressed his faith in the disinterestedness of the missionaries, ordered the captains to buy produce from settlers or from the missions, as might be most convenient, and declared that the Indians must not be taken from the missions under any pretext. Moreover, the Islanders were notified to fence in their fields,

---

17 Morfi, *Memorias*, Bk. VIII, paragraph 9; Joachín de Orobio Bazterra to the Cabildo of San Fernando, August 25, 1743, in Béxar Archives, Bahía, 1743–1778 (The Cabildo had asked for funds to defray the expenses of the deputation); *Año de 1735. Real Cedula que inserta el Brebe de Su Santidad p^a. que en los Dominios de Yndias no puedan los Religiosos ni clerigos Seculares tartar, ni contratar, aun p^r. interposita persona. El Brebe de S. S. es de 22, de Feb^o. de 1633; Patente del R. P. Barco p^a q^e. no se vendan los generos de los habios. 1740 as.*

abstain from killing the cattle of the Indians, and from trading with them without permission from the friars.[18]

The dispute now took the form of a quarrel over lands, the villa demanding that the missions should retire, move, or be converted into two, and complaining of the damage done to the crops of the citizens by the stock of the Indians.[19] In return the missionaries demanded the removal of the villa of San Fernando. The case went again before the viceroy. Instead of waiting, however, for the matter to be settled at the capital, the two parties decided to come to an agreement between themselves. On August 15, 1745, therefore, the "very Illustrious Cabildo, having assembled in the buildings which serve for an Ayuntamiento," in company with Father President Santa Ana, as representative of the missionaries and Indians, a covenant was made. Each party maintaining its right, it was agreed in writing that the demands should mutually cease. The site of the villa and the lands to the west of the river were to be regarded as belonging to the villa; to the lands between the house of Juan Banul and the mission of San Antonio the villa was to make no claim. Acknowledging the prior right of the missions, the lands to the north were to be divided by a line, those to the west belonging to the villa, and those to the east to the mission. The parties jointly and severally agreed to drop the dispute forever; and this agreement was not to be affected by any subsequent decision which might be made of the case in the Superior Tribunal, "because the complainants wish to have, now and in future, peace, union and harmony."[20] Quarrels continued, however, in spite of this

---

[18] Morfi, *Memorias*, Bk. VIII, paragraphs 16–17.

[19] In 1733 complaint had been made by Father Espinosa, from Querétaro, on behalf of the missionaries, regarding water rights in Arroyo de San Pedro and the San Antonio River, but no serious trouble ensued, it seems (MS entitled *Del Sᵒʳ. Casafuerte sobre el repartimtᵒ. de los Aguas a los Ysleños*. A. C. S., K, leg. 4, no. 6).

[20] The line was drawn north from the creek rising in the valley running to the Llano de las Viboras (*Tanto y testimonio de Vna escritura de Concordia Entre Los Señores Ysleños y las Misiones, 1745*). The viceroy de-

solemn agreement, much to the detriment of the community.
Since wrangling and conflicting reports were the rule, it is not
surprising that the government in Mexico was often greatly deterred from giving the needed assistance to the province.

3. *Campaigns Against the Apache.*[21]—Whatever had been
accomplished in the western district of Texas had been done in
the face of serious Indian depredations. From the time when
San Antonio was first established the missions and settlers were
subjected to raids upon their stock, frequently accompanied by
loss of human life. No doubt the cupidity and lawlessness of the
white man was as much to blame for Indian hostilities here as
elsewhere in American history. The Indians committing these
depredations were principally the Eastern Apache, particularly
the Lipan, the Natagés, and the Mescalero, tribes living in general
west of San Antonio and south of the upper Colorado River. The
same enemies infested the highways leading from San Antonio
to the Rio Grande, to Los Adaes, and to La Bahía. Under these
circumstances settlement and missionary work in the province
were attractive undertakings only to people endowed with the
true frontiersman's spirit. But such men were not lacking
among either seculars or friars.

To check the outrages, the missionaries used their utmost
powers of persuasion, and furnished mission Indians to aid the
soldiery; the troops of San Antonio usually stood on the defensive; but occasionally they made campaigns into the enemy's
country, and as a rule with telling results. The first formal
campaign from San Antonio had been made in 1723. As a result
of various outrages, including the murder of a Franciscan lay

cided in favor of the citizens and the dispute went on (*Satisfacción del
R. P. Lector Prado al exmo. sobre la quexa De la Villa de Sⁿ. Ferndo. De
que los Padres se extendian fuera de la jurisdicción de las tierras de las
Misiones*).

21 This section is based mainly upon William Edward Dunn's excellent monograph entitled *Apache Relations in Texas, 1718–1750*, published
in the Texas State Historical Association *Quarterly*, vol. XIV, 198–274.
That study was based upon manuscript materials gathered by the present
writer.

brother named Pita, near the San Xavier (San Gabriel) River. In the year cited Captain Flores made a punitive expedition, with thirty soldiers and thirty mission Indians. Going north and then west one hundred and thirty leagues, he encountered a ranchería of Apaches, killed thirty-four Indians, captured twenty women and children, and recovered one hundred and twenty stolen mules and horses.[22]

During the succeeding decade Apache outrages were interspersed with friendly visits and peace agreements, and there was little open warfare. Meanwhile the garrison was unfortunately reduced, on the advice of Brigadier Rivera, from fifty-three to forty-three soldiers, a measure which brought forth a storm of protest from the missionaries.[23] These protests proved well founded, for immediately after the coming of the Canary Islanders and the three new missions in 1731, the Apache renewed their depredations. In the fall of that year a hard-fought battle between the soldiers and the Indians took place just outside of San Antonio. In the following year a campaign was made by the new governor, Bustillo y Zevallos. With a force of one hundred and fifty-seven Spaniards, sixty mission Indians, and nine hundred horses and mules, Bustillo went by way of the San Xavier River to a stream which was apparently the San Sabá. Here he encountered several hundred Indians of the Lipan and other Apache bands, protected by leather breastplates. After a five-hour conflict the Indians were defeated, some two hundred being killed, thirty women and children captured, seven hundred stolen horses and mules recovered, and one hundred mule-loads of peltry and other booty confiscated. The expedition lasted two months.[24]

---

[22] Dunn, *Apache Relations in Texas*, 206–207; *Autos hechos Texas, no 11; Autos á consulta hecha del Pᵉ. Fr. Joseph Gonˢ. contra Don Nicolas Flores; Autos Sre. diferentes puntos Consultados por el Govr. de la Provincia de los tejas; Muerte de un Correo y otros materias, 1724.*

[23] Dunn, *ibid.*, 207–224.

[24] Dunn, *ibid.*, 232–233; *Autos sobre las providencias dadas pr. su exa. al Governador de la Provincia de Texas pa. la pazificazn. de los Yndios Apaches y sus aliados. Año de 1731.*

This campaign was followed by a succession of flimsy peace-pacts and friendly visits, alternating with raids upon the settlements and highways. Some of the outrages were of the most diabolical sort. On account of the serious situation, Governor Sandoval, who took office in 1734, made his residence at San Antonio, and strengthened the garrison by contingents drawn from Los Adaes, La Bahía, and the Rio Grande.[25] To protect the presidial horse ranch, it was moved to a more secluded site, on Arroyo del Cíbolo, sixteen leagues from San Antonio, and guarded by a small garrison. But two raids there in 1737 caused the removal of horses and garrison back to San Antonio.[26]

In the fall of this year depredations were temporarily checked by the capture of Cabellos Colorados, one of the principal Lipan chiefs, who, after being kept in prison several months, was deported to Mexico. In 1739 Captain José Urrutia made another campaign to the San Sabá River, in which many captives were secured. This expedition seems to have been the first to be made directly through the northwestern mountain range, for Urrutia claimed to have discovered the pass in the mountains through which the Lipan made their forays. As a result of the expedition he asked for an increase of ten men for his garrison and suggested a presidio on the upper Guadalupe.[27] In 1743 a

---

[25] Dunn, *Apache Relations in Texas*, 234–242; Morfi, *Memorias*, Bk. VIII, par. 3. The fear of the Apache at San. Antonio is reflected by the *Parecer* of the royal fiscal, Juan de Oliván Rebolledo, July 18, 1733, stating the exposed condition at San Antonio; by the consequent order of July 30, 1733, empowering the governor of Texas to call on the garrison at Adaes, San Antonio, and Rio Grande for aid; and by the order of acting governor Joseph Antonio Fernández de Jáuregui Urrutia, October 19, 1737, commanding that no citizen of Béxar shall fire off a gun unless he sees Indians entering the place, and that in case a shot is heard it is to be the signal for all citizens to arm themselves to resist the Indians (Béxar Archives, Béxar, 1730–1736).

[26] Dunn, *ibid.*, 243–244; *Testimonio de Diligencias sobre Ynfidelidad de Los Apaches.*

[27] Dunn, *ibid.*, 244–248; Morfi, *Memorias*, VIII, paragraph 3: *Auttos fechos por el Govr. de Texas Sobre la Remision de el Capn. Cabellos Colorados y otros treze Yndios e Yndias de Nacion Apaches, a la Rl. carcel de Cortte, etta; Expediente sobre la Campaña q a su costa ha de hacer en la Provᵃ. de Texas Nuevas Philipinas pʳ. el mes de Abril del sigᵗᵉ. año Dⁿ.*

campaign was made from Coahuila against the Apache in which, it is said, a force of two hundred men led by the governor fell into ambush and was badly cut to pieces.[28]

Conditions at San Antonio had become so bad that citizens could neither take the road for Coahuila nor even work in their fields except in large parties.[29] Captain Thoribio de Urrutia, son of the former captain, desired to undertake another campaign, but was strongly opposed by the missionaries, who were now trying to bring peace to the province by founding an Apache mission. At last, in 1745, after much delay, Urrutia secured permission from the authorities and made the expedition. With some fifty Spaniards, and accompanied by Father Santa Ana, president of the Querétaran missions, he marched northward some seventy leagues and crossed the Colorado. Here he defeated a settlement of Lipans and Natagés and secured a number of captives. The engagement was apparently near the San Sabá River.[30] In 1748 Pedro de Rábago y Terán, governor of Coahuila, made an expedition into the Apache country, exploring and claiming to discover the Florido (Concho) River, which, of course, had been well known to the Spaniards of New Mexico in the seventeenth century.

Thus, since 1731, three formal campaigns had been made against the Apache by the soldiers and citizens of San Antonio. By means of them the Spaniards had become well acquainted with the region about the San Sabá River, the central haunts of the Lipan. Going thither at first in a roundabout way, by following the edge of the prairies, later they had penetrated the hill

---

Joseph de Urrutia Cap^n. del Presidio de S^n. Antonio de Bexar, etc; Autos a consulta de D^n. Thoribio de Vrrutia Cap^n. del Presidio de S^n. Antonio de Vejar en la Provincia de Texas, sobre aumento de Soldados, y ottras providencias que pide para contener los Ynsultos que hazen los Yndios Apaches; sobre que tambien insto D^n. Joseph de Vrrutia Su P^e. difunto. Sup. Gov^no. 1741.

[28] Dunn, *Apache Relations in Texas*, 251.
[29] Morfi, *Memorias*, Bk. VIII, paragraph 10.
[30] Dunn, *Apache Relations in Texas*, 250–252.

country of the upper Guadalupe and the Llano. In the course of these expeditions they had learned of mineral deposits in the Llano country, and were thus stimulated to later activities in the same region.

Although Apache hostilities were unquestionably bad, as has been indicated, the missionaries saw in these campaigns other motives than a mere desire to afford protection for the settlements. In 1740 Father Santa Ana wrote: ''If the campaigns which they make were conducted with more discipline, and with a better and a more disinterested purpose, it would not be difficult to secure peace with them in their own country. . . . Of what took place in the present campaign Rev. Father Fray Felipe will give a good account. I can only say that it is very important that others like it should not be made, for neither God nor the King gains anything, while the hatred of the Indian is increased, the peace of the province in this way becoming more disturbed. On account of the unseasonable time when the campaign was made, and the disorders which the soldiers were allowed to commit, many were left so heavily in debt that for a long time to come they will have nothing to eat or to use; the expedition was profitable only for those who had horses and other goods, which they sold at excessively high prices; and it is ridiculous that these same persons should claim certificates as servants of the King our Lord, when they were interested in what I have stated, and had greater hopes of a considerable prize of horses, hides, and Indian men and Indian women to serve them. These are the purposes of the campaigns and the ones entertained by most of the citizens who join the soldiers in such operations; and since the purpose is so vile, so is the outcome.''[31] ·

From this time forward the Lipan became more friendly toward the Spaniards on account of the terrible ravages made upon their tribe by the southward-moving Comanche. They now

[31] Santa Ana, *Descripción*, 206.

desired the protection of the Spanish arms. This turn of affairs
gave the missionaries an opening which, combined with other
forces, resulted finally in the founding of a mission for the Lipan
on the San Sabá River.

4. *The French Border.*—In western Texas the settlements had
succeeded moderately with their work of conversion and civilization of the coastwise tribes, and the settlers had about held their
own against the hostile Apache. In eastern Texas the frontier
outposts were less successful, from the standpoint of their purposes. On that frontier the question of defence against the Indians was of slight importance, because the natives were friendly,
but the missionaries failed almost completely to convert and
educate the Indians, while the military outposts and the missions
together failed to prevent French encroachments on territory
claimed by Spain.

The principal matters of international interest connected
directly with Texas during this period were the question of the
dividing line between French and Spanish territory, and that
of French traders among the Texas Indians. After the War of
the Spanish Succession Franco-Spanish relations generally tended
toward an increasingly close friendship. In 1733 was signed a
family compact which marked the definite union of France and
Spain to withstand the colonial and commercial aggression of
England. Nevertheless, this did not prevent Spain from regarding the Louisiana border with a high degree of jealousy.

A case in point occurred in 1732. In that year the governor
of Campeche heard that thirty companies of infantry were about
to be sent to Louisiana. He reported the news to the king, who
ordered the viceroy to investigate; the viceroy, in turn, reported
the rumor to Governor Bustillo, of Texas, surmising that such
an increase, if a fact, was for the purpose of extending the
Louisiana boundaries. Since Los Adaes would be the first point
of attack, he ordered Bustillo to be on his guard, to keep his

men under strict discipline, and, if possible, to ascertain through Indian allies the basis of the report.[32]

A more interesting example of border jealousy occurred in 1735. Shortly after the establishment of Los Adaes in 1716 the French post of Natchitoches had been built on an island in the Red River, where a trading house had been erected three or four years before. On the western bank of the western arm of the stream French settlers had houses, orchards, and corrals, their ranches extending westward to Arroyo Hondo and La Gran Montaña, natural features about midway between Natchitoches and Los Adaes. Because of the overflow of the river, and perhaps because of the diminution of the Spanish garrison in 1730, in 1735 Saint Denis, the French commander, moved his post to the western side of the river.

Ensign José González, commander at Los Adaes, and Father Vallejo, president of the eastern missions, reported the matter to Governor Sandoval, who was then living at Béxar on account of the Apache depredations. Sandoval had received strict orders from his government to resist by all means any effort of the French to pass beyond their boundaries, but not to come to an open breach without first reporting to the viceroy. The incident was therefore the occasion of a spirited correspondence between Saint Denis on the one hand and Sandoval and González on the other, which lasted until August, 1736, and which involved mutual threats of a resort to force. Sandoval claimed the Red River as the boundary, but he was ill-posted on the history of the frontier, and Saint Denis easily got the better of the historical argument, showing that the Natchitoches settlement had existed west of the Red River since 1716, at least, without protest by Sandoval's predecessors. In the course of the dispute Sandoval issued a proclamation curtailing all communication with Natchitoches, greatly to the annoyance of the residents of Los Adaes, who

---

[32] El Marqués de Casafuerte, viceroy, to Gov. Juan Antonio Bustillo y Zevallos, Feb. 3, 1733, Lamar Papers, no. 66.

depended largely upon the French for a supply of grain. Meanwhile Saint Denis went ahead with the transfer, building a stockade, church, and some fourteen houses for the garrison and the citizens.

Shortly afterward Sandoval was arrested, without warrant, by his successor, Colonel Franquis, one charge against him being culpability for having permitted the removal of Natchitoches. Sandoval's case going to Mexico, in 1740 he was fined for having moved his residence to San Antonio, although he apparently did so under orders. A royal order of 1741 required the viceroy to oppose any advance of the French beyond their limits. To learn the facts concerning the boundary the viceroy ordered an investigation. Witnesses were examined, both at Adaes and in Mexico, and it was concluded that La Gran Montaña and Arroyo Hondo had always been the accepted boundary between Natchitoches and Los Adaes. Sandoval was therefore absolved of his charge, and in 1744 the boundary question was dropped for the time being.[33] The discussions had all been local or within the respective governments, no attempt having been made between the home governments of Spain and France to settle the matter.

More important than any question of the precise boundary was that of the activities of French traders among the tribes of Texas. While the expedition of the Marqués de Aguayo to eastern Texas in 1721 had determined the ownership of Texas— or of what is now southern Texas—in favor of Spain, it did not by any means give the Spaniards undisputed sway over the natives. The missionaries, unsupported by an adequate mili-

---

[33] The original correspondence concerning the episode is contained in the Archivo General y. Público, Mexico, Sección de Historia, vol. 524. My transcript of the *expediente* comprises sixty-nine typewritten pages. A very good summary of the case is contained in Altamira's *Testimonio de un Parecer*, 1744. A translation of the part of this document relating to Sandoval, by Elizabeth Howard West, is published in the Texas State Historical *Quarterly*, VIII, 72–78. Garrison's *Texas*, pp. 81–83, contains a good brief account based on that of Altamira; Morfi, *Memorias*, Bk. VIII, paragraphs 71–75, also follows Altamira closely.

tary force, failed almost completely to convert the Indians of eastern Texas, and they rightfully regarded this failure as due in no small degree to the baneful influence of the neighboring French. The men of the latter nation were skillful Indian traders, and readily affiliated with the savages. On the other hand, the narrow commercial policy of Spain permitted trade with the Indians only under the strictest regulations, and entirely prohibited supplying them with firearms. As a consequence the Indians of eastern and northern Texas continued to look to the French for their weapons, ammunition, and most of their articles of commerce, for which they gave in exchange their peltry and, to some extent, their agricultural products. As time went on the complaints, in Spanish circles, of French trade and French influence among the Indians of Texas, increased.[34]

The French traders operated even among the Hasinai, in whose very midst the Spaniards were established, though not without liability to apprehension and punishment, for such trade was strictly forbidden by law. Northern Texas the Spaniards scarcely entered before the middle of the century, and there the French traders were practically unimpeded. Among the Cadodacho the French had founded the Nassonite Post in 1719. This establishment, which was maintained till after the Louisiana cession in 1762, was an effective barrier to the Spaniards. A regular trail led from Natchitoches by way of the Sabine to the Cadodacho. Depots were established at the villages of the Petit Cado and Yatasí, further down the Red River. These trading stations, together with the influence of Saint Denis, the imperious and blustering French commander, were the basis of an almost undisputed French domination over the Caddoan tribes of the northeastern Texas border. More than once the Spanish authorities contemplated driving the French from the Cadodacho village, and erecting there a Spanish post, but the thought was

---

[34] For a fuller statement of this phase of border history see Bolton, *De Mézières*, I, 28–61.

never carried into action. Indeed, any attempt to curtail the French trade among the natives was made at the risk of bringing down upon the Spaniards the wrath of the Indian tribes.

French influence was scarcely less firmly established among the Witchita. In 1719 La Harpe had visited the Witchita tribes on the Canadian River. By the middle of the eighteenth century some of them had moved southward into northern Texas. During all this time they were frequented by French traders from the Arkansas and Nassonite posts, and in 1763 it was boasted that a French flag had been flying at the Tawakoni village for forty years. During the same period, the Tonkawan tribes of northern and central Texas, either directly or indirectly, received French arms and ammunition. Immediately after the founding of New Orleans in 1718 French traders began to push westward along the Gulf coast among the Chitimacha and Attacapa. Before 1730 they are known to have begun to pass the lower Sabine and to work among the Orcoquiza.

From the foregoing statements it is seen that while the eastern boundary of Spanish Texas as actually occupied in the middle eighteenth century lay near the Red River—at one point at least—and far to the east of the later Sabine River boundary, northern Texas was really in the hands of the French, and was not occupied by the Spaniards at all. In the boundary questions which arose in the nineteenth century attention was fixed upon the eastern and the western borders, whereas the northern boundary might equally well have furnished another ground for controversy.[35]

---

[35] Indeed, such a controversy did occur between the provincial officials of Texas and Louisiana just on the eve of the transfer of Louisiana. *Ibid.*, 51; *Carta del Comte. Mr. Macarti de Nachitos sobre una yndia española llamada ysabel qe. no remitio sino pidio 200 ps. por su rescate, como en ella consta.* Adaes, Sept. 23, 1763 (Lamar Papers, no. 172); *Copia de Carta del Comte. de Nachitos Mr. Marcartij en qe. exhorta se suspenda todos y qualesquiera proyectos qe. halla en los Tahuacanas ô otra nacion pertenezte. a los Españoles, por lo qe se dio qta. con ella á El Exmo. Sr. Marqs. de Cruillas.* Nov. 17, 1763 (Nacogdoches Archives).

What was taking place on the eastern border in the period under consideration is illustrated by a single incident better than by any amount of narrative. In April, 1737, Jean Legros, of Natchitoches, was sent by Saint Denis to trade among the Cadodacho. He had a passport, secured in February from Fermín de Ybiricú, lieutenant at Los Adaes, permitting him to go through Spanish territory. While on his way he was arrested twelve leagues from Nacogdoches by Sergeant Antonio Losoya, of Los Adaes, under orders from Ybiricú. When arrested he had a typical trader's outfit; he was accompanied by an Ais squaw, and had three horses, one of which he rode and two of which were laden with packs of goods. He was taken to Los Adaes, put in the stocks, and ordered given a ramrodding, but someone interfered. His goods were confiscated and a part of them burned by Ybiricú, in the presence of witnesses.

Legros was soon released, however, and returned to Natchitoches. When he told Saint Denis what had happened, the French commander was furious, and on April 17 he addressed a wrathful epistle to Ybiricú. It was written in Latin in Saint Denis' own hand. "Perhaps we are at war [he wrote], or perhaps you mean to prevent us from going to Kadodachos. What is meant that five soldiers should be sent by a sergeant to arrest one of my Frenchmen who was going to Kadodachos by the direct road? Did you know that he was sent by me? For, if you were ignorant, you should know that he was. You confiscated all his goods; on what grounds? You put him in the stocks; perhaps he is a Spaniard! You wished to ramrod him; where is your justice? You were wise that you did not do so, that's all I've got to say!" He proceeded to demand that all the confiscated goods be restored at once. "Otherwise [he continued] I will close all commerce with you from today, and will pursue you in the name of my king even to the viceroy, or even to the king himself, if that should be necessary."

Soon after these events Governor Franquis arrived at Los Adaes. A complaint being made by Saint Denis in the name of "Joannes Baptista Legros," Franquis investigated the matter. In the course of the testimony it came out that Legros had used his passport as a license for trading with Texas tribes. Whether his arrest was caused by this fact, or by a quarrel which he had had with Ybiricú over the squaw whom he took on his journey, is not clear. At any rate, Saint Denis evidently browbeat Franquis into compliance. Ybiricú was charged with undue intimacy with the French at Natchitoches, and with keeping French women at Los Adaes, and was thrown into prison for illegal acts.

The coercive force exercised by the Indian tribes on the frontier is illustrated by another incident of the same series. Fourteen Indian chiefs, incensed at the arrest of Legros, went to Saint Denis and complained at the interference with their trade. But as restitution had already been made, Saint Denis told them that he was satisfied and counseled them to go away content, which they did. Father Vallejo, president of the missions, who reported this occurrence, thanked Franquis for so prudently placating Saint Denis. Manifestly, it seems to have been thought best not to incur the enmity of the aggressive French commander.[36]

Still another phase of the French border question was that of trade between the soldiers of Adaes and the citizens of Natchitoches. From the first establishment of Los Adaes it was customary for it to depend partly upon the supplies purchased at the neighboring French post. In 1730 the viceroy ordered all trade with Louisiana cut off. Governor Bustillo replied that he would enforce the order, but that it had always been customary

---

[36] The correspondence concerning this case is in the Archivo General y Público, Mexico, Historia, vol. 524. Among the documents is an interesting list of the goods confiscated from Legros, written in Spanish in the hand of Saint Denis. The list includes powder, French cloth, a flag, three fusils, axes, adzes, knives, kettles, a hat, and shirts.

and necessary to purchase maize, beans, and other provisions from the French, and, in view of the hardship imposed by the order, asked for further instructions. On the advice of Mariscal de Campo Pedro de Rivera, who in 1727 had visited Texas, the viceroy ordered Bustillo to consider the feasibility of moving to a site where sufficient crops could be raised to make the garrison self-supporting. Bustillo set out in June to investigate, but after fifteen days' exploration he reported that between the Sabine and the Red rivers he could find no better location than the one already occupied. The one suggested by Rivera, on the other side of the lake, he reported as marshy and subject to overflow. Commenting on this incident a few years later, the Marqués de Altamira sarcastically remarked that a site "was not found in all that district examined for fifteen days; but perhaps other settlers more interested would have found one in less time."

In consequence of the unfavorable report, in December, 1733, the viceroy gave orders that for the present the presidio should remain where it was, and that, in case of necessity, maize, beans, and other food stuffs might be purchased at Natchitoches for the presidio of Los Adaes, but that beyond this, commerce should not go.[37] This permission was of course liable to great abuse, and troubles over illicit trade continued. In 1740 another order to cut off the trade was issued. But Governor Orobio repeated the plea made by Governor Bustillo ten years before, with the result that this decree was likewise rescinded, the reason given being the excessive cost of transporting provisions all the way from Saltillo. Hence traffic in food stuffs for the presidio was regularly permitted. It continued to be subject to great abuse, however, and a cover for extensive contraband trade.[38]

[37] El Marqués de Casafuerte, *Oficio, Para que el Governador de la Provincia de Tejas mantenga, por ahora el Presidio de los Adayis en el Parage, en q se halla, y execute todas las demas providencias, que se previenen en este Dpacho; en la forma q se expresa*, Mexico, Dec. 17, 1733; royal decree for extinguishing illicit trade in Spanish dominions in America, June 19, 1730.

[38] El Duque de la Conquista, viceroy, to Governor Prudencio de Orobio Bazterra, Feb. 3, 1741. Lamar Papers, no. 50.

In spite of these various forms of border friction, the relations of the two lonely outposts, Los Adaes and Natchitoches, were, on the whole, friendly, as might well be expected. When, for example, Bustillo, the new governor, arrived in Texas in 1731, the French officials went to Adaes to pay their compliments. When in the same year the Natchez Indians attacked Natchitoches, Saint Denis appealed to Bustillo for help. In response the Spanish governor sent eleven soldiers and a contingent of Indian allies. For twenty-two days they took part in the defense of besieged Natchitoches, one Spanish soldier being killed. Out of gratitude for this aid, Saint Denis sent Bustillo a present of some captive Indian women, which, however, the Spanish governor declined with thanks.[39] In after years the aid thus given by the Texas Indians against the Natchez seldom failed to be recalled in the oratory of the border councils.[40]

The anger shown in the official correspondence between González and Saint Denis over the boundary question seems less terrible when we learn from the local marriage records that on April 8, 1736, at the very time of the dispute, seventeen-year-old Victoria González, daughter of the Spanish commander at Los Adaes, went to Natchitoches and was married to Jean D'herbanne, one of Saint Denis' soldiers; that with another pair love overbore international hatred when on July 17 of the same year Juanita Victoria García, of Los Adaes, married François Lemoine, soldier at Natchitoches; and that in the very family of Saint Denis, the

---

[39] Gov. Bustillo y Zevallos to the viceroy, Adaes, Nov. 26, 1731, in Lamar Papers, no. 49. For an indication of the excitement caused on the Texas border by the Natchez war in Louisiana, see a letter by Governor Mediavilla y Azcona to the viceroy, Adaes, April 5, 1730, in *Tantos de Memoriales y carta del R. P. Sevillano al exmo. Sor. Virrey, para qe. se den las providencias al resguarda de las misiones, y misioneros, y a esto se erija el Presidio de Texas. Año de 1729; Ynforme al R. Discreo. de los PPs. Pree. y Misss. de Tejas en que piden salir al Rio de S. Xavier.* Adaes, March 18, 1730.

[40] See a harangue by De Mézières in 1770 at Cadodaches, in Bolton, *De Mézières*, I, 210; De Mézières to Croix, Feb. 20, 1778, *ibid.*, II, 173; De Mézières to Bernardo de Gálvez, May, 1779, *ibid.*, 249.

French commander, most of the marriages and baptisms of children and grandchildren were performed by Spanish *padres* of Los Adaes. Indeed, when, in June, 1744, the long career of Saint Denis came to a close, prominent among those who assembled at Natchitoches to assist in the funeral honors were Governor Boneo and Father President Vallejo, from Los Adaes, across the international boundary line.[41] And yet, when a few days later Boneo reported the occurrence to his viceroy he did so in terms which meant, in effect, "Saint Denis is dead, thank God; now we can breathe easier!"[42]

---

[41] MS church records at Natchitoches, examined by the writer in January, 1912.

[42] On August 8, 1744, the viceroy wrote to Boneo in reply to a letter of June 15, stating among other things, "that Dn. Luis de Sn. Deny, commander on that frontier for the crown of France, had died, and that from his death there was promise of living with less dread and some comfort in the future." Lamar Papers. I have not seen Boneo's letter, but learn its contents from the reply.

CHAPTER II

EXPANSION ACTIVITIES ON THE EVE OF THE LOUISIANA CESSION (1745–1762)

The period between 1731 and 1745 had not been one of large geographical expansion, but rather one of gradual development along the lines previously drawn. The next seventeen years, down to the transfer of Louisiana by Spain to France, was, on the other hand, a period of numerous and considerable expansion efforts.

Prominent among the motive forces bringing this about was the zeal of the missionaries to enter new fields, the tribes within easy reach of the older missions being depleted. In response to this motive, coupled with the real or supposed danger from the French, the very unfeigned danger of the settlements from the Apache, an interest in a new mining prospect, and a desire on the part of the government to advance the outposts from Coahuila and Texas toward New Mexico and the Red River, the missionaries were supported in the founding of new missions among the Apache and Tonkawan tribes of central Texas. In this way the frontier was extended a long distance to the north and northwest. On the other hand, the establishment of missions and presidios among the Apache gained for the Spaniards the hostility of the foes of the latter, and entailed a long and bitter war and a harmful division of policy.

The need of subduing the lower Gulf coast for the safety of the adjacent settlements, combined with a growing fear of the English in the Gulf of Mexico, led to the founding of the colony of Nuevo Santander, which lay across the Rio Grande and included the Texas coast as far as the San Antonio River. Its founding involved renewed missionary activities among the Karankawa. Continued incursions of the French traders revived the international boundary question, made necessary the defence of the lower Trinity, and resulted in the establishment there of a mission and a presidio, and in an attempt to found a civil colony. Underlying all these enterprises was the very sincere desire of the Spanish government to civilize the Indians and to attract to the rich province of Texas colonies of Spaniards and half-castes.

Thus in the decade and a half before the cession of Louisiana changed the course of events, four new regions within the present Texas were entered for missionary work, defense, and colonization. With varying degrees of success, in the course of the period eight new missions and four new presidios were established within the region. New districts were explored, new trails opened, and new tribes brought into notice or under control. Within the same period occurred the nearest semblance to a mining "boom" of which Texas could boast in Spanish days.

1. *The San Xavier Missions*—Most of these expansion activities took place simultaneously, a fact which may serve to suggest the magnitude of the demands upon the Spanish government at a single time in holding and developing the frontiers of a single one of its many provinces in the Americas. The first of the enterprises in its inception was the plan for the establishment of the missions on the San Xavier (the present San Gabriel) River by the friars of Querétaro.[1] The San Xavier River had been known to the Spaniards since 1716, and, being near the highway, had

[1] The following sketch of the San Xavier missions is based mainly upon the detailed study presented in Part II of this volume (pp. 137–278), where references to the primary authorities will be found. The first half of that study is a reprint, somewhat revised, of an article which appeared in the *Southwestern Historical Quarterly*, XVII, 323–378. Apart from that article, almost the only printed account of the episode is that contained in Arricivita's *Crónica Seráfica y Apostólica* (Mexico, 1792). Considerable space is given to the subject in Morfi's unpublished *Memorias para la Historia de Texas*.

been frequently visited. The region adjacent to it was known as a superb buffalo country, and more than once there had been talk of establishing missions or a colony on the stream. During the period the natives of the surrounding district had become known, notably the Mayeye, Deadose, and Yojuane tribes, and the conglomerate aggregation known as Ranchería Grande. Various attempts had been made to reduce these tribes to mission life at San Antonio, but without success. Prominent among the missionaries who had visited them was Father Mariano de los Dolores. As time passed the reduction of the Ranchería Grande, in particular, was of increasing importance, through its having become a famous asylum for deserters from the missions. But all efforts to take its inhabitants to San Antonio failed, and in 1745 a new plan was set on foot.[2]

In June of that year four chiefs of the tribes named went to San Antonio, with a band of followers, and asked Father Mariano for a mission in their own country. The matter was put before Father Francisco Xavier Ortiz, at that time on an official visitation of the missions at San Antonio, and through him before the College of Querétaro. Father Mariano urged that the request of the chiefs be granted, since it offered great possibilities. It would be a means not only of saving souls, but of defense against the Apache also, and, in case of war, against the French. To save expense for the necessary protection of the desired missions, he urged transferring to them thirty soldiers from the garrison at Los Adaes.

While awaiting the decision of the college and the viceroy, Fray Mariano did his best to keep the petitioners favorably disposed, and to prepare the way for the proposed establishments. For more than a year he and his associates labored without financial aid from the central government, and still another year before that government could be induced to authorize the missions. A

---

[2] See below, pp. 137–148.

site was selected on the San Xavier River, near the present Rockdale, and early in 1746 Father Mariano, accompanied by soldiers and mission Indians from San Antonio, planted crops for the support of the petitioners, and erected temporary buildings. By February, 1747, Father Mariano had spent over five thousand *pesos* in the enterprise. During a part of that time, at least, he was assisted by two missionaries, enlisted at San Antonio. In the spring of 1747 Eusebio Pruneda, a layman, was sent to San Xavier with mission Indians and seed grain, to plant another crop. He was assisted by the natives, but in the midst of their work they were attacked by Apaches. In consequence the Coco tribe, who had joined the original petitioners, withdrew.[3]

Meanwhile affairs were taking their slow and uncertain course in Mexico. The project of the San Xavier missions was favorably received by the College of Santa Cruz de Querétaro, none the less so because the mission of Lampazos had recently been relinquished to the secular clergy. Aided by Father Mariano and his associates, the College made a persistent struggle for authority to found the missions and for funds to support them. The presentation of the case to the viceroy was entrusted to Father Ortiz.

Don Pedro de Vedoya, the fiscal of the Real Audiencia, approving the plan, proposed two or three missions, to be protected by moving to the San Xavier the garrison then at Santa Rosa del Sacramento, a presidio in Coahuila. The matter being referred to the Marqués de Altamira, the *auditor de guerra*, he requested an opinion from Bustillo y Zevallos, ex-governor of Texas, and now an official in the City of Mexico. Bustillo flatly opposed the plan. He praised the efforts of the missionaries; but, he

---

[3] Ortiz, *Satisfaccion de los Missioneros; copia de Autos seguidos en el superior governo,* 1745; *Despacho q sin provecho se saco el año de 1746 el qual no so presento, ni aprobecha;* Ortiz, *Visita de las Missiones,* 1746; Bustillo y Zevallos, *Memorial,* May 28, 1746; *Memorial del P^e. Anda al Exmo Sor Virrey sobre. S^n. Xavier;* Arricivita, *Crônica,* 321–324; Morfi, *Memorias,* Bk. VIII, paragraphs 18–19. See also pp. 149–161, below.

maintained, the tribes in question were small; they were interested in missions for material rewards only; the San Xavier River was not a suitable site, for it lacked facilities for irrigation and was exposed to the Apache; moreover the alleged danger from the French in central Texas was imaginary. On the other hand, danger from the French in eastern Texas was very genuine, and the garrison at Los Adaes should not be reduced, unless part of it were to go to Cadodachos. As a substitute for the San Xavier plan, he proposed moving the petitioners to the Neches River or to the Angelina and placing them in missions with the Hasinai.

Bustillo's opposition became the focal point of much of the struggle which followed. The missionary college parried by calling upon Don Melchor de Mediavilla y Azcona, another ex-governor of Texas, who defended the plan as warmly as Bustillo had opposed it. In his view, the four tribes in question were tractable; the San Xavier was suitable; the French danger was unfeigned; the presidio of Sacramento was useless where it was, and might well be moved to Texas. On the other hand, with rather unconvincing logic Mediavilla maintained that while Bustillo's plan of moving the petitioners to the Hasinai country was impracticable, the Hasinai might be taken to the proposed missions on the San Xavier.

Vedoya was unmoved by Bustillo's argument, and he reiterated his former opinion. But Altamira was still doubtful, and since a call had come for troops to help to establish the new colony of Nuevo Santander, he suggested that the decision should be suspended. Father Ortiz being asked, meanwhile, to suggest some other plan, he proposed a civil colony of one hundred settlers at San Xavier, supported for eight years, or a garrison of presidials maintained for a term of years, on condition of remaining as settlers thereafter. Either plan, he argued, would result in a much-desired civil colony. Acting on Altamira's advice, early in 1747 the viceroy ordered all discussion suspended. But as a temporary measure he commanded that the missionaries be reimbursed for what they had spent at San Xavier, and that a temporary garrison of twenty-two soldiers be sent thither from Los Adaes and San Antonio.

This temporizing decision of the viceroy was followed immediately by an appeal by Father Ortiz directly to the king. On the other hand, the order to send to San Xavier a temporary guard was opposed both in Texas and by the college. Captain Urrutia, at San Antonio, supported by the cabildo of San Fernando, objected to losing his soldiers, on the tenable ground of Apache hostilities. Father Trinidad, speaking in Mexico for the college. insisted upon a regular presidio. These objections drew from the viceroy a new despatch, dated July 27, 1747. It rescinded the former order and required sent to San Xavier thirteen soldiers from La Bahía and seventeen from Los Adaes. To compensate La Bahía, the nine soldiers from there serving at the San Antonio missions were to return to their garrison. As was to be expected, this provision called forth a new storm of opposition. The missionaries at San Antonio resented the loss of their customary guard, and the college again demanded the protection of a regular presidio at San Xavier. As Urrutia had objected before, so now the captain at La Bahía and the governor at Los Adaes demurred, finding new objections to the San Xavier plan, and proposing, as a substitute, a mission near the Trinity River, where a new danger from the French had recently arisen.

But all these objections came to naught, for on December 23, 1747, after more than two years of discussion, the viceroy formally authorized the establishment of three missions on the San Xavier River, and made provision for defraying the initial expenses of founding them and for paying the annual stipends of the missionaries. In the following March, after much protest, Lieutenant Juan Galván was sent to San Xavier with the garrison of thirty soldiers borrowed from La Bahía and Los Adaes, as ordered by the viceroy, and in April the missionary project was approved by the king.

The situation is an interesting example of the actual workings of the Spanish government in the distant frontier provinces. Since the summer of 1745 the missionaries of the College of Santa Cruz had been asking permission to establish missions at San Xavier. Meanwhile they had proceeded without this authority to found a mission—a provisional one, it is true—as early as the spring of 1746. In February, 1747, the viceroy had furnished temporary financial aid, but for the formal erection of the missions he had withheld his consent. In December, 1747, he had given that consent, without awaiting the approval of the king. In February, 1748, as will appear, one of the missions had been already founded with due formality, in the king's name; and now, in April, two months afterward, comes the king's solemn order to the viceroy to found the missions if, after due investigation, they should be considered desirable. It was apparently but another instance in which the local authorities and leaders, and especially the missionaries, took the initiative, and forced the central government reluctantly to sanction what had already been done. In the Spanish as well as in the English colonies a certain measure of independence in actual government was wrested from the central authorities by virtue of the very necessity for local initiative due to distance.[4]

Consent and a promise of support having been given, the college proceeded at once to found the new missions. Fray Mariano was put in charge of the work on the ground, and Father Juan Joseph Ganzábal was sent from Texas to look after interests in Mexico. As soon as Fray Mariano heard the good news he set out for the San Xavier River, taking from San Antonio on his own credit goods and stock to the value of over

---

[4] See below, pp. 162–184; Arricivita, *Crónica*, 322–325; Morfi, *Memorias*, Bk. VII, paragraphs 20–25.

$5,000. At this time Galván had not yet arrived with the garrison of thirty soldiers. In February the first mission was formally founded, with the name of San Francisco Xavier. To enter it, or at any rate to take advantage of the expected distribution of presents and food, there assembled not only the original petitioners, but Cocos from the lower Colorado and Orcoquiza and Bidai from the lower Trinity. Indeed, the hungry crowd was larger than Fray Mariano could feed, and he was forced to discourage more from coming.

The mission was beset by more than the usual quota of tribulations. In April Fray Mariano suffered an accident which caused him to return to San Antonio, leaving Fray Francisco Cayetano Aponte y Lis in charge. Subsequently President Santa Ana went from San Antonio to take Fray Mariano's place. Scarcely had Fray Mariano left when the mission was attacked by Apaches, and before the end of the year it was raided three more times by the same enemy. On the first attack appeals for help were made to Captain Urrutia, but without avail. Some aid was given in May by Governor Pedro del Barrio, but it was offset by the adverse report which he made of the mission site. This report caused renewed hesitation on the part of the authorities in Mexico and consternation to Father Ganzábal, who was at the capital urging the provision of a presidio. To counteract the damage done by Barrio, Ganzábal now appealed to the frontier missionaries for favorable reports from San Xavier. In spite of these difficulties and set-backs, however, the new mission was ordinarily prosperous during the first year of its existence.

The founding of the two remaining missions was delayed for still another entire year. The college made the first regular assignment of missionaries in March, 1748, and they arrived at San Antonio in June; but the first caravan of supplies did not reach that place until December, and without them nothing could be done. As soon as the supplies arrived, Father Santa Ana and the missionaries went with them to San Xavier to establish the other missions and to secure testimony regarding the site, in answer to Father Ganzábal's appeal. Distributing the Indians on the basis of their linguistic affiliation, Mission San Francisco was reserved for those of Tonkawan stock—the Mayeye, Hierbipiame, and Yojuane tribes. To the second mission, named San Ildefonso, which had been established by the end of February, 1749, were assigned those of Attacapan stock—the Bidai, Deadose, and Orcoquiza. The third mission, called Nuestra Señora de la Candelaria, was reserved for the Coco and other Karankawan tribes from the coast region. Its formal establishment was delayed by the desertion of the Coco to their native haunts, whence they were recovered only by the heroic efforts of Father Santa Ana, who went for them in person. By May the third mission had been founded. The three missions were located short distances apart on the south side of the San Xavier (San Gabriel) River, above its junction with Arroyo de las Animas (Brushy Creek). Near the junction was San Ildefonso; two or three miles above, on Kolb's Hill, was San Xavier; a mile or so still further up stream stood Candelaria. From the standpoint of numbers at least, the beginnings were propitious, for when late in May Governor Barrio made another inspection there were three hundred and three persons under instruction at the three establishments.[5]

The struggle for a regular presidio had not yet been won, and it was now made more difficult by the personal hostility of Governor Barrio. But in March, 1749, Father Santa Ana and his associates sent in favorable reports of conditions at San Xavier, and Altamira was convinced. He therefore urged the provision of the desired presidio, and of a subsidized civil colony. But as

---

[5] *Memorial del Pe. Ganzabal, pidiendo fuerzas para el resguardo de las missiones de Sn. Xavier; Memorial del R. P. Preside. al capn. de Sn. Antonio,* May 7, 1748; *Escrito presentado al Govr. Dn. Pedro del Varrio sobre Sn. Xavier,* 1749; *Carta Ynforme qe. hizo a Su Exa. el Rdo. Pe. Preste. Fr. Benitto,* June 24, 1748. *Carta del P. Galzaval,* Jan. 22, 1749; *Varios papeles de Tejas.*

it would take some time to make plans for the presidio, he recommended advertising in the interim for colonists, and increasing the guard by eighteen men, to be secured through a characteristic juggling of several of the garrisons of Coahuila. In spite of some opposition by the fiscal to the auditor's plan for a civil colony, on July 7, 1749, the viceroy approved Altamira's proposal.

This approval was a promise of a presidio, but its realization was still far in the future. In August, after a quarrel with Father Mariano over Barrio's inspection, the governor again made an adverse report on the site at San Xavier. Another contest ensued between the two over the appointment of a commander for the enlarged garrison. Governor Barrio had his way in the matter, but he made the quarrel the occasion of another hostile report, in which he complained of Father Mariano's interference, and proposed removing the missions to the San Marcos River.

Father Santa Ana now set out for Mexico to conduct the fight in person, and by a new memorial, made there in November, he completely discredited Governor Barrio at the viceroy's court, with the result that Altamira and Dr. Andreu, now fiscal, agreed that the governor's opposition was ill-founded. And yet, before giving final consent for the presidio, they proposed a new investigation of the site on the San Xavier. To make the survey Lieutenant José de Eca y Músquiz, of the presidio of Sacramento, was appointed, in February, 1750. But Father Santa Ana again interposed. Fearing another long delay, and that the investigation could not be fairly made while Barrio was governor, he lodged a new memorial. It proved effective, and in April the viceroy ordered the work of Músquiz suspended until another governor should enter office in Texas.

The last order seems to have been countermanded, however, for in June, 1750, nearly a year before Barrio's successor came, Músquiz arrived in Texas and began his survey. After examining the San Xavier River and its banks for a distance of seven leagues above its junction with Arroyo de las Ánimas (Brushy Creek), he made a favorable report. This new testimony put an end to the doubt which had stood in the way of final consent to establishing the presidio. Another factor of some weight was the rumor of new dangers on the French frontier, and the consequent need of restoring to Los Adaes the soldiers who were at San Xavier. In a junta of March 11, therefore, a presidio of fifty soldiers was authorized for the protection of the new missions. Felipe de Rábago Terán, who had been appointed by the king more than a year before to the first vacancy which might occur, and was now in Mexico, was made captain. He was ordered to go at once to the frontier, recruit his company, and send the soldiers of the present garrison to their respective commands.[6]

Meanwhile the missionaries had been laboring under all the difficulties usually attendant upon the founding of new missions with inadequate and unsympathetic help, on a remote frontier, among wandering, barbarian Indians. The miserably housed soldiers, separated from their families, were insubordinate, and set an evil example to the Indians whom they were expected to subdue and instruct. The natives, restive under restraint, were prone to desert. In October, 1749, for example, San Ildefonso was abandoned and the missionary left entirely alone. In the following summer a terrible epidemic of smallpox swept through the missions, during which forty adult Indians died, but during which the friars remained at their posts like heroes. In August of that year the neophytes of San Ildefonso again deserted, being led off by a contingent of visiting Indians from eastern Texas,

---

[6] *Copia de una Carta del P. Guard^n. al S. Aud^r., año de 1749; Parecer de el S^{or}. Auditor para la fundacion de S^n. Xavier,* April 23; *Varios papeles de Tejas; Ynforme q^e. hizo D^n. Pedro del Varrio Govr. el año de 1749* (Sept. 11); *Dictamen fiscal,* Jan. 7, 1750; Morfi, *Memorias,* Bk. VIII; *Despacho para que no se continuaran las dilig^s. del Rio de S^n. Xav^r.,* Apr. 8, 1750; *Testimonio de los Autos fhos sre. la erecion del Precidio de S^n. Xavier,* 1751. See also pp. 185–248.

bound for a campaign against the Apache. They remained away until December, 1751. Before that time the Indians of Mission Candelaria had absconded, but they soon returned. Desertion was no doubt encouraged by shortage of supplies, for this drawback sometimes made it necessary for the neophytes to hunt their own food in forest and prairie. The exchange of Governor Barrio for Governor Barrios y Jáuregui was regarded by the missionaries as no improvement. Barrios came in June, 1751, with instructions to remove the seventeen soldiers belonging to Adaes, but to replace them with others. The first part of the order was duly fulfilled, but the second was not, and in consequence the garrison was weakened.

Yet all was not dark. When in July, 1750, Músquiz inspected the missions, he counted in the three churches four hundred and eighty resident Indians, and the books at that time showed two hundred and sixty-six baptisms. These results were not inconsiderable, for they were first among the things which to the missionaries meant success. Some progress was made also in buildings and agriculture, and in October, 1750, the construction of a ditch and a dam were begun, through the labor of the Indians, encouraged by extra rations, presents, and a necessary show of force.[7]

It was December, 1751, before Rábago arrived at San Xavier with his presidial garrison. But this was all too soon for the peace of the missionaries. For six years they had been clamoring for a presidio, and now that they had secured one it proved to be their very undoing, for, wherever the blame, Rábago's coming sounded the deathknell of the San Xavier missions. Rábago had not been there three days before a dispute arose over the mission guards. He had been there scarcely a month when he recommended consolidating the three missions into one, moving it to the San Marcos, and establishing there a civil colony, for which,

---

[7] See pp. 219–240, below.

on his journey northward, he had already secured volunteer settlers. In return Father Miguel Pinilla, who served as chaplain of the presidio, reprimanded Rábago for immorality. Father Mariano, who had led the long fight for the presidio, being disgusted with the captain's conduct, proposed within a month of Rábago's arrival that the presidio be withdrawn and defence provided by a civil colony.

To do what was possible to prevent further hostilities, the College of Santa Cruz ordered Father Mariano replaced, as president, by Father Alonso Giraldo de Terreros, and Father Pinilla, as chaplain, by Father Joseph López. But this attempt at conciliation came too late, for before it could take effect matters had come to a crisis. Friction continuing, Rábago ordered Pinilla to cease his functions as chaplain. In return, Father Pinilla declared Rábago and a part of the soldiers excommunicate. Though absolution was sought and granted, bitterness remained. In May, 1752, Father Ganzábal and a citizen were murdered as they stood in the doorway of Mission Candelaria, and all but one of the remaining missionaries fled to San Antonio. The matter being investigated, a mission Indian confessed that he and four soldiers had committed the murder at the instigation of Captain Rábago. To facilitate further investigation, Rábago was removed and replaced by his brother, Don Pedro. After eight years of tedious litigation Don Felipe was acquitted and reinstated, but the missionaries were never convinced of his innocence.

Meanwhile the missions struggled on, but after the murder of Father Ganzábal their usefulness was practically over. A part of the missionaries returned, however, and Mission San Francisco continued in operation. In the winter of 1752–3, Father José Pinilla made an expedition to recover the Coco, who had fled just before Ganzábal's murder. Somewhat later the Coco, Bidai, and Orcoquiza returned and entered Mission Candelaria.

But they afterwards fled intermittently, and sometimes offered deadly resistance to recovery.

When Don Pedro Rábago arrived in August, 1754, he at once urged the abandonment of the whole San Xavier undertaking, and by this time the missionaries, with whom the new commander was popular, were ready to agree. The few neophytes, Rábago thought, might be taken to the missions at San Antonio, and the soldiers and missionaries transferred to the Apache country, on the San Sabá or the Florido (Concho) River, which he had explored in 1748. Because of bad seasons the site at San Xavier had proved unhealthful, and to this drawback were added tales of horrible manifestations of nature. In consequence, after several unavailing appeals for permission to move, in the summer of 1755 the soldiers, missionaries, and a few neophytes, went with their belongings, but without permission, to the springs of the San Marcos River. Thus ended ten years of effort to establish and maintain missions on the San Xavier River, in the country of the Tonkawa.[8]

2. *The Reorganization of the Lower Gulf Coast.*[9]—Just at the time when the movement was begun by the missionaries to

---

[8] See pp. 248–280; Arricivita, *Crónica*, 330–338; Morfi, *Memorias*, Bk. IX, paragraphs 6–35. The circumstances of the removal were as follows: In July, 1755, the soldiers and missionaries made several petitions to Captain Rábago, asking permission to move from San Xavier to San Marcos, whither a part of the Indians had already gone to escape a pest caused by stagnant water. On July 23 Rábago granted the petition, as a temporary measure taken through necessity, and sent Diego Ramón with ten soldiers, one missionary, and twenty Indians to erect temporary buildings. On August 16 Rábago followed with the remaining missionaries, soldiers, neophytes, and belongings of the settlement. Arrived at San Marcos they were soon besieged by a thousand hungry Apache Indians asking that the missionaries and soldiers go to their country on the San Sabá or the Florido. (*Testimonio de los Autos fechos sobre la Reduccion de los Yndios Gentiles de la Nacion Apache y establecimiento de el Precidio de San Saba*).

[9] The following sketch of Spanish activities on the Gulf coast after 1745 is based mainly on the detailed study presented in Part III of this volume (pp. 281–324), where references to the primary authorities will be found. A portion of the ground is covered in Bolton, ''The Founding of Mission Rosario: A Chapter in the History of the Gulf Coast,'' Texas State Historical Association *Quarterly*, X, 113–139, and Bolton, ''Tienda

enter central Texas, another set of forces was making necessary the subjugation of the Gulf coast region, lying between Lavaca Bay and Tampico. This region was still unconquered and little known, but it had long been a menace to the prosperity and the security of the settled districts surrounding it.

The founding of the mission and presidio of La Bahía near Lavaca Bay, in 1722, had been followed immediately by trouble with the fierce Karankawa, and shortly afterward by the removal of the establishments to the country of the Tamique and Xaraname, farther inland. But the Karankawan tribes continued to be hostile and to give trouble to their Spanish neighbors. Indeed, they soon acquired and long maintained the reputation of being unconquerable.[10]

Even more troublesome was the coast district farther south, lying east of Nuevo León and north of Querétaro. This country, sheltered in its southern portion behind mountain ranges on the west, had long been the asylum of multitudes of broken-down bands and tribes, pushed northward and eastward by the progress of the Spanish conquest, or by more powerful Indian neighbors. Into this region little advance of settlement had been made since the sixteenth century. Efforts to subdue the southern end of the district, the Sierra Gorda, were made in the seventeenth century by Franciscan and Dominican missionaries, and in the early eighteenth century by the soldiery of Querétaro, but still with little permanent result, for the Indian bands continued to sally forth and to exact tribute from most of the towns of the Querétaran frontier. Efforts to subdue the coast region lying north of Tampico and south of the Rio Grande were likewise made in the early eighteenth century, by Francisco Barbadillo,

---

de Cuervo's Ynspección of Laredo, 1757,'' *ibid.*, VI, 187–203. The former article is reprinted, with revisions, in the present volume, pp. 281–324. A valuable account of the founding of Nuevo Santander is contained in Alejandro Prieto, *Historia, Geografía, y Estadística del Estado de Tamaulipas* (Mexico, 1873), and in Father Vicente Santa María's MS *Relación Histórica de la Colonia del Nuevo Santander* (1760).

10 See pp. 281–286, below.

especially commissioned for that purpose, but likewise with no lasting result.

These general conditions in the Seno Mexicano, as the coast district was called, made it imperative that the region be subdued. In 1738 the reduction of the Sierra Gorda was successfully begun by José de Escandón, aided by Franciscan missionaries. At the same time several proposals were made for conquering the coast region farther north. War with England broke out in 1739, and there was now some uneasiness lest the unoccupied Gulf coast be seized by that power. Effective action was delayed until 1746, however, when the task was entrusted to Escandón, who by then had completed the conquest of the Sierra Gorda. The missionary work of the new enterprise was entrusted to the College of Guadalupe de Zacatecas. Escandón's commission gave him ample powers and required the frontier garrisons to render him all possible aid. The territory assigned him to conquer and colonize, extending from Tampico to the San Antonio River, was called Colonia del Nuevo Santander.[11]

In 1746 and 1747 Escandón personally explored the country as far north as the Rio Grande, selecting sites for settlements, while under his orders Captain Joaquín de 'Orobio Bazterra, of La Bahía, explored the region from the Guadalupe to the Rio Grande. The explorations having been made, Escandón proposed founding in his colony fourteen Spanish villas, or towns, and as many missions as might be necessary. Twelve of the settlements were to be located south of the Rio Grande, and two north of that stream. The two northernmost towns proposed were to be Villa de Vedoya, at the mouth of the Nueces, composed of fifty families, and Villa de Balmaceda, on the Lower San Antonio, composed of twenty-five families. Near the former Escandón proposed founding a new mission, and to the site of the latter he proposed moving the mission and presidio of La Bahía.[12]

---

11 See below, pp. 287–292.
12 See below, pp. 292–294.

The execution of Escandón's plans was one of the most notable events in the entire history of the colonization of the northern frontiers of New Spain. At Querétaro the empresario raised seven hundred and fifty soldiers, and advertised for civil colonists. Because of the leader's fame, the response was ready and the results most gratifying. In December, 1748, Escandón was able to leave Querétaro with a colony comprising more than thirty-two hundred soldiers and settlers, while others joined him on the way or met him on the frontier. The colonists, a mixture of Spaniards, half-castes, and civilized Indians, carried their household goods, and drove before them great herds of horses, cattle, burros, sheep, and goats. The caravan must have resembled those of the Oregon and California migrations of a later date and another people.

Going northwest to San Luis Potosí, there Escandón turned eastward into his province. As he passed through it he planted, at the sites already selected, little colonies and garrisons, beside which the friars founded missions. Reaching the Rio Grande, on its southern bank he founded in March, 1749, the villas of Camargo and Reynosa, with families from Coahuila and Nuevo León, who had met him there by appointment. In 1750 Revilla, and in 1753 Mier, were founded, also on the southern bank of the Rio Grande.

North of the river Escandón's plans were executed entirely by his lieutenants. In 1749 the presidio and mission of La Bahía were moved, according to program, to the San Antonio River, where they were re-established at the present site of Goliad. A colony sent under Captain Diego González to found the Villa de Vedoya, at the mouth of the Nueces, backed out through fear of the Indians, recrossed the Rio Grande, and became the founders of Soto la Marina. Villa de Balmaceda failed to be established through lack of funds.

Near the Rio Grande the results were better. In 1750, at the same time that Revilla was being founded by Coahuila families on the southern bank of the stream, Rancho de Dolores was established across the river by Captain Borrego, whose ranch soon became the nucleus of a considerable settlement. In 1754 Tomás Sánchez was sent by Escandón to the Nueces River, with a view to making another attempt at settlement there. Returning with an unfavorable report, in 1755 he founded instead the Villa de Laredo, on the north side of the river, at a crossing which at once became important on the highway to Texas. Meanwhile, the missionaries at La Bahía had established a new mission for the Karankawan tribes near the San Antonio River.

By October, 1755, Escandón had founded in Nuevo Santander twenty-three settlements, most of which persist today. In them he had established over six thousand colonists. Beside the presidios and towns the Zacatecan friars had founded fifteen flourishing missions. North of the Rio Grande there were the Villa de Laredo, with thirteen families, the *población* of Dolores, with twenty-five families, and further down the river a string of ranches. This district fast became a stock-raising country, where thousands of cattle, sheep, and goats grazed on either side of the stream. Under Escandón's encouragement, ranching gradually extended northward, and within a few years had reached the Nueces.[13]

An important phase of all this work of reorganizing the Gulf coast, and the one most intimately connected with the development of what was then called Texas, was the renewed effort to bring the Karankawan tribes under missionary control. The mission of Espíritu Santo de Zúñiga, which was moved in 1749 to the San Antonio River, along with the presidio of Loreto (La Bahía), was devoted still to the welfare of the Tamique and Xaraname tribes. But the principal aim of Escandón's work of reorganization in the northern part of Nuevo Santander was to

---

[13] See 291–303, below; José Francisco Sotomayor, *Historia del Apostólico Colegio de Nuestra Señora de Guadalupe de Zacatecas* (Zacatecas, 1889), 187–190, contains an account of the missions in Nuevo Santander, copied verbatim from Father Hierro's *Informe.*

subdue the insubordinate Karankawan tribes living along the coast, and both missionaries and officers were instructed accordingly. This end was in part, though but momentarily, realized through the entrance of some of the Coco into the missions at San Xavier.

The activities of the Zacatecan friars at La Bahía on behalf of the Karankawa were quickened by the pushing of the Querétaran friars of San Antonio into the same field. An epidemic at San Antonio had carried off many neophytes and made room for new recruits. Moreover, the Querétaran missionaries at San Antonio were now under the presidency of the aggressive Father Mariano de los Dolores y Viana, founder of the San Xavier missions. Consequently, in 1750 plans were made to take the Karankawan tribes, particularly the Cujane, to San Antonio, where a few of them were already under instruction. The immediate work was entrusted by Fray Mariano to Fray Diego Martín García, one of the most intelligent and zealous of the missionaries. Knowing the prior claims of the Zacatecans to the Karankawa region, permission to enter it was first secured from the viceroy, and from Father González, head missionary at Espíritu Santo.

Nevertheless, some friction occurred over the matter. When the first delegation of fifty-four Cujanes started for San Antonio in response to a message and presents from Father García, they stopped, in passing, at the mission of Espíritu Santo, where they remained. Fray Mariano believed that force or persuasion had been used in order to profit by his efforts. Another attempt had a similar result, and Fray Mariano protested to Father González. After what he regarded as a third encroachment upon his rights, Fray Mariano appealed to his college, and through Father Santa Ana, then in Mexico, to the viceroy. Father Santa Ana made a vigorous protest at the viceroy's court, asking that the disputed field be turned over entirely to his own college. The whole situation greatly irritated Altamira, the *auditor,* and brought forth his emphatic assertion that nothing permanent would ever be accomplished on the frontiers without more settlers. Finally, after two years of discussion by fiscal, *auditor,* and missionary authorities, the viceroy discreetly, and no doubt wisely, exhorted both colleges to put aside their differences, and to co-operate in the important work of subduing the Karankawa.[14]

Meanwhile, little progress was being made at the mission of Espíritu Santo with its new charges. They frequently deserted, and trouble ensued between them and the soldiers. Nevertheless, the missionaries persisted with laudable zeal, and secured some worthy results. They were generously aided in their work by Captain Piszina, who made the enterprise an occasion for an appeal for more supplies and more soldiers.

In view of the difficulties of the situation, by the end of 1753 the friars of Espíritu Santo conceived the project of founding a separate mission for the Karankawan tribes. To promote this plan Father Camberos was sent to Zacatecas and from there to Mexico. The undertaking was defended on the ground of the hostility of the Karankawa toward the Tamique and Xaraname, tribes of a different language, and of their reluctance to going, as well as the impolity of trying to take them, to a mission outside their native land. Again the plan of substitution was suggested. To save expense Father Camberos proposed transferring the Ais mission, with one of its missionaries, to the new site, the other friar going to reside at the mission of Nacogdoches. The eastern missions, he argued, had never succeeded, and never would succeed, while all the aid possible could be rendered the Ais from Nacogdoches, especially if the tribe, of less than forty families, were moved to their relatives, the Aixitos. Though hesitant at

---

[14] See pp. 303–308, below; Morfi, *Memorias,* Bk. IX, paragraph 37; Fray Simón Hierro, *Informe de las Misiones de Texas,* January 8, 1762; Sotomayor, *Historia,* 191–192. Sotomayor's account is based on the *Informe* of Father Hierro just cited.

first, the fiscal and the *auditor* became convinced, and in June, 1754, the viceroy authorized the transfer.

But now the voice of dissent was heard from eastern Texas. Father Vallejo, president of the missions there, supported by the governor, protested to his college. In his view, the mission of Los Ais was not useless, by any means. In thirty-six years one hundred and fifty-eight precious souls had been saved there by baptism; the missionaries were useful as physicians and nurses for the Indians, and must be near at hand in order to perform these duties; there was still reason to hope that the Ais tribe would settle down to pueblo life; and finally—the old and threadbare pretext—the mission would be important in case of a French invasion.[15]

Father Vallejo's protest put an end to the effort to suppress the mission of Los Ais. In turn, the Zacatecan college proposed a new mission for the Cujane, a plan which, with unwonted promptitude, was approved by the viceroy in April, 1755. Already, in consequence of the order to transfer the mission of Los Ais, Father Camberos, who was back in Texas, had begun in the previous November to found the new mission. It was located west of the San Antonio River, some four leagues from La Bahía. While awaiting a final decision from the government, funds were supplied by the missionaries, Captain Piszina, and private benefactors. The name given the new establishment was Nuestra Señora del Rosario. By January 15, through the aid of Captain Piszina, fields had been opened and buildings erected. Two years later a stone and mortar dam fifty varas long had been built across an arroyo, and, sooner or later, a strong wooden stockade was erected. Though funds and forces were limited, and the Indians barbarous, the enterprise enjoyed some measure of success. In the course of the first few years the number of

---

[15] *Autos fhos. Apedimento* . . . [de] *Frai Benitto de Santa An*[a] . . . *que se le manden restitu* [*ir a la Mision de*] *Sn. Antonio* . . . *los* [*con*] *Bersos Indios de la Nacion* [*Cujan*] *que se hallan agregados a* [*la*] *de Santa Dorothea,* 1751–1758.

natives who lived, at least intermittently, at the mission, was considerable, although only twenty-one baptisms were performed during the first four years.

The viceroy had been prompt to authorize the new establishment, but he was slow to provide adequate funds. However, after four years of appealing by Father Camberos, the college, Captain Piszina, and Governor Barrios, in 1758 the government authorized more liberal supplies for the mission, and ten additional soldiers for the presidio. With this belated aid the mission became more prosperous.[16] Although it was situated within the limits of the colony of Nuevo Santander, it depended on the presidio of La Bahía, and was administered as a part of Texas.

3. *The French border and the defence of the lower Trinity.*[17] —Almost simultaneously with the beginning of the San Xavier missions and of the colony of Nuevo Santander, the Spaniards were forced by foreign aggression into the region of the lower Trinity River. Strange as it may appear, after more than half a century of exploration in Texas and after nearly thirty years of continuous occupation of several points within the province, this district seems to have been almost unknown to the Spaniards.[18] But now they were compelled by French encroachments to occupy the region, in order to defend it and to maintain the allegiance of its natives.

---

[16] *Autos fhos. Apedimento;* see also pp. 308–324.

[17] This sketch is based mainly upon the detailed study presented in Part IV of the present volume (pp. 327–374). That study is a reprint, with revisions, of an article in the *Southwestern Historical Quarterly,* XVI, 339–377. A brief résumé of the subject is given by I. J. Cox, *The Louisiana-Texas Frontier,* in the Texas State Historical Association *Quarterly,* X, 21–24. A brief account of the mission on the Trinity River is given by Sotomayor, *Historia,* 192. It is based on Father Hierro's *Informe.*

[18] A commentary on this point is found in the letter of Governor Prudencio de Orobio Bazterra, written at Adaes, July 8, 1740, to Father Santa Ana, president of the missions at San Antonio. He says: ''With respect to the rivers Colorado, Brazos de Dios, Trinidad, and Sabinas, I only know, and it is certain, that they empty into the Gulf of Mexico, and that it is false that the exploration of any of this has been made

As early as 1741, it is stated, Governor Prudencio Orobio Bazterra, hearing of French advances, urged the placing of a presidio on the lower Trinity. In 1745 Joaquín Orobio Bazterra, captain of the garrison at La Bahía, reported to the viceroy rumors of a French settlement near the mouth of that stream. In reply Orobio was ordered to proceed with all haste to verify the rumor, and, if it proved well founded, to expel the French. The prevailing ignorance of the geography of the coast region to the eastward of La Bahía at this time is illustrated by Orobio's difficulties in deciding upon a route thither. At first he attempted to go by land along the coast. Next he contemplated building a fleet of canoes and going by the Guadalupe River and the Gulf. Finally, in December, he set out over the Los Adaes road, planning to go to the Trinity crossing, thence to descend to the river's mouth. Arriving at the ford he changed his plans, and continued to Los Adaes, to confer with Governor García Larios. On the way, at the Trinity, at the Neches, and at Nacogdoches, the rumors of French traders were confirmed. Returning from Los Adaes to Nacogdoches, he thence set out southwest over the Bidai Trail, the best available route.

Passing among the Bidai, he crossed the Trinity and continued southwest to the Orcoquiza villages on the western branches of the Aranzazu (San Jacinto) River. Both the Bidai and the Orcoquiza claimed never to have seen Spaniards before. Among them both, however, the rumors of French activities along the coast were fully confirmed. Not only did the traders freely

---

either by Don Pedro de Rivera or anyone else, or that it would be impracticable, because if for this purpose the matter were to be considered with the necessary reflection, and his Excellency were to be informed with sincerity of purpose, and he who were to undertake the enterprise of its exploration were not moved by vanity, private interest, or other depraved intentions which should frustrate the aim, there is no doubt that what this coast contains from La Bahía to the mouths of all the rivers named would not be hidden from our notice, nor, likewise, what there is between said coast and the Camino Real which we travel from here to La Bahía.'' (*Varias Noticias por lo q mira a franzeses—dadas el año de 1740*). In writing thus Orobio was of course cognizant of the intense hostility of the missionaries toward Rivera.

come and go, but they were said to be preparing to make a settlement the very next year at a site already chosen near the mouth of the San Jacinto River. Orobio visited the site, but, seeing no signs of a settlement, he returned to La Bahía, by a more direct route.[19]

Captain Orobio, and those who in succeeding years visited the tribe, found the Orcoquiza living in four or five scattered villages near the San Jacinto and the lower Trinity, the center of population being near Arroyo de Santa Rosa del Alcázar (Spring Creek). East of the Trinity the tribe extended part way to the Neches. The Orcoquiza practiced some agriculture, but lived mainly on fish, game, and wild fruits. It was their trade in peltry and bears' fat which had attracted the French. The tribe was not large and its organization was loose, a fact which greatly complicated the question of control in subsequent years.

Before leaving the Orcoquiza Orobio talked to the Indians of missions, to enter which they showed some willingness. A year or two later, as has been seen, a part of the tribe, together with some of the Bidai, entered the San Xavier missions. Shortly after his return to La Bahía in 1746, Orobio seems to have made another visit to the lower Trinity to look for Frenchmen, but to have found none. During the next few years Spanish agents, in the capacity of traders, were regularly sent among the Orcoquiza and the Bidai. Of this trade the chief beneficiary, for several years after 1751, appears to have been Governor Barrios y Jáuregui. From the evidence available it seems that he and his personal agents completely monopolized the traffic. The goods were secured at Natchitoches, in open violation of the law, and were carried in pack trains, conveyed by small guards of soldiers. Among Barrios's chief lieutenants in the business were Marcos Ruiz, Domingo del Rio, Juan Antonio Maldonado, and Jacinto de León. In exchange for merchandise, the Indians gave maize,

---

[19] *Diligencias Practicadas por Don Joaquín de Orobio Capn. de la Bahia Sobre establecimiento de Franceses.* See also pp. 332–337, below.

hides, and horses, the latter usually having been stolen from the Spaniards farther west.

But the French traders did not cease coming to the lower Trinity. Whether or not they came with the collusion of Governor Barrios, as was charged, is not very clear. At any rate, in October, 1754, Joseph Blancpain, one of these merchants, was arrested by Marcos Ruiz at the governor's order. Blancpain's goods were confiscated and divided among his captors; he and his assistants were sent to Mexico and thrown into prison, where Blancpain died. Incidentally to the arrest, Ruiz was told that a French colony was coming soon to settle among the Orcoquiza.[20]

The arrest of Blancpain and the consequent defense of the Lower Trinity was intimately connected with Franco-Spanish relations on the whole frontier from New Mexico to the Texas coast. On the New Mexico border French intrusions had recently become alarming. As the French traders and official explorers had pushed west in the early years of the century, they had looked with covetous eyes toward New Mexico. But there were two obstacles to expeditions bound for that country. One was the jealous and exclusive policy of Spain, which made the reception of such Frenchmen as might reach Santa Fé a matter of uncertainty; the other was the tier of Indian tribes which stood in the way. The Red River highway was effectually blocked by the Apache, mortal enemies of all the tribes along the lower valley; the Arkansas and Missouri River avenues were impeded by the Comanche for analogous reasons. As the fur-traders and official explorers pushed west, one of their constant aims was to open the way to New Mexico by effecting peace between the Comanche and the tribes further east. In 1739 a trading party

---

[20] *Diligencias Practicadas por Dn. Joaquin de Orobio Capn. de la Bahia Sobre establecimiento de Francesces; Testimonio practicado sobre si D. Jasinto de Barrios tuvo comercio con Muniziones de Guerra con los Yndios Barbaros de Esta Prova. y fuera de ella; Autos de Residencia de Barrios y Jauregui; Dilixensias sobre Lanpen.* See also pp. 337–339, below.

of eight or nine men, led by the Mallet brothers, ascended the Platte River and made their way through the Comanche country to Taos and to Santa Fé. After being detained several months in friendly captivity, six or seven of the party returned, unharmed by the Spanish authorities, and bearing evidence that the residents of New Mexico would welcome trade. Four of the men descended the Canadian and the Arkansas rivers, the others going northeast to Illinois.

The Mallet party had succeeded in getting through the Comanche country to New Mexico and had returned in safety and with good prospects for trade—two important achievements. Immediately there was renewed interest in the New Mexico border. In 1741 Governor Bienville sent a party under Fabry de la Bruyère up the Arkansas to try to open trade with Santa Fé, but it did not reach its destination. Shortly afterward a new military post was established on the Missouri at the Kansas village, and the Arkansas route was made safe by effecting in 1746 or 1747 a treaty between the Comanche and the Jumano, who lived on the middle Arkansas. The effect of the treaty was immediate, and at once there were new expeditions to New Mexico by deserters, private traders, and official agents. Early in 1748 thirty-three Frenchmen were reported among the Comanche near Taos. A year later three Frenchmen, called Febre, Satren, and Raballo, accompanied the Comanche to Taos to trade, having ascended the Arkansas in a party of twelve. Within the next year seven others from Louisiana arrived at Santa Fé at different times, part of them at least entering by the Arkansas route. In 1751 four traders from New Orleans reached New Mexico by the Missouri River. In 1752 arrived two others, named Chapuis and Feuilli, members of a party of ten who had left Fort Chartres with official sanction. They boldly proposed opening a caravan trade, under military escort, from Illinois to Santa Fé.

The Mallet party had been permitted to return to Louisiana unimpeded and to tell what they knew of New Mexico. The evil

results of this policy were seen, and the Febre party were retained in Santa Fé as artisans, without permission to return.
The 1751 and 1752 parties, on the other hand, were sent to Mexico
in captivity, with the governor's reports that the alliance between
the French and Comanche was dangerous. The former were sent
to Spain late in 1752. After Chapuis and Feuilli had lain in
prison a year, they too were sent to Spain, early in 1754.[21]

The French intrusion into New Mexico found an echo in far
western Sonora. On March 2, 1751, Fernández Sánchez Salvador,
Captain of Caballos Corazas of Sonora and Sinaloa, cited the
French advance as a reason for haste in the Spanish occupation
of the Colorado of the West. He was convinced that the French
traders had ulterior ends, and that they would soon reach the
Colorado and descend it to the South Sea and California unless
impeded by a Spanish advance northward from Sonora.

The French advance through the Comanchería at this time,
encouraged as it was by the Louisiana officials, and coupled with
the strengthening of the Louisiana forces and with the increasing French aggressiveness on the Texas border, gives significance
to the proposal of Governor Kerlérec, in 1753, to break through
the Apache barrier and open up trade with the more interior
provinces of Mexico. In a *mémoire* addressed to the King in
that year the new governor spoke of Spain's jealous policy, the
weakness of her outposts, and the ease with which the mines of
Coahuila and Nuevo León could be conquered. As a base for
securing them, in case of any rupture, he proposed taking possession of the Apache country, at present dominated neither by

---

[21] The above account of French aggressions on the New Mexico border
is based on two *expedientes* in the archives of Mexico as follows: (1)
*Autos fhos sre averiguar que rumbo han ttraido ttres franzeses que llegaron
al Pueblo de taos con la Nazⁿ Cumanche q benian a hazer sus aconstumbrados
resgattes* (1749–1751). Archivo General y Público, Mexico, Provincias
Internas, vol. 37. (2) *Testimonio de los autos fhos a Consulta del Govᵒʳ.
del Nuebo Mexᶜᵒ sobre haver llegado dos franzeses cargados de efectos que
conduzian de la Nueba Orleans* (1751–1754). Archivo General y Público,
Mexico, Provincias Internas, vol. 34.

France nor Spain. But unless peace were established between the Apache and all their numerous enemies to the eastward, access to their country would be impossible. He proposed, therefore, to remove the barrier by securing an alliance between the Apache and these intervening tribes. What action was taken in France regarding the proposal[22] is not known, but the fact that it was made at all is significant.

While these developments had been taking place in New Mexico, there were disturbing reports of increasing dangers on the Texas border, which again brought forward the quiescent boundary question and led to interesting investigations. In 1750 the military strength of Louisiana was considerably augmented, and it was reported in Mexico that the new arrivals were destined for the frontiers bordering on New Spain. In February, 1751, the viceroy reviewed the situation, stated that the French had already passed eighty leagues beyond the Mississippi, their true boundary, and ordered Jacinto de Barrios, the new governor of Texas, to investigate rumors of contraband trade and of the French advance. The combined reports from Louisiana and the frontiers of Texas and New Mexico in turn elicited a royal order, dated June 26, 1751, which still further crystallized interest in the boundary question. It provided that Frenchmen entering Texas or New Mexico should not be permitted to return to Louisiana under any pretext, that the viceroy should carefully watch the French, and that in case of any effort to advance they should be ordered to evacuate Natchitoches, though no force should be used, in view of the alliance between the two nations.

As soon as he reached Los Adaes, in July, 1751, Barrios investigated the charges of contraband trade against his predecessor, which were not sustained. In October he held an in-

---

22 The account of Kerlérec's proposal of 1753 is based on the document entitled *Projet de Paix et D'Alliance avec les cannecis*, etc., in *Journal de la Société des Américanistes de Paris*, Nouvelle Série, III, 67–76. For the report by Sánchez, see his *Cuarta Representación*, in *Doc. Hist. Mex.*, 3d ser., vol. III, 662–663.

quiry regarding the boundary and the reports of the French advance. The witnesses, residents of Los Adaes, generally agreed that the true boundary was the Red River, and verified the reports of new military forces in Louisiana, asserting that part of them were destined for Natchitoches and Cadodachos. Their testimony regarding the operations of the French among the Indians shows clearly that Louis de Saint Denis, the younger, since 1744 had succeeded to the position of his more famous father, and was absolute master of the frontier tribes. As an illustration it was shown that in the preceding year the Indians had openly rebelled and threatened to expel the Spaniards merely because Governor Barrios had interfered with the trading operations of Saint Denis. In the following year Barrios sent Manuel Antonio De Soto Vermúdez among the tribes to report on the operations of the French. In attempting to go from the Nasoni to the Nadote village, where Saint Denis had a trading post, he was driven back by the Nadote chief. Immediately after De Soto left, an assembly of five hundred warriors gathered at the Nadote village and threatened to massacre all the Spaniards on the frontier, but they were calmed by Saint Denis.[23]

Meanwhile a *junta general* was held in Mexico, in September, 1752, to consider the question of the Texas border. It debated the establishment of a garrison on the San Pedro River, recommended by Barrios, to watch the French, the sending of an engineer to mark-the Texas-Louisiana boundary, the raising of the Los Adaes presidio to the rank of that of Vera Cruz, and the assembling of documents to determine whether the Mississippi River or the Red was the true international boundary. All of these points except the last were decided in the negative, but Governor Barrios was ordered to investigate the boundary ques-

---

[23] See *Testimᵒ. de Autos de Pesquiza sobre comercio Ylicito y Demas que expresa el Superior Despacho que esta por caveza de ellos.* (Béxar Archives, Adaes, 1739–1755); an *expediente* concerning the investigation made by De Soto Vermúdez (Archivo General y Público, *Historia*, vol. 299; also in Provincias Internas, vol. 181).

tion further, and to expel the French from any territory they might have usurped, if possible without using force.

In February, 1753, Barrios made the required investigation. Twelve witnesses were examined. They generally agreed that the Red River was the true boundary, but their testimony showed that since 1736 Arroyo Hondo or Gran Montaña had been the accepted limit. The land usurped by the French was stated to be a stone's throw or a gunshot in width. It is clear, therefore, that while the higher authorities were debating between the Red and the Mississippi rivers as the boundary, to the frontier residents the only matter of doubt was between Red River and Arroyo Hondo or Gran Montaña. Just at the time when Barrios was making his investigation, César de Blanc, commander at Natchitoches, wrote to protest against a rumored plan of Barrios to establish a presidio at the Nadote village, and to state that the boundary must be left *in statu quo* until the two sovereigns should determine it. In reply Barrios told Blanc that his protest was ill-founded and his advice unnecessary.

To Barrios the results of his investigation seemed inconclusive, but he reported that the Spaniards of the frontier were at the mercy of the French, since at a word, in case of war, the Indians would massacre them all, which was probably the case. He therefore again urged the establishment of a presidio on the San Pedro, asserted the necessity of competing with the French in the Indian trade, and asked permission, in case of war, to offer freedom to all slaves absconding from Louisiana, as an offset against the Indian allies of the French.

Such was the situation on the Texas and New Mexico borders at the end of 1753. In January, 1754, it was decided to send the last two French intruders, Chapuis and Feuille, to Spain. Immediately afterward (January 21–22) another junta assembled, and considered matters in the light of Barrios's report. It was decided not to try to expel the French from Natchitoches, since there was doubt as to whether the Red River or Gran Montaña was the boundary; not to plant the San Pedro garrison without more information; and not to grant Barrios's request regarding slaves, because it was neither "advantageous nor decorous." On the other hand, Barrios was again instructed to keep watch that the French should not overstep their boundaries; to order Saint Denis to withdraw his commission to the Nadote chief; to require the commander of Natchitoches to recall French interpreters from the Indian villages on Spanish soil; and to "prevent the commerce of the French with the Indians of Texas, observing what the governor of New Mexico had practiced in the matter, with the idea of preventing the Indians from communicating with them."

In response to the report of the junta of January, 1754, the king of Spain issued an instruction to the viceroy (July 30, 1755) in which he stated that "boundaries between Spaniards and French in that region have never been a subject of treaty, nor is it best at present." But as a preparation for such a measure, or any other, he ordered the viceroy to employ engineer Don Agustín de Cámara Alta, whom he had just sent to Mexico for the purpose, to make a map of northern New Spain, from Louisiana to the Pacific Ocean, in order to determine "the confines and distances." Since a detailed study of the whole frontier would be a matter of years, he was ordered to make an exact map only of "the situation of the province of Texas, that of the Rio Colorado and its borders, the presidio of Nachitóos which the French possess, and the provinces intervening as far as Mexico," estimating the rest of the district as far as California.[24]

The decision of the junta in Mexico bore fruit also in the arrest by Governor Barrios, in the fall of 1754, of Blancpain and

---

[24] *Testimonio de Autos fechos en Virtud de Superior Decreto . . . a 26 de Sepre. de 1752*, etc. (Béxar Archives, Adaes, 1739–1755); *Instrucción Reservada que trajo el Marqués de las Amarillas*, July 30, 1755, in *Instrucciones que los Vireyes de Nueva España Dejaron a sus sucesores*, pp. 96–97; *Expediente sobre la aprehencion . . . de tres Franceses, y dos Negros*, etc. (Archivo General de Indias, Seville, Guadalajara, 103–106–123).

his associates. Thus the whole French border question, from California to the mouth of the Trinity, was bound together.

Barrios reported Blancpain's intrusion to the viceroy, and, as a means of defense, recommended establishing on the Trinity a presidio, a mission, and a civil settlement, the latter to be recruited at Los Adaes and given the usual subsidy assigned to new colonies. At the same time, he sent Domingo del Rio to the Trinity to make a new investigation. Del Rio reporting, when he returned, that other Frenchmen had been among the Orcoquiza since Blancpain's arrest, in the summer of 1755 the governor sent a temporary garrison of soldiers to the danger point.

Blancpain's examination before the viceroy was held in the royal hall of confessions in February, 1755. For a year, however, nothing was accomplished by the superior government but to discuss and refer the matter back and forth. Barrios's proposal went in the course of the spring and summer to the fiscal, the *auditor*, and a *junta de guerra*, but no agreement could be reached. The controversy turned upon the size of the garrison and the question of subsidizing the proposed colony. It was mainly a matter of expense.

The arrest of Blancpain and the establishment of the Spanish garrison on the Trinity called forth a protest from Kerlérec, governor of Louisiana, who laid claim to the site in the name of the Most Christian King. This important phase of the matter being reported by Barrios in September, the case was again taken up in Mexico. But another delay was now caused by a change of viceroys, and when the Marqués de las Amarillas arrived at the end of 1755 the question of the defence of the lower Trinity was still demanding attention. Amarillas took the matter up promptly, however, and in a junta of February 4, 1756, it was settled, mainly in accord with the opinions of Barrios and of Valcárcel, now the *auditor*, who, like Altamira, his predecessor, was a strong believer in civil colonies and in the elimination of the soldiery as soon as possible.

The junta, whose views were approved by the viceroy, recommended a garrison of thirty soldiers and a mission, both to be
established for the present on the site of Blancpain's arrest. As
soon as possible a permanent site must be selected for the presidio
and mission, and for a subsidized colony of fifty families, half
of Spaniards and half of Tlascaltecan Indians, both classes to
be enlisted at Saltillo. At the end of six years the presidio was
to be suppressed, the soldiers remaining as citizen colonists. The
mission was to be conducted by Franciscan friars of the College
of Guadalupe de Zacatecas. Barrios was ordered to proceed at
once to found mission and presidio, select the permanent site, and
report upon the subsidy required.

In the summer of 1756, by royal appointment, Barrios was
made governor of Coahuila, and Don Angel Martos Navarrete
governor of Texas, but in order that Barrios might complete the
work already begun, the two appointments were temporarily interchanged, and Barrios was in consequence retained in Texas
three more years.

The governor at once set about founding the presidio, which
was established by midsummer, 1756. The soldiers were recruited mainly at Los Adaes, and Domingo del Rio was made
lieutenant in command. In honor of the viceroy the presidio
was named San Agustín de Ahumada. At the same time Barrios,
aided by Father Romero, of the mission of Los Ais, took the preliminary steps toward founding the new mission of Nuestra
Señora de la Luz. Before the end of January, 1757, Fathers
Bruno Chavira and Marcos Satereyn arrived from Zacatecas to
take charge of the work.[25]

Meanwhile extensive explorations were made on the Trinity
and on the San Jacinto for a permanent location, and in August,
1756, the governor and the missionaries agreed upon a site at the
Arroyo of Santa Rosa del Alcázar. In January it was approved

---

25 Hierro, *Informe*. This account contains some important data which
I have not seen elsewhere.

by the viceroy, and orders were given for the transfer of the mission, there to reduce both the Orcoquiza and the Bidai. At the same time the presidio was ordered transferred, on condition that each week a squad of soldiers be sent to El Orcoquisac to look for French intruders. But the Indians at El Orcoquisac opposed the transfer, and it was not made. Missionary work was continued, therefore, at the original site, and the presidio remained unmoved.

On the recommendation of Barrios, the government appropriated $30,000 for equipping and transporting the prospective colonists, and ordered three swivel guns for the defence of the presidio, to take the place of the cannon which had been borrowed from Los Adaes. The actual work of recruiting and transporting the families from Saltillo was entrusted by Barrios to Diego Giraud, a merchant of Mexico.

Up to this point the prospect had seemed good for a much-needed new civil colony in eastern Texas. But now ensued a period of disheartening inactivity, flimsy excuse-making, and pernicious quarrelling which in the end killed the entire project. The plan for a colony had originated with Barrios, who, until June, 1757, had appeared favorable toward it. But from that time forward he changed front. His opposition took the form of procrastination, which he defended on the ground of the lack of a suitable permanent location. Although he had approved the site of Santa Rosa, in October, supported by President Vallejo, he denounced it, saying that he had been deceived by Bernardo de Miranda, his surveyor. Instead of Santa Rosa, Barrios proposed a site called El Atascosito, on the Trinity above El Orcoquisac. Early in 1758 Father Caro, now missionary at El Orcoquisac, supported by Father Vallejo, demanded the removal of the mission, preferably to El Atascosito, alleging the terrible unhealthfulness of the present location, which, indeed, had caused the death of Father Chavira. In response Barrios went to El Atascosito, selected a site, and ordered crops planted and a new presidio erected. At the same time, he reported to the government that none of the places recommended would support a colony of fifty families. For some unknown reason the last essay at removal was not effective. Twice more in 1758 Barrios was ordered to seek a permanent site and make the transfer, but when he left the province, in 1759, the removal had not been made.

When Martos y Navarrete came, early in 1759, he in turn set about moving the mission and the presidio. Together with Father Abad, now in charge of the mission, he visited Santa Rosa and El Atascosito, but decided against them both. Instead, he favored either Los Horconsitos or Los Piélagos, two places a few leagues above the presidio. But Father Abad, perhaps reflecting the wishes of his neophytes, now opposed the transfer, saying that the fault was not with the site but with the laziness of the soldiers and the unfitness of Del Rio, the commander, and that the buildings and crops, secured at great cost, should not be lightly abandoned. Martos now recommended still another site, and President Vallejo, in spite of Father Abad's objection, declared the removal imperative. But still the matter dragged on; during the ensuing years various endeavors were made to transfer the mission and the presidio, but the removal was never made.

Meanwhile, in December, 1759, Governor Martos had asked to be relieved of responsibility for founding the colony. In the following year the request was provisionally granted, until a permanent site should be chosen. Since a site was never agreed upon, the project for the colony went by default. The usual difficulty of the struggling frontier province was to get funds to provide for its needs. But in this instance, after an appropriation of $30,000 had been made by the authorities, the governor was either unwilling or too shiftless to take advantage of it.

International interest in the new Spanish settlement continued. Governor Kerlérec's protest at the occupation of the lower Trinity was followed by other correspondence. Kerlérec maintained that only with difficulty had he been able to prevent the Attacapa Indians from destroying the Spanish settlement, and proposed a joint commission to consider the question of ownership of the soil. Barrios, of course, refused the proffered aid, and to his superiors he expressed the fear that Kerlérec intended to establish a post near San Agustín. Kerlérec likewise carried the matter to his home government. News of this step reaching the viceroy, in 1757 he proposed the erection of a presidio on the west bank of the Mississippi, opposite New Orleans, "to protect the boundaries." The map which he sent with his proposal shows Texas as extending to the Mississippi. Disputes over the boundary continued, in provincial circles at least, until after the Louisiana cession.

The establishment of the presidio on the Trinity had greatly disturbed the French traders, but they continued, nevertheless, to operate. Some of them even asked permission to settle at San Agustín, but the request was emphatically refused. In 1759 it was reported that they were trading at the mouth of the Brazos and preparing to establish a post there. In the following year Saint Denis was accused of having formed a plot to induce the Indians to destroy San Agustín. The charge was not completely substantiated, but the investigation brought out damaging evidence.[26]

Of the internal history of the mission of Nuestra Señora de la Luz during all these troublous times, we have, unfortunately, only very incomplete data, and yet we are able to ascertain the general character of its career. Whatever chance for real prosperity it might have had was destroyed by the continued uncertainty regarding a change of site and by the boisterous career of the nearby presidio. As was usually the case at new missions, at the outset the Indians were friendly, and they aided the

---

[26] *Diligens. Practicadas*, 1755; *Test. del Dictamen de Valcarcel*, Oct. 11, 1755.

fathers in the construction of buildings and the planting of crops. Until 1758 the missionaries worked without the customary *ayuda de costa,* or initial subsidy, and had to depend for support on the governor.[27] In June, 1757, Father Chavira died from the unhealthfulness of the place, and his companion sought asylum at Los Adaes. In the following year two new missionaries were sent from the College, provided with the necessary outfit. By the time of Chavira's death the mission had completed a fairly substantial wooden church, plastered with clay and moss. Later this structure was replaced by a better one. The Indians were docile as a rule, but there is no evidence that they ever actually submitted to mission discipline of the kind enforced at San Antonio and on the Rio Grande.

4. *The Apache missions, and the war with the northern tribes.*[28]—Of far more importance to the actual settlers in Texas than all the efforts to check the encroachments of wandering French traders were the endeavors of the missionaries and seculars to stem the depredations of the Apache. For a quarter of a century the principal means employed to this end had been war. That agency now for a time gave way to an attempt to reduce the hostile tribe to mission life. By 1743 several proposals had been made by the Texas missionaries looking toward

---

[27] Hierro, *Informe;* Bonilla, *Breve Compendio,* in Texas State Historical Association *Quarterly,* VIII, 57; Declaration of Calzones Colorados, Jan. 2, 1765; La Fora, Nicolás, *Relación del Viaje,* entries for Oct. 8–9; *Papeles pertenecientes al Orcoquiza; Testimonio de la Declaracion que hicieron los principales Indios de la Nacion Orcoquiza ante Don Marcos Ruiz,* 1765.

[28] This section is based mainly upon two scholarly monographs by William Edward Dunn, namely, ''Missionary Activities Among the Eastern Apaches Previous to the Founding of the San Sabá Mission,'' Texas State Historical Association *Quarterly,* XV, 186–200; and ''The Apache Mission on the San Sabá River; its Founding and its Failure,'' *Southwestern Historical Quarterly,* XVI, 379–414. Those studies were based mainly on manuscript materials gathered by the present writer and contained in his collection. Much of value has been found also in Morfi's *Memorias,* and Arricivita's *Crónica Seráfica.* A brief sketch of the history of the San Sabá mission is given in Fray Francisco Palou, *Relación Histórica de la Vida y Apostólicas Tareas del Venerable Padre Fray Junípero Serra,* etc. (Mexico, 1787), 40–43.

the conversion of the Eastern Apache, but with little result. The heavy pressure which the Comanche then began to exert upon the Apache had made them more friendly toward the Spaniards, and led to new proposals for missions. Another incentive, appealing to other Spaniards than the friars, was now furnished by rumors of rich mineral deposits in the Llano River country.[29] The government was moved, in addition, by a desire to advance the frontier into the wide vacant space between San Antonio and Santa Fé, and to establish communication between Texas and New Mexico.

In 1749, after the Natagés had murdered Father Silva and a party of companions, an elaborate treaty of peace was celebrated at San Antonio with the Lipan, who renewed their requests for missions, asking to be permitted to enter those at San Antonio. Father Mariano de los Dolores, then in charge in the absence of Father Santa Ana, proposed establishing the petitioners temporarily on the Guadalupe River, urging haste to prevent them from seeking communication with the French through the Cadodacho. Captain Urrutia supported the proposal, but through the influence of the Marqués de Altamira, the *auditor*, action was deferred, to await further information. Father Santa Ana, who was at the time in Mexico City, made a different proposal. He urged founding missions for the Apache on the Pedernales River, the gateway to the Apachería, removing thither the presidio of San Antonio, and founding nearby a pueblo of Spaniards. But when, to the displeasure of Father Santa Ana, the matter was referred back to San Antonio for investigation, it was strongly opposed by both Father Mariano and the junta called to consider it. These conflicting views again delayed action in Mexico.[30]

29 Dunn, *Apache Relations in Texas*, 255–258; Dunn, *Missionary Activities Among the Eastern Apaches*, 188; Arricivita, *Crónica Seráfica y Apostólica*, 338 et seq.

30 Dunn, *Missionary Activities*, 189–196; Morfi, *Memorias*, Bk. VIII, paragraphs 35–47; Bk. IX, paragraphs 3–4.

Another step toward an Apache mission was taken in 1754. As a result of recent treaties made by the Coahuila authorities with the Natagés and other Apache bands, they asked for a mission near San Juan Bautista, and through the efforts of Governor Pedro de Rábago and of President Alonso Giraldo de Terreros, of the College of Santa Cruz, a mission named San Lorenzo was founded in December, near San Fernando de Austria, eighteen leagues west of San Juan Bautista. It was put in charge of Fray Martín García, formerly a worker in Texas. Some of the neophytes were Indians who had asked for missions at San Antonio. For a time the mission prospered, but in less than a year the Indians revolted, burned all the buildings, and deserted. This failure promoted the plan for missions in the Lipan's own country.[31]

Meanwhile Fathers Santa Ana and Dolores continued their efforts; interest in the reports of minerals in the Llano River country increased; and Captain Rábago, late in 1754, as we have seen, proposed moving the San Xavier presidio and mission to the San Sabá or to the Florido River, where he had formerly made explorations. As a result of this growing interest three new expeditions were made to the Apache country between 1753 and 1756. In June and July, 1753, Lieutenant Galván and Fray Miguel Aranda, under orders from the viceroy, and with a company raised at San Antonio, explored the Pedernales, Chanas (Llano) and San Sabá rivers, in search of a mission site, finding a highly desirable one on the San Sabá. This exploration was immediately followed by two or more expeditions by citizens of San Antonio to look for mines at a place called Cerro del Almagre, near the mouth of the Llano River. In December of the following year Captain Rábago and Father Joseph López, in response to an order by the viceroy, went to explore more minutely the site on the San Sabá selected by Galván and

---

[31] Dunn, *Missionary Activities*, 196–200; MS records consulted by the present writer in the archives of Saltillo, Mexico.

Aranda.[32]   On his return Rábago repeated his former recommendation with added emphasis.   Early in 1756 Bernardo de Miranda, under orders from Governor Barrios, investigated the rumored mineral riches in the Llano River country.

The expedition made by Miranda is of especial interest, in view of the fame which in later days became attached to the so-called San Sabá or Bowie Mine, which Miranda now opened. The presence of silver in the hill country north of San Antonio had long been vaguely known and frequently discussed.   The recent explorations of Galván and Rábago had increased interest in the matter. The current report was that near the upper reaches of the Colorado there were two rich deposits called Los Almagres, referring to the red hematite in which the metal was found.   One of the deposits was the Cerro del Almagre near the Llano River. The larger of the veins, called El Almagre Grande, was reported to be the farther away, and in or near the Comanche country. To explore these minerals more thoroughly Governor Barrios sent Bernardo de Miranda from Los Adaes with four soldiers in November, 1755.

At San Antonio Miranda added to his party twelve soldiers, five citizens, some peons, and an Indian interpreter, and on February 17 he set out.   For eight days he proceeded north and northwest, going sixty leagues and crossing streams which he called the Alarcón or Guadalupe, Blanco, San Antonio de Ahumada, Pedernales, San Miguelito, and San Miguel.   The last-

---

[32] Dunn, *The Apache Mission on the San Sabá River*, 381–384; Morfi, *Memorias*, Bk. IX, paragraphs 38–39; Arricivita, *Crónica*, 358. Rábago was accompanied from San Xavier by Father López. From San Antonio he took twenty-five men, including Indians.   Going essentially over Galván's trail to the San Sabá, he explored and approved the site, called Paso de la Cruz, returning by a more westward route. On the Llano he examined some mineral deposits. He reached San Antonio on January 8 and San Xavier on the 17th, having travelled 263 leagues. On January 30 he made a long report to the viceroy, strongly urging the removal of the San Xavier establishments to the San Sabá. *Testimonio de los Autos hechos sobre la Reduccion de los Yndios Gentiles de la Nacion Apache, y establecimiento de el Precidio de San Sabá.*

named arroyo was the modern Honey Creek, a branch of the lower Llano River. A fourth of a league north of the San Miguel he reached Cerro del Almagre, which he named San Joseph del Alcázar. Here a shallow shaft was opened and samples of ore taken out. In the neighborhood the five citizens accompanying Miranda denounced ten claims. A short distance above the mine Miranda explored Honey Creek Cove, of which he gave a graphic description. From Cerro del Almagre he explored westward ten leagues, then eastward down Honey Creek to the Chanas (Llano), down that stream to the Colorado, and some distance above the junction. Having accomplished everything possible under the circumstances, on March 4 Miranda set out for San Antonio, which he had reached by the 10th. On the way he explored the springs and arroyo of San Antonio de Ahumada and concluded that it was a good site for a settlement. While in the region of El Almagre he had been unable to find a single Indian, but on the Guadalupe he now met an Apache who gave him glowing reports of silver deposits six days above the Llano in the Comanche country. On March 29 Miranda sent his report to Governor Barrios, saying that ''the mines of Cerro del Almagre are so numerous . . . that I pledge myself to give all the inhabitants of the province of Texas one each, without anyone being prejudiced in the measurements.''

In July Governor Barrios forwarded Miranda's report to the viceroy, together with the samples of ore, and Miranda himself went to Mexico to arouse interest in the mines. At the capital the ore was given for assay to two rich mine-owners of Pachuca, Don Pedro de Terreros and Don Manuel de Aldaco. In January they reported that the small samples had proved very rich and that the prospects were very bright, but recommended, to make sure, that thirty mule loads of ore be sent for assay to Mazapil, a mining town between Zacatecas and Saltillo. Miranda meanwhile was busy promoting interest in Los Almagres, as the mineral veins were collectively called. On February 15 he addressed the viceroy, giving further details of his discoveries, all of which were favorable. One of the deposits, in the Comanche country and inaccessible, he declared, on hearsay, to be not mere ore but pure silver. To make further explorations and to take the suggested thirty cargoes of ore to Mazapil, Miranda offered his services free, on condition that the government should bear the expense and furnish soldiers, or that, in case the mines proved profitable, he should be made captain of the presidio established to protect it. Appointing as his agent the Mexican merchant named Diego Giraud, previously mentioned, Miranda returned to Texas, and engaged in the exploration of the lower Trinity River, where Barrios was trying to found a colony. After much discussion and further correspondence with Terreros, in November, 1757, the viceroy granted Miranda's request. But nothing further came of the project for the time being for reasons which will be made manifest by the following history of the missionary plans.[33]

While Miranda was exploring the Llano country, discussion of Rábago's proposal to move the San Xavier establishments had been taking place in Mexico, and on February 27, 1756, the matter was considered in a *junta general*. It was urged that the Eastern Apache were now friendly; that there was danger of French influence among them; that a presidio in the San

---

[33] This account is based on the original reports of the survey, entitled *Autos Fechos a consulta de Don Jacinto Barrios y Jauregui, Gobernador de la Provincia de Tejas, sobre Haber Descubierto en el Paraje Nombrado Los Almagres unos Minerales*. A transcript has been in my possession for a number of years. Another copy of these *autos*, made from the original in Mexico, September 30, 1763, is contained in Archivo General de Indias, Mejico, 92–6–22. Of the latter a transcript was secured for the writer by Mr. W. E. Dunn. In 1907 the present writer, with Miranda's report in hand, and accompanied by J. Farley, of Dallas, beyond question identified the mine opened by Miranda with the Boyd Shaft, near Honey Creek Cove. From Miranda's diary his route is easily traced from San Antonio to Honey Creek, and his description of Honey Creek Cove and the surrounding country is remarkable for its accuracy and its graphic quality. On the basis of the writer's identification the Los Almagres Mining Company was formed and purchased about seventeen hundred acres of land round about Boyd Shaft.

Sabá country would make it possible to open up the new mineral district of Los Almagres, and to establish commerce and communication with New Mexico. Finally, it was urged, the San Xavier establishments were useless where they were. The result was that Rábago's suggestions were adopted almost bodily. The San Xavier presidio, the junta proposed, should be increased to one hundred soldiers, and moved, with the missionaries, to San Sabá River, where three missions should be established, the few neophytes from San Xavier now at San Marcos being sent to the San Antonio missions. In a despatch of May 18 the viceroy ordered these recommendations carried out.[34]

Before this despatch was issued a munificent gift had been offered to the viceroy for the support of Apache missions, an event which greatly enlarged the prospects for frontier expansion. The offer came from Don Pedro de Terreros, who had become interested in the Los Almagres mine, and who was a cousin of Fray Alonso Giraldo. In its first form the offer was to support all the Apache missions which might be founded, up to twenty, for a period of three years, at an expense not exceeding $150,000. After four months of negotiation, an arrangement was effected by which the number of missions was unlimited. The missions were to be founded alternately by friars of the colleges of Santa Cruz de Querétaro and San Fernando de México, and of the whole enterprise Fray Alonso Giraldo de Terreros was to be made superior. The missions were to be protected by the presidio of one hundred soldiers already provided for, at royal expense. As a result of the new arrangement, the missionaries from San Xavier were released from their obligation to go to the San Sabá and were ordered to their college. As a reward for the munificent gift, Terreros was made Conde de Regla. Meanwhile Captain Pedro de Rábago had died, and Colonel Diego Ortiz Parrilla was put in his stead, with

---

[34] Dunn, *The Apache Mission on the San Sabá River*, 384–387; Morfi, *Memorias*, Bk. IX, paragraph 41; Arricivita, 365–366.

orders to add to the San Xavier garrison twenty-two soldiers from the San Antonio presidio and twenty-seven new recruits.

In December, 1756, Parrilla and the missionaries reached San Antonio with their outfit. Father Terreros brought with him Friars Joachín de Baños and Diego Ximénez, from his own college, and Friars José Santiesteban and Juan Andrés from the College of San Fernando. At Saltillo nine Tlascaltecan families were obtained to serve as teachers of the prospective neophytes. In San Antonio and vicinity a whole winter was passed in further preparation. In the meantime Parrilla removed the San Xavier garrison from the San Marcos and aided Fray Mariano in formally establishing a mission on the Guadalupe River for the remaining San Xavier neophytes. At San Antonio conferences were held with delegations of Apache. From the surrounding country fourteen hundred head of cattle and seven hundred sheep were assembled for the new undertaking. As a means of securing better pasturage and, perhaps, for other reasons, in March, 1757, the stock and nearly the whole outfit were moved to the San Marcos, whence the garrison had recently been withdrawn.

Meanwhile discord reigned at San Antonio. Fray Mariano, who through the Terreros gift had been supplanted in the Apache enterprise by Fray Alonso, complained because the new mission on the Guadalupe River was not allowed to participate in the endowment. On the other hand, Parrilla, who was skeptical of success, was charged by Fray Alonso with unnecessary and purposeful delay in setting out with the expedition.[35]

---

[35] Dunn, *The Apache Mission*, 387–395; Morfi, *Memorias*, Bk. X, paragraphs 1–25, 36; Arricivita, 366–367; *Testimonio de los Autos fhos a pedimento de Don Pedro Romero de Terreros sre que se le admita la obligacion, que haze de mantener de todo lo necessario las Missiones, que se fundaren en los Confines, y terminos de la Governazion de Coahuila siguiendo el rumbo del Norte Vajo de las condiziones, que Expressa. Qno. 8o. A.* This document contains the offer of Terreros as submitted by the viceroy to the fiscal on July 10.

In April the start was finally made. Leaving most of the supplies on the San Marcos, Parrilla returned to San Antonio, went to the San Sabá River by the direct route through the hill country, and there, near the present Menardville, located the settlement, where Galván and Rábago had already selected sites. On the north bank of the river the presidio of San Luis de las Amarillas was planted, and three miles below on the south bank the first mission, called Santa Cruz, was founded. In a short time fairly substantial buildings and stockades were under way at both establishments. The presidio settlement comprised some three or four hundred persons, over two hundred of whom were women and children.[36]

When the caravan first arrived no Indians were in sight, but through various embassies there was assembled in June a throng of some three thousand Lipans. They were not on mission bent, however, but were on their way to a buffalo hunt, and to attack their northern enemies; and they departed on these errands in spite of all efforts to detain them. Other bands which came and went were equally unwilling to remain in the mission, though they made many promises.[37]

Parrilla was soon thoroughly convinced that the whole project was impossible, and he proposed moving the presidio to the Llano River to protect the Los Almagres mines, letting the missionaries work from there if they chose. Most of the missionaries also despaired, and in the course of a few months three of them departed, leaving Fathers Terreros, Santiesteban, and Molina, the last-named having arrived in January. But at San Sabá Father Terreros, and in Mexico Don Pedro and the viceroy, loath to give up so brilliant a plan, held on with stubborn tenacity.[38]

[36] Dunn, *The Apache Mission*, 396–397; Arricivita, 368–369.

[37] Dunn, *ibid.*, 397–399; Arricivita, 369–370.

[38] Dunn, *ibid.*, 399–401; Morfi, *Memorias*, Bk. X, paragraphs 27–28.

The fact seems to be that the Apache were mortally afraid to settle at the mission, on account of the hostility of their northern enemies. That this fear was justified the outcome proved. After many disquieting rumors, in March, 1758, the Comanche and their allies appeared, to the number, it was estimated, of at least two thousand, mounted on horses, and carrying French weapons. After committing minor depredations, on the 16th of the month they treacherously attacked the settlement, killing Fathers Terreros and Santiesteban and six other persons at the mission, besides two members of a rescue party sent from the presidio.[39] The principal cause of the assault was clearly the hostility between the northerners and the Apache, and the feeling that by establishing the mission the Spaniards had become the allies of the latter. The northerners were also attracted no doubt by the fine opportunity for plunder afforded by the mission stores and the well-stocked ranches. The Spaniards firmly believed, moreover, that the French were guilty of complicity in the outrage.[40]

Three days after the attack an appeal for help, carried by a courier, reached San Antonio, and nineteen men were sent from there at once. Alarm was not confined to San Sabá, but spread rapidly to the other settlements of Texas, Coahuila, and Nuevo León. The little mission on the Guadalupe River was forthwith abandoned. At San Antonio, where Captain Urrutia was now left with only a handful of soldiers, there were wild rumors of oncoming hordes, to which was added fear of an uprising of the neophytes of the nearby missions. To prevent annihilation Urrutia sent appeals for help to the viceroy and to all of the principal settlements of Texas and Coahuila. The news of the attack reached Governor Barrios at Nacogdoches, and he,

---

[39] Dunn, *The Apache Mission*, 401–408; Morfi, *Memorias*, Bk. X, paragraphs 34–47; Arricivita, 375–378.

[40] Dunn, *ibid.*, 413; Morfi, *ibid.*, paragraph 34. Concerning the attack on San Sabá, preparation for, and the conduct of the Parrilla expedition, Mr. Dunn has unearthed a wealth of new documents in the Archivo de Indias, of which through his generous aid I have secured transcripts. As yet, however, they have not been thoroughly studied.

giving up a journey to Orcoquisac, hastened with a small squad to the defence of San Antonio, but was turned back by floods. The viceroy, in turn, sent hurried despatches to the frontier garrisons, asking for aid, but in view of the general fright everywhere on the frontier, assistance was slow in being sent.[41]

Parrilla now again proposed that the San Sabá project be abandoned, and suggested that the presidio be moved to the San Marcos, to the Guadalupe, or to Los Almagres. At the same time he offered to conduct a campaign to punish the northern tribes for their outrage. These matters being considered in a junta in Mexico in June, removal from the San Sabá was strongly opposed, as a confession of cowardice, and continued missionary efforts were planned. On the other hand, Parrilla's proposal of a campaign was regarded with favor. With renewed efforts in view, Don Pedro de Terreros was urged to provide funds, and the colleges to send new missionaries. Don Pedro consented. Accordingly, Fray Francisco Aparicio and Fray Pedro Parras were appointed for the College of Santa Cruz, and Fray Junípero Serra and Fray Francisco Palou for the College of San Fernando. To avoid unnecessary risk, the missionaries were urged to live at the presidio. The mission on the Guadalupe was ordered suppressed, but this was unnecessary for it had already been abandoned.[42] Because of new disasters at San Sabá, missionary plans were changed, and Fathers Serra and Palou were not sent to Texas. This change deprived the province of two unusual men. Later they both went to Alta California, of whose missions Serra became the illustrious founder and Palou the distinguished historian.

To make plans for the proposed campaign, Colonel Parrilla was instructed to call a conference of the leading men of the frontier. It met at San Antonio in January, 1759. Its mem-

---

[41] Dunn, *The Apache Mission*, 408–413.

[42] Morfi, *Memorias*, Bk. X, paragraphs 48, 49, 51; Arricivita, 379–380. Palou, *Relación Histórica*, 40–43.

bers were Barrios and Martos, governors of Coahuila and Texas, Colonel Parrilla, and Lieutenant Eca y Músquiz, now commander at San Antonio in place of Captain Urrutia. Governor Martos presided. The recommendations made by the junta reveal the slender defences of the frontier, and the long distances from which troops had to be taken for even a small military enterprise. After due deliberation it was proposed that for the campaign thirty presidials and fifty mission Indians should be raised in Texas, in addition to the San Sabá garrison, one hundred and ninety men in Coahuila, eighty-two in San Luis Potosí and Charcas, fifty in Parras, twenty-five in the Sierra Gorda, and one hundred in Nuevo León. These troops must be ready to report at San Antonio by the first of June. Each man must be supplied with two horses, the militia serving at a peso and the Indian allies at half a peso a day. The estimated cost of the campaign was 53,000 pesos. In April the plan thus outlined at San Antonio was approved by a junta in Mexico City.[43]

A new attack of the northerners on San Sabá in March, in which nineteen persons were killed and seven hundred and fifty horses stolen, was a fresh cause for urging haste, but it was the middle of August before the expedition was ready to leave San Antonio. When finally assembled, the company consisted of about three hundred and eighty militiamen and presidials, ninety mission Indians, thirty Tlescaltecos, evidently from Saltillo, and one hundred and thirty-four Apache allies—over six hundred men in all.[44] They were supplied with several cannon.

Going to San Sabá and then northeast, for one hundred and fifty leagues the way was unimpeded, for the enemy had fled from their rancherías. At that distance a Tonkawa village was encountered, attacked, and defeated, fifty-five warriors being

---

[43] Morfi, *Memorias*, Bk. X, paragraphs 52–56; Arricivita, 381.

[44] These were the respective numbers provided for, but Parrilla complained that some of the contingents were short. (*Testimonio de los Auttos fhos á consulta del Coronel Dⁿ. Diego Orttiz Parrilla . . . en q^c. dá cuentta de los sucessos de la Campaña*, etc. Quad^{no}. 5.

killed and one hundred and forty-nine persons captured. Not satisfied with this success, Parrilla continued northeast until, on October 7, he reached the Taovayas villages on the Red River, in the neighborhood of the present Ringgold. Here he was surprised to find a large body of Indians intrenched behind a strong stockade with breastworks, flying a French flag, and skillfully using French weapons and tactics. For four hours the Spaniards sustained an attack by Indians from both within and without the fortress. Two swivel guns were trained on the stronghold, but near nightfall Parrilla withdrew with a loss of fifty-two men, having inflicted an equal loss upon the Indians. Desertions having begun, it was decided in a council to retreat that night, leaving the two cannon and extra baggage behind. The enemy pursued most of the way to San Sabá, and in spite of all that Parrilla could do the retreat became a route. The presidio was reached on October 25, after a march of seventeen days. This repulse was long regarded as a disgrace to the Spanish arms.[45]

---

[45] Morfi, *Memorias*, Bk. X, pars. 67–71; Arricivita, 381–382. At 1 p.m. on the 7th the vanguard was attacked by a body of Indians, who retreated through the timber separating the prairie from the river. The Spaniards, pursuing, suddenly found themselves in front of the fortified village, "a pueblo formed of high thatched oval-shaped houses, surrounded by a stockade and a ditch, the road leading to it being surrounded in the same way, since it is *culebrado*, with the opening at the very river . . . and all the stockade on that side surmounted by Indians armed with muskets." Nearby were large and well fenced fields devoted to the raising of maize, beans, calabashes, and melons. Behind the Taovayas town was the camp of the Comanche allies. Outside the stockade the warriors, on horseback, were attended each by two footmen carrying and loading extra guns. In the skirmish the Spaniards killed a leading chieftain, and claimed renown for it afterward. "This heathen captain bore himself all the time during which the battle raged from one side to the other with well ordered valor and extreme dexterity in the management of horse and arms, those which he used being the lance and fusils, which the footmen or servants furnished him. He had a shield of white buckskin and a helmet of the same, with a plume of red horsehair, and he was mounted on a horse of the best qualities and properties for the mode of warfare which has been described. There were many [men] of similar qualities, but not of such unusual spirit and conduct." Parrilla tried to rally his men, but they were apparently terror-stricken, and he found it impossible. Some estimated the number of the enemy as high as six thousand, while Parrilla reported it to be at least more than his own army (*Testimonio de los Auttos . . . en q^e. dá cuentta de los sucessos.*

It was nearly twenty years before the abandoned cannon were recovered.

The defeat of Parrilla was followed by a division of the authorities between two wholly incompatible policies. At San Sabá the captain and the missionaries, backed by the government in Mexico, did their best to reduce the Apache to settled life. This meant continued warfare with the enemies of the Apache. In eastern Texas Governor Martos and Father Calahorra, the veteran missionary at Nacogdoches, made efforts to restore peace with the northern tribes and to establish them in missions, even if it involved war with the Apache.

Soon after the defeat of Parrilla the Tawakoni and Yscanis, two of the tribes which had taken part in the hostilities, visited Father Calahorra, asking peace, and offering to give up Spanish captives and Parrilla's cannon. This opportunity was seized upon by Governor Martos and the missionary. With an escort furnished by the governor in September, 1760, Father Calahorra went to the villages of the tribes named, on the upper Sabine River, met an embassy from the Taovayas, and held a peace meeting. He found the Indians constructing a fortification to withstand an expected attack of the Spaniards. In the following year he repeated the journey, taking presents and conferring titles of honor upon the chiefs. The Taovayas were not present at this council, but Father Calahorra was told that a short distance above their village there were five French houses, established with the pretext of hunting for the Arkansas post. As a result of these visits, Calahorra and Martos proposed founding missions for the northern tribes and moving the San Sabá presidio to the Tawakoni village or to the country between them and the Taovayas. The viceroy, being in doubt between the two opposing policies, required further investigation. Accordingly, in 1763, Father Calahorra made a third journey. He found the Indians still desirous of missions, but noted the ominous presence of a French flag planted there since his last visit by a trader from Cadodachos.[46] News of the transfer of Louisiana, it must be remembered, had not yet reached Texas.

The alternative policy of trying to gather the Apache in missions being adhered to by the government, nothing came of these efforts of Father Calahorra.[47] But evidence of the continued good will of the northern tribes toward eastern Texas was given in 1765 when the great Taovayas chief, Eyasiquiche, escorted to Nacogdoches Antonio Treviño, whom they had captured near San Sabá a few months before. Eyasiquiche offered

[46] The villages visited in 1760 were north of the north or Lake Fork of the Sabine, near the edge of the great prairies, and therefore not far from the line between Wood and Emory counties. Leaving Nacogdoches on September 16 with seven soldiers and five citizens from Adaes, Calahorra went to the Asinais (Hainai) village on the Angelina. Accompanied thence by one hundred Indians they crossed the Angelina, ascended it ten leagues, went fourteen leagues northward to the Neches, west and north one day to Arroyo Santa Bárbara (evidently the small stream in northern Henderson County); north four leagues to a great prairie; north eight leagues to the first branch of the Sabinas; four leagues north through the prairie to the Tawakoni village, north of the second branch of the Sabinas. From there it was five days' journey to the Taovayas. The Tawakoni village was composed of forty-seven houses of twelve families each, comprising two hundred and fifty warriors. Its four chiefs were brothers. Only a street separated this village from that of the Yscanes. Crops were raised here in abundance, even for sale. One of the Tawakoni chiefs was called Flechado en la Cara. El Flechazo was the name of the Tawakoni villages found on the Brazos in 1778 by De Mézières. The inference is that the people were identical and that in the interim they had moved from the Sabine to the Brazos. (Calahorra y Saenz, *Diario del Viage*, etc., in *Testimonia de los Auttos fechos a consultta del Governador de la Provincia de Texas en que de cuentta de haverle presentado, y pedido los Yndios, que ynsultaron la Mision de Sansaba se yntteresara, e intercediece por ellos, a fin de que se les concediese paz, vaxo de varias condiciones, Quadno. 10 A.* Most of the same documents except the diary are in *Testimonio de las Diligencias practicadas de Orn del Exmo. Sor. Marqs. de Cruillas ViRey Govor. y capitan Gral de la Nueva Espa. por Dn. Angl. de Martos y Navarrete (a quien se remitieron los orijinales) Govor. y capitn. de esta Nueva Espa., digo esta Prova. de Tejas, sobre la reduccion de los Yndios Tehuacanas e yscanis a Mission.*

[47] That the two policies were balanced against each other is shown in *Testimonio de los Autos fhos a Consulta del Capitan del Precidio de San Saba sobre el planteo de dos Missiones en el Valle de San Joseph, que se la augmente la Tropa a dho Prezidio, Qno. 24 A.* This document contains additional data regarding Father Calahorra's journeys.

to give up Parrilla's cannon and other captives, but refused to cease war upon the Spaniards of San Sabá. Treviño told of the regular trade of the French in progress at the Taovayas village; Governor Martos, in turn, promptly reported it to the viceroy with a warning,[48] for, though Louisiana now belonged to Spain, possession had not yet been taken.

Meanwhile the renewed efforts to reduce the Apache to mission life were in progress, and activities were soon transferred to the Nueces River. In 1760, after eight years of investigation, Captain Phelipe de Rábago was acquitted of the charges against him arising from the troubles at San Xavier, and was restored to his command, now at San Sabá. Determined that Rábago should not be reinstated, Father Mariano, who was still in Texas, and still pugnacious, went to Mexico to prevent it and to fight for Parrilla's retention. Instead, however, Parrilla was made governor of Coahuila.

Rábago took charge at San Sabá in October, 1760, and at once set about replacing the wooden presidio by a substantial fort of stone and mortar, which was nearly completed by November, 1761. Its remains are still to be seen at Menardville. Rábago also set about the reduction of the Apache. To this end he explored the country for new sites, held conferences with the Indians, and defended them against the Comanche by sending escorts with their hunting-parties. As a result of this friendly treatment several Lipan chiefs promised to enter missions, and Rábago appealed to Father Diego Ximénez, now president of the missions on the Rio Grande, to aid him in the work. The breach between Rábago and Father Mariano was evidently too wide to be healed, and subsequent missionary work with the Lipan was directed from the Rio Grande instead of from San Antonio.

---

[48] *Testimonio de dilix^as. practicadas sobre la debolucion que hizo de Ant^o. treviño el capitan principal de la nacion tagui;* Morfi, *Memorias*, Bk. XI, paragraphs 1–6.

Father Ximénez responded to the call, new explorations were made, a council with the Indians held, and several new missions projected. The site selected for the first one was called El Cañon. It was on one of the upper branches of the Nueces, then called Rio Nuevo de San Antonio, or Rio de San José. Other missions were planned for the Llano and San Sabá rivers. In the fall Father Ximénez returned to his mission of San Bernardino, corresponded with his superiors, and made preparations, while Rábago assembled the Indians. In January, 1762, the captain took thirty soldiers and a band of Lipans under Chief Cabezón to Rio de San José, where he was met by Father Ximénez and Father Joachín Baños with supplies. On January 23 the mission of San Lorenzo was founded at El Cañon, and was given a garrison of twenty soldiers. A few weeks later Rábago brought another band, under Chief Turnio, for whom another mission, named Nuestra Señora de la Candelaria, was founded four or five leagues down the same stream, on the opposite side.

The mission of San Lorenzo continued in nominal operation for about seven years and that of Candelaria for about four. But their existence was precarious and their results extremely meager. The Indians were fickle, deserted at will, and returned mainly if at all to get food and presents. For this they could hardly be blamed, for they were soon pursued to their new haunts by the northern tribes, and suffered frequent massacres in the very neighborhood of the missions.[49]

---

[49] On the subject of the Nueces River missions see Morfi, *Memorias*, Bk. XI, paragraphs 7–22; Arricivita, 382–389. A report on the missions dated January 25, 1763, is contained in *Testimonio de los Autos fhos a Consulta del Capitan del Presidio de San Saba sobre el planteo de dos Missiones en el Valle de San Joseph y que se la augumente la tropa a dho Presidio.*

On his way from San Fernando de Austria to San Sabá in July, 1767, the Marqués de Rubí passed through the El Cañon settlement, of which La Fora, diarist and engineer, gives the following description: "A league to the east of said arroyo [del Cibolo] there is a gap of medium elevation through which one goes to the Valle de San Joseph, commonly called El Cañon, through which runs the bed of the Rio de las Nueces,

5. *Progress of the older missions, 1745–1762.*—This sketch would be misleading if it left the impression that all of the Texas missions in this period had the same disastrous career as those on the San Xavier, the Trinity, the San Sabá and the Nueces rivers. It is true that those of northeastern Texas continued to lead the same helpless existence which they had experienced since the outset. Those on the San Antonio River, on the other hand, in the period under discussion, continued to prosper moderately and in many respects were a notable success. The material plants improved. In spite of high death rates and desertion, the number of neophytes was maintained or increased by new converts from new tribes. Numerous Indian families became thoroughly established in civilized life and became assimilated to the *gente de razón.* At most of the missions the neophytes became so well disciplined in industrial pursuits that white overseers were no

---

which often dries up. It flows approximately south at the base of the opposite hills, which form said valley, whose greatest width from east to west must be a league and a half and its length from north to south twelve leagues. In it there are many mesquites and thickets, and the scarcity of water makes it ill-fitted for agriculture or settlements. We ascended it to the north five leagues to the place of La Candelaria, where, on the banks of a little arroyo of very fresh and clear water, there was a house with a little chapel, and in front of it a large thatched house (*jacal*) which the Lipanes built, flattering the Fernandino missionaries that they would submit to live in a settlement, but they never did so, and only mocked their zeal and credulity.

"On the nineteenth we travelled four leagues, the first two and a half to the north-northeast, to the Río de las Nuezes, which we crossed at low water, but its bed shows how furiously it comes in flood time. Turning from here to the north, we found, at a league and a half, the little pueblo of San Lorenzo de la Santa Cruz, commonly known as the Mission of El Cañon, whose origin and progress are the same as those of La Candelaria. It serves solely to give employment to a detachment of thirty men and an officer of the Presidio of San Sabá, and to maintain two unprofitable missionaries [Fathers Rivera and Santiesteban], with no other advantages than to provide a stopping place for the pack trains which enter to supply that presidio. Its form and its bad location are manifest from the sketch which I made of this settlement, where they have two small three-pound cannons, one with a broken trunion, both mounted on unserviceable carriages, and without balls of proper caliber or implements to manage them" (La Fora, Nicolás, *Relación del Viaje que de orden del excelentissimo Señor Virrey Marqués de Cruillas Hizo el Capitan de ingenieros Dn. Nicolas de la Fora en Compañia del Mariscal de Campo Marqz. de Rubi.*

longer necessary, and the mission Indians became a trustworthy and useful contingent in the local militia.

Until 1749 Father Santa Ana continued to act as president of the Querétaran missions, both on the San Xavier and on the San Antonio. In that year he was succeeded by Father Mariano de los Dolores, who continued to play an important rôle for another decade. Both of these presidents were distinctly men of parts, and deserve to be better known. Between 1745 and 1762 some twenty or more missionaries served at the five missions at San Antonio. Among them were three writers, each of whom has left an important book. Fray Diego Martín García, of Mission San Antonio de Valero, wrote a *Breve y Legal Noticia*[50] of the customs of the Indians, still unpublished, which is a valuable treatise on missionary methods. Fray Bartolomé García, of Mission San Francisco de la Espada, wrote a *Manual,*[51] published in 1760, in both Spanish and Indian, which preserves for us our principal vestige of the Coahuiltecan language. After his return to Querétaro Fray Juan Domingo Arricivita, who served both at Mission San Antonio de Valero and at San Ildefonso on the San Xavier, wrote his *Crónica Seráfica*, which is still one of the great contributions to the history of the Southwest in the eighteenth century.[52]

By good fortune, reports of all the Texas missions, made in 1762, have been preserved. By an order of October 16, 1761, issued by Fray Manuel de Náxera, Comisario General, a report

---

[50] *Breve y Legal Noticia de las Calidades y Costvmbres de los Indios, Metodo, que han de observar con ellos, y consigo mismos, los Obreros Evangelicos que quieren ganar sus almas para Dios. Escrita por el P. F. Diego Martin Garcia, Predicador Apostolico, Hijo del Seminario de propaganda fide de la SSma. Cruz de Querétaro. Año de MDCCXLV. MS.*

[51] *Manual para administrar Los Santos Sacramentos de Penitencia, Eucharistia Extrema-Uncion, y Matrimonio: Dar Gracias Despues de Comulgar, y Ayudar a Bien Morir a los Indios de las Naciones: Pajalates, Orejones, Pacaos, Pacóas, Tilijayas, Alasapas, Pausanes, y otras muchos diferentes, que se hallan en las Misiones del Rio de San Antonio y Rio Grande* (Mexico, 1860).

[52] *Crónica Seráfica y Apostólica del Colegio de Propaganda Fide de la Santa Cruz de Queretaro* (Mexico, 1792).

was required on all of the Franciscan missions of New Spain. In response to the order, on March 6, 1762, the Querétaran missionaries in Texas despatched a report directed to Fray Francisco Ortiz, guardian of the College of Santa Cruz. It gives us a most excellent view of the missions on the eve of the Louisiana cession.

The administration books showed a steady growth of spiritual work since 1745. By 1762 over 4400 Indians had been baptized at the four Querétaran missions since their foundation. Of these about half had been baptized within the last seventeen years, the increase at San Antonio de Valero during that time being about equal to that of the other three missions combined. There were now living at the four missions eight hundred and ninety-two Indians, the numbers ranging from two hundred and three at San Juan Capistrano to two hundred and seventy-five at San Antonio de Valero. The newer tribes represented at the missions were mainly from the southwest coast region, including the Karankawa, Piguique, Borrados, and Malaguitas. The only heathen mentioned were Karankawa at San Antonio de Valero. This would not indicate a lively expansion at the time.

Since 1745 the mission buildings had improved, but had not reached their best. At San Antonio de Valero the church begun in 1744 had been completed, but the tower and sacristy had fallen down on account of the stupidity of the builder. Another church "of harmonious architecture." was now being built of quarried stone. At Mission Concepción the church was completed. It was thirty-two varas long and eight wide, built of stone and mortar, with vaulted ceiling, dome, and bells, and contained a sacristy and a chapel. At San Juan a well constructed apartment twenty-five varas long served temporarily as a church. At San Francisco a stone church was in progress; meanwhile a capacious and "decent" building served in its place.

Besides the church, each mission had its *convento*, or monastery, including cells for the friars, porter's lodge, refectory, kitchen, offices, workshops, and granary, usually all under a common roof and ranged round a *patio*. At San Antonio de Valero the *convento* was a two-story structure fifty varas square with two *patios* and with arched cloisters above and below. That at San Francisco de la Espada had seven cells, four above and three below; at San Juan there were five cells.

An important part of each mission was the workshop, for here the neophytes not only helped to supply their economic needs but got an important part of their training for civilized life. At each of these four missions the Indians manufactured *mantas, terlingas, sayales, rebosos, fresadas*, and other common fabrics of wool and cotton. At Mission San Antonio the workshop contained four looms and two store rooms with cotton, wool, cards, spindles, etc. At Concepción and San Francisco there were three looms each; at San Juan the number is not stated.

The neophytes of each mission lived in an Indian village, or pueblo, closely connected with the church and monastery. Of the four Querétaran missions we have the fullest description of the pueblo at Mission San Antonio de Valero. It consisted of seven rows of houses built of stone, with arched porticoes, doors, and windows. There was a plaza through which ran a water-ditch grown with willows and fruit trees. Within the plaza was a curbed well to supply water in case of a siege by the enemy. The pueblo was surrounded by a wall, and over the gate was a tower, with embrasures, and equipped with three cannon, fire-arms, and munitions. The houses were furnished with high beds, chests, *metates*, pots, kettles, and other domestic utensils. The pueblo at San Antonio was typical of all. At Concepción there were two rows of houses, partly of stone, partly of thatched straw, surrounded by a wall. At San Juan the houses were of thatch, but preparations were being made to replace them with stone structures. For defence the mission had two swivel guns, twenty muskets, and, presumably, a wall. At San Francisco the pueblo consisted of three rows of stone houses.

Agricultural and stockraising activities had increased since 1745. At the four Querétaran missions there were now grazing 4897 head of cattle, 12,000 sheep and goats, and about 1600 horses, and each mission had from thirty-seven to fifty yoke of working oxen. Of the four missions San Francisco raised the most stock, having 2262 head of cattle and 4000 sheep and goats. San Juan came next, and Valero next. At each establishment maize, chile, beans, and cotton were raised in abundance, besides a large variety of garden truck. At the time when the report was made (March 6) each of the missions had in its granary from 1600 to 2000 bushels of maize, and a corresponding stock of beans. Each mission had well tilled fields, fenced in, and watered by good irrigating ditches with stone dams. Each had its ranch, some distance away, where the stock was kept, with one or more stone houses, occupied by the families of the overseers, the necessary corrals, farming implements, carts, and tools for carpentry, masonry, and blacksmithing.[53]

In response to the order of 1761 a report was made for the Zacatecan missions by Fray Simon de Hierro, guardian of the College of Guadalupe. It was not nearly so satisfactory as that made by the Querétaran missionaries. In Texas the College of Guadalupe now had three missions on the San Antonio River, one on the lower Trinity, and three in northeastern Texas beyond the Angelina.

The two old missions on the San Antonio, San José and Espíritu Santo, were prosperous, and had recently been praised by the Bishop of Guadalajara after his visitation. The former was declared to be "one of the most flourishing, both as to temporal and spiritual increase," which the college had had in the forty-one years since its establishment. Its neophytes now numbered more than two hundred, of the Mesquite and Pastias

---

[53] *Ynformes de los PP. Misioneros sobre el estado de las Misiones,* Mar. 6, 1762, in *Memorias de Nueva España,* XXVIII, 162–183.

tribes. The church was described as very finely built and capable of holding more than two thousand persons. It was not, however, the final and more magnificent structure which in 1778 was called the finest mission in all New Spain. That edifice was begun in 1768. In the cemetery there was a chapel of the *Sacra Via*. The monastery was well built, with closed cloisters. The houses of the Indian village were of stone and "constructed with such art that the mission is a castle, and so that although it is in the greatest danger from the Apache, an enemy so bold that he has attacked the presidio by day, he has never dared to enter the streets of this mission." The mission owned more than two thousand cattle and harvested annually more than one thousand bushels of maize. It raised cotton, and the neophytes manufactured cotton and woolen fabrics, like the missions described above. Father Hierro estimated that the neophytes of the Mission of Espíritu Santo would number more than five hundred, but his data were not recent. The chapel of this mission was reported as large and "decent," the monastery and store rooms good, and agriculture and stockraising extensive, but nothing was said of manufactures.

The new missions of Rosario, on the San Antonio, and Nuestra Señora de la Luz, on the lower Trinity, had as yet made little progress and were still on trial. The three old missions in northeastern Texas were avowed failures. Of these Father Hierro wrote, "And, in truth, if we had not taken note of the fact that the Son of God in his gospel does not command us to convert, but only to preach, and that according to the Apostle the work of conversion is not that of the one who plants nor of the one who waters, but only of God, who gives the increase, it would have been an intolerable toil of forty years without that fruit which might have been reaped elsewhere . . . for, in all these years, if the time has not been altogether lost, it is because in the fulfillment of the divine decrees they have sent many infants to glory by means of holy baptism.'' The Indians had never consented to live in a mission pueblo, and there was not sufficient force to coerce them. Accordingly, there was no discipline in crafts or doctrine, and the only baptisms performed were administered *in articulo mortis*.[54]

---

[54] *Informe de las Misiones de Texas, hecho p^r. el P. Hierro*, Jan. 8, 1762.

CHAPTER III

READJUSTMENTS FOLLOWING THE LOUISIANA CESSION (1762–1788)

1. *The Louisiana cession and plans for readjustment.*[1]—The outcome of the Seven Years' War caused several fundamental readjustments in Spanish North America. It left Spain in a position where she must rehabilitate her colonial power or sink to the rank of a third-rate nation. Renewed war with England was regarded as inevitable. To prevent it from falling into the hands of England, western Louisiana was ceded in 1762 by France to Spain, but this was offset by the loss of Florida. The French barrier having been removed, Spain's hold on both Louisiana and the Pacific Slope was threatened by the English, advancing now from Canada as well as from the thirteen colonies. On the Pacific Slope, Russia was even more threatening than England. Added to all this, northern New Spain itself was being overrun by increasingly hostile border tribes. Poor and unprepared though she was, therefore, Spain was forced to get ready for another war with England, occupy Louisiana and Alta California, strengthen the frontier defences of New Spain against the Indians, and explore or re-explore the northern interior.

All these demands could be met only by the most heroic measures; but these were attempted by the energetic Carlos III. This king, a Bourbon, had come to the throne in 1759, after a long and successful reign as King of Naples. By the time of his accession, Spain had already profited much by the Bourbon re-

---

[1] This section is based largely on the detailed study presented in Part V of this volume, pp. 375–446, where reference to the sources will be found. That study is a reprint, somewhat revised, of a monograph which appeared in the Texas State Historical *Quarterly*, vol. IX, 67–137.

forms which from time to time had been instituted since the opening of the century. But the national revenue was still small, commerce stagnant, the army and navy weak, and colonial administration corrupt. Now came the new demands entailed by the outcome of the great war. To make the program of defence and expansion possible it was necessary to provide revenue. This could be done only by increasing commerce and by completely reforming the fiscal administration of the colonies. To carry out such reforms in New Spain King Carlos sent a corps of inspectors. Chief among them was José de Gálvez, who, as *visitador general*, was entrusted with a complete overhauling of the administration.[2] The Marqués de Rubí was commissioned to report upon the military defences of the northern frontier.

In their immediate effects upon Texas the changes due to the cession of Louisiana to Spain were especially marked. In the first place, Texas ceased to be the outpost against the French, a position which had given the province its character since its founding. Spain's eastern frontier was now the Mississippi and the buffer district was the newly acquired province of Louisiana. Texas became, in effect, an interior province, except for the Gulf coast, and it was possible now to withdraw the defences which had stood on the eastern frontier for half a century. On the other hand, with the English in possession of Florida, the Texas coast was exposed to encroachments by that nation. Moreover, Spain had to face the problem of controlling the Indians of the enormous province which she had just acquired. With respect to the Texas border, this meant the establishment of authority over the "Norteños," or Nations of the North, the tribes of the Red River Valley and the adjacent regions of northern Texas which hitherto had been almost entirely under the influence of the French. These changes were not all effected immediately,

---

[2] See Addison, Joseph, *Charles III of Spain;* Hume, Martin, A. S., *Spain, 1479–1788,* 392–411; Coxe, W., *Memoirs of the Kings of the House of Bourbon,* IV; Danvila y Collado, *Historia del Reinado de Carlos III;* Rousseau, François, *Regne de Charles III d'Espagne (1759–88).*

nor without much discussion and investigation. Indeed, though ceded in 1762, possession of Louisiana was not taken until 1766, and the province was not fully under Spanish control till 1769, with the coming of Alejandro O'Reilly.[3]

One of the first steps toward readjustment to the new situation was a series of explorations looking to the defence of the Gulf coast against rumored dangers from the English. In November, 1764, the viceroy, the Marqués de Cruillas, addressed the court at Madrid on the necessity of establishing a coast guard "to observe the movements of the squadron which the English maintain at the Bay of Pensacola."[4] In the following year rumors reached the missions at San Juan Bautista, through Indians resident there, that the English had settled on the islands along the coast, not far from the mouth of the Nueces River. When the news reached Mexico, Colonel Escandón was about to set out for his colony, and on November 2 he was ordered by the viceroy to investigate the rumors. At the same time the Marqués de Rubí was preparing to leave Mexico on his tour of inspection of the northern frontier, and he was likewise instructed to make investigations. But as Rubí set out northwest instead of northeast, in April, 1766, Colonel Parrilla was especially commissioned to reconnoiter the islands on the lower Texas coast, particularly the óne extending from the Rio Grande to the Nueces and called Malaguitas, from the tribe inhabiting it, or Isla Blanca, because of its composition of white sand.

---

[3] Shepherd, W. R., "The Cession of Louisiana to Spain," in *Pol. Sci. Quarterly*, XIX, 439–458; Bolton, H. E., *Athanase De Mézières and the Louisiana Texas Frontier, 1768–1780*, I, 66–71.

[4] A. G. M., *Reales Cédulas*, vol. 86, fol. 69, no. 53; vol. 89, fol. 44, no. 147; vol. 90, fols. 47–49, no. 34; vol. 91; fol. 127, no. 208; Cor. Vir. Croix, 1766–67, vol. 1/11, ff. 129, 367; Provincias Internas, vol. 110, no. 708; *Autos y diligᵃˢ. fhas pʳ. el Coronel Dn. Diego Ortiz Parrilla Sre. las sircunstancias de la Isla de los Malaguitas q. comumᵗᵉ. han llamado Isla Blanca.* A. G. M., Historia, 396, *Diligencias practicadas por el Coronel Don Diego Orttiz Parrilla en que dá punttual notticia de la Isla de los Malaguitaɛ* [*Culebra*] A. G. M., Historia, 396. Most of the same-documents, with a few additional ones, are in A. G. I., Audiencia de Guadalajara, 104–6–13. Of them I secured transcripts through Mr. W. E. Dunn.

In the course of the same summer reports reached Spain from two distinct sources in Louisiana to the effect that the English were fortifying the Gulf coast west of the Mississippi. According to one version they were establishing a chain of posts fifty leagues apart and had fortified and sent a settlement of Negroes to San Bernardo (Espíritu Santo) Bay. Governor Ulloa, one of the informants, expressed the fear that if the English were to occupy the mouth of the Rio Grande, as was rumored, they would make their way by that river to Santa Fé. In November, 1766, the viceroy reported that the English of Pensacola were carrying on extensive contraband trade with the missions of Nuevo Santander, and asked for two vessels to check the abuse. These reports caused some uneasiness in Spain and resulted in urgent requests for information.

Meanwhile active steps had been taken on the frontier to ascertain the truth of the rumors. As soon as he reached Villa de Santander, his capital, Escandón sent a party under Joseph de la Garza to make an exploration, and himself went to the coast to make inquiries. Garza explored along the coast from the Rio Grande to Santa Petronilla, the ranch of his father, near the mouth of the Nueces. In May and June (1766) Escandón made a report regarding the whole shore line from Tampico to the Trinity River, based mainly on the testimony of Joseph Garabito, a seaman who had been many times up and down the coast and was now at Bahía del Espíritu Santo. Not only were no English found, but Escandón concluded that there was no place on the whole coast where they might settle.

These investigations directed by Escandón were followed immediately by those of Parrilla. With coast Indians from the missions at San Juan Bautista and a troop of soldiers, twenty-five of whom were furnished by Escandón, Parrilla directed his march to Santa Petronilla, which he had reached by September 13. Descending to the Playa (Beach) de Corpus Christi, he sent a party of twenty-five soldiers and nine mission Indians to explore Malaguitas Island and the opposite coast. The party traversed the island its entire length, to the mouth of the Rio Grande, and examined the places, pointed out by the Indians, where in times past vessels had anchored and sent out boats to the natives. But nothing of especial interest was found.

Having completed the task for which he had been especially commissioned, Parrilla set about extending his explorations to La Bahía. On account of heavy rains he found it impossible to continue along the coast, and he decided therefore to go to La Bahía and make his investigations from that point. Ascending the Nueces forty-two leagues from Corpus Christi, he struck the La Bahía road and followed it to his destination, which he had reached by October 7. Arrived there, he learned that the roads from the Nueces to Orcoquisac were flooded from the rains and a hurricane which had swept the coast a few days before, and that it would be impossible to make the desired exploration for many days to come. He therefore took extensive sworn testimony regarding the coast from the Nueces to the Trinity, its native inhabitants, and rumors of strangers. Of greatest interest in the testimony, perhaps, is the evidence that the soldiery at Bahía were well acquainted with the coast-line between Matagorda Bay and the Nueces, and had made frequent expeditions there to reconnoiter wrecked vessels and to pursue absconding mission Indians. Returning to Mexico, in the following April Parrilla made a report on the Malaguitas and Culebra islands, with maps, and expressed the opinion that there was no danger of the English occupation of either.

To secure information on which to base a general reorganization of the northern outposts of New Spain, the Marqués de Rubí had already set out on his tour of inspection. Reorganization there was made necessary not alone by the transfer of Louisiana, but also by the Indian situation in the interior provinces, for the entire frontier had long been harassed by Indian troubles.

In 1751 the Upper Pimas had rebelled and had wrought havoc in Pimería Alta. In Sonora the Seris were in open revolt. In northern Nueva Vizcaya Apache depredations were almost incessant. In New Mexico, the Yuta, Apache, and Comanche, all or severally, committed outrages nearly every year. Coahuila, Texas, Nuevo León, and even Nuevo Santander, suffered greatly from Apache hostilities. In Texas the Karankawa had long given trouble, and now the western portion of the province was sorely infested by the Comanche and their allies, who were sweeping south in pursuit of the Apache.[5]

Leaving Mexico in March, 1766, Rubí passed through the interior establishments, arriving in Texas in August, 1767. Entering the province by way of El Cañon and San Sabá, he continued to San Antonio, Nacogdoches, Los Ais, Los Adaes, San Agustín de Ahumada (Orcoquisac), and La Bahía, going thence to San Juan Bautista. He was accompanied by Nicolás de la Fora, a capable engineer, who kept a diary and made a remarkable map of the whole district traversed.[6] Rubí found the northern frontier as a whole greatly infested by warlike tribes, as has been intimated. The missions of eastern Texas he regarded as utterly useless, since the Indians refused to live in them.

A few months after Rubí entered the province on his tour, Father Gaspár José de Solis was sent to inspect the missions of the College of Guadalupe de Zacatecas. His report of what he had seen was little more encouraging than that of the Marqués.[7]

Rubí's chief general recommendation was to rearrange the

---

[5] See pp. 374–381.

[6] La Fora, Nicolás, *Relación del Viaje*: For a description of the map see Bolton, H. E., *Guide to the Archives of Mexico*, 365. Another copy of the same map is in the Archivo General de Indias.

[7] *Diario q^e. hizo el Padre Fr. Gaspar Jose de Solis en la Visita que fué a hacer de las Misiones de la Provincia de Texas, 1767*, in *Memorias de Nueva España*, vol. XXVII, 248–297. From San Antonio both Rubí and Solis went southeastward and joined the Bahía Road to Adaes near the Guadalupe. The direct road from San Antonio to Adaes was evidently not in use at this time on account of Comanche hostilities.

northern posts in such a way as to form a cordon of fifteen, extending from the Gulf of California to La Bahía. Regarding Texas he recommended that Comanche-harassed San Sabá be abandoned; that the district of Los Adaes be attached to Louisiana, or that the presidios and missions therein be suppressed and the settlers and the capital moved to San Antonio; and that a war of extermination be waged against the Lipan, relying for this purpose on the aid of the northern tribes. The latter, of course, had long been hostile, but it was now a part of the plan to win their allegiance. Rubí's report went to the king, and in September, 1772, a plan of reorganization was adopted in the form of the ''New Regulation of Presidios,'' which was a practical acceptance of Rubí's proposals. It provided for moving the post of San Sabá to the Rio Grande, into the general line of presidios; Arroyo del Cíbolo was to be garrisoned, as an outpost between La Bahía and San Antonio; the garrison at San Antonio was to be increased from twenty-three to eighty men; the presidios of Los Adaes and Orcoquisac, with their missions, were to be suppressed and the neighboring settlers taken to San Antonio and given lands. To secure a more efficient military service, the order provided for an *inspector comandante* and two assistant inspectors. Hugo Oconor, who had been *ad interim* governor of Texas, was made the first *inspector comandante*, Antonio Bonilla, author of the *Brief Compendium* of Texas history, and Roque de Medina, being made assistants.[8]

Another phase of frontier readjustment had resulted from reforms of Carlos III. For reasons which are generally well known and need not be discussed here, in 1767 the king expelled the Jesuits from all the Spanish dominions. In New Spain this meant a general redistribution of the missionary forces of the

---

[8] See pp. 382–385. Extended reports of Rubí's inspection, of which I have made but little use, are in the Archivo General de Indias, Audiencia de Guadalajara, 104–6–13. I have secured transcripts of many of them through Mr. Dunn.

northern frontier. For more than a century and a half most
of the missionary work of the Pacific Slope and the Tarahumara
had been in the hands of the Jesuits. Their place in Lower
California was now taken by the Franciscans of the College of
San Fernando, in Sonora by those of the College of Santa Cruz,
and in the Tarahumara by those of the College of Guadalupe de
Zacatecas. To offset this new burden the College of Santa Cruz
in 1772 asked and secured permission to renounce its missions
in Coahuila and Texas. Those in Texas were taken over by the
College of Zacatecas and those in Coahuila by the Province of
Santiago de Jalisco. The same province assumed charge of the
Querétaran missions in Pimería Baja, or southern Sonora. To
offset its new burdens the College of Guadalupe relinquished its
missions in eastern Texas, Nuevo Santander, and the Sierra
Gorda. Thus, after 1772, all of the missions of Texas were under
the College of Guadalupe de Zacatecas.[9]

2. *The abandonment of San Sabá, El Cañon, and Orcoquisac.*
—Before these general plans for readjustment had been com-
pleted, Indian hostilities had made necessary the abandonment of
the establishments on the San Sabá, upper Nueces, and lower
Trinity rivers, thus reinforcing the recommendations of the
Marqués de Rubí.

For more than seven years after the establishment of the missions and garrison on the Nueces in 1762, Captain Rábago, at
San Sabá, sustained almost continuous warfare with the
Comanche and the other northern tribes, whose raids were made
chiefly in pursuit of the Apache. In the course of this time the
latter tribe was driven farther and farther south, until they
took refuge beyond the Rio Grande. In 1764 the depredations
became especially bad, and Rábago appealed for help. Rein-
forcements were sent from San Antonio and Coahuila, but after
a few months they returned to their presidios. Early in 1766 a

---

[9] Bolton, H. E., *Guide*, 386, 394; Arricivita, *Crónica*, 437–444.

hard battle was fought with the Indians by forty-two soldiers on the Llano. Rábago now proposed another campaign against the Taovayas fort, asking for a thousand men, but as the Marqués de Rubí was expected soon to reach Texas on his official visitation, the matter was deferred until he should arrive. Early in 1767 depredations became almost a daily occurrence at San Sabá, and the horseherd was sent to Coahuila for safety. Rábago again appealed for aid and again proposed a campaign. In April fifty men were sent from Coahuila, but were soon recalled on account of Indian troubles south of the Rio Grande, whither the Apache had fled.

When Rubí reached San Sabá in July, 1767, Rábago urged that the place be abandoned, maintaining that it could not long hold out. His prediction of further trouble proved true, for scarcely had Rubí left when the Comanche pursued the Apache to El Cañon, attacked the settlement there, and ran off a thousand horses. Part of the families at San Sabá were now moved to El Cañon, and new appeals were made for help. Early in 1768, after another attack at El Cañon, the horse-herd there was sent to the Rio Grande. In June still more alarming reports of an assembling horde caused Rábago to abandon his post without orders and to retreat to El Cañon. For this conduct he was sharply reprimanded by the viceroy, but he was not sent back. For nearly a year longer the garrison remained at El Cañon, when it was removed, early in 1769, to San Fernando de Austria, a settlement south of the Rio Grande. The mission of El Cañon was also withdrawn, and the Apache mission enterprise was now at an end.[10]

By this time the Apache had again become as troublesome as the northern tribes. Meanwhile the latter had extended their

---

[10] For the history of the last years of the San Sabá establishment my main reliance has been Chapter VI of a MS study prepared in my seminar by Mr. W. E. Dunn, entitled ''The History of Spanish Establishments in Western Texas, 1718–1722.'' That chapter is based largely on documents in A. G. M., Historia, vols. 94 and 95, La Fora, *Relación del Viaje;* and Arricivita, *Crónica,* 391–393.

hostilities to eastern Texas and to San Antonio.[11] When Governor Martos left Los Adaes, they threatened to destroy the eastern establishments, and the missionaries were warned by their French neighbors to withdraw. Hugo Oconor, who in 1767 succeeded Martos as *ad interim* governor, strengthened the garrison at San Antonio and acquired a reputation for cowing the Indians—fame ill-deserved, according to Father Morfi. So bad indeed were Indian hostilities at San Antonio that when Ripperdá arrived there as governor in 1770 some of the citizens had abandoned the place and others were about to follow. To cover the road to La Bahía and to protect the ranches of the neighborhood, in the following year Ripperdá found it necessary to plant the fort of Santa Cruz at Arroyo del Cíbolo.[12]

The settlements among the Apache had failed because of Indian hostilities. Those on the lower Trinity failed because of incompetence. After the Louisiana cession these outposts lost their international significance, but their maintenance was deemed still desirable as a check to contraband trade and as a center of control and missionary work among the natives; but even these advantages were almost lost through inefficiency and distressful wrangling.

Up to the end of 1763 the presidio of San Agustín was commanded by Domingo del Rio, who was responsible to Governor Martos. But in November of that year Captain Rafael Martínez Pacheco was appointed commander and made subject

---

11 For the fear of Comanche attacks on all the Texas settlements in 1763 see *Testimonio de los Autos fechos á consulta de Don Lorenzo Cancio, y Don Phelipe de Rabago: El primero Capitan del Prezidio de Santa Rosa, y el segundo del de San Saba sre. assegurarse que los Comanches meditaban el sitado Prezidio de San Saba.*

12 Writing in 1776 Ripperdá claimed the building of the "Fuerte del Zivolo" as one of his special achievements (Letter to José de Galvez, Nov. 15, A. G. I. Guadalajara, 103–5–21). On April 27, 1777, he wrote of the post as follows: "the pueblo of Santa Cruz del Cívolo, about half way between that presidio [La Bahía] and this [Béxar], and off the road about a league to the north, as I established it in the year 1771, though even yet it has not been built of stone, the site not having been determined." Bolton, *De Mézières*, II, 123.

directly to the viceroy, Del Rio remaining as lieutenant. The change, which seems to have been resented by Martos, was followed by one of the most disgraceful of the many disgraceful quarrels which marred the history of Spanish Texas. With the missionaries Pacheco was generally popular, but by his troops he was charged with arrogance, ill-temper, harshness, and avarice. Within a few weeks after his arrival in 1764 a mutiny was under way, and in August all but five soldiers deserted, going to Natchitoches and the mission of Los Adaes. Among those who remained was Del Rio.

Governor Martos made an investigation, declared Pacheco suspended, and sent Marcos Ruiz with twenty of the deserters to arrest him. Pacheco barricaded himself in the presidio, and for several days withstood a siege directed by Ruiz. In the course of the investment the presidio was set on fire and partly destroyed, but Pacheco escaped across the river and fled to the mission of San José, near San Antonio, going later to Mexico to stand trial. Del Rio was soon arrested as a partisan of Pacheco, and Ruiz was left in command of the presidio, but he in turn was shortly afterward removed, on the charge of burning the presidio, and was replaced by Afan de Rivera, commander at Bahía. Governor Martos also fell before the evil spell of the place. Being charged in 1767 with responsibility for the destruction of the fort, he was eventually found guilty and fined. An oasis in the desert of ignominy, Rivera's administration was highly approved. In 1769 Pacheco, having been exonerated, returned to his command. But in the succeeding year he was called to San Antonio with a part of his troops to aid in the defence against the Indians, and in 1771 the remainder of the soldiers followed.[13]

With such a garrison for its protection, it is not strange that the nearby mission enjoyed little permanent success. With the

---

[13] *Testimonio de los Autos* . . . *contra Rafael Martínez Pacheco, Año de 1764.* B. A. Adaes, 1756–1766. See also pp. 367–375, below.

coming of Pacheco and more liberal supplies in 1764, a missionary revival had occurred, under the direction of Fathers Luis Salvino and Bernardino Aristorena. It extended to the Orcoquiza villages, and the Bidai also expressed a desire for a mission, but having had one experience in foreign lands, on the San Xavier River, they stipulated that it must be in their own country. This wave of enthusiasm was temporary, and Pacheco's quarrel with Governor Martos and the stormy times which followed upset it all. Nevertheless, the missionaries continued to secure some spiritual fruit among the Orcoquiza, and extended their ministrations to the Bidai. They remained at their post until after the garrison was removed in 1771, and left it then only with reluctance.[14]

3. *Withdrawal of the northeastern frontier.*—When the New Regulation of 1772 was promulgated, several of its provisions relating to Texas had already been rendered obsolete by the events just described. The work of carrying it into effect was entrusted to the governor, the Baron de Ripperdá, by instructions which reached him in May, 1773. One of the most difficult tasks assigned him was the removal of soldiers, missionaries, and settlers from the northeastern frontier.

Setting out immediately on this errand, Ripperdá passed through Nacogdoches and Los Ais to Los Adaes. At Nacogdoches he was visited by Sauto, head Hasinai chief, who entreated him not to withdraw the Spaniards. At Los Ais and Los Adaes he found a population of more than five hundred persons, whom it was his duty to expel. Among the settlers was one who in ability and substance stood out far above his fellows. He was Antonio Gil Ybarbo (properly Gil y Barbo), a native of Los Adaes, and now about forty-four years old. He was owner of a large ranch "already a pueblo," at El Labonillo, on the highway

14 *Papeles pertenecientes al Orcoquiza* (Arch. Coll. Guadalupe de Zacatecas); *Testimonio del expediente formado á instancia de . . . Pacheco* (A. G. M., Cor. Vir., Bucareli, vol. VII).

west of the Sabine. He was also a trader, and during the reform administration of Oconor as governor *ad interim*, he had been imprisoned on the charge of contraband trade with Louisiana. Nevertheless, he was generally regarded as a substantial, trustworthy man, and was spokesman for his fellows.[15]   He was a type of the able men which the Spanish as well as the English frontier sometimes produced.

Ripperdá's task on the eastern border reminds one of the expulsion of Evangeline's people from Acadia a few years before. As soon as he arrived at Los Adaes he issued a proclamation declaring that in five days everyone must be ready for the march to San Antonio. This order caused consternation and commotion. More time was asked for and granted, and Ripperdá returned to San Antonio, leaving in charge the aged commander, Lieutenant José González. Most of the inhabitants prepared to emigrate, but a number of them fled to the forests or to Natchitoches. The removal involved the abandonment of all permanent improvements, and the urgency of the order gave insufficient time to prepare for the march. Ripening crops and part of the stock had to be abandoned. Gun carriages and other things which could not be transported were buried within the stockade of the presidio.[16]

On March 25 the journey began. At Ybarbo's ranch twenty-four persons, including members of his own family, dropped behind on the plea of illness. At Nacogdoches Lieutenant González died, thus ending a long career of service on the frontier. Two women also died here, and nine other persons dropped out with permission. As the rest proceeded, some, even women, had to go on foot for lack of horses. There was much suffering, and before they reached the Brazos ten children died. But here they were met by supplies and mules, sent by Governor Ripperdá. At the newly established garrison of Arroyo del Cíbolo a few more persons stopped. On September 26, two months after leav-

15 *Quaderno que Corresponde* (A. G. M., Historia, vol. 51).
16 *Ibid.* See also pp. 385–391, below.

ing Adaes, the remainder straggled into San Antonio weary and footsore. With the party had come four missionaries from Adaes, Los Ais, and Nacogdoches. The soldiers brought twelve four-pound cannons, drawn by oxen. Ripperdá had been instructed also to remove the presidio and mission from Orcoquisac, but, as we have seen, they had already been abandoned a year or more before.[17]

As soon as they reached San Antonio Ripperdá ordered the "Adaesaños" to choose lands within the villa of San Fernando, those who had remained at Arroyo del Cíbolo being permitted to select lands there if they chose. But they all promptly refused, and, with Gil Ybarbo as their spokesman, by petition they asked permission to return to Los Ais, there to recover their abandoned property and start life anew. The petition was of course sincere, but the location proposed reveals Ybarbo's hand in the matter. Los Ais was near his ranch at El Lobanillo, to which he desired to return.

Ripperdá could not grant the request; but he was strongly opposed to abandoning the eastern frontier, and he suggested that the petition be presented to the viceroy. This plan was acted upon, and Gil Ybarbo and Gil Flores were chosen by the *émigrés* to go to Mexico. They set out on December 10, carrying letters from Ripperdá to the viceroy and to Oconor. In them the governor expressed his approval of the petition which Ybarbo carried, and also recommended the sending of settlers to live among the Taovayas and the Tawakoni. On the way to Mexico Ybarbo wrote to Oconor, at Chihuahua, urging that a settlement be re-established on the frontier, to keep out the French who were now flocking into Texas. In February he presented his petition to the viceroy.[18]

The readiness of Viceroy Bucareli to reverse a definite policy of the king is, to say the least, surprising. In doing so Bucareli

---

[17] *Quaderno que Corresponde;* see also pp. 391–393.

[18] *Quaderno que Corresponde; Autos . . . Sobre que se les deje avecindar en la Misión de los Ais* (A. G. M., Historia, vol. 51).

was guided almost solely by Areche, the fiscal of the Real Audiencia, who in turn was guided by conflicting reports from San Antonio, La Bahía, and Chihuahua. Areche, to whom the petition was referred, at once approved the settlement of Los Ais as a means of checking Indian assaults; a *junta de guerra* called to consider the matter likewise approved, recommending the provision of a minister at royal expense, and that the *émigrés* be given the customary aid furnished new settlers. Bucareli concurred in the opinion and promptly ordered the plan put into effect.

But the situation was now suddenly changed through opposition by Oconor, writing from Chihuahua. He maintained that Los Adaes had long been the seat of contraband trade in arms and ammunition among the northern tribes, carried on in spite of repeated royal orders, and that Ybarbo and his co-petitioners desired simply to return to that traffic. The question being referred to Areche, he now advised rescinding the former action. On May 5 a new junta referred the matter to Oconor, with power to decide it; his decision could hardly be doubtful. Meanwhile the viceroy ordered Ripperdá to aid in settling the exiles temporarily in a "suitable place," at least a hundred leagues from Natchitoches. Thus on one and the same day Bucareli left the affair in the hands of two persons whose views were widely at variance. But, fortunately for the petitioners, Oconor was preoccupied, and by the time he was able to give the question his attention matters were beyond his control.[19]

The establishment of the exiles from Los Adaes in a settlement was thus left temporarily in the hands of Ripperdá, with only the restriction that the place must be not less than one hundred leagues from Natchitoches. In the performance of his commission Ripperdá again showed his sympathy with the desires of Ybarbo by sending the colonists as far from San An-

---

[19] *Quaderno que Corresponde; Autos Sobre Avecindar en los Ais;* see also pp. 394–404, below.

tonio and as near to Los Adaes as the terms of his instructions would permit. The site designated by him was at Paso Tomás, the crossing of the Adaes Road, apparently at what was later known as Robbins's Ferry. Among the reasons assigned for the choice, one was that it was a good location from which to watch French and English contraband traders; another, that it was protected from the Comanche by the Nations of the North; another, that it was a vantage point between the northeastern tribes and those of the coast. Ripperdá's enemies, however, chief of whom was Oconor, charged that the location was chosen because of the interest of Ripperdá and Ybarbo in the trade which they pretended to desire to curtail.[20]

Preparations for removal to the Trinity were made in August, 1774. Before leaving, the colonists were organized as a militia and into a pueblo, Ybarbo being named both captain and *justicia mayor*. In honor of the viceroy the pueblo was named Nuestra Señora del Pilar de Bucareli. Most of the "militiamen" enlisted were without guns and ammunition. Because of their poverty many of the exiles could not provide an outfit for the exodus, and only about seventy families went, but the rest proposed to follow later.

Near the end of August the party set out, escorted by a squad of soldiers. Having arrived at the site, Ybarbo took the lead in founding the settlement, setting the citizens a worthy example and aiding them with his substance. Making an expedition to Los Adaes, he brought from there nails, powder, shot, six cracked cannons, and old iron, to be used in the building and the defence of the pueblo. Two other cannons were secured from Orcoquisac. In a short while Ybarbo had a regularly formed town with a plaza, church, guard house, and mounted cannons. The place prospered rather better than was the rule with frontier Spanish towns more methodically founded. It was exempted for ten years from civil taxation and, after some discussion, from church

---

20 See below, pp. 405–432.

tithes. Some, at least, of the settlers who had remained in the east were taken to Bucareli, and various other odds and ends of humanity gathered there. In 1777, after an epidemic had removed some of the population, there were three hundred and forty-seven inhabitants. For more than a year the place was without a regular minister, but eventually Father José de la Garza was sent from Mission San Antonio de Valero. President Ramírez protested the loss of his missionary, but did not recover him. Ripperdá was anxious to gather the Bidai and neighboring tribes into a new mission, but this project did not succeed.[21]

Ybarbo was active in promoting friendly relations with the surrounding tribes and in watching the coast. During Bucareli's four years of existence, he made at least three friendly tours among the northern Indians and at least three journeys to the Gulf. Most noteworthy of these coast expeditions was that made in 1777 to the mouth of the Sabine River, in response to rumors of English traders there. In the course of it Ybarbo mapped the coast, reconnoitered a stranded English vessel in Sabine Lake, and picked up a wandering Englishman near the Trinity. Later in the same year he took part in an expedition which explored the coast from the Trinity to the Colorado.

When he first went to establish Bucareli, Ybarbo found among the Bidai Indians French traders from Natchitoches, and some of them, having Spanish wives, were allowed to settle on condition of giving up the trade. Among those who came to the place the most prominent was Nicholas de la Mathe, who built for it a new church to replace the first chapel. That some smuggling from Louisiana went on we know from actual instances.

Indeed, reports of contraband trade at Bucareli gave it a bad name with the authorities in Mexico, and set on foot an attempt to remove it from the frontier. Ripperdá warmly defended the place, while action was delayed by Oconor's preoccupation and

---

[21] *Expediente sobre que al vecindario de Pilar de Bucareli se le destine Parroco* (A. G. M., Historia, vol. 51).

then by a general reorganization of the northern provinces. The result was that before the permanent disposition of the Bucareli settlers was decided by the government, it was determined independently by accidental circumstances and by the frontier community itself.[22]

One of the advantages claimed for the site at Bucareli had been that it was sheltered by the Tonkawa and Tawakoni from the hostile Comanche. And this claim may have been well founded, for it was three years before the peace of the settlement was disturbed by that enemy's unwelcome presence. In May, 1778, however, a band of Comanche appeared in the neighborhood and were pursued by Ybarbo, three Indians being killed. In October of the same year another band drove off a herd of two hundred and seventy-six horses from the place. This raid was followed by rumors of threatened destruction, and the little village was terror-stricken. Ybarbo appealed to the governor for aid, or for permission to move eastward among the friendly Hasinai. In December, before help could be secured, a part of the settlers withdrew, with Ybarbo's permission. Soon after they left the Trinity overflowed and another Comanche raid occurred. Thereupon the rest of the families, led by Ybarbo, followed. Going to Nacogdoches, which they reached by April, 1779, there they settled down, Father Garza occupying the mission buildings which had been abandoned five years before. After much correspondence, the authorities approved what Ybarbo had done, and thenceforth Nacogdoches grew in importance as a center of Indian control and Ybarbo as an Indian agent.[23]

4. *De Mézières and the pacification of the northern tribes.*[24] —The acquisition of Louisiana had made unnecessary the de-

[22] *Quaderno que Corresponde.*

[23] *Expediente sobre el abandono de Pilar de Bucareli* (A. G. M., Historia, vol. 51); see also pp. 432–446.

[24] This section is based mainly upon Bolton, *Athanase De Mézières and the Louisiana Texas Frontier, 1768–1780* (The Arthur H. Clark Company, Cleveland, 1914), where De Mézières' correspondence and diaries are printed.

fences of eastern Texas. On the other hand, it had made more
urgent the problem of controlling the northern tribes. These
tribes had been hostile to the Spaniards and friendly to the
French, and it was necessary now to win them to Spanish allegiance, particularly if a general war were to be conducted
against the Lipan, as Rubí had proposed, and if the northern
tribes were to be kept free from contamination by the advancing
English frontiersmen. These northern Indians had long been
managed by the French through the fur trade. Being powerful
and warlike tribes, for Spain to attempt to control them through
missions, according to the time-honored system, and as was now
being done so successfully in the new province of Alta California,
was impracticable. The obvious plan for Spain to pursue was
to put the Red River district in charge of a Frenchman who
understood its native inhabitants and to continue the French system of control through the fur trade. This was done.[25]

Effective possession of Louisiana was taken by Alejandro
O'Reilly in 1769. One of his early acts was to confer the office
of lieutenant-governor of the Natchitoches district upon
Athanase de Mézières, a son-in-law of the elder Saint Denis, a
brother-in-law of the Duke of Orleans, and long a soldier in
the French service at Natchitoches. His field of activities in-
cluded the Red River Valley and the adjacent parts of northern
Texas, Arkansas, and Oklahoma. Thus, although theoretically
Texas was regarded as extending to the Red River, northern
Texas continued to be actually managed as a part of Louisiana.

In his instructions to De Mézières, O'Reilly provided that
licensed traders be appointed for the friendly tribes, but that
in order to coerce the hostile Indians all trade with them must be
cut off, whether conducted by Spanish subjects or by foreigners.
A special abuse to be suppressed was trade in stolen horses and
Indian captives. This evil was particularly prevalent at the

---

[25] Bolton, *De Mézières*, I, 66–75.

Taovayas villages on the Red River. When they were not at war, the Wichita tribes supplied the Comanche with French weapons and agricultural products. In exchange they secured horses and mules stolen from the Spanish settlements, Indian captives, among whom Apaches predominated, and Spanish captives from the frontier settlements. For the horses, mules and Indian captives they found a ready market with the French traders from Louisiana, where Apache slaves and stock bearing Spanish brands were common. The Spanish captives were held for ransom or taken for that purpose to San Antonio or Los Adaes.[26]

Carrying out these orders with notable efficiency, De Mézières appointed traders for the friendly Yatasí and Cadodacho, gave them presents in the king's name, and conferred medals of honor upon their chiefs, Tinhioüen and Cocay. On the other hand, he took vigorous and effective steps to expel from the tribes all unlicensed traders and vagabond whites.

As his principal mission, however, De Mézières undertook to secure the allegiance and friendship of the tribes of the upper Red River district and of the country adjacent thereto, in what are now Texas, Oklahoma, and Arkansas. With this in view, he summoned them to meet him at the Cadodacho village of San Luis, near modern Texarkana. The council met in October, 1770. Through the mediation of the powerful Cadodacho chieftain, Tinhioüen, it was attended by the chiefs of the Taovayas, Tawakoni, Yscanis, and Kichai. Others failed to attend through fear of vengeance. The assembled warriors were surly and suspicious, but by dint of bold threats and gentle coaxing, and the powerful aid of Tinhioüen, De Mézières extracted from them a profession of friendship and a promise to go to San Antonio to make peace with Governor Ripperdá. As a result of this expedition, and of an embassy by Father Pedro Ramírez and Pablo le Blanc, in 1771 treaties of peace were made at Natchitoches with the Tao-

---

[26] Bolton, *De Mézières*, I, 47–48, 88–92; 127–197.

vayas, Tawakoni, Yscanis, Kichai, and Cainiones.   The Comanche
and Tonkawa were still uncertain.[27]

To cement the alliance with the northern tribes still further,
to explore their country, learn their strength, and investigate the
current rumors of English traders among them, in 1772 De
Mézières made a tour of their country.   Leaving Natchitoches in
March with interpreters and a small escort of soldiers, he went
west to the Trinity River where, in the vicinity of Palestine, he
visited villages of the Kichai, Yscanis, and Tawakoni.   Continuing westward, passing through a Tonkawa settlement, near
the present Waco he visited two Tawakoni villages.   Proceeding
up the Brazos some two hundred miles, he visited the Wichita on
that stream, and communicated with the Taovayas of the Red
River.   From the Wichita he marched directly south three hundred miles over an unknown trail to San Antonio, where he arrived with seventy Indians in his train, after an expedition of
eighty-eight days.[28]

This was one of the notable explorations of the Southwest.
The report which De Mézières made of his tour is a monument
to his care and intelligence, and gives us our first intimate view
of the tribes which he visited.[29]   During his journey he learned
that the Taovayas were procuring English goods in exchange for
stolen horses, and that, on the other hand, the northern tribes
were being hard pressed by the Osage.   To meet this situation
he now urged the new allies to move southward under the protection of a Spanish presidio.   The Indians promised to comply
in the autumn, after harvest, and Governor Ripperdá seconded
De Mézières's plan of a presidio in northern Texas.   However,
the government in Mexico opposed the project, the Indians failed
to move, and the plan went by the board.   While De Mézières

---

[27] Bolton, *De Mézières*, I, 92–95; 199–282.   De Mézières's own account
of the expedition of 1770 is printed in *ibid.*, I, 206–220.

[28] *Ibid.*, I, 95–99; 283–351.

[29] It is printed in *ibid.*, I, 784–312.

was at San Antonio he and Ripperdá proposed to the viceroy a joint campaign with the northern tribes against the Apache, after the plan suggested by Rubí. On his way back to Natchitoches De Mézières used his influence to sever a dangerous friendship which had grown up between the Apache on the one hand and the Bidai and Hasinai on the other. As a result of the treaties and of his tour he established licensed traders from Natchitoches among the new allies. In the following years men like the Layssards, Du Chesne, and La Mathe occupied a place in northern Texas like that filled by La Clede, the Chouteaus, the the Robidoux, and Lisa in upper Louisiana.[30]

In the fall of 1773, while De Mézières was absent in Europe, a trader named Gaignard was sent from Natchitoches up the Red River to make peace with the Comanche, who had not yet joined in the treaties and who continued to make trouble at San Antonio. Going to the Taovayas, he found them in bad humor because the horse and slave trade with Natchitoches had been cut off, and because the presents promised by De Mézières had been delayed. They opposed Gaignard's passage to the Comanche, but early in 1774 the head chief of the Naytane, a branch of the Comanche, with four thousand warriors, met him at the Taovayas village and signed a peace compact.[31] In spite of this agreement, however, the Comanche continued to give trouble.

De Mézières, aided by Ripperdá, had done much toward solving the question of the control of the northern tribes. But Oconor and others cast suspicion on their motives and belittled the results of their work. It was asserted that the promises of the red men were not being kept; that the French traders, including De Mézières, were profiting by illicit commerce with the

---

[30] Bolton, *De Mézières*, I, 75; 100–110.

[31] *Journal kept exactly according to the orders of M. de Villier to make, with the help of God and the Holy Virgin, the journey to the Panis and the Naytane, begun at Natchitoche on the day of my departure, October first, 1773.* Printed in *ibid.*, II, 83–100; original in Bancroft Collection. The document contains a symbolic Indian drawing, in colors, to represent the compact.

Indians; and that Ripperdá was partial to Frenchmen and an accomplice in the traffic. As a consequence, the viceroy forbade to Ripperdá all communication with Louisiana, and eventually had him removed from office for non-compliance.[32]

In spite of these charges and suspicions, however, and of the fact that the Comanche continued hostile, the plan of De Mézières and Ripperdá to unite with the northern tribes to destroy the Apache was adopted, and De Mézières was chosen as the principal agent in carrying it out. This vindication was facilitated by a recent turn in the government. In 1776 the Interior Provinces of New Spain were put under a *comandante general* with his capital at Chihuahua. The first *comandante*, El Cavallero de Croix, arrived on the frontier in 1777. As his first great task, he set about checking Indian hostilities, particularly those of the Apache. It is indicative of the importance of that frontier that he began with Texas.

Croix's plans were outlined even before he left Mexico for the north, and they were linked with his friendship for Don Bernardo de Gálvez, the brilliant young soldier who had just taken possession of Louisiana, and who soon demonstrated his military genius by the part he played in the American Revolution. The essence of Croix's program was to unite the Nations of the North and three hundred *chasseurs* from Louisiana, commanded by Gálvez, with the soldiery of the Interior Provinces, commanded by Croix, in a joint campaign against the Eastern Apache.

To consider the project or to devise an alternative, Croix held a council of war at Monclova in December, 1777. In this meeting he presented for discussion sixteen questions ''regarding the

---

[32] Bolton, *ibid.*, I, 107–108; II, 13–81; Viceroy Bucareli to Arriga, April 26, 1776. ''El Virrey de Nueva España Repite la necesidad, que pulsa de que al Baron de Riperda se le releve del Govierno de la Provincia de Tejas que esta exerciendo.'' (A. G. I., Guadalajara, 103–5–21.) By November 15, 1776, Ripperdá had been notified of his transfer to Comayagua, Honduras, but it was 1778 before he left. (Ripperdá to José de Gálvez, November 15, 1776, *ibid.*).

Apache on the one hand, and the Nations of the North on the other hand, their divisions, habitat, fighting strength, and depredations; the feasibility of making an offensive alliance with the Apache against the other group, or vice versa.'' Croix's plan for uniting with the Nations of the North was approved, but its details were referred to a council to be held in San Antonio de Béxar.[33]

The appointed junta met at San Antonio on January 5, 1778. In it sat El Caballero de Croix, who presided; Colonel Baron de Ripperdá, governor of the province of Texas; Antonio Bonilla, adjutant-inspector and secretary of the commandancy-general; Captain Domingo Díaz, commander of the First Flying Squadron of Croix's expedition; and the presidial captains Rafael Martínez Pacheco and Luis Cazorla. With the expedition had come Father Juan Agustín Morfi, later the author of the *Memorias* for the history of Texas, but he did not sit in the council of war. This body also approved Croix's plan. To outline its details, however, and to prepare the minds of the Nations of the North for its execution, De Mézières was called from Louisiana.[34]

By February 20 De Mézières had reached San Antonio and drawn up his plan. He proposed assembling at the Taovayas villages one thousand Indian allies; to lead them to the Colorado, there to meet three hundred Spanish troops; and to march in two divisions to the Pecos and northern Coahuila, there to crush the enemy between them. To prevent the torture of captives and as a means of replenishing the missions, he proposed that the missionaries should buy all captives at a prearranged price.[35]

While the plan was being considered by the authorities, De Mézières went on another tour among the northern tribes. Leaving San Antonio in March, he went to the settlement of Bucareli,

---

[33] Bolton, *De Mézières*, I, 110–112.

[34] The report of the council held at Monclova and San Antonio is printed in Bolton, *De Mézières*, II, 147–170.

[35] *Ibid.*, I, 112–113. His report is printed in *ibid.*, II, 172–186.

on the Trinity, thence to the Kichai, the Tonkawa, and the Tawakoni on the Brazos. From there he followed the Cross Timbers to the Taovayas villages on the Red River, whence he sent a threatening message to the Comanche. Learning that the Taovayas had been visited the year before by English traders—for while Daniel Boone was pioneering in Kentucky other English frontiersmen were threading the wilds of Texas and Oklahoma—he wrote a dispatch to Croix urging a Spanish settlement there. Returning to Natchitoches he took with him Parrilla's cannons, leaving them on the way at Bucareli.[36]

From San Antonio Croix had gone to his capital at Chihuahua. Several councils of war held there approved the plan of De Mézières for a campaign against the Apache, but concluded that before it could be executed more troops must be provided. In the meantime De Mézières was sent from Louisiana to reside in Texas, that he might continue his work among the Nations of the North and try to secure the friendship of the still hostile Comanche. This permanent transfer of De Mézières, it would seem, signalized an attempt to transfer the control of the Nations of the North from Natchitoches to San Antonio, a change which Ripperdá had requested. De Mézières left Natchitoches for Texas in May, 1779, intending to make a tour among the northern tribes on his way to San Antonio. At the Atoyaque River he suffered an accident which delayed him three months. Continuing in August, he passed through the Nabedache, Kichai, and Tawakoni villages, going thence to San Antonio by way of the San Xavier River, holding councils and making presents on the way. Soon after he arrived at San Antonio he learned that he had been appointed governor of Texas, but before taking office he died, on November 2, 1779.[37] By this time Spain had en-

---

[36] Bolton, *De Mézières*, I, 113–116; the original reports of De Mézières are printed *ibid.*, II, 187–238.

[37] *Ibid.*, I, 116–122. De Mézières' report of this expedition are printed *ibid.*, II, 239–288.

tered into the American War, Gálvez was unable to leave Louisiana, and the necessary troops could not be had; consequently the
plan for a general war on the Apache was postponed.

On the other hand, the Apache question was partly solved
locally by Juan de Ugalde, governor of Coahuila. By diplomacy
the Lipan were turned against the Mescalero, and between 1779
and 1783 Ugalde made four campaigns against the Mescalero in
northwestern Coahuila and on the lower Pecos. As a result of
these exploits he won great fame.[38] Seven years later Ugalde,
then *comandante* of the eastern Interior Provinces, greatly en-
hanced his fighting reputation, and to a degree carried out Croix's
plans, by uniting with the Comanche, Taovayas, Wichita, and
Tawakoni, and inflicting a severe defeat upon the Apache at
Arroyo de la Soledad west of the San Antonio.[39] In commemora-
tion of Ugalde's exploits, the cañon of the Nueces River became
known as Cañon de Ugalde, corrupted later into Uvalde.

5. *The exploration of routes to Santa Fé.*[40]—The occupation
of Alta California and Louisiana had made necessary the exploration or the re-exploration of the vast country lying between them,
with a view to the establishment of lines of communication and
to the handling of the new Indian problems. To open routes from
California to Sonora and New Mexico, Anza and Garcés, Domínguez, Escalante, and Miera y Pacheco made extensive and difficult explorations in the years between 1773 and 1777. No less
important was the establishment of communication between the

---

[38] An unsigned relation of Ugalde's campaigns in *Monumentos para
la Historia de Coahuila y Seno Mexicano*, in *Memorias de Nueva España*,
vol. XXIX, ff. 154–194.

[39] The engagement occurred on January 9, 1790. In it forty-four
soldiers and fifty-two citizens from San Antonio took part. The northern
Indians had shortly before been defeated by the Apache on the Pedernales (Report of the battle, by Rafael Martínez Pacheco, March 11, 1790.
Lamar Papers).

[40] In writing this section I was greatly aided by a manuscript study
prepared from my documents in my seminar by Mr. Colin B. Goodykoontz.
It is entitled ''Spanish Exploration of Louisiana and the adjacent Borders of New Spain, 1762–1800.''

new province of Louisiana and the old outposts of New Spain. This work was taken up, though somewhat tardily, and with it the task of opening a direct route from San Antonio to Santa Fé.

In spite of the venerable antiquity and the relative propinquity of these two northeastern outposts, there was as yet no established line of travel between them. Throughout the eighteenth century such communication had been made impossible by the hostilities of the intervening Apache and Comanche. Few persons travelled from one place to the other; when they did they went roundabout through Coahuila, Nueva Vizcaya, and El Paso, or *vice versa*. Plans for opening direct communication between the outposts had been frequently considered, however. The matter was urged in 1751 by the Marqués de Altamira when discussing the dangers of French advance into New Mexico. One of the reasons for the founding of the San Sabá establishment in 1757 was that it might form a basis for direct communication and commerce from New Mexico to Texas and Coahuila. In 1762 an attempt was made to open communication with San Sabá by the governor of New Mexico, who sent a band of Indians for this purpose from the Pueblo of Pecos. But they did not reach their destination.[41]

For twenty years more the project remained unexecuted, when it was made feasible by the establishment of peace with the Comanche who had blocked the way. The principal agent in the work of exploration, when it was finally taken up in earnest, was Pedro (Pierre) Vial, a Frenchman who was well known to the tribes of northern Texas and who evidently had traded between Louisiana and the Taovayas village. An important preparation for Vial's work had been made by the explorations of De Mézières.

---

[41] *Testimonio de los Autos á Conz^ta. de Don Lorenzo Cansio Capitan del Real Precidio de Santiago de la Monclova, en que dá quenta de haver aprehendido dos Indios del Nuebo Mex^co. que aquel Gobernador embió á descubrir la comunicacion de aquellas Provincias con el Presidio de San Savá.*

In 1786 Vial was commissioned by Domingo Cabello, governor of Texas, to explore a direct route from San Antonio to Santa Fé. Setting out on October 4 with one companion, Vial went north, crossed the Llano and reached the Colorado, which he ascended for some distance. Suffering an accident through a fall from his horse, he now turned eastward to the Brazos, where he found succor at the Tawakoni village of Quisquate, with whom he remained six weeks. Continuing his journey on December 15, he ascended the Brazos sixty-two leagues, then turned north-eastward and crossed over to the Taovayas villages on the Red River, where Parrilla had been defeated seventeen years before.

Leaving the Taovayas on January 8, Vial set out west up the Red River, and on the next day reached the Comanche village of Chief Zoquine. Remaining here till February 18, he continued westward up the Red and Canadian rivers, accompanied by Zoquine, and arrived at Santa Fé on May 26, 1787, having passed through several Comanche villages on the way. To the Tawakoni, Taovayas, and Comanche alike Vial spoke plainly of the importance of keeping peace with the Spaniards. All were friendly, and the Comanche asked for a Spanish settlement on the San Sabá or the Pedernales River, as more convenient and safer trading points than San Antonio.[42]

Vial had made his way from San Antonio to Santa Fé, and had found the Comanche friendly, but his route was far from direct. For this reason Governor Concha sent out another party under Corporal José Mares. He left Santa Fé on July 31, 1787, accompanied by Cristóbal Santos and Alejandro Martín, the latter being an interpreter in the Comanche language. From

---

[42] *Diario que por la gracia de Dios, comienso á hacer desde este Presidio de San Antonio de Bejar hasta arrivar al de la capital Villa de Santa Fe por Comision de mi Governador Don. Domingo Cavello, Governador de la Provincia de los Texas, con expresion de las Jornadas desde el dia 4 de Octubre de 1787 [1786].* Santa Fé, July 5, 1787. The mis-dating of the official transcript of the diary led to an error in dating Vial's first journey on the map in my De Mézières (frontispiece). In that map Vial's first journey from the Taovayas to Santa Fé is not shown.

Santa Fé they went to the pueblo of Pecos. Setting out from that place on August 6, they followed the Pecos River half a day, and then, leaving it, took a route parallel to that of Vial, but in general considerably south of it, to the Taovayas villages, which they reached on August 5, having passed through several Comanche villages on the way. Turning southwest at the Taovayas, Mares crossed over to the Brazos, and from there went south across the Colorado, San Sabá, and Llano rivers, by a route similar to that taken by De Mézières in 1772, reaching San Antonio on October 8, 1787.[43]

Thus far Mares had not greatly improved upon the route of Vial, for he also had made a detour to the Taovayas. But on his return journey he did better. Setting out for Santa Fé in January, 1788, he went to the upper Red by a more westward route, striking it near the 101st meridian. Following his former trail from here, he arrived at Santa Fé on April 17.[44]

After reaching Santa Fé in 1787, Vial was sent by Governor Concha to explore a route to Natchitoches, with instructions to return by way of San Antonio. He was thoroughly competent to make the journey, for he had just come from the Taovayas, and it was said of him that he had frequently traversed the country between the Taovayas and Natchitoches. Pursuant to his instructions, in June, 1788, Vial set forth, accompanied by Francisco Xavier Fragoso and three soldiers, Fragoso going as diarist. They were escorted as far as the Taovayas by a squad of cavalrymen under Santiago Fernández. The combined party left Santa Fé June 24, two months after Mares had returned

---

[43] Ugarte y Loyola to Governor Concha, January 23, 1788; Mares, José, *Viaje ó descubrimiento de Camino desde la Capital del Nvo. Mexico a la de la Provincia de Texas, hecho p*r*. el Cavo de Ymbalidos Jose Mares.* San Antonio, October 19, 1787.

[44] Mares, *Derrotero y Diaro que comprende el numero de Leguas que hay desde la Capital de San Antonio de Bejar Provincia de los Texas hasta la de Santa Fe del Nuevo Mexico, que hago Yo Jose Mares Cabo Ymbalido de la Compañia de ella p*r*. los terrenos que me conducen los Yndios Amigos Cumanches, para descubrir camino en derechura.* Santa Fé, April 21, 1788.

thither. Going to Pecos, from there they pursued a direct course to the Taovayas, close to the routes already taken by Vial and Mares, though apparently not identical with either. The Taovayas villages were reached on July 20. After remaining there four days, Fernández and his party returned to Santa Fé, reaching their destination in August.[45]

The day after Fernández departed, Vial continued his journey with his three companions for Natchitoches. Going generally eastward, they struck the upper waters of the Sabine River, which they followed to the great bend near the 32nd parallel. West of the river, near that line, they passed a Nadaco village, and, a short distance away, on the other side of the river, a village of Bidai Indians. Going directly from the Sabine to Natchitoches, they passed on the way the ranchos of six Frenchmen and one Englishman. Natchitoches was reached on August 20.

After a stay of ten days Vial and his party set out for San Antonio, over the Camino Real. Los Adaes was not mentioned on the way, but west of the Sabine they passed "a rancho called Lobanillo, a settlement of Spaniards from the pueblo of Nacodoches." In other words, Gil Ybarbo's ranch had been reoccupied since 1773. Between there and Nacogdoches Spanish settlements were passed at the Atoyaque River and at El Atascoso. Nacogdoches was described as consisting of eighty or ninety houses, inhabited by two hundred or three hundred Spaniards and French. Here all of the party but Vial were taken ill with chills and fever and were detained thereby from September 4 to October 20. Between Nacogdoches and San Antonio only two settlements were mentioned. These were Rancho del Reten and Rancho Chayopines, seventeen and ten leagues southeastward

---

[45] Ugarte y Loyola to Concha, January 23, 1788; Concha to Ugarte y Loyola, June 20, 1788; Fernández, Santiago, *Derretero, diario y Calculacion de leguas que hago Yo el abajo firmado (Santiago Fernandez) en descubrimiento desde esta Santa Fé a los Pueblos de humanes por orden superior del Sor Gouernador Dn. Fernando de la Concha, á conducion y guia de Pedro Vial.* Santa Fé, December 16, 1788.

from San Antonio, respectively. Vial had come by the route followed by Rubí and Solis twenty years before.

Reaching San Antonio on November 18, Vial and his party were detained there seven months by illness. Setting forth on June 25, 1789, with four Comanches as guides, they went directly north to the Brazos by a route close to that taken by De Mézières in 1772 and therefore east of that by which Mares had returned. Turning northwestward at the Brazos, they reached Santa Fé on August 20, exactly a year from the day on which they had entered Natchitoches.[46]

The diary gave the distance from Santa Fé to Natchitoches as 361 leagues; from Natchitoches to San Antonio 201 leagues; and from San Antonio to Santa Fé 348½ leagues. Vial had travelled on the journey over 900 leagues, or some 2500 miles. Within the past three years, four distinct exploring journeys had been made between San Antonio and Santa Fé, one between Santa Fé and Natchitoches, and four between Santa Fé and the Taovayas villages. Of the first four each had been by a route somewhat more direct than the former. In the course of these expeditions the Comanchería, long regarded as a barrier, had frequently been passed and had become well known to written records. In all these expeditions the prominence of the Taovayas villages as a strategic point is made manifest.

Vial had taken the principal part in opening direct communication from Santa Fé to San Antonio and to Natchitoches. Three years later he was entrusted with exploring a route from Santa Fé to St. Louis, a task which he successfully accomplished in

---

[46] Fragoso, Francisco Xavier, *Derrotero, Diario y Calculacion de Leguas, que en descubrimiento por derecho desde esta Provincia del Nuevo Mexico hasta el Fuerte de Nachitoches y la de los Texas, de orden Superior voy á practicar en Compañia de Dn. Pedro Vial comisionado á este proposito, yo el abajo y á lo ultimo firmado (Francisco Xavier Fragoso), Villa de Santa Fé veinte y quatro de Junio de mil setecientos Ochenta y ocho.* Santa Fé, August 20, 1789. This journey of Vial from San Antonio to Santa Fé is not shown on the map in my *De Mézières.*

1792 and 1793.[47] Ten years later he was still operating among the Indians of the Louisiana frontier from Santa Fé as his base. He was not a great diarist, but he was a good frontiersman, and has left his name permanently fixed in the history of exploration.[48]

The expeditions of Vial may be said to close the half century of Texas history after the founding of San Fernando de Béxar, and to bring to an end the first series of readjustments of the Texas frontier resulting directly from the Louisiana cession. Since that event the eastern border had been abandoned, and then partially reoccupied by local initiative. The Apache frontier had been deserted. The policies regarding the Apache and the Nations of the North had been reversed. A war of extermination had been declared upon the former, to be waged by firearms and bad whiskey; the latter tribes had been converted into allies and a trading system had been established among them; and routes of communication had been explored between the outposts of Louisiana, Texas, and New Mexico. By this time the reconquest of Florida had helped to set in motion a new series of readjustments along the Gulf. José de Evía had undertaken coast explorations all the way between Tampico and West Florida. A new movement had been set on foot to subdue the fierce Karankawan tribes, through missions or through war. And officials had begun to consider the moving of the Louisiana boundary westward to the Sabine River, and the opening of a commercial port on the coast of Texas.

---

[47] Diaries of Vial to and from St. Louis. A. G. M., Provincias Internas, vol. 183, and also in Historia, vol. 43. The diary to St. Louis is translated in Houck, *Spanish Régime in Missouri*, I, 350–358, but so far as I know the diary of the return has not hitherto been used.

[48] I. J. Cox, *The Early Exploration of Louisiana*, 65.

II. THE SAN XAVIER MISSIONS

CHAPTER I

THE DAWN OF HISTORY IN CENTRAL TEXAS

It is not generally known that the San Gabriel River, in central Texas, was once the seat of Franciscan missionary activity. Yet such is the case, and slender remains of the mission establishments are still to be seen in the valley of that stream. If one will drive nine miles northwest from Rockdale to the Kolb Settlement, and then turn westward up the river for about a mile, he will come to what has long been known in the neighborhood as "Ditch Valley Farm," a name, the present writer has discovered and established beyond doubt, which comes from the fact that through the farm once ran an *acequia*, or irrigating ditch, constructed in the year 1750 to serve three Spanish missions which had recently been founded there. In the river near by are still to be seen at low water the remains of what has long been known as the old "Rock Dam," whose origin, it is now clear, was the same as that of the ditch.

The remains of the *acequia*, as well as of the dam, are still to be seen in dim outline. Crossing the main highway near the western end of the farm is a shallow ditch leading toward the river. North of the road it is quite distinct, being some eight feet wide at the top and two or three feet deep in the middle. The land on this side of the road is uncultivated, and in the bed of the ditch are growing hackberry trees nearly a foot in diameter. About one hundred feet from the road the ditch terminates in a natural arroyo or gully, which leads eastward into the river about two hundred yards away. South of the road the ditch leads into cultivated fields, where it is soon lost;

but forty rods to the southeast, where it crosses an unplowed lane, it is again distinct, and eighty rods farther away it can still be faintly traced across another lane.

In the bed of the river two hundred yards below the mouth of the arroyo the remains of the old "Rock Dam" are pointed out. They now consist of only a heap of large stones, stretching across the stream. A man fishing up the river at low water would certainly notice the stones, though he might not suspect that they are the remains of a dam. But the inhabitants of the neighborhood claim to remember when both ditch and dam were quite distinct—a claim fully supported by the long and commonly used names, "Rock Dam" and "Ditch Valley Farm." In the fields the *acequia* has been filled in by the plow, while most of the stones of the dam, I am told, have been hauled away and used for building purposes. Besides the ditch and the dam, tradition tells of the remains of old buildings of pre-American origin, once standing on Kolb's Hill, below Ditch Valley Farm.

Tradition ascribes the ditch, the dam, and the old buildings to the Spaniards, and neighborhood belief in the tradition is evidenced by perennial digging about the locality of the dam for pots of Spanish gold. But few or none have guessed, what is now established beyond question, that these archaeological remains are the vestiges of what were known in their day as the San Xavier missions.

1. *The obscurity of the history hitherto.*—The story of these missions is a little known chapter in the history of the labors of the Franciscan Fathers among the Indians northeast of the Rio Grande River. Writing a few years ago on "Some Obscure Points in the Mission Period" of the history of Texas, Dr. W. F. McCaleb said, with essential truth, "Though little is known of most of the eastern missions, still less is known of some others. Indeed, as to the three missions on the San Xavier River, no historian, so far as the writer's information goes, save Bancroft,

has even mentioned their names.''[1]   And Bancroft, he might have added, devotes to them only a little more than a page. Besides Bancroft, Dr. McCaleb should have excepted Shea, who devotes a few short paragraphs to the subject.[2]   Had the assertion been intended to include books printed in a foreign language, it would have excepted, also, *Arricivita's Crónica Seráfica y Apóstolica*,[3] a very rare work, which contains a fairly good, though in many respects unsatisfactory, account of the missions, in whose founding and administration the author took part.   Arricivita's worst defect is his utter disregard for chronology and geography.   There is, in addition, the still rarer treatise, for it is as yet unprinted, by Father Morfi, which devotes a considerable amount of space to the San Xavier missions.[4]   This history and that of Arricivita are the chief basis of the brief and obscure paragraphs of Bancroft and Shea.

Since Dr. McCaleb wrote the words quoted, no advance has been made in published works, with the exception of a minor contribution by the present writer.[5]   At the time when that was published, only Bancroft had even dared guess the identity of the San Xavier River, on which the missions were established. He conjectured that it might have been a branch of either the Colorado or the Brazos, a guess giving considerable latitude, since these streams are from fifty to seventy-five miles apart in their

---

[1] The Texas State Historical Association *Quarterly*, I, 221.

[2] See Shea, *The Catholic Church in Colonial Days* (1886), 500–501; Bancroft, *North Mexican States and Texas*, I, 623 (ed. of 1884).

[3] Mexico, 1792. Pp. 321–338.

[4] Morfi, *Memorias para la Historia de Texas*, cir. 1781. A copy is in the Bancroft Library, and is now being edited for publication.

[5] The reference is to the article by the present writer entitled ''Spanish Missions in the San Gabriel Valley,'' published in the *Williamson County Sun*, March 21, 1907.   This article correctly identifies the site of the missions and gives a general outline of their history, but it contains some errors and is indefinite at points where definite information is now at hand.   The same article was published contemporaneously in the *Rockdale Express*.   (Since the above was written the first half of the present study was published in the *Southwestern Historical Quarterly*, XVII, 323–378.)

middle courses.[6] Other features of the history of the missions have been equally or more obscure. Indeed, even the date of their establishment has not hitherto been correctly recorded.

And yet the reason for this obscurity is not that the missions were relatively unimportant, for they were more far-reaching in design, longer in duration, and more successful in operation than the San Sabá mission, for example, of which much more is popularly known. Nor has the reason been the non-existence of data for making the episode fairly plain, for these are abundant. It has been, rather, the inaccessibility of the data, and the fact that whereas considerable material remains of the San Sabá mission have been preserved, those of the San Xavier River have completely lost their identity. Recently, however, a large quantity of documentary sources for the history of the missions on the San Gabriel has been gathered from the archives of Mexico,[7] and the site of the missions and some of their remains have been identified. It is now possible, therefore, to construct with some degree of fulness, on the basis of the newly acquired material and a study of the site, the story of the precarious career of these shortlived but not unimportant missions.

2. Early knowledge of the San Xavier River.—The San Xavier River of Spanish days, it is now clear enough, was the San Gabriel of today, which joins Little River—the old San Andrés, or the first of the Brazos de Dios—some twenty-five miles before that stream disembogues into the main Brazos. The way in which the Spanish name became converted by a series of misspellings into the present form, with the resulting loss of the stream's identity in modern geography, is in itself an interesting bit of history, but it cannot be indicated here. The San Xavier River early became known to the Spaniards as one of the

---

[6] Bancroft, *North Mexican States and Texas*, I, 623.

[7] The larger part of them come from the archives of the extinguished College of Santa Cruz de Querétaro, which founded the missions. Specific references to the materials are given throughout this paper. Their location in the archives is indicated in the Bibliography, pp. 452–467, below.

streams of central Texas endowed with more than usually attractive surroundings. It was visited and given its name by the Ramón-Saint Denis expedition on June 1, 1716.[8] By the same party Brushy Creek, the principal tributary of the San Gabriel, was twice crossed and was given the name of Arroyo de las Benditas Ánimas[9] (Creek of the Blessed Souls) which it bore in somewhat shortened form almost continuously throughout Spanish days.

From 1716 forward the San Xavier River was frequently visited and mentioned. The expedition led by the Marqués de Aguayo in 1721 passed the Colorado near the mouth of Onion Creek and followed a northward course that took the party across Arroyo de las Ánimas, the San Xavier River, Little River near Belton, and thence to the Brazos about at Waco.[10] In 1730, when the Querétaran missions were removed from eastern Texas to San Antonio, the Zacatecan missionaries asked permission to remove their establishments to the San Xavier,[11] a fact which indicates some acquaintance with the stream. In 1732 Bustillo y Zevallos, governor of Texas, made a campaign against the Apache that took him to and beyond the San Xavier.[12] In 1744, during the perennial quarrel between the Canary Island settlers

[8] Espinosa, *Diario derrotero de la nueva entrada a la Prov. de los Tejas, Año. de 1716,* entry for June 1. It is seen that this expedition, led by St. Denis, did not by any means follow the ''Old San Antonio Road'' of later days.

[9] *Ibid.,* entries for May 28 and June 2.

[10] Peña, *Derrotero de la Expedeción en la Provincia de los Texas* (Mexico, 1722). This is the original government print. The copy in the *Memorias de Nueva España,* vol. 28, has numerous errors, and is there given a wrong title. I am indebted to the paper by Miss Eleanor Buckley on ''The Aguayo Expedition'' for the results of her study of Aguayo's route. This paper was her master's thesis written at the University of Texas, 1908–1909. Father Pichardo made a map of the route in 1811, which corresponds roughly to that made by Miss Buckley.

[11] *Ynforme al R. Discreo. de los PPs. Pres. y Misss. de Tejas en que piden salir al Rio de S. Xavier.*

[12] Bustillo y Zevallos, *Memorial del Govor. Bustillos en contra de la fundacion de Sn. Xavier,* May 28, 1746, paragraph 7; Cabello, *Informe,* 1784.

and the other inhabitants of San Antonio, it was suggested that one of the parties should move to the San Xavier,[13] but the proposal was not acted upon. Two years later it was asserted that the region of the San Xavier was well known to the inhabitants of San Antonio as a buffalo-hunting ground,[14] and anyone who has beheld the superb prairies between the Colorado and the middle San Gabriel can readily believe the assertion.

It is thus seen that in 1745, when the project of missions for the tribes of central Texas was broached, the merits of the San Xavier River and its surrounding country were not by any means unknown. Its natural advantages were many; its principal drawback was its proximity to the Lipan country, which lay beyond the rugged hills on the west.

3. *First contact with the tribes of central Texas.*—But what interested the missionary fathers in any region more than its fertility and beauty, of which they were extremely good judges, were its natives. In this connection, it may be remarked that without the writings of the Catholic missionaries our ethnological knowledge of many portions of America would be almost a blank. This would be true of central Texas in the eighteenth century. In the course of the passage of the Spaniards to and from eastern Texas and of missionary excursions from San Antonio, several tribes became known on either side of the Camino Real, in the region between the Colorado and the Trinity. Conspicuous among them were the four bands which played the chief part in the inception of the San Xavier missions, namely, the group called Ranchería Grande (Big Camp or Big village),[15] the Mayeye, the Deadose, and the Yojuane.

---

[13] Cabello, *ibid.,* par. 6.

[14] Ortiz, *Satisfaccion de los Missioneros á las objecciones hechas por el Govr. Bustillos contra las fundaciones de S^n. Xavier,* 1746. This is a memorandum of points by Father Ortiz and Father Espinosa relative to certain objections raised to founding a mission on the San Xavier.

[15] These tribes were sometimes collectively called at San Antonio ''the Eastern Indians.''

Ranchería Grande was a most extraordinary aggregation. At its basis the principal tribe was the Hierbipiame, or Ervipiame,[16] for whom a mission had been founded in 1698 between the Sabinas and the Rio Grande, about forty leagues northwest of Monclova.[17]. It will be interesting to note in passing that the name given to this first, as well as to the second and third missions founded for the Hierbipiame, was San Xavier. To just what territory the Hierbipiame were indigenous does not appear. In the formation of Ranchería Grande there had been added to this tribe (1) the remains of numerous broken-down bands from near and even beyond the Rio Grande who had fled eastward and joined the Hierbipiame for defence against the Apache and to escape punishment for injuries done the Spaniards of the interior, and (2) many apostate Indians from the missions at San Antonio and on the Rio Grande. Because of the prominence of the Hierbipiame in that group, it was sometimes called ''Ranchería Grande de los Hierbipiames.''[18]

Ranchería Grande was mentioned as early as 1707, when Diego Ramón, commander at San Juan Bautista, set out to punish it for disturbances at the missions on the Rio Grande.[19] It was then said to be near the Colorado River, at that day called the San Marcos. Again, in 1714 Ramón secured from it apostates who had fled from the San Juan Bautista mission.[20] In 1716 the Ramón expedition passed through it north of Little

---

[16] See articles by Bolton on ''Ranchería Grande'' and ''Ervipiame'' in Hodge, *Handbook of American Indians.*

[17] Portillo, Estéban L., *Apuntes para la Historia Antigua de Coahuila y Texas* (Saltillo, 1888), pp. 269–271. These pages contain the *autos* of the founding of the mission, copied from the archives of Coahuila. The name given to the mission and pueblo was ''San Francisco Xavier y Valle de Cristobal.''

[18] *Dilig^{as} q^e. hiso el Colegio año de 1729 para la Mudanza de las Mis^{es}. de Texas.*

[19] *Diario de la jornada que executo el Sargento M^r. Diego Ramon . . . á la parte del norte y lebante,* etc., 1707.

[20] *Dilig^{as} q^e. hiso el Colegio año de 1729 para la Mudanza de las Mis^{es}. de Texas.*

River and two or three leagues west of the Brazos, apparently near modern Cameron.[21] According to Ramón, it then contained more than two thousand souls.[22] In 1721 a chief of the Ranchería Grande, called Juan Rodríguez, was found by the Marqués de Aguayo at San Antonio, with a band of his people, asking for a mission. The marqués took him as a guide as far as the Trinity River, where he found the major portion of his people mingling with the Bidai and Agdoca (Deadose). Aguayo ordered the people of Ranchería Grande to retire across the Brazos, "where they were accustomed to live," promising to establish a mission for them near San Antonio on his return thither. True to his promise, in 1722 he founded for Juan Rodríguez and his band the mission of San Xavier de Náxera, on the outskirts of San Antonio, where the mission of Concepción now stands.[23] It endured, with little success, till 1726, when it was merged with that of San Antonio de Valero.[24]

Though reduced in numerical strength by the drain made by the missions, Ranchería Grande continued to give much trouble to the missionaries, since it afforded a refuge for apostates from San Antonio, who must have tended to replenish its population. The missionaries complained that it was a veritable "Rochelle," and they earnestly requested that it should be either destroyed or Christianized. Its pernicious influence was thus described in 1729 by Fray Miguel de Paredes: "Not only do they impede new conversions, but they also destroy the reductions already established . . . At present, Most Excellent Sir, since these Indians of the missions know that they have an open door, asylum, and protection in the Ranchería Grande, their flights have reached such an extreme that if their disorders are repri-

---

[21] Espinosa, *Diario*, 1716; Ramón, *Diario*, 1716.

[22] Ramón, *Diario*, 1716.

[23] Peña, *Derrotero*.

[24] See Bolton, "Spanish Mission Records at San Antonio," in The Texas State Historical Association *Quarterly*, X, 298–300.

manded or punished the least little bit, whether by the chiefs or by the missionaries, or if there should be any extraordinary labor—and many times without other cause than to seek their liberty—they flee to the said ranchería.''[25]

It has been seen that down to Aguayo's time this troublesome aggregation of Indians was ''accustomed to live'' west of the Brazos, near the timber belt (Monte Grande). But pressure from the Apache soon drove them to spend much of their time eastward of the Brazos. In testimony of this fact, Bustillo y Zevallos, who had been governor of Texas from 1732 to 1734, wrote in 1746 that ''of Ranchería Grande there remained in my time only the name, for their abode being the Monte Grande, they had already, because of their diminutive forces, retired to live in the distance, between the Yojuanes and Acdozas,''[26] that is, between the Trinity and the Brazos. This seems to have been their principal haunt in 1745, when our story begins.

The habitat and movements of the Mayeye were much the same as those of Ranchería Grande, in so far as those of either are known. In 1687 Joutel, La Salle's companion, heard of the Meghy as a tribe living north of the Colorado somewhere near the place where the Spaniards later actually came into contact with the Mayeye,[27] and it seems not improbable from the similarity of the names and locations that the two tribes were identical. In 1727 Rivera encountered the Mayeye at a spring called Puentezitas, fifteen leagues west of the junction of the two arms of the Brazos, that is, of the Little River with the main Brazos, and thirty-five leagues after crossing the Colorado. The place must have been somewhere near the San Gabriel River.[28] According to Bustillo y Zevallos, who was evidently speaking

---

[25] July 12, 1729. Doc. 15, K, leg. 19, Arch. Coll. Santa Cruz.

[26] He says, ''in the former time.'' He may mean the administration preceding his own. Bustillo, *Memorial*, May 28, 1746, par. 4.

[27] Journal, in Margry, *Découvertes*, III, 288.

[28] Peña, *Derrotero*.

of them as he had known them in his day, the Mayeye customarily came down from the Brazos de Dios to the Nabasoto (Navasota), and ranged from there to the Trinity. As he had seen them several times, he probably spoke with authority.[29] A critical document now in the archive of the College of Guadalupe de Zacatecas, written anonymously in 1748 by someone who had had wide experience in Texas, evidently a Zacatecan friar, says that the country of the Mayeye was on the east side of the Brazos, eighty leagues from San Antonio and twenty from the "place of San Xavier."[30] The two designations agree essentially with each other and harmonize with the testimony of other documents.

The Yojuane are less easily traced. They were a wandering Tonkawan band, as were the Mayeye, and their general history was much the same as the better known Tonkawa tribe.[31] They were mentioned by Casañas in 1691 as "Diu Juan," in a list of enemies of the Hasinai.[32] In 1709 fathers Espinosa and Olivares met a tribe called Yojuan near the Colorado River.[33] About 1714 they destroyed the main Hasinai temple near the Angelina.[34] The Joyuan tribe met by Du Rivage in 1719 near the Red River above the Caddodacho seem to have been the Yojuane.[35] Later on the Yojuane were closely associated with the Mayeye and the Hierbipiame, and for some time before 1745 they lived northward of these tribes between the Trinity and the

---

[29] Bustillo, *Memorial*, May 28, 1746.

[30] This document consists of a copy of the royal *cédula* of April 16, 1748, which authorizes the establishment of the San Xavier missions, and of critical comments on the tribes named therein. It is of great value for the tribal distribution of this region. It has no title, but will be referred to as "Anonymous Commentary."

[31] See Bolton, articles on "Tonkawa" and "Yojuane," in Hodge, *Handbook of American Indians*.

[32] Casañas, *Relación*, 1691.

[33] Olivares, *Diario*, 1709.

[34] Espinosa, *Chrónica Apostólica*, I, 424.

[35] La Harpe, *Relation* in Margry, *Découvertes et Establissements*, III, 616.

Brazos. Mediavilla y Azcona, governor of Texas between 1727 and 1730, stated that he frequently saw them on the road to eastern Texas. Bustillo y Zevallos, his successor in office, said that they lived "to the northwest, up the Trinity River, far distant from them [the Deadose and Mayeye] and neighbors to a tribe of Apaches called los Melenudos." Before the middle of the eighteenth century the hostility of the Yojuane for the Hasinai seems to have ceased, for thereafter the two tribes frequently went together against the Apache.

The sources for the history of the San Xavier missions establish the already conjectured[36] identity of the Deadose with the Agdocas of earlier times. The name is variously written Yacdoca, Yadosa, de Adoze, Doxsa, Deadose,[37] etc. The same documents also make it clear that the Deadose were a branch of the Bidai-Orcoquisa linguistic group.[38] On this point the anonymous document in the archives at Zacatecas cited just above says "Yadocxa ought to be called Deadoses. This is a band of Viday Indians who, being dismembered from its vast body, which has its movable abode between Trinidad and Sabinas Rivers, have lived for more than twenty years, for the sake of the trade afforded them by the transit of the Spaniards, on this [western] side of the River Trinidad, and, extending as far as Navasotoc, . . are accustomed to join the Mayeyes, who reside in the thickets of the River Brassos de Dios." According to the same document, the Deadose were habitually forty leagues east of the Mayeye.[39] These statements harmonize with various other detached items of information. In 1714, for example, the Agdoca were said to be twelve leagues south of the Assinai (Hasinai), that is, in the

---

[36] By the present writer.

[37] Penicaut (1714) gives the name "Aquodoces" (Margry, *Découvertes*, V, 504); Peña, 1721–1722, gives it "Agdoces" (Diario, in *Mem. de Nueva España*, XXVIII, 31); Espinosa, 1746, "Yacdocas" (*Chrónica Apostólica*); Morfi (*cir.* 1781), "Igodosa" (*Mem. Hist. Tex.*, II, 26).

[38] Several years ago the present writer conjectured that this might be the case. See his card notes on Texas tribes, under "Deadoses."

[39] Anonymous Commentary, Arch. Coll. Guadalupe.

country near the mouth of the Angelina River,[40] where Bidai
continued to live at a much later date. In 1721, as has been seen,
Aguayo found the Agdocas west of the Trinity, mingled with
Ranchería Grande.[41] They evidently had already begun to move
westward.

Bustillo bears testimony that both the Mayeye and the
Deadose were in his day already succumbing to the principal
enemy of the native American race, disease. He says: ''Both
of these tribes are small. I have seen them various times, the last
being in 1734, when I left that province. I do not believe that
they have increased since that time, because of the epidemics
which they are accustomed to suffer and which they were suffering, of measles and smallpox, which are their sole de-
stroyers.''[42] In 1745 the four bands, Ranchería Grande, the
Mayeye, the Yojuane, and the Deadose, were said to comprise
1228 persons.

Other tribes intimately connected with the history of the San
Xavier Missions were the Bidai, of the lower Trinity River, and
the Coco, a Karankawan tribe of the lower Colorado. Early
Spanish contact with these tribes has been discussed by the
present writer elsewhere, and will not need repetition here.[43]

---

[40] Margry, *Découvertes*, V, 504.

[41] Peña, *Derrotero*, 31.

[42] Bustillo, *Memorial*, May 28, 1746.

[43] See Bolton, ''The Founding of Mission Rosario,'' in the Tex. Hist.
Assn. *Quarterly*, X, 113–139; and ''Spanish activities on the Lower
Trinity River,'' *ibid.*, XVI, 339–377. See also pp. 281–283, 332–336, below.

CHAPTER II

TENTATIVE BEGINNINGS OF THE MISSIONS, 1745

1. The petition of the four tribes.—The establishment of missions for these tribes was due primarily to the zeal of Fray Mariano Francisco de los Dolores y Viana, missionary at the mission of San Antonio de Valero.[1] He had come to Texas in the year of 1733,[2] and had made occasional visits to central Texas, now to recover apostates, and again in search of new tribes from which to replenish the missions, ever in need of recruits because of desertions and the ravages of disease. In the course of these expeditions he had visited the Deadose, Yojuane, Mayeye, and the Ranchería Grande. The precise details of these visits, unfortunately, have not appeared. We are told, however, that with some of the tribes he had contracted friendship as early as 1734.[3] Presumably the first to be dealt with were the Indians of Ranchería Grande, since, as we have seen, with these the missionaries of San Antonio had frequent and early contact. We learn, again, that in 1741, when Fray Mariano accompanied Governor Wintuisen to the Trinity, he carried presents to the Deadose and the Mayeye and tried to induce them to enter his

---

[1] This priest signed his name Fr. María Ano Franco de los Dolores y Viana, though his associates and superiors always wrote it Fray Mariano. He has frequently been referred to as Father Dolores.

[2] In a memorial dated January 22, 1757, he said that he entered Texas in 1733, and began to journey northwest, east, and southeast. In a communication written in April, 1746, he said that he had been in Texas 13 years (*Escrito* by Fray Mariano addressed to the governor of Texas, April 16, 1746). In a letter to the viceroy written March 13, 1749, he said that he had been engaged in the work seventeen years, by implication, all the time in Texas. Father Ortiz wrote that Fray Mariano had had relations with the petitioning tribes before Bustillo y Zevallos left Texas, which was in 1734. (*Satisfaccion de los Missioneros á las objecciones hechas por el Gov*r. *Bustillos contra las fundaciones de S*n. *Xavier*).

[3] *Satisfaccion, ibid.,* fol. 1.

mission;[4] and, again, that for some time before 1745 he had been visiting all of these tribes and they him, "either every year or nearly every year."[5] Thus, contrary to what might be inferred from some of the documents, it is clear that a project to found missions for these four tribes was no sudden thought.

But it was not till 1745 that matters came to a head. On the second of June of that year, after numerous unfulfilled promises, it would seem, four chiefs of the tribes in question, with thirteen followers went to San Antonio and asked for a mission, requesting that it should be in their own country, at a site which Fray Mariano should select.[6]

2. *The appeals of Fray Mariano, June–July, 1745.*—It happened that just at that time the commissary visitor, Fray Francisco Xavier Ortiz, was at the San Antonio missions on an official visitation. Accordingly, although he had already passed by the mission of San Antonio de Valero, on his way down the river, Fray Mariano embraced the opportunity and asked Father Ortiz to return, recommending that the desired missions should be established, with a presidio of thirty soldiers to protect the missionaries from the Indians, and the latter from their enemy, the Apache. From such a step he prophesied great results. Not only would these Indians be brought to a knowledge of the true God, but their friends, the Texas, who had so long been obdurate, would also be converted. Moreover, great advantages would result in case of war with France, for the Indians, if converted, could be relied upon to aid the Spaniards, whereas, at present, they would be sure to join the French. To avoid unnecessary expense, he recommended that half of the garrison of Adaes be put under a captain and assigned to the proposed new presidio.

---

[4] Anonymous Commentary, Arch. Coll. Guadalupe.

[5] *Satisfaccion.*

[6] This is the story told by Father Mariano to Ortiz, June 12, 1745 (*Copia de autos seguidos en el superior govierno*) ; Francisco Xavier Marquéz to the viceroy, January 18, 1746, *ibid*. Note that the later documents imply that the Indians chose San Xavier at the outset.

To make possible the two or three missions that would be necessary for the 1228 souls which the four tribes were reported to comprise, he recommended appealing to the king for the required initial sum and a suitable annuity thereafter.[7]

Father Ortiz granted the request that he return to the mission of Valero, and, while the Indians were still there, had their petition formally examined by Thoribio de Urrutia, captain of the presidio, in the presence of the other officials.[8] We are told that Captain Urrutia tried to persuade the Indians to settle at San Antonio, where he would provide them a separate mission, but that they refused to go so far from their relatives, their lands, their friends, and their trade with the Texas, from whom they were accustomed to procure their weapons. Next, Captain Urrutia proceeded to test their sincerity, telling them that if they entered the mission they must be subordinate to the missionaries, labor in the fields, attend religious services, receive instruction, and fight the enemies of the Spaniards. When they consented to all this, he promised, in the name of the king, to aid them against all their foes, and again they repeated their request for a *padre* to go with them to their country, see their people, and instruct them as to what they must do in preparation for a mission.[9]

In addition to the appeal made to Father Ortiz, Fray Mariano addressed one[10] to the guardian of his college, Fray Alonso Giraldo de Terreros, a zealous soul who, a decade later, was to suffer martyrdom in Texas. In this appeal Father Mariano stated that, in view of the great number of Indians who would be likely to join the petitioning tribes, the opportunity of

---

[7] Fray Mariano to Fray Ortiz, June 12, 1745. The numerical strength of the tribes was learned from the four chiefs (*Copia de autos seguidos en el superior govierno*).

[8] *Despacho q sin provecho se saco el año de 1746 el qual no se presento, ni aprobecha.*

[9] Arricivita, *Crónica Seráfica*, 323.

[10] Dated July 26.

the college was the rarest it had ever had in Texas. "According to the reports and the names of the unknown Kingdoms which there are in all that region, making a conservative estimate, at the lowest figure there would not fail to be more than six thousand souls who in time could be reduced. It would be a pity to lose this opportunity, which would lead to another equally holy . . . It is a fact that on one of the occasions when I went inland, I came upon Indians of whom those which we have reduced had never heard at all. And thus the report which the Indians themselves give is made to appear credible. And even if it were not, it cannot be denied that, besides those who wish to be converted, there are large nations, none of which, we know, will ever become converted unless means be taken to establish missions for them in their own country or near to them, according as there are conveniences in the different places."

Continuing, Fray Mariano suggested that Fray Diego Ximénez, secretary of the visitor and present with him at San Antonio, be sent to assist in the new work, and that the conduct of the matter before the viceroy be entrusted preferably to Father Ortiz, and if not to him, then to Father Ximénez.[11]

Father Espinosa, in his *Chrónica Apostólica*, which was completed in 1747 (though its title-page bears the date 1746)[12] makes a statement which may furnish the real reason why the project of a mission for these tribes, which, as has been seen, had been known and dealt with for some time, came to a head just at the time when it did. He says that the mission of La Punta, or Lampazos, had just been secularized, and that the college wished to establish another in its place, and, therefore, promoted one on the San Xavier. As Father Espinosa was at the time chronicler of the college, and was then writing his now famous history, and

---

[11] Letter of Fray Mariano to the guardian, July 26, 1745, in *Copia de autos seguidos*. For more detailed information relative to Fray Ximénez, see Ortiz, *Visita de las Missiones hecha, de orden de N. M. R. P. Commo. Gral. Fr. Juan Fogueras, por el P. Fr. Franco. Xavier Ortiz, en el año 1745.*

[12] For evidence of this see Espinosa, *Chrónica Apostólica*, 467.

as he took some part in the struggle for the San Xavier missions, there is good reason for accepting his explanation[13] as at least a part of the truth. One of the opponents of the project went so far as to say, but evidently without foundation, that he believed that Father Ortiz's visit to San Antonio was for no other purpose than to see about establishing these San Xavier missions.[14]

3. A new embassy and the selection of a site.—While waiting for help and for approval of his project, Fray Mariano did his best to keep the petitioners favorably disposed, and to prepare the way for the establishment of the hoped-for missions. Indeed, for more than a year he and his college labored without help from the central government, and still another year before that government could be induced to authorize the missions, although for much of that time an inchoate mission settlement was in actual existence on the San Xavier.

Before the visiting Indians had returned to their homes, they had promised Fray Mariano that they would assemble their people at some specified place to await his coming at the beginning of the winter. When they departed they were accompanied by an escort of mission Indians, who returned in a short time reporting that the news carried by the chiefs had been joyfully received by the people of the tribes and that a search for a site had already been begun.[15] This report was made before July 26, 1745.

Sometime later, just when does not appear, the petitioners sent to San Antonio a delegation who reported that a site had been selected, and told of "many other nations" which had promised to join them in the proposed missions.[16] The names of these tribes, as given in the *autos* reporting this visit—as yet the

---

[13] Espinosa, *Chrónica Apostólica*, 367.

[14] Anonymous Commentary, par. 3.

[15] Fray Mariano to the Guardian, July 26, 1745.

[16] Our knowledge of this second visit of the Indians comes from the *Memorial* of Bustillo, dated May 28, 1746.

autos have not been found—are apparently those given later by
Father Ortiz in his memorial to the king.[17] His list was as follows: Vidais, Caocos, Lacopseles, Anchoses, Tups, Atais, Apapax,
Acopseles, Cancepnes, Tancagues, Hiscas, Naudis, Casos, Tanico,
Quisis, Anathagua, Atasacneus, Pastates, Geotes, Atiasnogues,
Taguacanas, Taguayas, "and others who subsequently asked for
baptism."[18] Among these we recognize the Bidai, of the lower
middle Trinity, who lived below the Deadose; the Coco and the
Tups, Karankawan tribes of the lower Colorado and the gulf
coast; the Naguidis, a little known branch of the Hasinai, of
eastern Texas; the Tonkawa, Kichai, Tawakoni, and Taovayas,
tribes then all living on the upper Trinity, Brazos, and Red
rivers,[19] beyond the Hierbipiame and Mayeye; and the Tanico,
a tribe near the Mississippi. The wide geographical distribution
of these tribes might cause one to be suspicious of the accuracy
of the report, but this doubt is lessened when we learn that later
on a number of the tribes named actually became identified with
the enterprise. The most that could be said in criticism of the
report is that the outlook was perhaps regarded with a somewhat
unwarranted optimism.

After making suitable presents to the delegation, Fray
Mariano set out with them, accompanied by some mission Indians
and soldiers, to visit the petitioners in their homes, and to view
the site which they had selected. The place, it seems, was beyond
the first or the second arm of the Brazos. The journey was
impeded by high waters, and Fray Mariano was forced to turn
back. But he sent forward some of the soldiers and neophytes,
who succeeded in reaching a gathering of Indians, of various

---

[17] Memorial of Ortiz to the king, after February 14, 1747.

[18] This list is copied in the royal *cédula* of April 16, 1748, granting the
petition of Ortiz, the spelling of which I follow, instead of that of the
copy of the Ortiz memorial (*Reales Cédulas*, vol. 68, 1748. Archivo General y Público, Mexico).

[19] For the identification of some of these tribes, see the Anonymous
Commentary.

tribes, who were awaiting them in the Monte Grande on the Brazos.[20]

Now, it seems, on account of the difficulties of passing the high waters, the place which had been chosen was given up, and the soldiers were conducted to the San Xavier River, instead, and shown a site there. There are indications also that one of the reasons for a change of site was the discovery by the Indians that in their immediate country the necessary water facilities were lacking. This could hardly have referred to a lack of water, but rather to a topography unsuited to irrigation.

On returning to San Antonio the soldiers reported that they had examined the site shown to them on the San Xavier and that they had found it satisfactory. Hereupon[21] new *autos* were drawn before the captain and the cabildo, giving an account of the occurrences just related, expressing a favorable opinion of

---

[20] The exact circumstances of the selection of the site are not quite clear. Some later statements make it appear that the San Xavier was designated at the outset, but putting all the evidence together, this does not seem to be the case. (1) In the two petitions of Fray Mariano nothing was said of the San Xavier and it was distinctly intimated that the site was as yet unchosen, while emphasis was put upon the fact that the Indians desired a mission in their own country. This, we have seen, was characteristically beyond the Little and the Brazos rivers. (2) The story given above of Fray Mariano's unsuccessful attempt to visit the site is given by both Bustillo and the Anonymous Commentary. While the former hints that there was some disappointment in regard to water facilities in the immediate country of the Indians, it gives the floods as the reason for change of site. The words are as follows: ''Tired of passing so much water, since the Indians were waiting in the Monte Grande, and in order that the soldiers might return, they [the Indians] showed them the Rio de San Xavier.'' (3) That the site was changed is definitely asserted by Fray Santa Ana, who at the same time was president of the missions at San Antonio, but he gives as the reason the lack of water facilities in the immediate country of the Indians. In a letter written to the viceroy on June 24, 1748, he explains the increased demands by Fray Mariano for military protection at San Xavier by saying that at first the Indians had asked that the missions be in their own lands; that none of them ''reside where they would be exposed to the invasions of the Apaches,'' and that, therefore, it was at first thought that thirty soldiers would be enough; but that when it was later learned that suitable water facilities were lacking in their country, the Indians insisted on gathering on the San Xavier, which, being a site exposed to the Apaches, required more protection (*Copia de autos seguidos*).

[21] Or, possibly, after Fray Mariano's first visit.

the site chosen, asserting, as a warning, that the petitioners had all come armed with French guns, and giving assurance that "through this establishment of pueblos the malice of the Apache nation will be punished and the communication of the French nation will be prevented."[22]

4. *The tentative beginnings of a mission, January–April, 1746.*—Various items of rather fragmentary information enable us to record the circumstances and to establish the date of the actual beginnings of tentative missionary work at San Xavier, both of which matters have hitherto been undetermined.

True to his promise, at the coming of winter Fray Mariano went to meet the petitioners at the designated site, where we find him in January, 1746, accompanied by the *alférez* of the San Antonio garrison, a squad of soldiers, and some mission Indians (and, presumably, with oxen and agricultural implements) making preparations for the hoped-for missions.[23]   Besides the original petitioners, he found at the site some of the Coco tribe, with whom he had communicated in the previous October.   They assisted in the preparations, promised to enter the missions, and returned to their native haunts for their families.[24]   A mission site was chosen on the south side of the San Xavier River, now the San Gabriel, a short distance above its junction with the Arroyo de las Ánimas, now Brushy Creek.[25]   Sometime before April 13, evidently, Father Mariano wrote to his president at San Antonio that, since the good intentions of the Indians had proved constant, "he had founded a mission to attract them, on

---

[22] Bustillo, *Memorial*, paragraph 1.   For a summary of the *autos*, see Bustillo, *ibid.*; and for the petition of the College based on the *autos*, see an *expediente* in the Lamar Papers entitled *Erecion de la Mision [Presidio] de Sⁿ. Xavier*, 3, and Terreros to Mediavilla, June 23, 1746.

[23] Fray Mariano tells us this in a document dated April 13, 1746.   See also documents dated June 10 and 11, 1746, in *Copia de Cartas del R. P. Guardⁿ.*

[24] See documents cited in notes 20 and 22, above.

[25] For the location of the site, see pp. 225–230.

the banks of the San Xavier,[26] in which enterprise he had spent all he possessed; that the place was most fertile, and its fields spacious and watered with good and plentiful water, that he had planted potatoes, and that though he had lost [them], he still had enough for another planting.''[27] The mission was regarded as having been ''founded,'' therefore, between January and April 13, 1746. Thus far, however, the founding seems to have consisted in little more than the selection of the site and the planting of crops. It had not yet been duly solemnized.

Before the middle of April, Fray Mariano returned to San Antonio, but he left some mission Indians from the latter place in charge, to plant and care for crops with which to support the prospective neophytes. When he departed he promised the assembled Indians that he would return with Spanish settlers and missionaries.[28]

The injury to the missionary cause which the fathers frequently had to suffer at the hands of the military authorities is illustrated at this point by Father Mariano's experience with the Coco tribe.[29] As some members of this tribe were returning

26 Fray Mariano says that ''many of them lacked even the leaves of the trees to cover their shame.'' Communication of April 16, 1746.

27 *Erecion*, 5, is the authority for this assertion. It is quite clear that the letter referred to must have been written during Father Mariano's first stay at the San Xavier, which ended before April 13, for he was in San Antonio thenceforward till June 11. The facts stated above are referred to in a document written near Querétaro on June 28.

28 Testimony concerning Cocos, April 13, 1746.

29 In October, 1745, he had communicated with this tribe, who lived on the lower Colorado, through the Bidais. Just at this time Capt. Orobio Bazterra, of Bahía, was about to undertake his expedition to the lower Trinity to look for a rumored settlement of the French. The Bidais, hearing that the expedition was to be directed against the Cocos, sent a delegation to San Antonio in the middle of October, to ask Father Mariano to request Orobio not to harm the Cocos. He did so, and took occasion also to ask Orobio to take the Xaranames, who were living with the Cocos, back to their mission at Bahía. In order that the Cocos might not become entangled in the trouble likely to ensue, he sent to them a request that they should separate from the Xaranames. No doubt he also told them of the San Xavier mission project, for a number of them met him at San Xavier and agreed to enter the missions there. (Communication of April 16, 1746).

from San Xavier for their families, they were attacked, apparently without provocation, by Captain Orobio Bazterra, of Bahía, who was on his return from the lower Trinity, whither he had been to reconnoiter French traders.[30]   In the course of the trouble two of the Cocos were killed and others captured.   On receiving the news of the occurrence on April 13, fathers Dolores and Santa Ana complained to Captain Urrutia, saying that they feared that the mission project would be sadly interfered with and that even an outbreak might result unless something were done, and requested that Orobio should be required at once to release the captives.   Captain Urrutia issued the order and also sent to San Xavier a delegation of mission Indians to make explanations and help to keep the peace.   The result seems to have been satisfactory, for later on, as we shall see, some of the Coco tribe entered one of the missions at San Xavier.[31]

Between April and June, evidently, there were no missionaries at San Xavier, for early in the latter month a delegation of Indians went from there to San Antonio again to urge Father Mariano to return with the promised friars and supplies.   Four days later the ''principal chief of all the nations'' went from another direction to San Antonio to complain of the delay in sending them missionaries.   Ethnologists would like to know to what tribe the principal chief belonged, but the information does not appear.   Fray Mariano took this occasion to send a new appeal for help, predicting that the Indians could not be expected to wait longer than till October before giving up in disgust.[32]   Meanwhile, the crops had been cared for by the new

---

[30] See Bolton, ''Spanish Activities on the Lower Trinity River,'' *The Southwestern Historical Quarterly*, XVI, 339–377. See below, pp. 327–332.

[31] Docs. of Apr. 13, 15, and 16, concerning the killing of two Cocos by Orobio.

[32] Fray Mariano wrote to the guardian of his college the following account of the event and of his helplessness to carry out his heart's desire: ''I would gladly refrain from further molesting your attention, for I assume that you are sufficiently occupied, but, knowing that these people understand the language of hands better than that of tongues,

tribes, who had remained in the vicinity in spite of Fray Mariano's absence.[33]

Sometime during the summer of 1746 the construction of mission buildings was begun. We learn this fact from an undated document of this year by Father Ortiz, who writes that "it appears from other letters that the said father [Mariano] has already begun a church, habitation, and other things necessary, in order that the religious may live there, and that they have planted maize, potatoes, and other grains, for which he took from his mission of San Antonio forty cargoes, yokes of oxen, Indian workmen, and others to escort him, besides the soldiers."[34] Before January 16, 1747, Father Mariano had spent $2262.50 in supporting and entertaining the Indians, and by February the sum had reached $5083.50.

---

and are more easily subdued by gifts than by words, I am compelled by my great poverty not to lose any opportunity to the end that the promptest provision may be undertaken there, and, in case delay is necessary, that assistance with the most necessary expenses may be solicited, for our lack of everything makes it impossible to send more now to the multitude of Indians which are to be reduced. This and what I noted in my former [letter] oblige me to inform you that on the fourth day of June there came to this mission of San Antonio some of the new Indians, and that on the eighth the principal chief of all the Nations came from a different direction to inform me that a multitude of people have gathered on various occasions to await me with the Fathers and Spaniards to establish missions for them, but, seeing my delay and being dissatisfied at the lack of provisions, they have again deserted. They told me that grass having grown up in the crops, the chiefs were obliged to go and assemble their tribes to clean them, aside from the fact that they are maintaining the post, not having been made cowards by fear of the Apaches, who had killed five Indians in that neighborhood, and that I should send them maize, tobacco and other *dogas* which they needed, for which purpose and the remission of which I have asked for mules. Since I was in San Xavier I have concluded that the greatest delay would be until October, for in more than eight months there would be sufficient time."

[33] Urrutia, certificates of June 10, 1746, in *Copia de Cartas del R. P. Guardⁿ.*; Fray Mariano to the guardian, June 11, 1746, *ibid.*; Fray Benito de Santa Ana to Urrutia, April 15, 1746, in *Dos testimonios de diligencias, sobre los Yndios Cocos;* also related documents of April 13 and April 16, 1746.

[34] *Satisfaccion de los Missioneros á las objeciones hechas por el Govr. Bustillos.* This must have been in 1746, for then was the time when the Bustillo fight was on.

In the spring of 1747 some of the prospective neophytes, twelve in number, were at San Antonio, probably to complain again of the delay. At any rate, near the end of March, Fray Mariano sent back with them some Indians from the missions of Valero and Concepción, together with a Spaniard named Eusebio Pruneda. Pruneda was provided with seed grain, and was instructed to plant crops and to "serve as a diversion for the people" until the viceroy should give the necessary orders for proceeding regularly. He found at San Xavier "Deadoses, Cocos, and Yojuanes." They welcomed him and turned in to help plant the crops, "the said Indians working in person"—a fact that was regarded as noteworthy. When half through with the task, however, the enterprise was broken up by the Apaches. A band of twenty-two Cocos, who had been sent out to secure buffalo meat for the assemblage, met the enemy near by, fought with them, and killed one. But seeing or learning of "many rancherías" of Apaches close at hand, at Parage de las Ánimas (evidently on Brushy Creek) they returned to San Xavier, where the whole body of Indians remained three days prepared for battle. At the end of that time, fearing an attack by a larger force of the enemy, and "fearful of the ruin which they might wreak upon them," they withdrew to the lower Brazos, designating a place where they might be found. Before leaving they sent word by Pruneda to Father Mariano that he had deceived them by his promises to send missionaries and other Spaniards; that until these should be forthcoming they would seek their own safety by retiring; but that when they should be provided not only would they be prompt to return, but several other tribes from *muy adentro* ("far in the interior") whom Father Mariano had not seen, would come also.[35]

---

[35] This account is based on an *escrito* presented by Father Mariano to Urrutia, telling of the event, May 4, 1747; the sworn declaration of Pruneda, of the same date; a *diligencia*, or opinion given by the cabildo, justicia, and regimiento of the villa of San Fernando, together with the officers of the presidio of San Antonio de Béxar, May 10, 1747. The story was confirmed by ten Cocos who went to San Antonio on May 7. (All in *Dos peticiones del P. Fr. Mariano sobre los Yndios de Sⁿ. Xavr. año de 1747*).

It would seem that during a part of this time Fray Mariano had with him two assisting missionaries, for later on the College of Santa Cruz asked for reimbursement for the stipend paid three missionaries for work at San Xavier during the full years of 1746 and 1747. It is clear, however, that during this period missionaries were at San Xavier at most only intermittently. One of the friars who assisted Father Mariano during this time was Mariano de Anda y Altamirano, a missionary formerly of the College of Guadalupe, who had served both at the Bahía mission and at San Miguel de los Adaes. In the summer of 1747, while at San Xavier, he was ordered to hasten to Mexico to assist in securing the desired license for the missions. He passed through Saltillo on his way south in July,[36] a fact which gives us a clue to the time of his departure.

We have thus been able to piece together some fragments of information concerning the circumstances of the beginnings of missionary work on the San Xavier; but practically all that we know of actual operations there between June, 1746, and February, 1748, is that the missionaries were there, from time to time at least, planting crops, catechising the Indians, and holding them until the project should be definitely authorized and supported, and something permanent undertaken.

---

[36] *Memorial del P^e. Anda al Exmo Sor Virrey sobre S^n. Xavier.*

CHAPTER III

THE STRUGGLE BEFORE THE AUTHORITIES

1. The approval of the college and of the fiscal obtained.—
Meanwhile affairs were taking their slow and uncertain course
in Mexico. If one does not care to follow the tedious details of
the persistent struggle made by Father Mariano and the College
of Santa Cruz for authority from the civil government to found
the desired missions, for a presidio to protect them, and for
funds to support them, he will do well to pass this chapter by.
But as a monument to the zeal and the dogged fighting qualities
of the Franciscans, and as a study in actual government in the
frontier provinces of New Spain, the struggle deserves to be
faithfully and somewhat fully recorded.

On leaving San Antonio in the summer of 1745, Father Ortiz
carried with him written evidence of all that had occurred there
relative to the request of the tribes for missions.[1] He evidently
did not reach his college at Querétaro until late in the fall, for
the report of his visitation was certified by his secretary at La
Punta, or Lampazos, on October 11.[2] The college heartily approved the plan of Father Mariano, and, as he had suggested,
entrusted the conduct of it before the viceroy to Father Ortiz.
He in turn through his agent, Francisco Xavier Marquéz, presented the two letters of Fray Mariano, and besought the viceroy's patronage for the enterprise. This was on or before
January 18, and on· that day the matter was referred, in the
regular routine of such affairs, to the royal fiscal, Don Pedro
Vedoya.[3] Just a month later this official advised the viceroy to

---

[1] Arricivita, *Crónica*, 323.

[2] *Visita de las Missiones.*

[3] Viceroy's decree of this date, endorsed on the memorial of Marquéz.

secure, before deciding so important a matter, from the governor of Texas, the officials of San Antonio, and the commissary general of missions, who was then at the College of San Fernando, ''detailed information regarding the advantages and the need of increasing missions and missionaries in those places, the nations named in the two letters, the distances [of San Xavier] from the presidios of San Antonio de Valero and los Adaes, and the direction to each.'' On the same day the viceroy ordered that Vedoya's advice should be acted upon.[4]

Before these orders could be complied with, the college presented a new memorial based on later news from Texas and urging haste. It told of the additional tribes which had offered to enter the missions, reported that the site selected was satisfactory, and asked for the establishment, in addition to missions, of a presidio of at least fifty soldiers to withstand the warlike Apache and to cut off their trade with the French.[5]

The matter was again sent to the fiscal of the Royal Audiencia, and on March 28, satisfied with the evidence and knowing the importance of haste while the Indians were in the right frame of mind, he gave his approval to the project. He proposed that for the present, until a larger number of Indians should congregate, two or three missions should be established and supplied; and that, in order to avoid additional expense for their maintenance, the garrison of Boca de Leones and the presidio of Cerralvo, in Nuevo León, should be extinguished. To provide defence for the missions and for the settlement of Spaniards who it was hoped might locate near them, instead of approving Fray Mariano's plan of dividing the garrison of Los

---

[4] *Dictamen fiscal*, February 18, 1746, and viceroy's decree of the same date. These decrees, the letters of Fray Mariano, and the memorial of Marquéz, constitute *Copia de autos seguidos en el superior govierno*.

[5] The memorial was evidently based on the new *autos* drawn at San Antonio after the second visit of the petitioning tribes, and drawn with a knowledge of the decree of February 18, therefore after that date. My knowledge of the memorial comes from the summary in *Erecion de la Mision de S^r. Xavier.*

Adaes, he recommended transferring to San Xavier the presidio of Santa Rosa del Sacramento, of Coahuila.[6]

This proposal of Vedoya to rob Peter to pay Paul, like that of Father Mariano, was altogether characteristic. They are but single examples of a policy widely practiced by the Spanish government on the northern frontier of New Spain. The government was always "hard up," and yet was desirous of distributing funds and forces where they were most needed. Demands for protection against the Indians and for money to aid the missionaries and colonists were multitudinous. Consequently, the officials were ever under the necessity of cutting off here in order to piece out or patch on there. The truth is, therefore, that many of the new enterprises of the eighteenth century represent transfers of effort from one scene to another rather than real expansion.[7] Actual increase in annual expenditures was in reality slight until after 1760.

2. *Opposition by Bustillo y Zevallos, May, 1746.*—Vedoya's *dictamen* was referred to the *auditor de guerra*, the Marqués de Altamira. He, in turn, on April 13, recommended that an opinion on all the matters involved should be obtained from Juan Antonio Bustillo y Zevallos, at the time *alcalde ordinario* of the City of Mexico.[8] Bustillo had been twelve years in Texas,

---

[6] My knowledge of this *dictamen* is gained from the summaries contained in the memorial of Bustillo y Zevallos and *Erecion de la Mision de Sⁿ. Xavier.* The former is in some respects clearer as to the points of the *dictamen.*

[7] Thus, the founding of the mission of San Antonio de Valero in 1718, considered in one light, was but the transfer of that of San Francisco Solano from the Rio Grande to the San Antonio. The establishment of the mission on the Guadalupe above Victoria in 1736 and that on the lower San Antonio in 1749 were but two transfers of the mission of Espíritu Santo from the Gulf coast. The establishment of the missions of San Juan Capistrano, Nuestra Señora de la Purísima Concepción, and San Francisco de la Espada at San Antonio in 1731, was in reality a transfer of three missions thither from eastern Texas. Finally, the establishment of the San Sabá mission was but the transfer to another site of the missions established at San Xavier. Numerous other examples might readily be cited.

[8] *Erecion de la Mision de S. Xavier,* 5; Bustillo, *Memorial,* par. 3.

seven of them as captain of the presidio of Loreto, or Bahía del Espíritu Santo, and three as governor of the province. As captain at Bahía he had assisted in the transfer of the Querétaran missions from eastern Texas to San Antonio. His administration as governor had been notable for the settlement of the Canary Islanders at San Antonio and for a campaign to the San Xavier and the San Sabá rivers led by himself in 1732 against the Apache.[9] Altamira's advice was followed by the viceroy, who in a decree of April 18 requested Bustillo to make the desired report.[10]

Bustillo's opposition to the San Xavier mission project, as manifested in his memorial of May 28, was the focal point of much of the tedious discussion of the matter which followed.[11] He began by paying a generous tribute to the zeal of the missionaries of Querétaro in the northeastern provinces and reviewing the history of the San Xavier matter to date. Then he proceeded to present objections to nearly every point which had been raised. According to him, the country along the highway between San Antonio and the Trinity was occupied by only the two small tribes of the Mayeye and the Deadose. The Yojuane lived far up the Trinity to the northwest, and the Ranchería Grande, now little more than a name, between the Deadose and Yojuane. All of these tribes were now beyond the Brazos, and by no means close to San Xavier, while they were applying for missions merely in order to get the material benefits, "since they will never receive the principal without the accessories."[12] The Bidai might some day be reduced, but, because of their

---

[9] For an account of this campaign see "Apache Relations in Texas, 1718–1750," by W. E. Dunn, in the Texas State Historical Association *Quarterly*, XIV, 225–237; Bonilla, "Breve Compendio," *ibid.*, VIII, 41–42.

[10] Bustillo, *Memorial*, par. 3.

[11] *Ibid.*

[12] On this point he was certainly borne out by the facts of missionary history among the wild tribes.

barbarity and their plentiful supply of food, he doubted very much whether their reduction could be speedily effected. The Karankawan tribes of the coast[13] could never be subjected to mission influence, a fact which had been proved by the failure of his own efforts and those of the missionaries covering many years. He doubted the feasibility of irrigating the lands of the San Xavier, because he had camped on it three days during his campaign of 1732 without noticing any facilities for irrigating ditches. Indeed, he had reported this opinion in December, 1744, when settlement on the San Xavier was being contemplated. As an example of the ease with which one could be mistaken on such matters without adequate information, he said, with truth, one had only to remember the disappointment of the missionaries in 1730 when they had attempted to establish on the San Marcos the missions removed from the east.

Moreover, said Bustillo, the San Xavier River was in a dangerous location, being on the highway by which the Apache sallied forth from their hills in the west. As to the possession of French guns by the petitioning tribes, they had not gotten them directly from the French, but from the Texas, who were the middlemen in this trade. The French themselves had never entered so far into the interior. The presidio of Los Adaes could not be reduced without great danger to the French frontier, and if any of the soldiers were to be taken away they might much better be stationed at Los Cadodachos, where the French had so long been established. Adaes was the capital of the province, and should be the residence of the governors. The only reason why governors had lived at San Antonio was to avoid the hard life at the frontier post. On the other hand, the garrisons at Cerralvo, Boca de Leones, and Sacramento were all needed in their respective places, as a defence against the Tobosos and Jumanes, and, besides, there was more hope of establishing a settlement of Spaniards at the last-named place than there ever could be at San Xavier.

---

[13] The Karankawa, Coco, Cujane, Guapite, and Cujane.

After all these objections to the San Xavier plan, however, Bustillo was ready with a substitute. The four tribes in question and the others which had been named, were, he said, nearer to "Texas"[14] than to San Antonio. Why not establish a mission for some of the petitioners at the village of San Pedro de los Nabedaches, as an example to the Nabedache tribe; and another at the Aynais village called El Loco, between the Angelina and Nacogdoches? In this way, he concluded, "three desirable ends, in my opinion, will be secured. First, that the moving of the Presidio del Sacramento may be dispensed with; second, that the Reverend Fathers may realize the object of their desire, and the Indians the wish which it is said they have manifested; third, and more important, that there may be restored to the poor Texas the consolation which has been taken away from them. Indeed, I am most certain that they will receive it with notable rejoicing, for many times I have seen them lament with tears the fact that they were deserted—not that I should say for this reason that they were weeping for the lack of access to our Holy Faith, for none of the Indians with whom I have communicated give this reason, but rather those of intercourse and of trade in their products."[15]

Withal, it would seem that Bustillo was a man of more than ordinarily sound sense and candor. His experience with the barbarian Indians had taught him their altogether too common motives to a profession of love for Christianity.

3. *Rebuttal by Mediavilla and the college.*—Again the matter went to the *auditor*. With the memorial of Bustillo was sent the news from San Antonio that the Indians had proved constant in their desires; that Fray Mariano had actually founded for them a mission and planted crops on the banks

---

[14] At this date the term "Texas," as a territorial designation, was still often restricted to what is now eastern Texas, then the country of the Texas, or Hasinai Indians.

[15] *Memorial*, par. 19.

of the San Xavier; that the place was extremely fertile and well watered, and that Father Mariano had spent his all on the work.[16] Hereupon, at the *auditor's* instance, Father Ortiz was called upon for a reply to Bustillo's objections.[17]

To prepare an answer, the college called into requisition a gun of like caliber, another ex-governor of Texas, indeed, Don Melchor Mediavilla y Azcona, who was then at Hacienda de Galera y Apaseo.[18] Mediavilla had preceded Bustillo as governor of the province. He had been in office at the time of Rivera's inspection in 1727, had sided with the missionaries in their opposition to that official's recommendation to reduce the Texas garrisons, and had supported their appeal in 1729 to be allowed to retire from eastern Texas. It was for these actions, according to Bonilla, that he had been removed from office in 1731.[19] Evidently the college expected hearty support from him, and it was not disappointed.

Fray Alonzo Giraldo de Terreros, at the time guardian of the college, wrote to Mediavilla relative to the matter on June 23.[20] In his reply, made at his hacienda on June 28, Mediavilla was as emphatic in his advocacy of the San Xavier project as Bustillo had been in his opposition to it. He said that he knew from personal acquaintance with them that the four tribes in question were docile, and that he believed them to be "domesticable." As they lived near the San Xavier, they could easily be taken there and settled. For such a purpose this river was the best place in the province, having good water facilities and fertile lands. Bus-

---

[16] *Erecion*, 5.

[17] *Erecion*, 6. The opinion of the *auditor* and the viceroy's decree carrying it out must have fallen between the date of Bustillo's memorial and June 23, when the opinion of Mediavilla was asked by the College.

[18] Bonilla, "Breve Compendio," Texas State Historical Association *Quarterly*, VIII, 41.

[19] *Copia de autos seguidos*.

[20] Archive of the College of Santa Cruz de Querétaro, K, leg. 6, No. 15. The *Erecion* gives the date of Mediavilla's letter as June 21, but this is evidently incorrect.

tillo, he said, could hardly be taken as an authority on this point, as he had crossed the river near the Brazos, and not near the proposed site; besides, he was rather frightened while in its vicinity on his campaign, and could not have been expected to make careful observations. As to taking the Yojuane and other tribes in question to San Pedro and the El Loco settlement, this was impracticable, for, to say nothing of other difficulties, they would be unwelcome, since they had different rites and customs from those of the Texas. On the other hand—and the delightful inconsistency did not disturb him—it would be most easy to settle on the San Xavier not only the petitioners, but also the Texas and the Nabedache, who, as Bustillo had said with truth, greatly lamented the departure of the missionaries from their midst. But Bustillo was wrong, he said, in supposing that the Yojuane and others did not trade directly with the French, for, as a matter of fact they were visited regularly by traders who came by way of Cadodachos and the Texas. Indeed, entry was so easy that in 1725 five hundred French soldiers (*genizaros*) had penetrated the country for a distance of ninety leagues, looking for a rumored mine on the Trinity, and had returned by the same route without even being molested.[21] It was clear, therefore, if for these reasons alone, that the province needed the protection of another presidio, whereas those of Sacramento and Cerralvo were not needed where they were, and were at best serving only a temporal purpose. Well might they be taken to the San Xavier to serve so important a spiritual end.

Supported by Mediavilla's opinion and by a paper of similar tenor written by Fray Isidro Felix de Espinosa, who had been for several years president of the Querétaran missions of eastern Texas and was now writing his famous chronicle,[22] Father Ortiz

---

[21] The present writer does not know to what event Mediavilla alludes.

[22] *Apuntes que dio el R. P. Fr. Ysidro,* undated, in *Satisfaccion de los Missioneros á las objecciones.* One paper drawn by Father Ortiz seems to have been a preliminary outline of a reply and not to have been presented. The copy which I have seen contains no date, salutation, or signature, but is labeled *Respuesta del P^e. Ortiz.*

prepared his answer. It was dated at the College of San Fernando on July 30. His reliance was mainly on the opinion of Mediavilla, which he submitted with his reply. Father Ortiz himself added to the discussion little that was new.[23]

Upon receipt of these opinions, the *autos* were remanded by the viceroy to the fiscal. This official was of the opinion that Bustillo was completely worsted in the argument, and, considering that he had no reason to change his original view, but, rather, strong additional ones for maintaining them, he reiterated his opinion of March 28.[24]

4. Delay due to the undertakings of Escandón.—Now arose a new cause or excuse for delay. A short time previously the king had charged the viceroy with the pacification and colonization of the coast country between Tampico and Bahía del Espíritu Santo, the last portion of the Gulf coast to receive attention by the Spaniards. To effect this important task, José de Escandón, Count of Sierra Gorda, was appointed by the viceroy on September 6, 1746. To enable him to explore, preliminary to colonizing it, the large stretch of country assigned to him, Escandón asked the aid of detachments from the garrisons at Adaes, Bahía, Sacramento, Monclova, Cerralvo, and Boca de Leones.[25] In view of these facts, the *auditor de guerra* gave the opinion[26] that with the garrisons thus occupied, none of them could be spared for the proposed San Xavier missions. He recurred, therefore, to his former opinion that neither could the

---

[23] *Memorial del R. P. Ortiz al Exmo. Sor. Virrey exponiendo las razones para fundar en Sⁿ. Xavier, año de 1746.* The memorial is signed also by Fray Alonso Giraldo de Terreros, guardian of the college, Fray Mathias Saenz de San Antonio, prefect of missions, Espinosa, and Fray Pedro Pérez de Mesquía, all of whom had served in the missions of the northern frontier.

[24] *Erecion,* 7. The date of giving this opinion does not appear, but it was between July 30 and September 24.

[25] See Bolton, ''The Founding of Mission Rosario,'' in the Tex. Hist. Assn. *Quarterly,* X, 119–122, for a sketch of the plans of Escandón. See also *Erecion,* p. 7, and pp. 291–294, below.

[26] The date was September 24. See *Erecion,* 12.

presidio of Sacramento be moved nor a new one be erected, and recommended that Father Ortiz be asked to propose some new means of securing the end so much desired.[27]

5. *New plans proposed by Father Ortiz.*—On September 28, the *auditor's* opinion was sent to Father Ortiz, and on October 10 he was ready with his reply. With the courage of convictions that usually marked these frontier missionaries, he dared to question the judgment of the *auditor* on matters of state, insisting that the garrisons of Sacramento, Coahuila, Boca de Leones, and Cerralvo were unnecessary, and slyly affirming that they could be diverted *either* to take part in the Escandón enterprise or to protect the proposed missions at San Xavier. Since a suggestion had been asked for, he submitted two alternative plans. One was for a volunteer civil colony, the other for a presidio which should become a civil settlement after a term of years. The first plan was to use the funds now being spent in supporting the Sacramento garrison, for the maintenance of one hundred volunteer settlers at San Xavier, assigning them lands, providing them with an initial outfit, and maintaining them for a term of eight years, after which they might be expected to support themselves. This would make a garrison unnecessary. The second alternative plan was that the company at Sacramento, or another of equal strength, should be maintained at San Xavier for a term of years, with the obligation to remain thereafter as colonists, having been supplied during their period of service with the means of pursuing agriculture. In either way, he said, a substantial village or city of Spaniards would be established at the end of ten years, while the missions would meanwhile have the necessary protection. It will be seen that both

---

[27] For a summary of this opinion, see *Erecion*, 7; for the date, see *ibid.*, 12. It is not absolutely certain that the two opinions referred to are identical but of this there seems little doubt. For more light on the contents, see the memorial by Ortiz, October 10, 1746, in response to the new request, I, leg. 19, No. 62. The autograph copy of this document has no title, but a copy of it is labeled *Instancia, y razones representadas al exmo. Sor Virrey para la fundacion de S*ⁿ*. Xavier.*

of these suggestions involved the use, for the defence of San Xavier, of the funds then being spent in Sacramento, and could hardly be regarded as entirely new plans, or greatly different from that of the fiscal.

Finally, in order that the Indians now gathered at San Xavier might be kept friendly and retained at the spot, Father Ortiz requested that, while the fate of the project was being decided, a sum of money should be assigned from the royal treasury for the purchase of presents and food, for "the eagerness (*moción*) of the Indians is such that the like was never before witnessed, and if these should fail . . . we do not know what would happen."[28]

Notwithstanding the suggestion of Father Ortiz, the advice of the *auditor* prevailed, and, in view of the operations of Escandón,[29] the viceroy ordered all discussion of the matter suspended. That Escandón's projects were the cause of the viceroy's withholding his decision is clearly stated in his dispatches of February 14 and July 27.

6. *Tentative approval by the viceroy: funds and a temporary garrison authorized.*—Nevertheless, the viceroy and the *auditor* were sufficiently convinced of its desirability to give the San Xavier project tentative support. On February 1, 1747.[30] as a result of another *escrito* from Father Ortiz,[31] and in conformity with a recommendation of the *auditor* made on January

---

[28] Father Ortiz to the viceroy, October 10, 1746; *Instancia, y razones.*

[29] The date of this order seems to have been February 1, 1747, but this point is not quite clear.

[30] The date, February 1, 1747, is fixed by Arch. Coll. Santa Cruz K, leg. 6, nos. 5 y 11; K, leg. 19, no. 67, is indefinite but corroborates the opinion.

[31] On January 16, 1747, Father Ortiz presented to the viceroy an *escrito* which he concluded by asking for the repayment to the College of the 2262 *pesos* 4 *tomines* already spent in attracting the Indians at San Xavier, and repeated his request for the assignment of a sum for like purpose till the matter should be decided. The date of the *escrito* and its contents are gathered from the viceroy's orders of February 14, 1747, requiring soldiers sent to San Xavier.

28, the viceroy ordered that the 2262½ pesos which had already been spent by Fray Mariano in attracting and maintaining the Indians at San Xavier should be repaid, and on February 14, in order to prevent the neophytes from deserting whilst the Seno Mexicano was being inspected, to protect them from the Apache, and to aid the missionaries in founding the settlement, he ordered the governor to send at once to San Xavier ten soldiers from Los Adaes and twelve from Béxar.[32]

Students should be guarded against an error at this point. An original despatch of the viceroy says that on December 26, 1746, the viceroy ordered the establishment of three missions on the San Xavier. From what has been stated above it will be seen that this is a mistake of the despatch, although it is official.[33]

7. *Father Ortiz appeals to the King, 1747.*—Perhaps in despair of success at the viceroy's court, or perhaps at the viceroy's suggestion, and to aid any effort which the latter might make, Father Ortiz now turned to the king himself. In a memorial written sometime after the viceroy's decree of February 14,[34] he reviewed the circumstances under which the tribes had asked for a mission, gave a list of those which had subsequently joined the first four tribes in their petition, recounted the efforts that had been made in Mexico by the college, and cited the fiscal's unqualified approval and the viceroy's tentative aid recently given. With great shrewdness he made much of the political advantages of the desired missions: ''even more

---

[32] Viceroy's decree of February 14, reciting the contents of the *auditor's* opinion of January 28 and the decree of February 1. See the letter of Ortiz to the king, 1747 (after February 14). Arricivita quotes an order of identical tenor, but gives the date as February, 1748. I suspect that he refers to this one of February 14, 1747 (*Crónica*, 325).

[33] The reference is to the document entitled *Erecion*, etc. See also the erroneous statement in *Memorias de Nueva España*, XXVIII, 179, to the effect that the mission were authorized on February 14, 1747.

[34] The decree is referred to in the memorial, and reference is made to ''this year of forty-seven.''

notable because these Indians and their broad, fertile, and
bounteous country are coveted by foreign nations, who anxiously
try to add them to their crowns, and with this aim maintain
commerce with them and supply them with guns, ammunition,
and other things which they know they like. It follows, therefore,'' he continued, ''that if they are not heeded, and if—God
forbid—France, on whose colonies they border, should become
hostile and, with the desire to gain their affections should maintain closer friendship with said Indians, and these should become
her partisans, she might without any difficulty get possession of
not only this province but of many others of New Spain.'' But,
by making the necessary provision for these Indian petitioners,
New Spain would be sufficiently protected and very much increased. Not only would these tribes enter missions (he added)
but the Apache, who so infested the province, and yet so many
times had asked for missions, would be forced to accept the faith
and attach themselves to the crown of Spain. ''And in this way
the Province of Texas will become a most extensive and flourishing kingdom, which may freely trade and communicate with
New Mexico and other provinces of New Spain and even with
others of your royal crown if this communication is sought by
sea.'' With not a little wisdom he argued, further, that by paci-
fying the Indians and peopling the country, many presidios
would become unnecessary, and the crown thereby be saved great
expense.

On the basis of this argument on political grounds, to which
he did not fail to add the obligation to extend the faith, Father
Ortiz proceeded to request not only permission to found permanently the missions already being provisionally established, and
all the means necessary for the purpose, but also asked permission and funds to establish a hospital in Texas, either at San
Xavier or other convenient place, to facilitate the broad missionary project under contemplation. It should serve as an

infirmary and a place of rest for sick and worn-out missionaries, and be the headquarters of the prelate of the San Xavier missions, who otherwise would be three hundred or four hundred leagues from headquarters with no means of succor or medical aid. In addition to the prelate, there would be necessary two missionary priests, to act as substitutes for the missionaries, care for the military, and serve civilian Spaniards, and two lay brothers, one to serve as nurse for the sick, and the other to act as financial agent, with the title of conductor of alms, to secure funds in Mexico to help on the project.

Father Ortiz closed by repeating his request for reimbursement of the sums that had been spent by the college in maintaining three missionaries at San Xavier in the work of catechizing and otherwise preparing the Indians for mission life.[35]

8. *Opposition to the plans for a temporary garrison.*—It was not enough for the viceroy merely to order a garrison sent to San Xavier, for excuses, or even good reasons for respectful argument were easily found and hard to resent. And thus it was with the order of February 14. It reached San Antonio on May 7, by a courier who had been delayed on the Rio Grande two months by Apache hostilities. This circumstance, coupled with recent occurrences at San Antonio and the situation at San Xavier revealed by the declaration of Pruneda, made three days before, augured ill for the execution of the despatch.

On the 9th Fray Mariano presented the document to Urrutia,[36] and asked for its fulfillment. Urrutia gave formal obedience, but wrote on Mariano's *escrito* several reasons why the detaching of the twelve soldiers should be suspended until further orders should be received from the viceroy. Apache hostilities were especially bad just then; in the preceding month the tribe had driven off the horse herds of three of the missions,

---

[35] Memorial of Father Ortiz to the king, after February 14, 1747.

[36] Fray Mariano to Urrutia, in *Escrito sobre los 12 Soldados, qᵉ avian de hir a Sⁿ. Xavier.*

and were now encamped near the San Xavier in large numbers; at that very moment he had in his possession a memorial of the cabildo on the subject, dated April 29, waiting till a courier could take it to Mexico; and a petition from the citizens asking him to request the aid of fifteen or twenty of the soldiers of Los Adaes to strengthen the defense.[37] To support this petition, on the next day he presented the matter to a joint meeting of the military officers, the cabildo, justicia, and regimiento of the villa of San Fernando, and this body issued a statement similar in tenor to that of Urrutia, adding to his reasons for suspending the order the shortage of supplies at San Xavier.[38] On May 19 the substance of the deliberations was embodied by Urrutia in a *consulta*, or opinion, and sent to the viceroy.[39]

While the immediate purpose of Fray Mariano was thus frustrated, the College of Santa Cruz seized the occasion to ask not for less but for more.   Fray Francisco de la Santísima Trinidad, joint agent with Marquéz at Mexico for the college in promoting the San Xavier plan, put in the appeal.   In a memorial to the viceroy he referred with evident approval to the reasons for not fulfilling the order of February 14.   He then argued at length on the importance of controlling the group of Indians for whom the new missions were desired.   They lived on the French border, secured their firearms from the French, and were in pernicious communication with that nation.   They were dextrous in the use of firearms, and in case of a breach with France it would be important to have them on the side of Spain. The only way to secure this allegiance was to "reduce" them to mission life; this done, they would defend the frontier against

---

[37] This *consulta* is summarized, also, in *Memorial del R. P.* (*ibid.*), and in *Presidente al Cap^n. de S^n. Antonio*, May 7, 1748.

[38] *Diligencias* of the cabildo, May 10, 1747, in *Dos peticiones del P. Fr. Mariano sobre los Yndios de S^n. Xav^r. año de 1747.*

[39] This fact is stated in the viceroy's despatch of July 27: "Todo lo qual me participio el citado capitan en consulta de diez, y nueve Mayo passado de este año."

both the French and the Apache, and perhaps bring that dangerous nation to Christianity. And to do this properly would require a presidio, not of twenty-two soldiers, but of sixty or more,
for which number he now asked.[40]

The matter now went again through the regular routine of
the viceroy's secretariat. It was first referred to the fiscal, who
replied on June 28; and then to the *auditor de guerra*, Altamira,
who gave his *dictamen* on July 4. Complying with Altamira's
advice, on July 27 the viceroy issued new despatches. By the
terms of these orders the nine soldiers belonging to the presidio
of Bahía but serving at the missions near San Antonio were to
return to their post; from the Presidio of Bahía thirteen soldiers
were to be sent to San Xavier, and from that of Los Adaes
seventeen. Each soldier sent was to be of good character and
suitable for the purpose. Though the captain of Béxar was
exempt from complying with the order of February 14 in form,
that place was to suffer a loss of nine soldiers borrowed from
Bahía. And the new order must be fulfilled without excuse or
interpretation, on pain of dismissal from office and fine of $6000
for any failure or violation. The viceroy was now showing his
teeth.[41]

---

[40] He continues with a statement of the duties of such a guard, which
might be interesting to quote (*Memorial, en q°. insiste pidiendo la licencia
para fundar en S*. Xavier*). The archive copy is undated, but it evidently fell between May 19, when Urrutia's *consulta* was written, and
June 28. The despatch of July 27 refers to a prolix memorial following
the *consulta* of Urrutia and preceding a document of June 28. ''Y Sabi-
dor de esto la parte del referido colegio insto an su pretension alegando
difusamente, quanto le parecio convenir a su derecho.''

[41] Altamira gave the opinion that if the missionaries were to ask for
a hundred settlers for San Xavier he would recommend a subsidy of two
hundred dollars apiece and liberal grants of land, exemptions, and privileges; but in order not to venture too freely the royal funds, and since
the presidio of Sacramento was destined for other purposes, he made
the recommendation which the viceroy adopted (Despatch of July 27
to the governor of Texas and the captain of Bahía). There is some doubt
as to whether the date of the despatch is July 17 or July 27. My copy
of the original despatch of February 24 to Governor Larios refers to
the order as of July 17. But my copy of the original despatch in the
archive of the College of Santa Cruz is dated July 27. In both cases

The missionaries were no better pleased with the new order for a temporary guard than had been the commanders in Texas with the former decree. The removal of the nine soldiers from San Antonio would be a hardship to the missions; and, besides, what the missionaries demanded was a regular presidio. This feeling was made known in August by Father Mariano de Anda y Altamirano, in a memorial to the viceroy.[42] As has already been stated, he had been assigned to the new missions on the San Xavier River, and had been to the site; he had been sent to Mexico to aid in securing the necessary license, and had heard of the order of July 27. His argument now was much like Father Trinidad's had been. In his memorial he prophesied that the governor of Texas and the captain of Bahía would give only formal obedience and then proceed to raise objections, with resulting delays. As for himself, he saw two difficulties. If the nine soldiers of Bahía doing duty at San Antonio were to be removed, either they must be replaced by soldiers from that presidio or the missions near San Antonio would be without protection. To take soldiers from the presidio would leave San Antonio exposed to attack. The presidio of Los Adaes, being on the French frontier and surrounded by Indians, could ill spare any of its sixty soldiers, most of whom were constantly needed to escort the governor, the missionaries, and convoys of goods from Saltillo, to cultivate the fields, or to guard the storehouse.[43] The presidio of Bahía was almost as much in danger from Apaches as was San Antonio; and the Cujane were bad.

Moreover, the garrison of thirty soldiers assigned to San Xavier was altogether too small. Twelve men would be needed

---

the words are spelled out in full, and I am of the opinion that the correct date is July 27. (See despatch February 24, 1748, Lamar Papers, and Arch. Coll. Santa Cruz, K, leg. 19, No. 71).

[42] *Memorial del Pe. Anda al Exmo. Sor Virrey sobre Sn. Xavier.* I infer the date from the reference in the document to the decision of the "past month," alluding to the order of July 27, 1747.

[43] Father Anda's paper gives an interesting statement of the duties of a presidial guard.

to guard the three missions being planned, and ten to guard the horse herd; this would leave only six to escort the supply train and the missionaries, making no allowance for desertions and deaths. Finally, any guard less than fifty soldiers would be too small in case of trouble with the barbarian tribes at the new missions or of attacks by their enemies.

The provision of one hundred settlers would not serve at present, since it would take a long time to secure them, especially if the task were left entirely to the missionaries, already over-burdened; besides, the allowance of two hundred pesos per family was too small, since in spite of the greatest economy the expense for one missionary going to Saltillo or Coahuila, with only one servant, was at least one hundred pesos.

A presidio at San Xavier, on the other hand, would be on the very frontier against the Apache, and would help to restrain the French, who were now entering by way of the Trinity River. Indeed, it was now well known that they had a large settlement on that stream, with a garrison and fifty or sixty cannon, and were supplying the very Indians of San Xavier.

In view of all the foregoing, Father Anda closed by urging, first, that the presidio of Sacramento be moved to the San Xavier River, and second, that thirty or forty men be added to it. If this could not be done, he urged that eighty or ninety men be detached from other presidios—not including those of Texas—and formed into a new presidio at San Xavier.

As Father Anda predicted, the disposition of the Texas commanders to comply was no better than before, though in saying this we would not wish to convey the impression that the military authorities did not have good grounds for resisting the reduction of their petty garrisons. But the resistance of Orobio Bazterra, the captain at Bahía, seems to have been in part inspired by ill feeling toward Father Mariano. The Apache situation, at least, was really serious. The captain set forth his objections in communications of November 1 and 21, and the governor, Fran-

cisco García Larios, voiced his in one of December 12.[44] From a
review of these documents given by the viceroy in a despatch of
January 29, 1748, it appears that the objectors maintained that
all of the soldiers were needed in their respective presidios; that
the San Xavier, though called a river, was only an arroyo, and
that their soldiers had refused to go there to live. The governor
added that he feared that if he should try to carry out the order,
the men would desert to Natchitoches. This argument might
appear frivolous if we did not know that twenty years afterward nearly the whole garrison of San Agustín did that very
thing. The captain concluded by saying, maliciously, it would
seem, or at least without foundation, that the favorable reports
given of San Xavier were false, and had probably been secured by
subornation or collusion of witnesses.

Captain Orobio had a substitute plan to urge as an excuse for
noncompliance, and he may have been sincere in his support of
it. In 1746, as we have seen, he had gone to the lower Trinity
and the San Jacinto rivers to investigate a rumor of a French
settlement in that region. While there he had become acquainted
with the Orcoquiza tribe and learned of the activities of French
traders among them and the Attacapa.[45] He now represented to
the viceroy that the ''Horquisa'' nation was composed of five
rancherías and three hundred families; that they had asked for
missions, promising to settle between the Trinidad and the
Sabinas rivers, ''which is their fatherland;'' and that they had
repeated their offer, promising to return (to Bahía, it seems),
in the following March. He concluded by proposing various
reasons for embracing and not depreciating this opportunity to
reduce Indians dexterous with guns, because of their nearness
to the Mississippi and of their communication with the French.[46]

---

[44] These objections are reviewed in the viceroy's despatch of January
29, 1748.

[45] Bolton, ''Spanish Activities on the Lower Trinity,'' in the *Southwestern Historical Quarterly*, XVI. See also pp. 327–332, below.

[46] Summary in the viceroy's despatch of January 29.

Fear that the viceroy might accept this plan, and that it would interfere with their own, sank deep into the minds of the missionaries, and they did not lose an opportunity to use their influence to head it off, offering as their best substitute a mission for the Orcoquiza at San Xavier.

9. *Three missions authorized by the viceroy* (*December 23, 1747.*)—But these arguments of Governor Larios and Captain Orobio came too late, for on December 23, 1747, before they had been received, the viceroy, conforming with two opinions of the *auditor,* dated December 10 and 19, ordered three missions founded on the San Xavier River within the next eight months.[47] In consequence of this determination, appropriations were at once made for a year's salary in advance for six missionaries, and for the purchase by the royal factor of the necessary ornaments and supplies for the three missions.[48] Thus, after two and one half years of petitioning and of heroic efforts at San Xavier, Fray Mariano and his college had the satisfaction of obtaining the permission and the help they had so zealously sought.

When the letters of Orobio and Larios were received by the viceroy they were sent, in the regular way, to the fiscal. But he gave them little weight, arguing especially that it would be foolish

---

[47] I get the contents from the summaries in *Erecion,* 8, and letter of Santa Ana to the viceroy, in K, leg. 6, no. 18.

The *Erecion,* page 8, says that on December 26, *1746,* in conformity with the *auditor's* opinions of December 10 and 17, the viceroy Horcasitas authorized the three missions. This cannot have been the case. In the first place, it is in conflict with the decrees of February 1 and July 27, 1747, in which the viceroy states that he is suspending final action until the outcome of Escandón's work is known, and of February 14, 1747, granting temporary aid, while the matter of approval was under consideration. In the second place, Espinosa, writing in 1747 of the San Xavier enterprise, says that "although it lacks the confirmation of the Most Excellent Viceroy" it appears to "have accepted his Catholic Zeal." (p. 467); in the third place, other contemporary documents besides the summary in *Erecion,* give the date December 23, 1747. See Fray Santa Ana to the viceroy, March 10, 1749, *dictamen fiscal,* July 21, 1748, in *Memorias,* XXVIII, 73.

[48] This had been done by January 23, 1748. See *dictamen* quoted in the viceroy's despatch of January 20, 1748, *Memorias de Nueva España,* XXVIII.

to give up a project of proved merit, like that of the San Xavier missions, for one which had not yet been investigated, like that suggested by Orobio. In consequence, the viceroy issued a dispatch on January 29, requiring the governor to carry out his former orders at once, and not to neglect that part which provided for the encouragement of as many families as possible to go to San Xavier to settle, in order that in time the garrison might be unnecessary. This despatch was enclosed in a letter of February 24.[49]

By virtue of this new order the thirty soldiers were sent under the command of Lieutenant Galván, of the Béxar company. He arrived at San Xavier on or about March 13, 1748. The married soldiers were followed by their families, who remained a short time.[50]

10. By the King, April 16, 1748.—Soon after the consent of the viceroy was obtained, the petition of Father Ortiz to the royal court separately bore fruit. The petition was considered in the Council of the Indies, and the resulting action shows that it struck the right chord in the royal breast. On the 16th of April, 1748, more than four months after the viceroy had ordered the missions established, more than two years after a tentative mission had actually been begun, and two months after one of the authorized missions had been formally founded, the king issued a *cédula* to the viceroy, setting forth that, although he had not sufficient information to form a wholly satisfactory opinion, and though the viceroy had not sent the reports which he might have sent, yet, ''considering that the gravity of the matter does not admit of delay, and that there are in the Province of Texas the nations of gentile Indians mentioned soliciting religious in order that they may receive holy baptism and attach themselves

---

[49] The original despatch is in the Béxar Archives, Miscellaneous, 1742–1793, and the accompanying letter in the Lamar Papers.

[50] Fray Mariano tells us in a document written about May, 1749, that the soldiers were followed by their families, who remained till May, 1749.

to the body of the Church (which is the principal object that I have ordered attended to and promoted), and considering that the country, because of its great extent, unpopulated condition, and nearness to the region where the French have intruded, merits greater care and vigilance; in order to prevent them from stirring up and attaching to their side the idolatrous Indians, it has seemed proper to order and command you'' to ascertain for certain that the Indians have made such a petition and that the establishment of the missions would be wise. Such being the case, the viceroy was to proceed at once to plant the requisite number of missions, furnishing the means for ornaments and other necessities usually supplied. And if the hospital asked for should prove absolutely necessary, that, too, was to be founded. Finally, the three missionaries must be paid for the time they had been serving at San Xavier.[51]

An opinion written in the College of Guadalupe regarding the royal *cédula* of April 16, 1748, shows that the Zacatecan college was not altogether pleased with the license permitting the sister college to enter the missionary field in central Texas.[52]

It stated that the College of Santa Cruz had four missions at San Antonio, the only ones in Texas at the time of the visit of Father Ortiz; that in the belief of the writer, Ortiz's visit had no other purpose than the founding of missions for the central Texas tribes; that the country of the Mayeye where the mission was to be founded was rough and bad; that the Tauacana, Quichay, Tancague, and Yojuan were too far to the north to be reduced at the proposed site; that the Yadoxa, from whom the *padres* had got their information, had included them ''not to secure Holy Baptism, as is supposed, but for the material benefit of clothing, tobacco, maize, and more than all this, in order that

---

[51] Royal *cédula* dated at Buen Retiro, April 16, 1748. Arch. Gen. y Púb., *Reales Cédulas,* vol. 68, no. 52.

[52] Anonymous Commentary.

the Spaniards in a presidio may restrain the boldness of the Apache; that it would be better for the sick of Rio Grande and San Antonio to come to Xacatecas than to go to an hospice at San Xavier; finally, if the Bidai wished missions they could enter that of Nacogdoches, where they went every year at harvest time and near which they lived; or to Los Ais; in either of which cases they would not need to leave their own country. The Tawakoni, Kichai, Tonkawa, and Yojuan might congregate there also and thus save the expense of new missions.

CHAPTER IV

THE FOUNDING OF THE MISSIONS

1. *San Francisco Xavier, February, 1748.*—After the viceroy's consent and promise of aid for founding permanent missions were received, things for a time went favorably with Fray Mariano's cherished plan. To look after preparations in Mexico, the College of Santa Cruz appointed Fray Juan Joseph Ganzábal, who was destined four years later to suffer martyrdom at one of the missions he was helping to establish.[1] He went from San Antonio to Querétaro, arriving there at the end of March.

In February, probably as soon as he received the good news from Mexico, Fray Mariano proceeded to the formal founding of the first mission—presumably that already tentatively established—taking for the purpose from San Antonio, on his own credit, while the royal funds were forthcoming, goods to the value of $5083.50.[2] The date of the formal founding is fixed by a letter written by Fray Mariano himself to Captain Urrutia on May 7, 1748, and is thus put beyond dispute.[3] In the same communication Fray Mariano called the mission "Nuestra Señora de los Dolores del Rio de San Xavier." This is the earliest name I have seen applied to it, but otherwise it is always called San Francisco Xavier. Perhaps the former name is the one by which the temporary mission had gone.

The progress made at the mission is shown by the report dated March 18, by Lieutenant Juan Galván, who was sent, as

---

[1] Communication of Ganzábal, June 14, 1748, in *Memorias*, XXVIII, 70.

[2] *Ibid.*, 72.

[3] Memorial of Fray Mariano to Urrutia, May 7, 1748. The same date is also given in Músquiz's report, based on the original baptisimal records of the mission.

has been said, in command of the thirty soldiers who had been ordered there.[4]   Galván stated that when he arrived at San Xavier the missionaries were without a single soldier. He found already provided a strong wooden stockade, huts to live in, and supplies of seed, stock, working oxen, and clothing for the Indians. At the mission there were many Indians, of Ranchería Grande (Hierbipiame), Yojuane, Tonkawa, Mayeye, Deadose, Bidai, and Orcoquiza, and others daily coming. It will be seen that most of the tribes named here were of the original peti- tioners. At the very moment when he was writing his report there arrived a band of Bidai, who reported that six leagues away there were more than four hundred others on the way.[5] An Orcoquiza chief offered to bring numerous Indians of the neighboring tribes. Indeed there were more Indians than could be supported, in spite of the supplies which Fray Mariano had brought; and before the end of March he was constrained to tell the neophytes not to solicit any more tribes, to refuse food to all of those already there except such as were actually helping in the fields and at the missions, and to send word to the tribes on the way to remain at a convenient distance.[6]

In reconstructing the picture of life at the new establishment the imagination is assisted by the statement that of the twenty- eight soldiers there—two of the thirty assigned were lacking— one was usually employed to supervise the Indians with the

---

[4] Arricivita, *Crónica*, 325. There are some indications that Arricivita confused the orders of February, 1/47, for soldiers with that of January, 1748. The order of 1747 provided for sending soldiers from San Antonio and Adaes, that of 1748 from Bahía and Adaes.

[5] *Memorial del Pe. Ganzábal, pidiendo fuerzas para el resguardo de las missiones de Sn. Xavier;* report by Galván, in Ganzábal's memorial (Ar- ricivita, 325). Also in *Memorias de Nueva España*, XXVIII, 71, where I find this date. Fray Mariano states that at the end of March there were at San Xavier the Ranchería Grande Indians, Yojuanes, Tancagues, and others; the Deadoses, Bidai and other nations were at the Brazos, on the way; while the other promised tribes were gathering to come.

[6] *Memorial del R. P. Preside. al capn. de Sn. Antonio.* May 7, 1748. It was impossible to take from San Antonio more than 500 fanegas of maize, and by May 7 this had not all been transported.

stock, one assisting in the labor of the fields, six guarding the
horse herd, ten guarding the missions and the families, and ten
escorting the supply trains that brought maize from San Antonio
for soldiers and neophytes.[7]

Galván filed with his *diligencias* a certificate that he did not
regard the thirty soldiers provided sufficient for the protection
of the three missions planned, but that a presidio of fifty men
would be sufficient. The college made Galván's report the basis
of new requests, and before the end of the year Father Ganzábal,
in Mexico, presented a memorial reviewing progress at San
Xavier, requesting the repayment of the 5083 pesos 4 reales, and
the erection of a regular presidio of fifty men.[8]

2. Apache attacks and new appeals for help.—Shortage of
provisions was not by any means the only trouble that beset the
struggling mission early in its career. In April, 1748, in the
midst of his pious task, Fray Mariano suffered an accident which
compelled him to retire to San Antonio for several months, delayed the completion of his work, and caused it to devolve largely
upon Father Santa Ana.[9] When he withdrew he left in charge
Fray Francisco Cayetano Aponte, apparently the first minister
of the permanent mission (as Fray Mariano was minister at San
Antonio de Valero) and one of those who had been there temporarily, since the six provided by the viceroy did not arrive
till much later, as will be seen. Scarcely had Fray Mariano
reached San Antonio when bad news from San Xavier overtook him.[10] On May 4 Fray Cayetano wrote him that two days
before more than sixty Apache had attacked the place, ransack-

[7] *Memorial del R. P. Preside. al capn. de Sn. Antonio.* May 7, 1748.

[8] *Memorial del Pe. Ganzabal, pidiendo fuerzas para el resguardo de las
misiones de Sn. Xavier.* See also Arricivita, *Crónica,* and *Mem. de Nueva
España,* XXVIII, 71. Galván's report is described as "7 foxas utiles."

[9] Fray Mariano to the viceroy, March 13, 1749. Santa Ana to the viceroy, March 10, 1749. The nature of the accident does not appear. After
reaching San Antonio other ills beset him, almost depriving him of the
use of his right arm, and extending the duration of his incapacity.

[10] Fray Mariano, *Memorial,* May 7, 1748.

ing the houses, and attempting to stampede the horses. The soldiers and mission Indians, of whom there were more than two hundred present, made resistance, and succeeded in driving the horses into the corral, whereupon the Apaches, seeing themselves outnumbered, withdrew, but not without threatening to come again, with a larger force, to destroy the place. This threat was understood by a Yojuan who had been a captive among the Apache. In retiring the Apache killed two mission Indians who were encountered returning with buffalo meat. The mission Indians, seeing their danger, now began to contemplate withdrawing to the woods for safety.[11]

Before the end of the year three other Apache raids were made on the mission. In each the raiders ran off horses belonging to Spaniards and Indians. Incident to the four attacks three soldiers and four new converts were killed—not a great number, indeed, but manifestly large enough to cause the missionaries to fear for their personal safety and to lessen the enthusiasm of the tribes for residence at the site. The main facts of the first attack are told by Fray Mariano in a memorial of May 7. Subsequent events are described in a paper written by him about a year later.[12] A second report to Fray Mariano from Fray Cayetano told that on May 5 the Indians made good their threat, returned in a great multitude, and ran off the horse herd, ''the settlement retaining its existence solely through divine providence.''

On receiving the second notice Fray Mariano, who was still sick at San Antonio, repaired by petition[13] to Captain Urrutia for help. Urrutia replied that he could not give it because sixteen of his men, all indeed except those actually occupied in guard duty, had gone to Bahía to escort the new governor. Pedro

---

11 Fray Mariano, *Memorial*, May 7, 1748.

12 Communication to the governor. In it he speaks of a year having elapsed since the Apache attacks. I infer that the document was written as late as May, 1749.

13 *Escrito* of May 7.

del Barrio, to Los Adaes.[14] Urrutia forwarded the petition with
his *proveido* to Governor Barrio, at Bahía, while Father Mariano
waited for the expected aid. Instead of giving it, however,
Barrio wrote a sharp reply to Captain Urrutia for having received and forwarded the petition, saying that the king was more
in need of Urrutia's sword than of his pen.[15] This attitude on
the part of Governor Barrio, at the opening of his term, was
quite in keeping with all of his subsequent dealings with Fray
Mariano. Indeed, the hostility between these two prominent men
was one of the leading threads of the history of the San Xavier
missions for more than a year.

Fray Mariano was forced, under the circumstances, to make
the trip to relieve Fray Cayetano with only one soldier and some
mission Indians. Arriving at San Xavier he found that most
of the mission Indians had fled to the woods, frightened,[16] and
threatening not to return till there should be adequate protection.
Fray Mariano sent for them, and they were found so near by
that they returned on the second day, bringing more than had
run away. After that, according to Fray Mariano, they remained
steadfast up to the time of his writing. We thus infer that the
mission continued in operation.

In spite of his sharp reply to Urrutia, to Fray Mariano
Barrio wrote that he would hasten to San Xavier. He did so,
arriving on May 26 and remaining two days. During this time
he conducted an investigation, about which we shall hear in
another connection. Before leaving he ordered the soldiers to
send their wives and children away, the inference being that he
did so on account of danger from the Apache. He also sug-

---

[14] *Memorial del R. P. Preside. al Capn. de Sn. Antonio pidiendo fuerzas para la defensa del Presidio, y misiones de S. Xavier.* May 7, 1748. The word "Presidio" in the title, which is an archive label, is misleading.

[15] *Escrito presentado al Govr. Dn. Pedro del Varrio sobre Sn. Xavier,* 1749. Fray Mariano later wrote that at the time he attributed this position of Barrio "not to passion but to his recent arrival." (*ibid.*).

[16] *Cf.,* letter of March 13, 1749, for these events. Arch. Coll. Santa Cruz, K, leg. 6, no. 18.

gested, as a means of increasing the temporary defences, that Father Mariano bring from San Antonio fifteen or twenty mission Indians.[17]

Fray Mariano continued ill[18] for a year or more after April, 1748, and could not carry on the work at San Xavier, but Father Santa Ana supervised it, and it seems that one or more missionaries spent a part of the time with Father Aponte.[19]

By March, 1749, Father Santa Ana was able to report a good beginning for the first mission. He wrote on the tenth of that month: "The mission of San Xavier, having some established form, has been situated on this river since February of last year. Not counting those who have died Christians, there are listed in it of the nation of the Mayeye thirty-two men, and among them only two old men, one of sixty and the other of eighty years of age. The women number only forty-one, because this nation has been attacked by the Apaches. The youths, maidens, and children, likewise number only thirteen, for the same reason. Of the nation of the Hierbipiamos there are thirty-one men, there not being any old men among them; women, twenty-one, boys and girls, eleven. This nation suffered the same assaults as the former. Of the nation of the Yojuanes twenty-six men, none of them old; women, twenty-three; boys and girls, seven; youths, twenty-eight. With these three nations there are some Tanchagues who struggle with the Apaches, whom they attacked last year before the governor of Coahuila did so."[20]

---

[17] *Escrito presentado al Govr. D^n. Pedro del Varrio sobre S^n. Xavier,* 1749; and *Carta del P. Galzaval.*

[18] Santa Ana wrote to the viceroy March 10, 1749, that Fray Mariano was entirely free from blame for any shortcoming at the new missions, having been since the month of April of last year gravely ill; "for which reason I was obliged, from that time, to continue with the matters pending relative to the three new missions of said river. But as soon as he is restored from his illness he will perfect and complete what he has begun." *Dictamen del Auditor de guerra.*

[19] My evidence for this is given further on.

[20] *Dictamen del Auditor.* For the attack by the governor of Coahuila, see Dunn, "Apache Relations in Texas," 254.

3. *Assignment of regular missionaries.*—At the end of March, 1748, the first regular assignment of missionaries was made by the college. On the 31st of that month the newly elected guardian, Fray Francisco Xavier Castellanos, himself a former worker in Texas,[21] wrote to the president, Father Santa Ana, in regard to his plans. The new missions had been erected into a presidency, and Fray Mariano, of course, made the president. Six new missionaries were to be provided for Texas, but three of them were to change places with three of the "antiguos" (old missionaries) at the San Antonio missions, two from Mission Valero and one other. With these three men already in Texas, three of the new ones were to go to San Xavier, the rest to be distributed elsewhere, as President Santa Ana should see fit.

The Valero missionaries at this time were Fray Mariano and Fray Diego Martín García. The latter had been in Texas since 1741, at least.[22] It is to him that we owe the preservation of the earliest records of the Texas missions. Later he saw service in the missions of northern Sonora. The missionaries named in the guardian's letter were Friars Alonso Giraldo de Terreros, Juan de los Angeles, and Saluad de Amaya, all of whom had formerly served in Texas;[23] and Juan Hernández, Mariano Anda, and Fray Domingo, referring by the last name, no doubt, to Fray Juan Domingo Arricivita, later known as the historian. The document does not state in terms that all of these men are among the missionaries to be sent, but such is the implication. It will be seen later on that some of them did and some did not operate at San Xavier. In addition to these six new missionaries, sent in the name of the three new missions, Father Castellanos promised to send others to supply deficiencies.

21 He had been at the mission of Valero twenty years before. See Schmidt, *Franciscan Missionaries in Texas,* 7.

22 See Schmidt's list, *op. cit.*

23 Terreros had been at Valero in 1730 and 1731; Amaya was in Texas during the period 1728–1734 (Schmidt, *op. cit.*) ; and Los Angeles in 1744 (Schmidt, *op. cit.*).

Of the new workers the guardian specifically assigned to stations only two. They were Fathers Terreros and Hernández, who were to take the places of the Valero ministers. Two of the appointees seem to have been considered hard to get along with. President Santa Ana was instructed to see to it that all did their full duty, and to send them back to the college for discipline if necessary. *"Hoc dico sub sigilo* with reference to the Fathers Preachers Anda and Amaya, for the others I have no doubt will conduct themselves well."

"With respect to Father Preacher Anda, your Reverence will see whether it is proper for him to remain in those missions or those of San Xavier, and with your accustomed prudence will decide the matter; for I desire to relieve your Reverence as much as possible of the cares which the reverend fathers presidents are caused by the lack of congeniality and agreement of the missionaries."[24]

To aid in their work, the missionaries were to take from the missions of San Antonio, or from the Rio Grande if necessary, as many families of converted Indians as might be needed. Cattle and other supplies were also to be secured from these places, at a fair price it was hoped, and the new missions were to pay them back "when, how, and in what" was possible. Matters not specifically provided for in the instruction were to be decided by the two presidents in conference.[25]

4. The supplies delayed.—The missionaries were all supplied and ready to go when the above communication was written, and presumably they soon set out.[26] On June 13, they reached San Antonio, but through slowness in the despatch of the supplies, and Fray Mariano's illness, there was another half year's delay. The situation on June 24 is stated in Father Santa Ana's

---

[24] Castellanos and Amaya had been in Texas about the same length of time.

[25] Castellanos to Santa Ana, March 31, 1747.

[26] "Por hallarse ya los Ministros en vn todo hauiados, y para salir a las nuebas conversiones." *Ibid.*

letter of June 24 to the viceroy: "I am obliged to make known to your Excellency that on the 13th of June I found myself with the religious who ought to be in the missions of San Xavier, and the simple notice that within eight months the reduction of the Indians in three missions should be effected.

"This appears to be a decree of December of the past year, but it is morally impossible to put it into effect until the supplies come (which will be in the month of October or November) for it is certain that among these Indians there is not a thing with which they can sustain and maintain themselves unalterably in that place, since their sustenance depends on the chase.

"And thus the entry of the religious and the supplies must be provided for, certainly with six hundred fanegas of maize for each one of the conversions, and also some cattle, sheep and goats. All of this up to the present it has been impossible to provide, now for lack of pack mules, and the unavoidable cost of freightage; now because the enemies, as I suppose the ministers of your Excellency have reported, make it impossible to travel the road without difficulty. And thus, with great humility, I will do what your Excellency orders, but only at the most opportune time and by the best means.[27]

"In case of founding in fact the missions of San Xavier there will be necessary an order from your Excellency to the effect that the governor of this province or another official[28] assist at this act with the accustomed formality, giving in your

---

[27] At this point the president explained why the demand for thirty soldiers had been changed to one for fifty, the reason given being the change of site from the country of the petitioners to the San Xavier.

[28] *Carta Ynforme q^e. hizo a Su Ex^a. el R^do. P^e. Prest^e. Fr. Benitto.* June 24, 1748. The main contents of this communication are quoted in a letter of Santa Ana to the viceroy dated March 10, 1749. He there states: "In June of the past year there came to my hands a simple copy of the decree of your Excellency issued in December, of the year 47, and at the same time entered the religious who were to assist in the three missions of the Rio San Javier, and without loss of time I made supplication from this decree in the following terms," quoting what has been given above.

Excellency's name possession of that country to the Indians which, all being recorded by juridical *diligencias,* may be sent to the Secretaría de Govierno, as a means by which your Excellency may be informed of the number of souls entering each one of the conversions.''[29]

Although the documents are not explicit on this point, it seems that some of the new missionaries went to San Xavier during the course of the summer of 1748, in spite of the delay of the supplies. At any rate, we know that ''padres and soldiers'' lived there during the ''rigor of the drought'' of that summer. We have seen that Father Aponte was alone in May, when Father Mariano went to aid him, and that Father Mariano was sick at San Antonio on June 24. Therefore it is evident that someone went to San Xavier to aid Father Aponte after that date,[30] otherwise the plural ''padres'' could not be used. So much, at times, are we forced to depend upon inference.

5. *Barrio's unfavorable report, 1748.*—It has been seen that after endless investigations, which we have painfully followed, the viceroy in December, 1747, definitely authorized the founding of the missions on the San Xavier River, and that early in 1748 one of the missions had been duly established. And yet in May, 1748, Barrio went to Texas with instructions to inspect and report on the site which had already been approved—an indecision which resulted in reopening the whole troublesome matter.[31]

While at the mission settlement in the latter part of May, Barrio looked over the site, apparently without showing Fathers Mariano and Cayetano his commission. On the next day Fray Mariano, knowing his hostility, presented him a petition requesting his assent to four points, namely, that the region was unsafe

---

[29] Santa Ana, *Carta Ynforme.*

[30] Letter of Santa Ana to the viceroy, March 10, 1749.

[31] Ganzábal states that he had secret instructions. *Carta del P. Ganzabal.*

from the Apache, that the lands were good, and the water was
sufficient, and that the Indians desired missions and were there
voluntarily. Barrio replied that as it was the common opinion
in Mexico that the friars wished to control everything, Fray
Mariano had better make an official report on those points.
Nevertheless, at the friar's request, Barrio assembled the Indians
in the presence of the two missionaries and other Spaniards, and
through an interpreter questioned them about their desires regarding missions. Fray Mariano claimed a year later that,
although he did not know what Barrio wrote in his *diligencias*,
as they were not shown to him, yet the answers were all favorable, some of them emphatically so; that Barrio found no fault
with the site; and even showed his approval of it by his request
that Fray Mariano should supplement the military force with
mission Indians from San Antonio.[32]

On the basis of this investigation Governor Barrio wrote the
auditor an adverse report.[33] Father Ganzábal, who was in
Mexico fighting for the success of the missions, saw the document and was greatly alarmed by it. He was already sick at
heart over the endless host of opponents, and now a new one had
arisen. "The person who has caused the greatest backset and
damage," he wrote to Fray Mariano on January 22, 1749, "is
Governor Barrio; for this person, when he went in, bore secret

---

[32] Our knowledge of the investigation comes from a statement made
by Father Mariano a year or more after the event (*Escrito presentado
al Govr. Dⁿ. Pedro del Varrio sobre Sⁿ. Xavier, 1749.* K, leg. 19, no. 79).
Barrio did not wish the missionaries present at the examination, but the
other Spaniards urged it. Several Indians had told Fray Mariano and
Fray Cayetano that some Spaniards had told them that when the governor should ask them if they desired missions they must say, No. But
Fray Mariano at the time attributed it to the desire of the soldiers to
escape from the place. Later he suspected another cause. (*Ibid.*).

[33] One of his reports was dated July 20, 1748. I cannot say whether
or not this was the main one. Morfi, Bk. 8, paragraph 27, discusses this
report. On July 25 he wrote a *consulta* in which he set forth the difficulty of supplying the detachment from Adaes for San Xavier—they had
to be supplied by the governor—and suggested that the San Xavier missions look for aid rather to San Antonio than to Los Adaes. Morfi, Bk.
8, paragraph 29.

orders to inspect San Xavier, and after such an investigation as your Reverence certifies that he made, he wrote to the Señor *auditor* a letter that deserves to be consigned to the flames, for it was entirely hostile to the new foundations.'' The report stated, Father Ganzábal continued, that the land at San Xavier was rough and unsuited to cultivation; that the river was not permanent and irrigation facilities not good; that the Indians, in the investigation, had said that they did not desire missions, but wished to live like the Tejas; that when the San Xavier missions should become a fact, he would give his head, ''and, finally, a multitude of other absurdities.''

After a hard fight Father Ganzábal secured a new despatch, dated January 10, 1749, and a *carta órden*, addressed to Father Mariano, requiring a report on the situation at San Xavier.[34] In recounting the matter to Fray Mariano on January 22, Ganzábal exhorted him to give the lie to all these false reports by counter testimony, taken without the governor's presence. ''And with this alone, with the rest which the enclosed certified copy [of the order] requires, and whatever else your judgment tells you should be sent, your Reverence will attain the end which we all desire; and then we shall not be discredited and without means for other conquests, but, on the contrary, our opponents will be overthrown.''[35]

In the same communication Father Ganzábal revealed the state of his mind over the whole situation. He had returned the day before from Mexico where he had been struggling for eight months, achieving nothing but animosities, broken health, and the order for another report.

6. *The founding of Mission San Ildefonso, February, 1749.* —The appeal of Father Ganzábal arrived at a most opportune

---

[34] The dates are learned from *Dictamen del Auditor de Guerra.*

[35] *Carta del P. Galzaval*, January 22, 1749. The *Erecion* states that Barrio reported the site unfit. Father Mariano summarizes what Ganzábal wrote him. *Escrito presentado al Govr.*

time, for it found the missionaries at San Xavier in the midst
of establishing the second and third missions. Because of the
illness of Father Mariano, the founding of them had fallen to
Father Santa Ana. As he had predicted, it was December before
the supplies arrived at San Antonio. With them he proceeded
to the San Xavier, reaching the place on December 27.[36] There
were now nine missionaries on the ground,[37] and prospects looked
bright.

The time between December 27 and February 25, Santa Ana
and the missionaries spent in founding the second mission,[38]
which they placed down the river, near the mouth of Brushy
Creek, and which was given the name of San Ildefonso. Since
adverse reports had been made with respect to the suitability
of the site, Father Santa Ana, immediately on arriving, took
testimony of the soldiers and missionaries who had lived on the
San Xavier during the dry season, as to the volume of water
during the drought, and then proceeded to explore the river himself, up to Apache Pass. Though the soldiers and missionaries
agreed that the water supply was plentiful, when Father Santa
Ana came to request them to swear to the statement they refused
to do so, from which he suspected that they had sworn to the contrary for their officials.[39]

Santa Ana's statements as to what he did in respect to the
distribution of the tribes among the different missions is of high-

---

[36] Santa Ana to the viceroy, March 10, 1749, in *Dictamen del Auditor,*
''Llegando a esta pais de Sⁿ. Javier al mismo tiempo, que los avios, y
fue el dia 27 de Diz^re. del año pasado.''

[37] This is not mere inference; Father Santa Ana states the fact. *Ibid.,*
12. He does not state that there were not more than nine.

[38] ''En confianza de dha. dilijensia, y aver entrado en diz^re. los avios,
a las Misiones de Sⁿ. Antº. y Sⁿ. Javier, en 27 de dho mes, no se pudieron
asertar las tres conversiones tan prontas como la deseava, y mas no
teniendo dia asentado asta el dia 25 de fro; en que se conocio alguna
serenidad, y todo efectuo.'' (Report to the viceroy, March 10, 1749, in
Dictamen del Auditor de Geurra). In the same report he twice says that
he was just finishing the founding of this mission on February 25 when
a despatch reached him.

[39] *Dictamen del Auditor de Guerra.*

est value for the ethnology of some of the tribes and for specific
information regarding mission beginnings. Following the prescribed practice, not always observed, he separated the various
bands on the basis of racial and linguistic affiliation. At the
mission of San Francisco Xavier he left the Mayeye, Hierbipiame, and Yojuane, all related to and allied with the Tancahue
(Tonkawa), a few of whom were there also. Noting that the
Bidai, Deadose, and Orcoquiza were camping together, that they
spoke the same language, and were closely intermingled by marriage, he took them to a site about three quarters of a league
(he says about a league, but a later survey called it three quarters) down the river from the San Francisco Xavier mission and
founded for them that of San Ildefonso, which was nearly completed on February 25.[40]

When he reported the result of his work on March 10, there
were at the mission of San Francisco Xavier fifty-nine Mayeye,
seventy Hierbipiame, and eighty Yojuane, a total of two hundred
thirteen persons; and at the San Ildefonso there were sixty-five
families, or two hundred and two persons, comprising fifty-nine
Orcoquiza, eighty-eight Bidai, and fifty-five Deadose.[41]

---

[40] "I observed that among the Indians who were at San Xavier and
who wished to enter in the missions there were some Horcoquisas Indians
who camped among the Vidais and Deadoses; that the language of these
and the Horcoquisas was the same; and finally, that many Orcoquisas
women were married to the Vidais and Deadoces, and that the women
of these nations [have] relations with the Horcoquisas Indians (*Indios*).
Accordingly, as soon as I began the foundation of the mission of San
Yldefonso, which is distant from the already founded San Xavier about
a league, going down to the east, I decided that all of the souls of the
three said Nations should go to said new foundation of San Yldefonso
which they have done." *Ibid.*, p. 9.

[41] "There are in it [San Ildefonso] 65 families; of the Orcoquisa
nation, 21 families, which, with men, women and children comprise the
number of 58 souls, including their captain, who is the oldest of all,
being about 69 years old; of the Vidais nation there are 26 families,
which include 26 men, 32 women, and 30 boys and girls, making all together 80 persons, in which are included eight old women. Of the nation
of the Deadoses there are 18 families, composed of 18 men, 21 women,
16 boys and girls. In all 65 persons, and of the three nations the number
of persons with which this mission was founded appears to be 199."
Ibid., 10.

The president reported that of the Tonkawa alone he might proceed to the founding of the third mission, but concluded that since they were related to and allied with the Indians of the San Xavier mission, they might be reduced there, leaving the third establishment to be located above the first, for the Coco and their allies from the coast.

In regard to the outlook Santa Ana was hopeful. If what Orobio had said was true, the Orcoquiza alone would supply three missions; since the Coco had mastered the former tribes, they must have been at least as numerous; while the mission of San Francisco Xavier would yield nothing to the others in point of numbers. "And thus there can be no doubt of the copious fruit which is hoped for in the three missions of the River of San Xavier, and on this score everything that the Father Preacher Fr. Mariano de los Dolores has written to the Superior tribunal is confirmed." Of the water supply there was no doubt; irrigation would be easier even than at San Antonio; and as to the fertility of the soil, it would support not only three missions but all the Indians of the whole province of Texas and as many Spaniards besides. The climate was good and the natural fruits of the country bountiful and useful. One drawback, however, was the fact that the soldiers did not have with them their families, for there were only two women at the post, a situation which would have a very bad effect on the Indians. Finally, a regular presidio was needed.[42]

7. *Desertion of the Cocos and the founding of Mission Candelaria, 1749.*—In the midst of their labors the missionaries were dismayed by the desertion of the Coco Indians to their native haunts. The reason given was the bad conduct of the garrison. They were in ill humor through bad fare and hardship, "and knowing that anything they could do to contribute to

---

[42] *Dictamen del Auditor de Guerra.*

the ruin of these missions gave pleasure to their captains, they treated the Indians with excessive insolence, inflicting upon them serious and continued extortions, the supplications of the religious not being sufficient to restrain them.'' Under these circumstances the Coco, who were being maintained at San Ildefonso until their mission of Candelaria should be completed, deserted early in 1749 and fled to their own country.

This was a heavy blow to the missionaries, who feared that the fact of the desertion would be used by their opponents as a weapon against them, and that the example of the Coco would be followed by the other tribes. But Father Santa Ana did not give up in defeat; on the contrary, he set out alone in pursuit of the Indians, in spite of the personal danger presaged by soldiers and neophytes.

After extreme fatigues Father Santa Ana succeeded in finding the Coco, in their haunts between the Colorado and the Brazos. At the time the tribe was suffering from measles and smallpox. The friar succeeded in his errand, and it was agreed that those not yet infected should accompany him, the others following when they had recovered. He took back with him eighty-two persons and with them as a nucleus founded the mission of Nuestra Señora de la Candelaria. The Coco chief sent three of his sons to Mission Valero to learn the Spanish language, and later they became interpreters for the missionaries.[43]

On April 14, Fray Mariano reported from San Antonio to Father Ganzábal that he had news that the third mission had been founded of Coco, Tusos (Tups) and other Indians. Even the Jaraname wished to enter it, he said.[44] On August 11th the new guardian, Castellanos, wrote a long memorial to the viceroy reporting the evidence that the third mission had been established, and asked for the payment of $5083.50 spent by Fray

---

[43] I have these details from Morfi, Bk. VIII, paragraphs 30–33.

[44] Memorial by the guardian, Fr. Francisco Xavier Castellanos, July. 1749. Presented August 11, 1749.

Mariano in 1748 before the arrival of the funds; for $2700 for the maintenance of three missionaries at San Xavier during the whole of 1746–1747; and for the erection of the hospice. This, he said, should be established at San Antonio, and would cost about $14,000.00 besides running expenses. He closed by reiterating the need of a presidio.[45]

8. *Mission progress.*—We get some very intimate details of conditions at San Xavier just after the establishment of the second and third missions through the reports of an inspection made of them in May, 1749, by Governor Barrio. The governor counted in Mission San Ildefonso forty-six adult men, forty-eight women and thirty-one children; in Mission San Francisco Xavier there were fifty men, thirty-three women, and thirty-seven children; in Candelaria, twenty-four men, twenty-five women and twenty-two children, a total of three hundred and twenty-two persons. Besides these, some were absent with permission hunting buffalo and eating wild fruit in the woods.[46] The missionaries were still complaining that the lack of supplies was such that they had to turn away numerous Indians who would be glad to enter the missions, "for neither God, the King, nor reason permits the Indians to be congregated merely to be killed by hunger and to be made to work. And thus we have in the missions only those whom we can support well."

At this time Fray Mariano wrote; in the course of a dispute with the governor, that "In all the missions the Indians say prayers morning and afternoon. They live congregated in pueblos, and labor insofar as their wildness permits, making their fences and clearing their corn patches. In Texas (i.e., eastern Texas) they are not congregated, much less do they say prayers. At the same time, they are in the missions without your lord-

---

[45] Castellanos, Memorial, presented August 11.

[46] Morfi, Bk. 8, paragraph 56. This shows that Mission Candelaria was founded by May, 1749, and that Músquiz was wrong in his report on this point, wherein he says it was founded in July.

ship having ordered them called or the soldiers bringing them. Therefore, it is because they desire it. It is thus manifest that these missions are a fact, and that the Indians do not live like the Texas up to the present.''[47]

Sometime before this the lands of the river had been inspected with a view to opening irrigating ditches. This had been done by Fathers Mariano and Pedro Ysasmendi, for, as Fray Mariano wrote, ''Of all there are in the province, we alone understand [surveying] both theoretically and practically.''[48]

The garrison which had been taken there in March, 1748, was now under a *cavo* named Phelipe de Sierra, from whom Governor Barrio withheld even the right of *jurisdicción ordinario*. It was not up to its full quota of thirty men, for during much of the past year from two to four of the seventeen assigned from Los Adaes had been lacking.

In the previous May Barrio, during his first visit, had ordered the families of the soldiers sent away, perhaps on account of the Apache hostilities. The order had been carried out, and during the whole year the soldiers had been without the comforts of family life, at which they complained, especially since it increased their labor, for, ''having no one to prepare a mouthful for them, they were obliged to do it themselves, their ordinary food being maize, boiled and toasted.''[49] The Indians, too, Fray Mariano complained, were displeased, since they concluded that with the families there, the Spaniards would better defend the place against the Apaches, which was one of the cardinal points to be considered. Documents of a later date show that, according to the usual custom in founding new missions, Christianized Indians from the San Antonio missions were taken to San Xavier to serve as teachers and interpreters. Among them were Sayopines, Cocos, Pajauaches, and Orejones.

---

[47] *Escrito presentado al Govr. Dn. Pedro del Varrio sobre Sn. Xavier.* 1749.

[48] *Ibid.*

[49] *Varios papeles, de Tejas,* pp. 15–17.

9. A New trail to Los Adaes.—The founding of the missions on the San Xavier led to the opening of a new road to Los Adaes, crossing the San Xavier, the San Andrés, and the Brazos. It is well known that in 1721 the Marqués de Aguayo crossed the San Xavier and continued north to the region of Waco. Father Santa Ana, writing in 1752, stated that since 1722 no one had crossed the San Xavier on the way to Adaes, because of the murder of Father Pita between that stream and the Brazos. He adds that the new route was opened in 1748, and that Governor Barrio followed it when he went from the San Xavier missions to eastern Texas.[50]

---

[50] *Consulta* of Fr. Benito Fernández de Santa Ana, on or before July 5, 1752, in *Test. de los Autos fhos Sre. la erecion del Presidio de Sⁿ. Xavier.* A. G. I.

THE GARRISON INCREASED: DIFFICULTIES WITH GOVERNOR BARRIO

1. Altamira convinced.—Father Ganzábal's appeal from Querétaro, made in January, for help to counteract the hostile report by Barrio, was answered by Father Santa Ana's report dated March 10 and Fray Mariano's dated at San Antonio, March 13. With these documents went a report of a survey of the site by the father conductor of supplies.[1] In his communication Father Santa Ana defended his college for delays; recounted in full what had been done, as related in the previous chapter; reported the second mission already founded and the third about to be established; stated that the river and the lands had been surveyed and found ample; and reiterated the need of a presidio. In his letter Fray Mariano told of his illness, as explaining why he was not at San Xavier, and echoed the appeal for a presidio.[2]

These documents must have been sent in great haste, for before the end of March they had reached Querétaro and the guardian had transmitted them to Altamira, as the best evidence of "the honesty of our pretension, and that we have no other interest than the honor and glory of God, the increase of the Catholic Faith, and the welfare of souls who anxiously desire to drink the healthful waters of baptism." In his letter the guardian emphasized the dissatisfaction of all the missionaries, in both the old and the new missions. "I fear they may fail in

---

[1] The first two documents are in *Dictamen del Auditor de Guerra.* I have not seen the report of the survey.

[2] Santa Ana to the viceroy, March 10, 1749; Fray Mariano to the viceroy, March 13, 1749. More of their contents is given in connection with the founding of the second and third missions.

patience," he said, "some being ill, others asking to retire, as
is already the case with the most important missionaries, among
them being Fray Mariano de los Dolores." He appealed elo-
quently to Altamira to "give special attention to San Xavier,
certain that it will be the most pleasing [mission] of these times,
. . . I trust in God that your Lordship will perfect the work
begun for the welfare and consolation of so many souls, since
we have been groaning under the tyrant hand of such unjust
opposition, whose malice has so greatly indisposed your Lordship's good will and cooled your good wishes, in the perplexity
of so many and various reports and opinions designed to obscure
and confuse what is patent and clear."[3]

Altamira was now convinced that regarding the site the missionaries were right and the governor wrong. In his *dictamen*
given April 23, 1749, he stated that, although the reports of
Fathers Santa Ana and Mariano were irregular in form, not
having been duly authenticated by the governor or the captain
at Bahía, as had been ordered, nevertheless "it would be temerity
to doubt the good condition, state, and progress of said establishment, there being already planted the mission of San Xavier and
that of San Ildefonso a league from the first; or that by now is
also founded that of Nuestra Señora de la Candelaria, another
league from the first mission of San Xavier, in the opposite
direction." The reports showed that even during the drought
of the past year the water was plentiful; that the San Andrés
River,[4] two leagues away, was even larger and better, having
lands enough for all the Indians of Texas, and better irrigating
facilities than were possessed by even the San Antonio River. It
was true, moreover, as Father Santa Ana had said, that Governor
Barrio was ill disposed toward the new missions, resenting the
detachment of his soldiers, who had also become infected with

---

[3] *Copia de una Carta del P. Guard^n. al S aud^r. año de 1749.* It is
labeled "March, 1749."

[4] Little River.

the hostile feeling—reasons why the proper procedure at San Xavier had been impossible.

2. *A plan for increasing the garrison.*—Being thus fully convinced of the justice of the cause of the missionaries, Altamira proceeded to make recommendations in their favor. They should be thanked for their zeal, and assured that they would be assisted in their important work, "for your Excellency cannot doubt but that these reverend fathers, with the same most commendable zeal and laudable efficiency as heretofore, will completely dissipate the opinions hostile to the establishment of these missions."

Next, he urged that measures should be taken to establish a regular presidio of fifty soldiers at San Xavier. But as this would take some time, he recommended that meanwhile the temporary garrison be increased to forty-eight men, and that provision be made for securing citizen settlers for the place. To provide the forty-eight soldiers, he proposed a roundabout procedure which is quite typical, and illustrates the slender means available for the northern frontier of New Spain. The thirty men from Adaes and Bahía, he recommended, should be retained. To provide the additional eighteen he suggested that four soldiers from Monclova and ten from Sacramento be sent to San Juan Bautista to serve; that from the last-named garrison sixteen men be sent to Béxar; while from Béxar eighteen should be sent to San Xavier, to remain till further orders should be received, "assisting very particularly the reverend missionary fathers and aiding them in the instruction and direction of those Indian neophytes." In each case the men were to continue to draw their pay and support from their regular headquarters. To provide officers he recommended that Captain Urrutia, of San Antonio, should appoint a lieutenant and an *alférez* to command the entire detachment at San Xavier, unless there were already there officers of like rank and longer tenure. In case of doubt, the appointment should be referred to the governor of Texas. With the letter of thanks to Father Santa Ana should go a charge to admonish the soldiers to live uprightly, aid with the neophytes, defend them against the enemy, and prepare a site for a new presidio.

3. *A plan for securing settlers.*—Besides recommending an increase of the temporary garrison, Altamira urged sending citizen settlers to San Xavier. As a beginning, the soldiers already there should be ordered to take their families, and the governor and captain required promptly to assist them in doing so. In addition, the captain and missionaries at Béxar should be urged to solicit at the villa and the presidio settlers for San Xavier, promising them ample lands, water rights, the privileges of first settlers and, if necessary, a hundred pesos per family from the royal treasury, to assist them in going and settling, on condition of remaining five years, building adobe houses, and cultivating the soil.

The matter was now referred to the fiscal. This official approved Altamira's plan for increasing the temporary garrison and for the presidio; but he opposed enlisting and subsidizing citizen settlers, on the grounds both of expense and of the impolity of associating Spaniards with neophytes.[5]

On July 7 the *auditor* made a sarcastic reply to the fiscal's objections. That officer was willing, he said, to spend twenty thousand pesos a year on a presidio for San Xavier, but he hesitated to increase the amount by six hundred pesos a year, at the most, for settlers.[6] The fiscal feared the evil example of the citizen settlers upon the Indians; he therefore must think that the soldiers, whom he approved sending, were ''of angelic nature and quality, unlike Spaniards and people of other classes.''

---

[5] The fiscal's opinion has not been seen by the present writer, but is inferred from the summary of it in Altamira's reply to it.

[6] He stated that the *vecinos* (heads of families) at San Fernando and Béxar would not exceed sixty (not counting the presidials, I suppose), and that at most he would not expect more than four or six volunteers.

At this point Altamira put on record an official opinion throwing much light on the whole matter of Spanish frontier garrisons. As it comes from one of the ablest of New Spain's officials, it is of great weight. "It is certain," he said, "that in spite of the greatest care in the military discipline, the books are full of the irregularities of soldiers; and for the presidios of these frontiers are found only the least temperate Spaniards and non-Spaniards, who, in order not to work, or for worse reasons, seek such asylums; and yet they are the apostles well received, desired, and acclaimed for the edification, instruction, and good example of the tender plants recently converted from heathen Indians.

"Christianity would cease in this New Spain today if from the beginning the Indians had not been mixed with or in sight of Spaniards and *gente de razon,* at whose example they should become docile, subject themselves to instruction, and apply themselves to labor and commerce. They will lack everything without Spaniards and *gente de razon;* for in their natural velleities, inquietude, and uprisings, only respect for the Spaniards and *gente de razon* restrains them; and experience has taught . . . that without Spaniards or *gente de razon* it is impossible to trust the Indians in anything, as is shown by the provinces of Sinaloa, Nuevo Mexico, Nueva Vizcaia, Coahuila, Nayarit, and Texas; for in this New Spain within ten years or less the missions became *doctrinas* and curacies, whereas in those provinces some missions are over one hundred and sixty years old, and yet never, according to their present state, will cease." [7]

On the same day, July 7, the viceroy approved the *auditor's* plan in all respects, and on the ninth issued to the missionaries, the governor, and the captain at Bahía, the corresponding orders. [8]

---

[7] *Parecer de el Sor. Auditor para la fundacion de Sn. Xavier,* April 23 and July 7.

[8] *Ibid.,* also *Varios papeles, de Tejas,* p. 17.

4. A presidio promised.—To Father Santa Ana the viceroy wrote acknowledging the report of March 10, admitting the validity of his reasons for not having reported earlier, thanking him warmly for his zeal and fervor in so important a work, reporting what had been done to increase the temporary garrison and to provide settlers, and assuring him of a presidio. "As your Reverence will see by the same certified copy, steps will be taken with all celerity for the establishment of the presidio of fifty soldiers, but it will be necessary to solemnize these steps with *juntas de hacienda y guerra.*" Santa Ana and the officers were instructed to admonish the soldiers, among other things, "to select the most appropriate location for the new presidio which is to be founded." On the same day the viceroy wrote a similar but briefer letter to Fray Mariano.[9] Thus, the decree of July 7 was a virtual promise of a presidio. But its establishment was still a long distance in the future, for between the promise and its fulfillment the usual slow routine of administrative procedure had to be passed through.

5. New reports from Governor Barrio.—In May, 1749, Governor Barrio went on his own authority to San Xavier to make another inspection. While there he was made to feel the wrath of Father Mariano. Before he left San Antonio, President Santa Ana denied his right to make the inspection,[10] and immediately on his arrival at San Xavier Fray Mariano renewed the protest. It charged Barrio with having refused an escort in May, 1748; with having made false reports in Mexico; with having expelled the families of the soldiers, and with excluding them

---

[9] The viceroy to Santa Ana and to Fray Mariano, July 9, 1749. Both were sent to Fray Mariano to be forwarded to Santa Ana at San Xavier. On July 9, 1751, they were transmitted to the college by Fray Mariano, from San Antonio.

[10] Unfortunately, the copy of the document on which I here rely, in the Santa Cruz archive, is not dated, as was the case with many of the documents there. Consequently I cannot fix the date of this visit. Since Santa Ana had known of Barrio's plan, it is quite possible that the visit was made after Barrio had been in Béxar in August and September.

during the entire subsequent year; with failure to provide two and sometimes four of the seventeen soldiers due from his presidio; with failure to appoint a commander of the guard, as his orders required;[11] with denying the corporal in charge the right of ordinary jurisdiction; and with anger because in a certain emergency a *cavo* had been appointed at San Antonio, without his authority, to conduct supplies. Alluding to the reports made by Barrio in Mexico, Fray Mariano declared that, as could be seen by the governor, the Indians were congregated and in regular attendance at religious services—evidence that they did not ''wish to live like the Tejas;'' and that the lands were good and water plentiful, as had been proved by the survey made in the present year by himself and Father Ysasmendi. He charged the opposition on the part of the soldiers to a mere desire to escape from a disagreeable post, and on the part of their officers to a desire to recover their detached soldiers.

Barrio having ordered the Indians assembled for counting, Fray Mariano repeated the protest in his president's name, declaring null and void whatever investigation Barrio might make regarding lands, water, or Indians. Though he obeyed the order to assemble the Indians, he did so under protest, and insisted that Barrio must count not only those present, but also all those who were with permission hunting buffalo or wild fruits, and those who had been turned away for lack of supplies.[12]

On August 2 the governor sent to the viceroy a report of his visit to San Xavier. It arrived too late to be considered in the *junta* of July 7, which dealt with increasing the garrison, but it entered into the deliberations regarding a presidio. Barrio reported that several times the principal personages at San Xavier had told him that in that region there were neither lands, nor

---

[11] It was in charge of a *cavo* named Phelipe de Sierra.

[12] *Escrito presentado al Govr. D^n. Pedro del Varrio sobre S^n. Xavier,* 1749. The exact date is not given, but it was clearly before August 31, when Barrio appointed a commander for the garrison.

water, nor Indians suitable for a mission, and that as he had heard that it was being planned to erect a presidio at the expense of the royal treasury, he had proceeded to investigate the site, as was his duty. According to his statement, he cited the missionaries to the inspection, but they obstinately refused, without giving their reasons for doing so. Consequently the investigation was witnessed by the military authorities only. The inspection was at the governor's instigation, and he forwarded the report at his own expense "for whatever value it might be to the royal service."[13]

6. *An unwelcome commander.*—The appointment of a commander for the enlarged garrison gave a new opportunity for the hostility between Governor Barrio and Fray Mariano to manifest itself.[14] It will be remembered that provision had been made that Captain Urrutia should appoint a lieutenant and an *alférez* for the enlarged garrison, unless there were already there officers of equal rank and longer service, or unless there was doubt, in which case the governor was to decide the matter. On August 28, 1749, the new detachment of sixteen soldiers from San Juan Bautista arrived at Béxar, Governor Barrio being there at the time. Without consulting Barrio, Urrutia appointed as lieutenant, Diego Ramón, and as *alférez*, Ascencio Rasso. To provide them with salaries, he removed two soldiers. Barrio was angry because his advice had not been asked; and Urrutia, taken to task, was haughty. Thereupon Barrio proceeded to restore the displaced soldiers and to appoint as officers of the garrison Lieutenant Juan Galván, who had been at San Xavier in 1748, and Pedro de Sierra, *alférez* at Adaes, who was then at Béxar to escort the new detachment to San Xavier.

---

13 Morfi, *Memorias*, Bk. 8, paragraph 34.

14 On the authority of the viceroy's communication of July 9, Fray Mariano, in two petitions, demanded that Governor Barrio should aid the families of the detachment of Los Adaes to go to San Xavier. The dates are not given, but presumably the first of them was written soon after the viceroy's despatch was received.

Barrio claimed that he saw Father Mariano's hand in Urrutia's appointments. He said that Ramón was a mulatto who, with his descendants, had been degraded for offences committed by Ramón while he was an officer at Bahía. Rasso was brother and companion of a famous thief. Neither could read, and the lieutenant could write only "under the direction and counsel of the Rev. Father Fray Mariano de los Dolores."[15]

Whatever his part in their appointment, Fray Mariano greatly resented the removal of Ramón and Rasso and the appointment of Galván, and he accordingly raised objections.[16] He repeated his protest made at San Xavier, for, said he, to admit as commander there a subordinate of Barrio, would be to put an end to the prosperity of the settlement. He prayed, therefore, that the appointment of Ramón and Rasso might stand.[17]

Against this interference Barrio complained to the viceroy, and gave his view of its origin. In reporting the matter on September 11, he appealed for aid to "restrain the boldness and proud spirit of Father Mariano, who with no other reason than because I despised his gifts, designed to keep me from reporting to your Excellency regarding the sterility and unfruitfulness of the post of San Xavier, has tried by the worst of methods to impede the administration of justice, trying by illegal methods to have me confirm the two officers whom this captain had appointed at his direction in order that he might continue, through neither of them knowing how to read, with his false reports and certifications."[18] As evidence of the missionary's importunities Barrio enclosed two *escritos* which Fray Mariano had presented to him.

In spite of the emphatic discredit with which Altamira and the viceroy had received his former report, Barrio, in the same

---

[15] *Ynforme qᵉ hizo Dⁿ. Pedro del Varrio Govʳ. el año de 1749* (September 11).

[16] Evidently before September 11, when Barrio reported to the viceroy.

[17] Fray Mariano to Barrio.

[18] *Ynforme qᵉ. hizo Dⁿ. Pedro del Varrio Gobʳ. el año de 1749* (September 11).

letter of September 11, made bold to open again the question of the suitability of the site at San Xavier. His opposition now took a new form. His suggestion was that the actual neophytes at San Xavier (the Mayeye, Hierbipiame, Yojuane, and Deadose —the Bidai and Coco Indians he regarded as unstable) be moved to the San Marcos River, which he had examined with the express purpose in view and had found satisfactory in every respect. Barrio was a betting man. He had once wagered his head that missions would never succeed at San Xavier. Now, as evidence of his good faith, he offered to provide irrigation facilities on the San Marcos in one year, without remuneration, whereas, on the other hand, if they should be provided successfully at San Xavier, he would willingly lose two thousand pesos from his salary.[19]

Notwithstanding Fray Mariano's objection, Barrio sent Galván to San Xavier. Thereupon Fray Mariano registered another protest. Relying on the orders that the soldiers sent there should be of good character, he complained that in San Xavier everything had been done contrary to the king's orders, particularly since Galván's arrival. "According to the evidence, he is doing his best to ruin and annihilate the new settlement, or at least to make the Indians unmanageable and without respect for the fathers." He therefore begged Barrio to recall Galván and appoint to the command Diego Ramón, or some person "not of your alliance."[20]

7. Santa Ana in Mexico; Barrio discredited.—In order to offset the hostile reports of Barrio, as well as to promote his plans for an Apache mission, President Santa Ana set out for Mexico. When he reached San Juan Bautista he received the favorable despatch of July 9. He continued on his way, how-

---

[19] *Ynforme,* September 11, 1749.

[20] *Varios papeles de Tejas que parece son posteriores al año 1746.* It is clear that the date is after September 11, and the inference is that it was after 1749.

ever, and on November 11 presented a memorial in which he alleged the inspection by Barrio to be defective, the witnesses not being competent and the missionaries not being present. Moreover, he charged Barrio with bribery.[21]

Barrio's opposition was now entirely discredited in Mexico, where all had been favorable to the missionaries since April. On January 7, 1750, Dr. Andreu gave his opinion. He recited that, notwithstanding the fact that after long deliberations the government had been convinced of the desirability of the missions and of the suitability of the site, and that the missions had been established, a temporary garrison provided, and a presidio resolved upon, yet "the governor now stirs up the matter of the unsuitability of these missions." Barrio, however, the fiscal maintained, had not furnished sufficient evidence to warrant suppressing the missions. His report had been made without authority, without due formality, and without the presence of the friars; moreover, the witnesses contradicted themselves, and some of the testimony was untruthful; indeed the report itself proved the sufficiency of the water and the presence of three hundred and sixty-seven neophytes at the missions. Finally, in view of the disinterested zeal of the missionaries, "it is incredible that they should attempt to locate missions in a place where the reduction of the Indians would be most difficult and most troublesome to their apostolic institute. . . . Withal, it appears that this matter is settled without any sort of doubt." Nevertheless, before authorizing a new presidio, he deemed it wise to have another inspection of the site made by some suitable person not of Barrio's jurisdiction and without that officer's interference.[22]

Three weeks later the Marqués de Altamira, the *auditor*, gave his opinion, in which he fully concurred with that of Andreu. The investigation made by Barrio he characterized as "the

---

21 Morfi, Bk. 8, paragraphs 49, 57; Bk. 9, paragraph 29.

22 *Dictamen fiscal*, January 7, 1750, quoted in full by Morfi, Bk. 8, paragraphs 50–60.

exaggerated, hostile, and gratuitous proceedings enacted by the governor of that desert and remote province.'' Altamira confessed that for more than two years he himself had opposed the San Xavier missions, but as they had been established ''with reasonable probability of their permanence'' he had yielded. The principal doubt in his mind now arose from Fray Mariano's failure to report, in a letter of December 6, whether the Indians who had deserted the mission of San Ildefonso in October had returned, as they had promised to do before November 9.

Altamira approved Dr. Andreu's recommendation of a new investigation before establishing the presidio. But who was to make it? For someone of the court of Mexico to go would be too expensive, while between the capital and San Xavier there was no competent person, ''as much for lack of means as because the *auditor* assumes that the governor of Texas must be suspicious of the governors of the Kingdoms of León and Cohaguila, on account of other constant incidents; and the same is true of the captain of the presidio of San Juan Bautista del Rio Grande.'' All things considered, he could think of no more suitable person than Lieutenant Don José de Eca y Músquiz of the presidio of Sacramento, whom he had met in Mexico City and whom he thought well of. To Músquiz there might be assigned, in addition to his own salary, the pay of a soldier who had been temporarily dismissed from Los Adaes, and thus no expense would be involved. If this choice of Músquiz were to be approved by the viceroy, he should be put in charge of the San Xavier garrison, and as *juez comisionado* instructed to measure most thoroughly and carefully the lands and water of the San Xavier River, wherever he should think it best or the missionaries request; to explore the San Andrés River; to make a census of the Indians of the mission, and to do anything else necessary for the purposes in view.[23]

---

[23] *Dictamen* of Altamira, quoted in full by Morfi, bk. 8, paragraphs 61–70.

8. A new survey ordered, and then suspended.—Complying with the opinions of Andreu and Altamira, on February 3 the viceroy issued ·a commission to Músquiz. In addition to the duties recommended by Altamira, he was to examine the San Marcos River. This is evidence that Barrio's last report had carried weight, in spite of the cavalier treatment which it had received.

Father Santa Ana, who was still in Mexico, hearing of the order, presented an *escrito,* or memorial, in which among other things he maintained that the survey would merely cause delay, and demanded that the proceedings should stop.

The opinions of Andreu and Altamira were apparently the occasion also of an appeal by Father Santa Ana for help from Texas, for on April 12, just about the time after March 24 for a rapid express to reach San Xavier, Father Mariano, writing from mission San Ildefonso, appealed to Lieutenant Galván. It is possible, however, that the appeal was made by Father Santa Ana as soon as Barrio's report of September 11 was received in Mexico. "I have received letters from the outside," Fray Mariano wrote, "in which they tell me of some new turns which have taken place regarding these missions of San Xavier." As he was on the point of going to San Antonio to make a full report to the viceroy, he desired Galván's opinion on certain matters. The fear now was that an attempt would be made to move the missions to the San Marcos River, and it is clear that it was Barrio's report of September 11 which was now causing the flurry, for the two main questions were raised by that document.

One of the points regarding which the court was in doubt, Fray Mariano said, was whether or not the Coco tribe could be subdued. It was plain enough that they could, he continued, for they were even now remaining quietly in the missions. Indeed, the Coco were the most docile and teachable of all the tribes there. The Bidai were a little bold because of their plentiful supply of firearms, and they had not given up their *mitotes* and other native customs; but the reason was that they had not been properly subjected, "for it is impossible to the missionaries alone without the favor of the king's agents," that is, the soldiers.

Another point being debated at the court was whether or not the San Marcos River was better than the San Xavier. That it was better he admitted, and that perhaps much might have been gained had the missions been founded there in the first place, or should they be moved thither now. Nevertheless, the San Xavier had ample lands and water—superior indeed to those at San Antonio. With a presidio to assist, the irrigation ditches might have been opened in three or four months, though they would never be finished unless the Indians could be subjected. Moreover, it must be remembered that San Xavier was a gateway for all the Texas tribes; that they had selected this place when they promised to receive Christianity; and that perhaps they would not consent to move to the San Marcos. The missionaries would of course go if the viceroy so ordered, but on condition that the governor be obliged to move the neophytes and keep them there, and that the soldiers be under obligation to keep the missions supplied with heathen. Indeed, the missionaries would be quite content to confine their labors to spiritual guidance, leaving it to the king's agents to subject and civilize the Indians, and make of them loyal subjects.[24] The nature of Lieutenant Galván's reply and of Fray Mariano's report, or the effect they had in Mexico, has not been ascertained by the present writer.

The decision at the court, however, did not await news from the frontier. Father Santa Ana's report was referred to the fiscal and the *auditor*, who gave opinions on March 14 and 24. Conforming with their advice, on April 8 the viceroy issued a

---

[24] Fray Mariano to Galván, April 12, 1750, *Ynforme del the. Galvan sobre Sn. Xavier y carta escrito al dho el año de 1750.* The *Ynforme* is not present.

despatch in which he maintained that Father Santa Ana had given no good reason why the investigation should not be made, especially since meanwhile the missions were to go on without change, and since the purpose of the investigation was to give them greater stability and to set at rest the doubts which had beset the foundation from the beginning. Yet, in view of the fears expressed by Father Santa Ana that the investigation could not be properly conducted during the term of Barrio, on account of his influence, and since Barrio was only *ad interim* governor and was soon to retire, the viceroy ordered the investigation suspended for the present. If Músquiz had begun the investigation regarding the missions he must stop at once, and report what he had done. He was, however, to take charge of the garrison and execute all his other commissions.[25]

---

[25] *Despacho para que no se continuaran las dilig^r del Rio de S^n. Xav^r. el q^e. no tuvo efecto,* April 8, 1750. Also Morfi, Bk 8, paragraph 75.

CHAPTER VI

MISSION PROGRESS AND PROBLEMS, 1749–1751

As Father Arricivita expressed it, it was no Adamic Paradise in which the missionaries worked at the San Xavier River.[1] What with the physical hardships of the task of opening a new agricultural settlement, the shortage of supplies, the slowness of the government in providing funds, the hostility of the governor, the insubordination and low morals of the soldiers, the hostility of the Apache, the fickleness and barbarous habits of the neophytes, the bad influence of neighboring tribes, and the horrors of an epidemic of smallpox, life was indeed anything but a pleasant dream. Morfi writes of this period, "Through the open persecution which oppressed them, the missions of San Xavier could make no progress. The reports of the governor, the frequent surveys of water and land, and the expressions with which he and his companions prophesied the short duration of that establishment, asserting that an order would soon arrive from Mexico to destroy it, or to move it to another site, added fear to the natural lukewarmness with which the Indians regarded work. Even the religious themselves were now doubtful of its permanency."[2]

1. Trouble with the soldiers.—Not the least of the tribulations of the missionaries was the unsatisfactory character of the garrison, and the soldiers, in turn, had their own share of grievances. The men of the garrison were poorly fed, miserably housed, far distant from their paymasters—since they were paid at their regular headquarters—and without their families. It is probably true, therefore, as charged, that they were desirous of escaping from a disagreeable post, and were not unwilling to

---

[1] Arricivita, *Crónica*, 328.
[2] Morfi, Bk. 8, paragraph 48.

assist in bringing about the suppression of the missions as a means of escape.

The garrison was improperly officered and ill disciplined. Until Galván arrived in the fall of 1749 it was under a mere corporal (Phelipe de Sierra) who, into the bargain, had been deprived by the governor of ordinary jurisdiction. From the fall of 1749 until Músquiz arrived in June, 1750, it was under Lieutenant Galván. There is no evidence that the families of the soldiers were restored or settlers provided until the end of 1751, with the coming of Captain Rábago. Indeed, up to that time the friars frequently demanded that previous orders to these ends be carried out.

Complaints of the conduct of the soldiers were loud and frequent. On July 5, 1749, Father Santa Ana wrote that, not content with maltreating the neophytes, the soldiers openly encouraged them in desertion. After Galván came it was complained that things were worse than before, and that Galván was doing his best to destroy the settlement, or at least to make the Indians unmanageable. In February, 1750, President Santa Ana wrote that the discipline of the garrison was so lax and the soldiers had become so familiar with the Indians that they even lived in the houses of the neophytes and assisted them in their daily tasks. In April Fray Mariano wrote that the Indians were living in insubordination and that the missionaries had not power to restrain them, since it was natural that the Indians, seeing the King's agents living without fear or respect, should resist the imposition of Christian customs upon them and the rooting out of their "diabolical" rites. By excessive coaxing on the part of the missionaries, he said, something was being accomplished; but by no amount of persuasion could they prevent the Indians from destroying the cornfields as soon as roasting ears were ready.[3]

---

[3] Morfi, Bk. 8, paragraph 48; *Varios Papeles;* p. 15; Fray Mariano to Galván, April 12, 1750.

In October Fray Mariano recited that the duties of the mission garrison had not been observed, "a reason which has caused the heathen to be living in the missions as if they were in the woods, since it is impossible for the fathers, unless they have respect for arms, to check their abominable rites or dispose them to the labor indispensable to the preservation of life. Therefore we have been caused excessive trouble; and even the very little which has been accomplished has been effected through the force of supplication, unaided by the least respect for the soldiery; and thus it is that up to the present the Indians have recognized no authority."[4]

2. *Mission San Ildefonso deserted, October, 1749.*—Whatever may have been the cause, it is certain that desertion by the neophytes was one of the evils which the missionaries suffered. On the night of October 23, 1749, at eight o'clock, a courier reached San Antonio with the news that San Ildefonso, the most populous of the three missions, had been abandoned; that one of the missionaries was gravely ill; that he had asked Lieutenant Galván for an escort to San Antonio, but that Galván had denied the request on the ground that he could spare no soldiers, since seventeen or eighteen of his men were already absent in service.

Immediately upon receipt of the news, Fray Mariano wrote to Governor Barrio, who was still in San Antonio, stating that on the next day he or some other friars must go to San Xavier to relieve the sick brother. Accordingly, he asked for an escort "suitable to our character and persons, bearing in mind what might befall us or the mules" of the packtrain, which was also to set out, and without escort.[5] The incident serves again to illustrate the ill feeling between the two parties. For the governor refused to receive the letter and returned it unopened.

---

[4] Fray Mariano to Francisco de la Cerda, K, leg. 6, no. 26, Arch. Coll. Santa Cruz. About the middle of June, 1750, Carabajal arrived at San Xavier from Los Adaes to exchange the detachment from that place.

[5] Fray Mariano to Barrio, October 23, 1749 (*Escritos presentados al Govr.*).

But the case was urgent, and on the same night Fray Mariano wrote to Captain Urrutia, enclosing the letter to Barrio, with the request that Urrutia deliver it and return a written report of what might happen. Urrutia did as was requested; Barrio received the letter, but only stormed at the missionaries, taking no steps to relieve them.[6]

Regarding Fray Mariano's procedure after this treatment we have no data, except that he made a record of the occurrence. As to the fugitives, it appears that some of them, subsequent to their desertion, promised that all would return by the 9th of November. But when Fray Mariano wrote to Mexico on December 6, he said nothing of having heard of their return, and was for this reason criticised by the *auditor*.[7]

3. *A shortage of supplies and an appeal for alms.*—The constant assertion of the missionaries that provisions were short, making it impossible properly to maintain the Indians already assembled or to admit the many more who would be glad to come, led in 1750 to an appeal for alms from the other missions of the Texas-Coahuila frontier. The situation, too, was complicated by the new enterprise of an Apache mission, which Father Santa Ana was now promoting with might and main. The two new enterprises led the college to propose giving up their missions on the Rio Grande in order to concentrate their attention on the frontiers of western and central Texas.

Early in 1750 (before April 12) Father Santa Ana wrote from Mexico City to his college that the royal officials of the exchequer had flatly refused the viceroy's request for aid for

---

[6] Fray Mariano to Urrutia, October 23; certificate by Fray Mariano, October 25 (*Ibid.*).

[7] *Parecer* of Altamira, January 30, 1750. Morfi, Bk. 8, paragraph 64. At this point Altamira took occasion to remark that ''it is a sad thing that, the presidio of San Antonio de Bejar being three hundred and seventy leagues and the new mission of the San Xavier four hundred and thirty leagues distant from this capital, news and information must come mutilated, and affairs jumbled up with one another without that plain, simple, and complete narration that even the least cultured practice in their familiar letters.''

the Apache missions. On April 12 this news was reported by Father Castellanos, the guardian, in a letter addressed to the missionaries of the presidencies of the Rio Grande and San Antonio. Another recourse, he added, had also failed. Sometime previously Father Thoribio had been authorized to ask the commissary general for a license to solicit alms for the new missions, but a negative reply had come. Father Castellanos was much disturbed, the right to solicit alms being, he said, "the only means whereby I might escape from such anguish." In view of the situation he now appealed to the presidents and other missionaries to aid the new establishment with such gifts as they were able to supply, "remembering that we all should keep in mind one purpose, namely, the glory of God and the conversion of the heathen . . . not only those who live near or in our respective missions, but the whole world, if it were possible." He added that he realized that some of the missions were better subjects to receive than to give aid, but that such were not included in the appeal.[8]

4. Smallpox at the missions.—In the summer of 1750, about May it seems, a terrible epidemic of smallpox—that scourge of the Indian race—swept over the neophytes of the Mission San Ildefonso. Because of the lack of supplies, most of the neophytes had been foraging in the woods, and were camped about two leagues from the mission when the epidemic came upon them. So virulent was the disease, according to Father Ganzábal, who was there at the time, that when removed from the tents the dead bodies literally fell in pieces. The scenes of suffering must have been horrible. But the missionaries worked bravely through them all, giving material aid where they could, and rejoicing at the opportunity to baptize the dying savages. The number of deaths reached forty, mainly among the adults, but none died

---

[8] Fray Francisco Xavier Castellanos to the missionaries of the Rio Grande and San Antonio, April 12, 1750.

without baptism. The greatest victory of the zealous missionaries was the baptizing, on the death-bed, of a shaman "versed
in the superstitions of the Texas."

The force of the epidemic over, the Indians returned to the
missions, many of them still suffering with gangrenous sores.
It was these Indians who were counted in the *padrón* of Mission
San Ildefonso made in the following July by Músquiz.[9]

5. *Músquiz's survey, June–August, 1750.*—As we have seen,
orders had been given that Músquiz should suspend his survey
at San Xavier until a successor to Barrio should arrive; this
order seems subsequently to have been countermanded, however,
for Músquiz began his work in June, whereas Barrio's successor
did not arrive till the next year. The report of the survey, still
extant, is a document of thirty-six folios,[10] and gives us full
details as to the location and other circumstances of the missions.
Every step in the procedure was carefully written down and
formally attested before witnesses. The record is so important
and so interesting that it is drawn upon here at length.

On June 16 Músquiz was at San Antonio, where he called
upon Captain Urrutia, asking him to nominate intelligent and
experienced men to aid him in his work. They must be men
without bias against either the governor or the missionaries. In
view of Urrutia's former relations with the two hostile parties,
it would seem that this was a difficult task to put upon him.
He complied, however, and named one soldier and two citizens.
They were Francisco Delgado, Gerónimo Flores, and Juan Diego
de la Garza. The last two "inteligentes y practicos" could not
sign their own names.[11] Before leaving San Antonio Músquiz
called also upon Fray Mariano, asking him to be present at the

[9] Arricivita, 328–329.

[10] *Testimonio de diligencias, Executadas sobre los dos Rios de S^n. Franc^o. Xavier y San Andres, y demas que dellas consta, prozesadas por mi D^n. Jph. Joaquin de Ecay Muzquiz, por Comision del Exmo. Señor Virrey de esta Nueba españa.*

[11] *Test. de diligencias*, folio 1.

survey; but instead of going himself Fray Mariano delegated Father Arricivita, minister at the mission San Ildefonso.[12]

By June 30 Músquiz had reached the San Xavier River settlement, for on that day, in an *exhorto* dated at Mission San Ildefonso, he notified Father Arricivita to be ready on the morrow to help begin the survey.[13] Work was got actually under way on July 2, and began with administering to each of the commissioners an oath to perform his duty honestly and without bias.

The survey was begun at the junction of the San Xavier River and Arroyo de las Animas—the San Gabriel River and Brushy Creek of today. Between July 2 and July 6, surveys, or measurements, were made at five different points along the San Xavier. The first was made July 2, at the junction of the two streams; the second, on the same day, half a league above the junction; the third, next day, at Paso de los Apaches, a point about nine thousand varas, or some five miles, above the junction; the fourth, on July 5, at Santa Rosa de Viterbo, a crossing two leagues higher up; the fifth, on the next day, at Santa María de la Visitación, a point two leagues still higher up. This last place was estimated as being about seven leagues, or some eighteen miles, above the junction of the two streams. Descriptions were given of the lands adjacent to the river, on both sides above Mission San Francisco Xavier, and on the south side below that point.

From the report of the survey we learn with great precision the location of the three missions, which have completely passed from memory and whose material remains have almost disappeared. All of the missions and their fields were on the south side of the San Xavier River. Mission San Ildefonso was situated on a knoll or hill an eighth of a league from the junction. On the slope of the hill there were growing three fanegas of maize, beans, and chili, all of which were doing well,

---

12 *Test. de diligencias*, folio 5; Fray Mariano's reply was dated June 20.
13 *Ibid*, folio 5.

though the season had been dry.[14]   Three fourths of a league, or some two miles, up the river above San Ildefonso, stood Mission San Francisco Xavier de Horcasitas, on a hill and surrounded by a fence or wall.   Between this enclosure and the junction extended a great flat or plain, five thousand varas (about two and one-fourth miles) long, and one thousand eight hundred varas wide at Mission San Ildefonso.[15]

Above, that is up stream from Mission San Francisco Xavier, extended a plain twelve hundred varas long and three hundred varas wide, on which were growing three fanegas of maize belonging to the last-named mission.   This plain was terminated at its lower end by the ridge on which stood Mission San Francisco Xavier, and at its upper end by another ridge or hill on which stood the third mission, Nuestra Señora de la Candelaria. Stretching up stream above this mission lay a great plain, or flat, nineteen hundred and sixty-one varas (about a mile) long and eight hundred varas wide, on which were planted, in front of the mission, three fanegas of maize.   On the same plain, at a distance of sixteen hundred and sixty-one varas from Mission Candelaria, was established the garrison of forty-eight men who were guarding the missions.   As was reasonable, it was established in the direction from which Apache attacks might be expected. Above the plain of Mission Candelaria, and separated from it only by an arroyo, was still another flat, or plain, one thousand varas long, three hundred and seventy-eight varas wide, and terminating a short distance below Paso de los Apaches.

Adjacent to Santa Rosa and Santa María similar plains were described on the south side of the river.   Ample water was found at all points where measurements were made.   The best opportunities for irrigating were encountered at Santa María and Santa Rosa; none were found at the junction or at the point of the second measurement.

---

14 *Test. de diligencias,* 8.

15 *Ibid.,* 7.

On August 2 the exploration of the San Andrés River was begun, near the junction with the San Xavier at Paso de los Vidays. In this locality facilities for one mission were found. From here the surveying party continued up a stream for eleven leagues, but finding the country constantly rougher, made no measurements.[16]

An item of interest in the report is the statement that from the crossing of Arroyo de las Animas (by the road, I suppose), to the junction, it was twelve leagues, or some thirty miles. This would place the ford anywhere from Rice's Crossing to Round Rock, presumably at the former place.

6. *Topographical identification.*—The present writer has three times explored the San Xavier between the junction of the San Gabriel River and Brushy Creek and a point nine miles above, twice before he discovered the report of Músquiz's survey, and the last time with a transcript of that document in hand. On the last occasion he was accompanied and assisted by Rev. Mr. Ander, then residing within a few miles of the historic spot. He was also given valuable assistance by other residents of the locality, especially after he succeeded with great difficulty in convincing them that his quest was not for hidden Spanish gold. Independent of archaeological evidences, which have already been mentioned, the principal points in the topography of the region described between the junction and Paso de los Apaches are clearly recognized by the explorer. For a distance of some two and one half miles above the junction of the streams the land between them consists of a great alluvial flat, whose width where it is traversed by the highway leading from Rockdale to the San Andrés Crossing is about a mile and a half. West of the highway the plain terminates in a steep-sloped highland, which extends to the westward parallel with the San Gabriel River and Brushy Creek and is bordered by the valleys of these

---

[16] *Test. de diligencias,* 35–36.

two streams. The northernmost projection of the highland at its
eastern end is that known as Kolb's Hill, on which now stand
Kolb's residence and store.   This hill or projecting ridge is
clearly that on which stood Mission San Francisco Xavier, a
conclusion which is borne out by other data than the survey.
Westward of Kolb's Hill about three fourths of a mile is another
projection of the highland known as Cemetery Hill.   Between
Kolb's Hill and Cemetery Hill extends a flat or plain which is
clearly that described by Músquiz as the one on which were
growing the crops of Mission San Xavier in 1750.   Cemetery
Hill was undoubtedly that on which mission Nuestra Señora de
la Candelaria was situated.   West of this hill extends a great
level valley more than a mile in length, near whose western end
lies what is known as Ditch Valley Farm.   Near the eastern end
of this valley, no doubt, were the fields of Mission Candelaria
described by Músquiz.   In the same valley, some three fourths
of a mile from the mission, was situated the garrison.   Near
the northward turn of the road, beyond Ditch Valley Farm and
just above the Old Rock Dam, a dry arroyo runs eastward into
the San Gabriel.   Up stream beyond this arroyo extends another
flat which corresponds with that described by Músquiz as terminating, on its western end, near Paso de los Apaches.   It is now
covered with a magnificent forest growth.

   The exact site of Mission San Ildefonso is not so easily determined, because of the timber growing above the junction of San
Gabriel River and Brushy Creek.   But there are two elevations
above the junction, either of which might have been the site of
the mission.   The first of these is the site of the old Witcher
house, which is about half a mile by direct line above the junction and therefore at a distance from the junction corresponding
to that of Mission San Ildefonso.   The distance to Brushy Creek
at this point, however, is too small to fit the description.   About
a third of a mile west of the Witcher house is another elevation

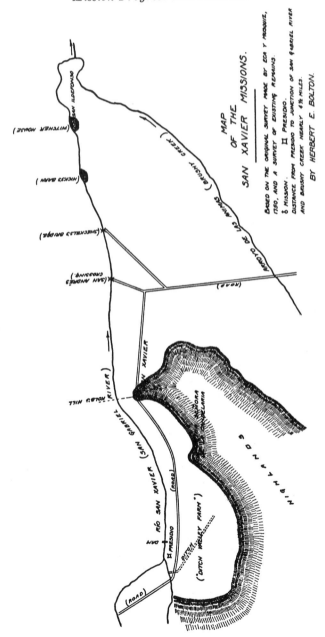

MAP
OF THE
SAN XAVIER MISSIONS.

BASED ON THE ORIGINAL SURVEY MADE BY ECA Y MÚSQUIZ,
1750, AND A SURVEY OF EXISTING REMAINS.
⊞ PRESIDIO.
☦ MISSION.   DISTANCE FROM PRESIDIO TO JUNCTION OF SAN GABRIEL RIVER
AND BRUSHY CREEK NEARLY 4½ MILES.

BY HERBERT E. BOLTON.

on which stands (or stood in 1909) Hicks' barn. At this point the distance between the two streams is about three fourths of a mile, which corresponds well with the eighteen hundred varas given as the width of the plain opposite mission San Ildefonso. Hicks' barn, moreover, stands on a much more "likely" spot than the Witcher house. However, in point of distance from the junction, the Witcher house fits the description better than Hicks' barn. I have therefore indicated this as the probable site of Mission San Ildefonso. It may be slightly incorrect, but at most it cannot be more than a few hundred yards out of the way.[17]

7. *The inspection of the missions*—On July 11 Músquiz issued an *exhorto de citación,* notifying Father Arricivita that on the 13th a *padrón,* or census, would be made of the Indians of each mission, and requesting that they be congregated and prepared for the occasion, and that all the missionaries be on hand to assist.[18]

The inspection began with Mission San Xavier. At six o'clock on the appointed morning, at the sound of the bell, the Indians gathered in the church for their accustomed worship. Prayer and the *alabado* being over, they were detained in the church to be listed, one by one, by tribes and classes; first the men, then the women, then the children. The count showed for this mission one hundred and fifty-three persons, consisting of ninety-nine adults and fifty-four children. Besides these, eight others, at the time absent, belonged to the mission. The children present had all been baptized, but of the adults only one, the Hierbipiame chief. had embraced that rite. Of the ninety-nine adults forty-one were Hierbipiames, forty-one Mayeyes, eight Yojuanes, two Navidachos, one Tops, three Asinais, and three of other tribes. Next was witnessed the customary daily distribution of maize by the hand of the missionary, each neophyte, large and small,

---

[17] *Test. de diligencias,* 35–36; see the map, p. 229.
[18] *Ibid.,* 18.

being given a gourdful equal to a double handful. The only other allowance was a bull killed and distributed once every twelve or fifteen days. Músquiz took the chiefs aside, beyond the presence of the missionaries, to ascertain whether they desired to move elsewhere; but all maintained that the site was good, buffalo and wild fruits plentiful, and relatives near, and that here they would stay. Músquiz next told them that they must give up their *mitotes* and dances, or be punished, to which they assented. Thereupon they were dismissed.

An examination of the records showed that since February, 1748, when the mission was founded, seventy-seven persons had been baptized, of which eleven were adults, the rest infants. All the adults had been baptized *in articulo mortis,* and three of them had died. Of infants seven had died.

The missionary, whose name is not given, stated upon inquiry that there could be added to the mission the Yojuane, Tancague, Asinai, and Nabedache. Of four of these tribes a few were already present. The Yojuane had been among the first petitioners and had lived there more than a year. But after the first distribution of presents when the first supplies were brought, they went to the woods, "solely on account of their natural inconstancy." Subsequently they had returned several times, but had not been admitted because of a lack of provisions.[19]

On the fourteenth the same procedure was gone through at San Ildefonso and on the fifteenth at Candelaria. At San Ildefonso, where Father Ganzábal was head missionary, there were one hundred and sixty-five Indians present, eleven being absent. Of the one hundred and seven adults present, sixty-five were Bidai, ten Patiri, and thirty-two Orcoquiza and Deadose, counted as one tribe. The books showed that since January, 1749, when the mission was founded, there had been one hundred and fifty-one baptisms, one hundred and one being adults. Of

---

[19] *Test. de diligencias,* 25–26.

these, two-thirds had been Bidai baptized during illness or *in articulo mortis.* Of the forty deaths thirty-six had been of adults. These figures clearly indicate that an epidemic had wrought havoc among the adult Bidai. Among the Bidai present there were numerous adults who had been baptized. These were of course recorded in the census by their Christian names, the others being called simply "gentiles." Among the Bidai present we recognize chiefs Tomás and Agustín, who are later met in connection with the mission on the Trinity. Father Ganzábal reported that all three of the bands of the Bidai and all five of the Orcoquiza might be added to the mission if there were only means for their support.

At Mission Candelaria there were present sixty adults and thirty children, twelve persons being absent. Of the adults thirty-five were Coco, twenty-one Tops, and four Carancaguas. Since July, 1749, when the mission was said by the report to have been founded, there had been fifty baptisms, fourteen of adults and thirty-four of children. Of the adults eight had died, and of the children five. Fray Bartolomé García, oldest minister at the mission, said that the Cujane, relatives of the Coco and Tops, as well as the rest of the Carancaguas, might be secured for the mission.[20]

8. *Mission San Ildefonso again deserted, August, 1750.—* About the middle of June, 1750, Carabajal arrived at San Xavier from Adaes to exchange the squadron detached from that presidio.[21] With him came four Nabedaches, who remained till August, when, as Arricivita writes, "a more pernicious pest" than smallpox seized upon the Indians of Mission San Ildefonso.

From the time of the arrival of the Indians from the east there were rumors abroad that the interior tribes were assembling for a campaign against the Apache. On August 2 the Ais and

---

[20] *Test. de diligencias,* 29–34.

[21] At least, I suppose that it was to make the exchange. The word is "mudanza."

Hasinai tribes arrived, followed by some Cadodacho, Nabedache, and Yojuane, saying that the "capitan grande," called Sánchez Teja, was near by, bringing the Tawakoni, Yatasí, Kichai, Nazoni, Tonkawa, and a multitude of others. They held meetings with the mission Indians, particularly at Mission San Ildefonso, by day and by night. The campaign did not take place, but the mission Indians deserted in small detachments accompanied by bands of the visitors, until Father Ganzábal was left alone. The persuasive force had come in part, at least, in the form of trade in guns, vermillion, and other articles. While the blow was the hardest at San Ildefonso, Father Ganzábal reported that he doubted not that the other missions, especially San Xavier, also suffered. He saw in the affair an occult power which he could not divine. But there was another force not so occult. Among the Indians from the east, Father Ganzábal wrote, was a person who looked like a Frenchman. He wore a three-cornered hat, and refused to speak with the missionary, but among the Indians of the missions he was very officious.

The Indians promised to return in two months. That they would do so Father Ganzábal expected, since they would return through necessity or because of the advantages of mission life, if for no other reason. Nevertheless, he maintained that their fickleness should be punished, even though they had been coaxed away. As late as October 12 the Indians had not returned, and Father Ganzábal was still waiting alone for them.[22] But he had long to wait, for they did not return till December 20, 1751, when, "recognizing their error," twenty-six leading Bidai, Deadose, Orcoquiza, and others, put in an appearance, and, being caressed by their minister, promised to return and stay in their own mission. It was implied in a letter of January 12, 1752, that they were there.[23]

---

[22] Ganzábal to Fray Mariano, August 20, 1750; K, 6, no. 26; Arricivita, 329.

[23] It is possible that they had returned since August, 1750, and absconded again. *Memorial del R. P. Viana al exmo Sor Virrey, 1752.*

Before the neophytes of San Ildefonso returned, those of
Mission Candelaria—the Coco, Tops, and Carancaguas—deserted.
The explanation given was that a soldier had frightened them
away by telling them that many Spaniards were coming to kill
them, and that, believing the story, they had fled. This was in
August, 1751. They did not go far, however, and their ministers were easily able to reassure them. Accordingly within a
few days the principal chiefs, with their bands, it seems, returned to the mission, where they still were in January, 1752.
The remainder of the fugitives, joined by newcomers, also returned to the neighborhood, but by January they had not entered
the mission.[24]

9. The beginning of the acequia, October, 1750.—While
Músquiz and Arricivita were examining the site, Fray Mariano
had been at San Antonio, co-operating in the effort to move the
presidio of San Antonio to the Pedernales River, to protect the
proposed Apache missions which Father Santa Ana was in
Mexico struggling to promote.[25] But when he received a copy
of the record made by Músquiz, he hurried to San Xavier to see
if it were really true that the sites of Santa Rosa and Santa
María were better than that where the missions were already
established. Having made a personal examination, he concluded
that such was not the case, and that the missions would better
remain where they were.

This point determined, it was of first importance to open the
irrigating ditches, in order, even in case of drought, to assure
each Indian of a full stomach, "which," he said, "is the God to
whom these miserable creatures pay the tribute of their hardest
labor." With a view to determining the location and course
of the ditch he several times examined the river, and concluded
that the best opportunity for opening a channel was through the

24 *Memorial del R. P. Viana.*

25 *Memorial presentado por el R. P. Preside. Fr. Mariano de los Dolores.*
September 17, 1750.

arroyo near the garrison called by him San Francisco, since the arroyo itself would serve for a goodly portion of the ditch, which could be continued easily through the fields of Mission Candelaria to the neighborhood of all three pueblos. This one ditch, he concluded, would serve for all the missions, since it could be made to irrigate a stretch of untimbered land more than a league in length and half a league in breadth.[26]

On October 12 he formally made known his plans to the missionaries, reminding them that since all were of one brotherhood and were working towards the same end, they should not object to the common use of a single irrigating plant. This done, he proceeded to order the ministers to be prepared to assist in the work on the fifteenth, each mission providing as many yokes of oxen as it might have, seven bars, fifteen picks, four axes, and one cauldron. In excess of the regular rations, which would be continued, each mission was asked to provide each week during the continuance of the work, a tierce, or half a mule load, of salt, six bulls for slaughter, two handfuls of tobacco, and whatever else was possible. Fray Mariano promised to provide for distribution each day a fanega, or two hundred pounds, of hominy. All of the *ladinos*, or instructed Indians, must be sure to be on hand, to assist in giving instruction to the *bozales* or untrained neophytes.[27] Since Fray Mariano had many other duties to attend to, both at San Xavier and at San Antonio, he appointed Father Ganzábal superintendent of the work, with the duty of assigning the tasks and taking care of the tools and supplies. To the order formal obedience was given on the same day by Fathers Ganzábal, of Mission San Ildefonso, Joseph Anda y Altamirano, of Mission San Xavier, and Acisclos Valverde and Bartolomé García, of Mission Candelaria. Father Ganzábal, in giving obedience, called Fray Mariano's attention to the fact

---

26 Fray Mariano to the missionaries, October 17, 1750, in *Diligencias practicadas por el R. P. Presidᵗᵉ.*

27 *Ibid.*

that though his mission was still without Indians, yet they might return, and he ought to be present in such an event to receive them.[28]

All this extra food and tobacco was to be provided as a means of encouragement to the neophytes. But it could not be expected that mere coaxing would alone suffice. There must be a show of force as well. Accordingly, on October 14, Fray Mariano addressed the commander of the garrison, Francisco de la Cerda, calling for the assistance of the soldiers. He prefaced his request by a statement of the functions of mission garrisons. Their business, he said, was not merely to protect the neophytes from their enemies, but also to assist in disciplining the neophytes in civilized and Christian life, eradicating their heathen rites, "cooperating with the missionaries in everything, both in what relates to instruction in the doctrine and rudiments of the faith, and in their peculiar function of making them show due respect and veneration and of giving them practical direction, teaching them the necessary tasks and occupations, which they ought to follow in order to continue in the civilized and Christian life which they should observe." In all this the soldiers had failed up to the present, but, trusting in Músquiz's upright conduct, he assumed that appropriate orders had been left for giving proper assistance henceforth.

With this preface, Fray Mariano asked that one soldier be charged, during the work on the ditch, with caring for the tools, and another with looking after the oxen sent to work on the ditch and to haul stone for the dam. Cerda was asked to give orders that the horses of the Indians be kept under guard so that the Indians could not flee or wander away, taking care that no soldier be allowed to mount the horses and thus anger the Indians; to send to each mission daily "enough soldiers to cause respect," and to set the Indians at work at the proper time and

---

[28] Fray Mariano to the missionaries, Oct. 17, 1750.

keep them at it. The missionaries, he said, would provide all the attractions possible in the way of extra food, but coercion must be left to the soldiers, "since for the missionary fathers to assume the task would be to make themselves odious to the Indians, which is a serious impediment to their receiving the faith, and, besides, few would go, and there is risk that they would lose respect, because of their bad instruction up to the present." Cerda was asked to give orders that the soldiers keep guard by night to prevent nocturnal flights. When buffalo should appear in sight, soldiers must go with the Indians to pursue them, to insure the return of the Indians. Finally, the soldiers must be required to instruct the Indians in their work.[29]

Such were the preparations for opening the irrigating ditch and building the dam. We have found no report of the execution of the plan, but since Father Mariano remained at San Xavier till November (he arrived at San Antonio on his return on November 11), and since both ditch and dam were made, we may fairly assume that their construction was begun at this time.[30] We know, on the other hand, that the work went slowly, for on January 22, 1752, that is, a year and more later, it was still unfinished. On that day Fray Mariano complained that since June, 1751, when Barrios y Jáuregui took away his seventeen soldiers, "no hand has been put, up to the present, on the dam and the acequia, which they were making with due preparation to gather this year the fruit of their past labor." Meanwhile, the frequent desertion of soldiers had lessened the available supply of help.[31] In view of the calamities that befell the settlement early in 1752, it is doubtful if the ditch was ever wholly completed.

10. Barrios y Jáuregui and the missionaries.—The new governor was no less obnoxious to the missionaries than Barrio

---

[29] Fray Mariano to Francisco de la Cerda, October 14, 1750, *ibid.*
[30] *Memorias*, XXVIII, 118.
[31] *Memorial del R. P. Viana.*

had been. Father Morfi states that he became their avowed
enemy as soon as he left Querétaro; that he insulted Father
López, who traveled with him to Texas, by denouncing the missionaries in the friar's presence; and that at San Antonio he
accorded similar treatment to Father Cayetano, when the latter
broached the subject of Apache missions.[32]

Fray Mariano heard that Barrios came with orders to "clear
up the truth" regarding the missions, lands, and water at San
Xavier. What was the basis of this report I cannot say. At
any rate, Fray Mariano presented the governor a petition on the
subject of the tiresome quarrel. Prefacing it with a statement
that it was his duty to defend the reputation of his college, that
he desired only that the truth should prevail, and that he welcomed an investigation, he outlined the correct procedure in the
case. Relying on a similar experience at the Lampazos mission,
he maintained that this would be, (1) to cite the interested
parties and, (2) to ascertain whether Músquiz's investigation had
been duly thorough. He insisted that, other things being equal,
the missionaries would gladly move to a better site. San Marcos
doubtless had advantages, but the Indians were at San Xavier.
Let the opponents obligate themselves to move the Indians and
prepare suitable irrigating ditches for three missions, the missionaries being the judges, and gladly would they consent to this
benefit. Not only would they go to San Marcos, but anywhere
else, providing that the truth were made known regarding the
assertions of the missionaries relative to the site at San Xavier.[33]

Barrios apparently made no response to this memorial, perhaps because he had no instructions regarding the matter. He
reached San Xavier on his way to Los Adaes in the latter part
of June. While there, as we have seen, he carried out that part

---

[32] Morfi, Bk. 9, paragraphs 1–4.

[33] *Escrito presentado en S[n]. Xavier a D[n]. Jacinto Gob[r]. y nada respondio
1751 a[s].;* also *Varios papeles, de Tejas.* The archive label says: "presentado en S[n]. Xavier," but I infer from the language that it was before
Barrios left San Antonio.

of his orders which provided that he should remove the seventeen Adaes soldiers. But he did nothing to fulfill his orders requiring them replaced.[34] While at San Xavier, according to Morfi, the Apache matter was twice presented to him, once by Father Anda and again by Fray José Pinilla, but in each case he refused to listen.[35]

11. A thousand goats for San Xavier.—Compelled by the necessities of the San Xavier missions and the urgent demands for new ones among the Apache, in the fall of 1751 the college decided to give up to the secular clergy the two old missions of San Juan Bautista and San Bernardo, on the Rio Grande, and so notified the viceroy. In the taking of this step Fray Giraldo de Terreros, then president at the Rio Grande missions, played an important part. The decision having been made, the college planned to utilize the opportunity for the better support of the San Xavier missions. Writing to Father Terreros on November 28, 1751, the Discretorio of the college stated that they had no doubt the offer would be promptly accepted, in view of the reputation of those missions for excessive wealth. They then ordered the president and his subordinates to extract with due caution from the two missions a thousand head of female goats,[36] to. be divided among the three San Xavier missions, "in order that, with this subsidy, those new sons of the church may have the means with which to continue Christian and civilized life." With the letter was enclosed an order to Fray Mariano requiring him to send at once a religious prepared to conduct the animals, giving it out in San Antonio that he was going to buy that amount of stock, in order not to set tongues wagging. "This," the Discretorio added, "will not be objectionable, for it has been done this way many times."

---

[34] *Testimᵒ De Autos de Pesquiza sobre comercio Ylicito.* Béxar Archives, Adaes, 1739–1755.

[35] Morfi, Bk. 9, paragraphs 1–4.

[36] The order says "ganado menor," meaning in this case probably goats, and not sheep and goats.

Father Terreros was also to use his judgment as to what other things from the old missions might be of use to the new. These orders were to be kept secret, that no obstacle might be placed in the way of delivering the missions.[37] This communication was evidently not sent till February 21, when the order was repeated and the conduct of the stock entrusted to Fray Miguel Pinilla, who with Father Felix Gutiérrez Varaona was on his way to the San Xavier missions. It was added now that each mission should send some horses to San Xavier, together with the other things which might be spared.[38] It was still twenty years before the Rio Grande missions were secularized. But the order to send the goats was not conditioned upon secularization, and, therefore, though we have no record of the arrival of the stock, we may assume that it went.[39]

---

[37] Discretorio to Terreros, November 28, 1751.

[38] Discretorio to Terreros, February 21, 1752.

[39] Bolton, *Guide to the Archives of Mexico*, 386.

CHAPTER VII

THE PRESIDIO ESTABLISHED

1. Músquiz's report.—The next important step in the history
of the missionary enterprise at San Xavier was the establishment of the presidio. The missionaries had clamored for it from
the beginning. In July, 1749, it had been approved by the *junta
de guerra* and promised by the viceroy. But, as an extra precau-
tion, its final approval had been deferred until another report
should be made upon the San Xavier site, a task which was
assigned to Músquiz.

Bonilla writes of the work of Músquiz: "He fulfilled his
charge with such pleasure and satisfaction to the interested
parties," etc. Hereupon Morfi exclaims with justice, "This is
a strange way of reconciling those parties! Far from being
satisfactory to the opposing parties, it was very contrary to
their desires, for it made conspicious the falsity of what Bonilla
calls a demonstration."[1] The report by Músquiz was, indeed,
generally favorable to the site at San Xavier and to the maintenance of the missions there; and it put an end to the doubt
in the minds of the government officials which had stood in the
way of final consent to the establishment of a presidio. Nevertheless, it was still eight months before this consent was formally
given and orders issued for the erection of the new post.[2]

2. Danger from the French.—Another force working in
favor of an independent presidio for San Xavier came in the

---

[1] Morfi, Bk. 8, par. 78.

[2] After Músquiz made his report, Fray Mariano made another, which
I have not seen. It is referred to in *Erecion*, p. 9, as one of the *antece-
dentes* to the junta of March 11. I conjecture that it may have included
a reply to Músquiz's report that the best facilities for irrigation were
to be found at Santa Rosa and Santa María.

form of reports of French activities on the Louisiana frontier. In July, 1750, the commander of Ysla de Santa Rosa, Punta de Sigüenza, had reported the arrival in Louisiana of four shiploads of soldiers and colonists and thirty-six vessels laden with merchandise. The French were progressing inland, had now for the first time organized a squadron of cavalry, and were conducting illicit trade with their Spanish neighbors. Moreover, large numbers of Spanish soldiers and citizens were accustomed to descend to New Orleans to trade. Apart from this report, another had come to the effect that Governor Barrio had shamefully engaged in illegal commerce with the French.

Pointing in the same direction was the communication written by Jacinto de Barrios y Jáuregui, the new governor of Texas, on December 31, 1750, on the event of his departure to his province. He stated that he had come from the court of Spain especially instructed by the Marqués de la Ensenada to put the presidio of Los Adaes in first-class order just as soon as possible, as a safeguard against French aggression. Though there was peace at present between the two courts, a breach might unexpectedly occur at any moment, when advantage would certainly be taken of the woeful weakness of the Spanish defences. Barrios reminded the viceroy that of the sixty soldiers of the Los Adaes garrison fifteen men were always employed in guarding the horse herd, seven assisting the missionaries, and fifteen in escorting the annual caravan of supplies from Saltillo, a round trip of some two thousand miles. Counting out the seventeen men now at San Xavier, there remained actually at the presidio the pitiful guard of only six soldiers. It was urgent, therefore, that he restore the detachment to their headquarters, as a first step toward fulfilling his orders.[3] This request was referred to the fiscal and the *auditor de guerra,* and on February 10, 1751,

---

[3] Barrios y Jáuregui to the viceroy, December 3, 1750. *Testim⁰. de autos de Pezquiza sobre comercio Ylicito.* Béxar Archives, Adaes, 1739–1755.

the viceroy granted the petition, on the ground that a presidio had already been resolved upon, and in view of the danger on the eastern frontier. But Barrios must replace the seventeen men at San Xavier, either by detaching the number from Béxar or Bahía, by enlisting new recruits, or by borrowing from a neighboring province. The same order required Barrios to investigate the charges against Governor Barrio, and thereby an unsavory chapter in Texas history was introduced.

As we have seen, when, in June 1751, Barrios reached San Xavier, on his way to eastern Texas, he immediately fulfilled the part of his orders requiring him to restore the seventeen soldiers to Los Adaes. On June 23 he executed a formal *auto* of obedience, and then issued an order that the soldiers be removed at once, without waiting for their replacement, in view, he said, of the necessary haste and of the inquietude of the Apache:[4]

3. The junta of March 11, 1751.—The question of the presidio had already been referred, with Músquiz's report, to the fiscal and the *auditor*, who gave opinions on February 1 and 8, 1751. In consequence of these opinions, on March 11 a *junta de guerra, real hacienda, y prácticos*,[5] was held to consider the question. In this meeting sat Domingo Salazar y Formento and Francisco López Adam, knights of the Order of Santiago, members of the Royal Council, and *oidores* of the Audencia, of which the one was also deacon and the other sub-deacon; Juan de Albuerne, Marqués de Altamira, member of the Council and of the Audiencia, and *auditor general de la guerra* of the Kingdom of New Spain; Doctor Antonio de Andreu y Ferras, member of the Council and *fiscal de lo civil;* Juan Chrisóstomo Barroetta, regent of the Tribunal y Real Audencia de Cuentas of New Spain; Miguel de Varrio y Saldinar, Conde de San Mateo de Valparaiso, *contador mayor* of the same Tribunal; Ignacio

---

[4] *Testim⁰. de autos de Pesquiza sobre comercio Ylicito.* Adaes 1751. Béxar Archives, Adaes, 1739–1755.

[5] Report in *Erecion.*

Joseph de Mazo Calderón, treasurer of the *caxas reales*. As *prácticos*, or men of experience in the particular matter at hand, sat General Juan Antonio Bustillo y Cevallos, ex-governor of Texas and now *alcalde ordinario* of the most noble City of Mexico, and Captain Joaquín de Orobio Bazterra, formerly captain at Bahía. The last two members had long before made known their position regarding the matter in hand.[6]

In the council a review was given of the history of the San Xavier missions, of the opposition to them, "and, in very great detail," of the report by Eca y Músquiz.[7] In view of everything, it was resolved that "since by the investigation by which Don Joseph de Eca y Músquiz . . . shows patently that all the difficulties which were embarrassing the establishment of the presidio on the banks of the Río de San Xavier have been vanquished, steps shall be taken at once to erect it in the manner proposed by the Señor Fiscal and approved by the Señor Auditor under dates of February 1 and 8 of this year." What that manner was can be inferred from the specifications which followed. The presidio was to be located at the point which the captain and the friars should select as "most suitable and dominating in that region;" it was to be composed of fifty men drawing a salary of four hundred pesos each, that of the captain being six hundred.[8]

4. Despatches of the viceroy March 26 and March 30.— More than a year before, the king, by a despatch dated at Buen Retiro on March 6, 1750, had appointed as expectant captain of the presidio Don Felipe de Rábago. Accordingly, on March 26, 1751, the viceroy approved the resolution of the junta and ordered that Rábago, who was now in the City of Mexico, should go as soon as possible to take possession of the presidio, and send the existing garrison to their respective companies. The

---

[6] *Erecion*, 9–10.

[7] *Ibid.*, 13.

[8] *Ibid.*, 13–14.

same despatch provided that the missionaries should be requested to seek, by all possible means, Spaniards and *gente de
razón* to go to settle near the new presidio; and that to the same
end the governor of Texas and Captain Rábago should be ordered
to publish a proclamation, advertising for settlers and promising
them lands, water rights, and the privileges of first settlers.[9]

On March 30, by decree, the viceroy formally "erected and
established" the presidio with the name San Xavier. As the
junta had stipulated, it was to be erected where the captain and
missionaries might choose; and the captain was to receive six
hundred pesos a year, and the soldiers four hundred, paid from
the same branch of the Real Hacienda as the salaries of other
interior presidios. Rábago was empowered to publish a proclamation to recruit soldiers and settlers, using all possible care to
select as soldiers only those of good character and expert in
arms. With these soldiers and the friendly Indians he was to
proceed to erect the presidio, with the understanding that it
could be moved, if necessity required it, to a more advantageous
place; he was to erect a fortification for the protection of the
garrison and another for the church (the presidial church, I
infer), "with its plazuela." He was to assign *solares*, or house
lots, to soldiers and settlers; *cavallerías de tierra* to the soldiers,
that they might engage in agriculture when not employed in military pursuits; and lands to the citizen settlers. For *dehesas*
and for pastures for the horses of the soldiers, reserve was to
be made of the best lands near the presidio.

The presidio was to be within the jurisdiction of the governor
of Texas; but the collection of the pay of his soldiers and the
purchase of their supplies was to be in the hands of the captain,
the governor not being allowed to meddle in these matters;
he could, however, hear complaints of the soldiers and remedy
abuses. Thus the captain was made, in effect, company con-

---

[9] *Erecion*, 14–15.

tractor, and given an unusual opportunity for what in this day we call graft. Regarding prices of goods for soldiers, and other matters, Rábago was to be governed by the *reglamento* recently issued by the viceroy Marqués de Casafuerte. A copy of this document must be furnished Rábago, and he must read it in public annually to the men, for their protection.

Finally, Rábago must take special care that his soldiers be well equipped and disciplined, prompt for any service for the defense of the frontier and the reduction of the Indians to the Faith, "which he must attend to as the principal concern, exerting himself in every way in order that this end so much desired may be achieved." He must look to the instruction of the neophytes in Christian doctrine and civilized life; prevent the soldiers from abusing them, and from reducing them to personal service, under pain of severe punishment.[10]

In answer to an inquiry whether the lieutenant, *alférez*, sergeant, and corporals of the company were to be included in the fifty men or not, and whether a chaplain would be appointed for the company, as was the case at Sacramento and San Antonio de Béxar, the viceroy, after consulting Altamira, replied affirmatively in the former case and negatively in the latter, saying that one of the missionaries might serve as chaplain, the obventions ·being paid privately by the captain and soldiers, as was the rule in most of the interior presidios, Sacramento and Béxar being exceptions.

In the same communication Rábago had asked for a year's pay in advance for himself and men, and for six thousand dollars cash in advance for the material construction of the presidio. Regarding this request Altamira recommended that before acting a report as to what was customary be secured from the *oficiales reales,* but remarked that in case Rábago recruited his soldiers outside of Texas, Nuevo León, and Coahuila, it would be just

---

10 *Erecion,* 16–18.

to advance the year's pay. On April 1 the viceroy ordered the report made; I do not know what the result was, but I infer that the advance was made in both cases.

At the same time that these instructions were issued to Rábago, a copy of them was sent to the new governor, Barrios y Jáuregui. To the missionaries the viceroy issued a request, *de ruego y encargo,* that they seek Spaniards and *gente de razón* for the formation of a settlement near the presidio.[11]

5. *The establishment of the presidio.*—Through the writings of the missionaries we get glimpses of Rábago's journey to the frontier. He stopped at Querétaro, where he entered into a compact with the College of Santa Cruz. The agreement provided, as a means of keeping petitions and complaints from going to the viceroy's court, that each party should first make known its grievances to the other, and that each should do its best to give satisfaction. Charges were later made by the missionaries that on the way to Texas Rábago was guilty of unbecoming conduct at every one of the important cities where he stopped. The specific nature of the misdeeds with which he was charged before reaching San Antonio does not appear. Some of his doings at that place will be evident from the following chapter.

The details of enlisting the company by Rábago—how, when, or where—likewise have not come to light, but it is evident that some at least of the soldiers were enlisted at San Antonio. While there Rábago published a *bando* calling for colonists, and twenty families volunteered.[12]

---

11 The despatch was formally "obeyed" at Los Adaes by Barrios on December 30, apparently the day when he took possession there, and ordered published on the first holiday at the *cuerpo de guardia* after mass. It was published on January 1, 1752.

12 A document of February, 1752, contains the names of the following persons, part of whom were soldiers and part citizen inhabitants of San Xaxier; Joseph de Salinas, Antonio Cambray, Don Manuel Cos, Jⁿ. Victor Rodríguez, Nicholás Caravajal, Joaquín Valle, Jph. Antonio Estrada, Joseph Francisco Yruegas, Thomas Yruegas, Francisco Xavier de Zuñiga, Joseph Thoribio de Terán, Joaquín Antonio Flores, Francisco Ramírez, Juan Antonio Ramírez, Christóbal Vela, Joseph Flores, Antonio Cadena,

Rábago was delayed in his journey, especially at Monclova, and it was December 11, 1751, when he arrived with his company at San Xavier, accompanied from San Antonio by Fray Mariano. He found there Lieutenant Músquiz, eighteen soldiers, and five friars. The soldiers were all who remained of the forty-eight who belonged in the garrison. The friars were Joseph López, Mariano de Anda, Joseph and Miguel Pinilla, and Joseph Ganzábal. Músquiz and the friars gave formal obedience to the despatches which Rábago carried, but the missionaries protested regarding the arrangement which had been made for the payment of obventions.

On December 13 Músquiz formally delivered the post, the guard house, and the hut which served as commander's quarters. Rábago detailed six soldiers to help at the three missions, but the friars insisted on having nine, asserting that it was their business to herd the stock, cultivate the soil, and aid the missionaries. Although he differed with the friars regarding the point, he yielded, as he said, to avoid dissensions till he might get superior orders.

Next day Rábago held a review of the Indians at the missions. At San Francisco Xavier he found and listed seventy adult heathen and thirty-nine baptized Indians under twelve years of age, of the Hierbipiame and Mayeye tribes. At Candelaria, where Fray Miguel Pinilla was missionary, there were eighteen adult heathen and seven converts under twelve. At San Ildefonso, where Father Ganzábal was missionary, there were no neophytes, and there had been none for seventeen months. It is evident that this mission had been moved up the river from its first site, for all three missions were within a quarter of a league of a given point.

Vizente Ferrer Montalvo, Gerónimo Rodríguez, Cayetano Ulibarri, Miguel and Joseph de Sosa, Joseph Manual Martínez, Pablo Joseph Carmona, Phelipi Neri Valle, Pedro Joseph de Herrera, and Marcos Minchaca (Pinilla, Fray Miguel, decree of censure, February 19, 1752, K, leg. 12).

On the second day after his arrival Rábago sent a request to Captain Urrutia, at San Antonio, for three expert surveyors to assist him in selecting a site for the presidio and the town. Urrutia complied at once, saying that he had no experts but sending the best men he had, namely Joseph Flores, Gerónimo Flores, and Antonio Ximénez. By the 22nd they had reached San Xavier, and on that day and the next, accompanied by Rábago, the missionaries, and soldiers, they explored both banks of the river to Santa María and Paso de los Apaches. All agreed upon a site for the presidio on a hill within a quarter league of all the missions, but when they surveyed the lands with a view to irrigation, the surveyors and six other witnesses unanimously declared the place unsuitable for settlement.

Concurring in this opinion, Rábago immediately went to the San Marcos River to see what it offered. On January 16, having already returned to San Xavier, he despatched the *diligencias* to the viceroy, accompanied by a letter. In view of the small number of neophytes, he was of the opinion that one mission would suffice at San Xavier, thereby saving the pay of four missionaries. He believed that the place offered "absolutely no advantages" for missions, presidio, or settlement, and that the Indians, far from desiring conversion, wished only to "traffic freely with the Spaniards as they are doing with the French, who provide them with what they need." But the San Marcos River possessed what the San Xavier lacked. At the springs "above the Pass which they call Paso de los Texas" he had found abundant facilities for missions, presidio, and settlements. The twenty families who had volunteered to form a settlement, he was sure, could be induced to go to San Marcos, but not to San Xavier.[13]

---

[13] *Testimonio de los autos fhos sre. la erecion del Precidio de S^n. Xavier en las Margenes del Rio y Consulta hecha por D^n. Ph^e. de Ravago y Teran,* etc., 1751. When, on February 13, Rábago's report was handed to Altamira he reviewed the history of the San Xavier missions, but vouchsafed no opinion. When it went to Andreu, the fiscal, he, on March 9, asked that an opinion be secured from Father Santa Ana, who was still in

This report of Rábago's does not convey an altogether correct idea of the situation at San Xavier, for before it was written the breach between Rábago and the missionaries had become much more serious than he intimated.

Mexico. On or before July 5 the desired opinion was submitted. Father Santa Ana maintained that Rábago had gone to his post with his mind already made up regarding the San Marcos, having simply adopted the plan of Governor Barrio. He had shown his bias in the investigation by not taking the opinion of a single missionary. The plan was not worthy of a soldier like Rábago, for to colonize San Marcos would scarcely advance the frontier, which could be effected, without the aid of a single soldier, by the very families Rábago had enlisted at San Antonio. Músquiz's report had fully demonstrated the advantages of the San Xavier for a settlement, and it was clear that some of the testimony submitted by Rábago was falsified, as he would prove if but given a chance to cross-question the witnesses. The matter being submitted again to Dr. Andreu, he, on August 5, recommended that none of the missions be suppressed; but in view of the fact that all the earlier investigations had been made without respect to a colony he advised a new investigation be made, with the assistance of the missionaries, and under the supervision of Governor Barrios y Jáuregui. What action was taken at this juncture by the viceroy does not appear. Meanwhile things on the San Xavier had taken a serious turn (*ibid.*).

CHAPTER VIII

THE QUARREL WITH CAPTAIN RABAGO

"In the apostolic road," says Father Morfi, "there are only crosses, and if some day the sky is cloudless, it is to make the tempest which follows it more dreadful by comparison. The religious saw the truth triumph and their missions favored. They knew that the former persecutions had their birth in the fact that the soldiers of different garrisons there were idle; they believed that by restoring them to their posts and establishing new troops there, they would be able to devote themselves in peace to the functions of their institute. This caused them to desire and ask for the creation of the new presidio; but they did not know, nor could they know, that this would scarcely be erected when they would see the work of many years demolished in a few days, their beloved Indians scattered, their funds destroyed, their honor wounded in the most sensitive point, and their blood spilled by the hands of those whom the piety of the king honors and maintains precisely for the purpose of defending it."[1] This paragraph is a fitting introduction to the stormy chapter which followed the establishment of the new presidio at San Xavier.

1. Scandalous living, and the right of sanctuary.—When Captain Rábago arrived at San Xavier in December, 1751, he carried with him a person who was the occasion of a vile scandal which had much to do with the ruination of the ill-fated missionary enterprise. The person was the wife of Juan Joseph Zevallos, a citizen of San Antonio who enlisted in Rábago's

---

[1] Morfi, Bk. 9, paragraph 5.

company. Before leaving San Antonio Rábago had met this woman and formed a liaison with her, and when he went to his new post he took both her and her husband with him. On the way the husband protested in defense of his honor, and threatened to do violence to the captain, in return for which he was maltreated and carried to San Xavier a prisoner.[2]

At San Xavier Captain Rábago continued his relations with Señora Zevallos, the scandal becoming public, and known even to the Indians of the missions. To put an end to it Father Miguel Pinilla, whom Fray Mariano appointed chaplain of the presidio, urged Rábago to send the woman back to San Antonio, at the same time privately urging her to go. After much recrimination this arrangement was effected, but it left bitterness between Father Pinilla and Rábago.[3] Meanwhile, Rábago kept Zevallos in prison and under a torture that consisted of his being tied prostrate on the ground to four stakes at hands and feet and three at his neck.[4] But on Christmas Eve he managed to escape to Mission Candelaria, where he sought sanctuary. On the following day the wrathful captain went with a squad of soldiers, entered the church on horseback, violently recovered Zevallos, took him back to prison, and put him again under torture. Thereupon Father Pinilla went to the captain, explained to him the enormity of his crime of violating the right of the sanctuary, and put him under censure. At the end of ten days Rábago restored the prisoner to the mission.[5]

---

[2] *2ª Consulta remitida a su Exª. en 13 de Junio de 1752 aˢ.;* Arricivita, 331. On his arrival Rábago read the viceroy's despatch requiring the missionaries to serve as chaplains of the presidio, and on December 10 Fray Mariano appointed to that office Miguel Pinilla, of the mission of Candelaria. Fray Miguel took his office seriously, as was soon learned. Pinilla to Mariano, March 1, 1752.

[3] *2ª. Consulta;* also *Ex. San Sabá,* 1763, p. 10. In the former document, written June 13, 1752, Fray Mariano makes it appear that the woman was sent home after Zevallos escaped. In the latter, written in 1760, he more distinctly inverts the incidents.

[4] *2ª. Consulta;* Arricivita, 331; *Ex. San Sabá,* 10.

[5] Arricivita, 331; *2ª. Consulta,* p. 2; *Ex. San Sabá,* 11.

2. Appeal of the missionaries to the college.—Apart from Rábago's flagrant misconduct regarding Zevallos, his general bearing toward the missionaries was to them most objectionable, as was stated in a communication dated January 12, signed by all of the friars and directed to the Discretorio.[6]

They recited that Rábago had been guilty of imprudent and even rash conduct on the way to Texas. In spite of this they had received him with more than the usual respect and esteem; but in return they had been accorded the extremest disrespect and illtreatment. Notwithstanding Rábago's scandalous living and his harsh treatment of Zevallos, they had offered to forget the past for the sake of the future. They had yielded on every point consistent with honor; knowing that Rábago favored moving to the San Marcos, they had consented; knowing that he desired the site of one of the missions for the use of the presidio, they had agreed to move the mission. Yet nothing had availed, and they had been repaid only with insults. For these reasons they begged either to be recalled to Querétaro or that "the head of this serpent be crushed," so that they might work unmolested, "for the indecent rage of Don Carlos de Franquis, the impostures of Barrios, the craft of D". Jacinto, the plots of the Islanders, the machinations of D". Juachin, and the entanglements of the provinces, all combined, are outdone by the malice of this man." With their petition Fray Mariano sent a plan to be submitted to the viceroy, which all had approved. and Fray Pinilla sent a detailed report of occurrences.[7]

3. A substitute for the presidio proposed.—In his memorial Fray Mariano complained that instead of employing the garrison in the interest of the missions, Rábago used the soldiers for his own purposes, "for, contenting himself with assigning two or three soldiers to each of the missions, the chief considers his

---

[6] *Carta de los Pad^{es}. de Sⁿ. Javier al Discret^o. dando razon de las cosas de Rábago.*

[7] *Carta de los Pad^{es}.* See Morfi, Bk. 9, paragraphs 10–19.

obligation discharged, and reserves the rest for escorting pack trains and convoys. In this work ten are regularly engaged; an equal number in guarding the horse herd; and the same number in keeping guard, which makes thirty; ten in erecting barracks, and [the] others in various occupations which concern the convenience and interest of the same chief.'' From this it could be seen, said Fray Mariano, that nothing could be expected from the present arrangement.

Convinced of the futility of the presidio, Fray Mariano made the radical and surprising proposal that it be abolished and a civil colony established to protect the mission in its stead. His plan was to retain the forty-eight soldiers as settlers at a salary of two hundred and forty pesos each annually, instead of the four hundred and fifty pesos which they were receiving. Over the settlement let there be put a judge or superintendent, charged with jurisdiction over Spaniards and Indians and authorized to assign lands. Let sixteen of the soldiers settle at each mission, acting as a guard. Let all be granted the rights of first settlers. Let such as might so desire, enjoy water rights in the mission ditches, on condition of giving up their salaries, their places as soldiers being filled by newcomers.

It was of first importance, he said, that the salaries be paid in cash at the settlement, instead of in goods, as at present. Under the present system the whole twenty-two thousand dollars due the company was spent in the interest of the captain. For the presidio usually eight thousand dollars were spent for horses and clothing outside the province, the rest going into the pocket of the captain. By his plan the cash would circulate at the settlement, merchants would be attracted, Indian trade in peltry would spring up, and stock ranches and industry would flourish. Moreover, the settlement would take root and be permanent, whereas the few artisans—the tailor, the barber, the leather-jacket makers, the blacksmith—who would gather round the presidio, would move if it moved. The advantages of the plan were obvious: the crown would save ten thousand dollars a year; the missionaries would have an escort sufficient to gather and restrain the heathen; and the Indians would have instructors in agriculture. The saving, in fifteen years, might be diverted to founding two villas containing one hundred and fifty settlers, each of whom could be given one thousand pesos outright as an inducement.

Fray Mariano concluded by asking the viceroy, in case the plan were not approved, to provide some means of relieving the missionaries of their temporal cares.[8]

4. A policy of conciliation attempted.—When these documents reached the College of Querétaro, that body, weary of endless bickering over the San Xavier missions, and realizing that the college must do its best, now that the government had at last granted its support, made a strenuous effort to stop complaints and to install a reign of peace, in order that the missions might have some chance to prosper. With this in view, it had taken advantage of the passage of Rábago, the new captain, to make a compact to refrain from sending unnecessary complaints to Mexico. On its part the college had agreed to give satisfaction for all complaints made to it.[9] It was in pursuance of this policy of conciliation that on February 18, 1752, after the complaints had come from the frontier, Fray Mariano was "promoted"—this is the word used by the guardian—to the presidency of the Rio Grande missions, and Father Terreros put in his place. In other words, the two presidents were to be interchanged.[10]

Three days later the Discretorio of the college issued its instructions to Father Terreros, a document which throws light

---

[8] This plan is summarized in full by Morfi, Bk. 9, paragraphs 10–19. Compare with a report by Fray Mariano, January 12, 1752. See also *Memorias*, XXVIII. 94.

[9] The Discretorio to Terreros, February 21, 1752.

[10] The guardian to Terreros, February 18, 1752.

on the existing situation. It recited that never before was the college so much in need of the wisdom and prudence which had brought peace and safety to Father Terreros' missions. Never before had the college wavered as at the present time. In view of the obligation under which the recent belated measures of the government had placed the college, Father Terreros, "sole remedy and recourse in the exigencies of the time," was ordered to take charge of the missions of San Antonio and San Xavier. He was to go at once, leaving in charge at San Juan Bautista Father Miguel Placido de Alaña. Arriving at San Antonio, he was to deliver to Fray Mariano the corresponding order to go to the Rio Grande to take charge.

The keynote of the instructions was tolerance. "By virtue of the agreement that the college would remedy everything reported," wrote the Discretorio, "this policy has been followed to the end that, innocence being justified, envy and malice should be silenced, event which your Reverence will keep in mind, so that violence may not be used to vindicate what God permits to try the patience; for means which do not accomplish their ends are always ill chosen, and there is little wisdom in fighting with a sword when it is known that it will not cut."

Father Terreros was authorized to choose any mission he might elect as his residence, and any missionary as his companion. Nevertheless, it was believed that he would find it necessary to go to the San Xavier in person to live, for "we consider your Reverence the benevolent rainbow of peace who, with your prudence and discretion, will pacify the violent tempest which has caused such consternation to the fatigued laborers." He must at once take all necessary measures for "the greatest peace, tranquility, increase and stability" of the San Xavier missions. One of these means was to install Father Joseph López as chaplain of the presidio in place of Father Pinilla, against whom complaints had been made. Full instructions must be given Father López for his conduct, providing that he restrain indiscreet zeal, "for he must not attempt to remedy what cannot be remedied," and he must do nothing on his own responsibility, without referring it to the president. He must also immediately put some one in place of Father Anda in Mission San Francisco Xavier, sending Father Anda to San Antonio as companion of Father Lector Prado and subordinate to him.[11]

To remedy a complaint that mass was said at San Xavier on holidays so early and hurriedly that most of the soldiers could not attend it, he was to order expressly that both at the missions and the presidio of San Xavier mass be said between eight and nine in the morning and that great care be taken in explaining the doctrine. Father López must minister to the presidio from his mission of San Xavier. The Pinilla brothers were to retain charge of Candelaria. Father Terreros must look after the moving, "which, as we are informed, is necessary and altogether advantageous and profitable to the purposes and greatest lustre of this College." As a means of putting an end to the past dissension, Terreros must interest himself in the liberation of the refugee criminal, and in restoring peace between Zevallos and his wife.

With Father José Pinilla was being sent Father Felix Gutiérrez Varaona, "a religious who, besides the many talents which adorn him, has a disposition most lovable, very docile, and tolerant in everything, for which reason he is being assigned to the mission of San Xavier in company with Father López, a combination which we judge will be agreeable to both, and under the present circumstances very advantageous." In case Father Terreros should not choose to live at Mission San Francisco de la Espada and should choose Fray Bartolomé as his companion, that mission was to be put in charge of Father Arricivita.

---

[11] Father Anda had recently been reprimanded for being careless in his accounts, which may explain this provision.

Since the San Xavier missions had no other recourse than those of San Antonio, Terreros was charged to make charitable subsidies of Indians from San Antonio to instruct those of San Xavier and of supplies, tools, etc., for their support and commerce. Finally, under the present urgent circumstances, the missionaries must not be permitted to take on any new charges, "lose what we may, or come what may."

5. *Rábago declared excommunicate.*—Whatever its possibilities had this step toward conciliation been taken earlier, it came too late. Before it went into effect the breach had become too wide.

It was complained by the missionaries that Rábago failed to furnish the missions with the soldiers necessary to guard the stock, cultivate the fields, and instruct the Indians, and that each day he caused mortification to the missionaries.[12] A matter of more concern was that of the morals of the garrison. The captain was not the only one whose standards were below par. A number of the soldiers had come without their families, and it was not long before rumors were rife that some of them were implicated in concubinage. Father Pinilla complained to the captain. Rábago claimed to know nothing of the scandal, but authorized Father Pinilla to enter the presidio by day or by night to root out the trouble.[13] Father Pinilla also begged Rábago to send for the families of the soldiers, which he promised to do, though without keeping his word.[14]

The month of February was filled with wrangling. A soldier named Arrucha complained to Pinilla of undue intimacy between his wife and Corporal Carabajal, a close confidante of Captain Rábago. The wife confessed, and thereupon Carabajal raised a storm against Father Pinilla, charging him with de-

---

[12] *2ª. Consulta.*

[13] He requested him to do this by a letter of February 1. *Carta de los Pad^es.* Pinilla to Fray Mariano, March 1.

[14] *Ibid.*

famation of character. Father Pinilla demanded that Rábago hold an investigation. This demand was answered by a document, inspired by Rábago and signed by some thirty soldiers, charging Father Pinilla with breaking the seal of secrecy in the confessional. The complaint was accompanied by an order from Rábago that Father Pinilla cease the administration of the presidio.

Father Pinilla now consulted with his companions, and they concluded that he should declare the captain and soldiers excommunicate. He did so, and on February 19 Father Ganzábal, as notary, appointed by Father Pinilla for the purpose, posted the pronouncement on the presidio.[15] The document was defaced and burned by the soldiery and immediately answered by a petition demanding absolution. The demand was denied; thereupon, Rábago assembled the soldiers with drumbeat and held a conference, wherein the soldiers threatened to desert, in order to seek absolution at Guadalajara. The assembly ended by sending as couriers to Mexico two of the excommunicates and chief offenders, Thoribio de Guevara and Carabajal, a collection being taken up for the purpose.

After one or two more parries the soldiers and captain, with due penitence, besought absolution and received it from Father Ganzábal at San Ildefonso, with the authority of Father Pinilla. This incident was now closed, but Rábago declared that he was sorry that he had not ejected Father Pinilla.[16]

On February 22 Guevara and Carabajal reached San Antonio on their way to Mexico, where they gave óut the nature of their mission. Thereupon Fray Mariano addressed to Rábago a petition, charging him with responsibility for the complaint, asking him to withdraw it, offering to go at once to San Xavier

---

[15] A copy of the *carta* with the names is in Pinilla's decree of censure, February 19, 1752.

[16] A full account is given by Pinilla, March 1, 1752. See also Arricivita, 331; *Ex. San Sabá*, 11; and *2ª. Consulta*.

to do justice to both parties, and demanding a formal statement of the charges. On March 2 this petition was presented to Rábago by Fray Diego Martín García, in the presence of Fray Joseph López, minister of Mission San Francisco Xavier, but the captain made no reply, though one was asked.[17]

6. *The murder of Father Ganzábal.*—When news of the censure of Rábago by Father Pinilla reached Mexico, the viceroy arrived at a similar though more far-reaching solution of the trouble than the one proposed by the college, for he issued an order that all the missionaries should retire, others being assigned to their places.[18] But by the time this order reached Fray Mariano, in June, it was already too late, for a crisis had been reached.

The crisis referred to was the murder of Father Ganzábal and the refugee Zevallos. It seems that on account of some disturbance at the mission, Rábago gave orders that no Indian should enter the presidio armed, and that a Coco Indian, of Mission Candelaria, unwittingly violated the order and was in consequence beaten. Thereupon, the whole Coco contingent at the mission fled. Shortly afterward a report was given out that the Coco were on the war-path, and Rábago sent to Béxar and Bahía for help, which in both instances was refused. A few days later, on the evening of May 11, as Fathers Ganzábal and Pinilla, together with the refugee Zevallos, were standing in the door of the mission of Candelaria, Zevallos was killed by a blunderbuss shot, and immediately afterward Father Ganzábal fell pierced to the heart by an arrow.[19]

---

[17] *Petizn. Al Capn. de Sn. Xr.*, February 22, 1752.

[18] This is inferred from *2a. Consulta.*

[19] *2a. Consulta.* Arricivita, *Crónica,* p. 334, gives essentially the same account, clearly from the same document which I am following. Fray Mariano in this document distinctly says that Rábago was especially angry at Ganzábal for his part in the censures; but Morfi, on what ground I know not, says that Rábago was especially friendly toward Ganzábal. Bk. 9, paragraph 23.

Soon after the murder—before June 13—all of the missionaries but one, fearing further violence, fled. The one who had the courage to remain was Father Anda y Altamirano, in whom the college had shown a lack of confidence. The flight of the Coco left but one mission—San Xavier—for him to serve.[20]

7. *Investigation of the murder.*—Rábago immediately despatched a messenger to San Antonio for help, and a few hours after the murder he went to the mission and began an investigation, whereupon the Indians fled.[21] It was not long before an arrest was made in another quarter. The night before the messenger sent by Rábago reached San Antonio, there appeared at San Juan Capistrano a Sayopin Indian named Andrés. He belonged to Mission Capistrano, where he had been raised from boyhood by Father Ganzábal, who took him to San Xavier as a personal servant and interpreter. Two days before the murder Andrés and his wife had disappeared from the missions. On his arrival at Capistrano he gave out news of the murders, charging them to the Cocos. Next day the courier arrived calling for help. Suspicion pointing to Andrés, Captain Urrutia went to San Juan Capistrano, accused him, and he confessed, without torture. His version of the story was that at the instigation of Rábago he and four soldiers—among them Sergeant Miguel de Sosa and Manuel Carrillo—had committed the murder.[22]

---

[20] See also Bolton, *Guide*, 390, for other data in Querétaro. On May 13, 1753, Miguel de la Garza Falcón, captain and *justicia mayor* of the royal presidio, and Músquiz were at San Xavier as commissioners to investigate. Fray Mariano was there with them. Shortly afterward Captain Piszina took testimony at Bahía.

In his reply Fray Mariano stated that, "of six ministers belonging to those conversions God was pleased to call one home: another was maliciously killed, together with a refugee, and of the other four, three have fled for fear lest they may meet the same fate, and one has barely remained there to assist the Indians of the mission of San Xavier, which is the only one inhabited now." *Ibid.*

[21] Morfi, Bk. 9, paragraph 24. There is some contradiction here. Morfi states that the Cocos had all fled some days before. Now he states that when Rábago made his investigation they fled.

[22] This account of the investigation and the confession of Andrés is from Fray Mariano's *consulta* of June 13, 1752. Arricivita's *Crónica*, 334–335; and Morfi, *Memorias*, Bk. 9, paragraphs 25–26.

This was but the beginning of a long and tedious investigation, which cannot be followed here. Urrutia drew up a *proceso*, and Governor Barrios sent a commissioner to San Xavier to conduct an inquiry. He was removed, and others were appointed and removed in a long succession, among them being the most prominent men of the frontier. To facilitate the investigation Rábago was removed and made captain of the presidio of Santa Rosa, where he made for himself an unsavory reputation. His place was taken at San Xavier by his brother, Don Pedro de Rábago y Terán, who proved to be very popular with the missionaries. The investigation lasted eight years, being terminated in the viceroy's court in June, 1760. Rábago was acquitted, and at the same time the missionaries were declared by the viceroy to be free from all charge of guilt or misconduct in the case.[23]

---

[23] Arricivita, 334–335; Fray Mariano to the viceroy, Oct. 28, 1760. *Ex. San Sabá;* Morfi, Bk. 9, paragraphs 25, 26; Report of Fray Mariano, June 13, 1752; *Expediente* in Béxar Archives, Béxar, 1751–1769.

CHAPTER IX

THE REMOVAL TO THE SAN MARCOS AND TO THE GUADALUPE

1. Continued work with the Indians.—The usefulness of these ill-fated missions was now largely at an end, and their subsequent history was made up mainly of an investigation of the murders and of efforts to move to another site. However, missionary work did not altogether cease, and more than three years elapsed after the murder of Ganzábal before the place was abandoned.

Although all but one of the missionaries had fled, Fray Mariano at once talked of and planned for restoring the missions, and before long missionaries were sent to replace those who had left. Among those who returned were Fray Joseph López, Fray Sebastián Flores, and Fray Francisco Aparicio. In his letter of June 13, 1752, to the viceroy, Fray Mariano wrote that even though the Indians were scattered and the fields neglected, it would still be possible to recover the Indians of San Ildefonso and Candelaria, and that the zeal of the fathers would cause them to seek them out. In the case of San Ildefonso, he said, this would be easy, since the neophytes had settled in a ranchería not far from the mission and had frequently been visited there by their missionary.[1]

Arricivita, in discussing events after the murders, states that the missionary of San Ildefonso went several times to visit and minister to the apostates in their nearby ranchería, and that they volunteered to return to their mission, but that their minister wisely put them off for lack of supplies and because of the bad

---

[1] *2ª. Consulta* of Fray Mariano.

state of affairs at San Xavier. With his customary indefinite-
ness, Arricivita gives no names or dates, and one wonders if he
is not referring to events before the murders, as indicated in
Fray Mariano's statement given above. In that case, Arricivita
knew all about the matter, since he himself was at that time missionary at San Ildefonso.[2]

That Fray Mariano knew whereof he spoke regarding the
zeal of the missionaries is shown by the efforts of Father José
Pinilla to recover the Coco. In the winter of 1752–1753 he went
with a guard of soldiers from Bahía to the Colorado to recover
the members of that tribe who had fled from San Xavier, as well
as to secure some apostate Xaraname from Bahía. According
to testimony given in May, 1753, incident to the investigation of
the murders, they went to the Xaraname ranchería on the banks
of the Colorado, where they found a Coco woman. Choosing
her as an intermediary, they sent her across the Colorado to
where her tribe were living, to inform them that Father Pinilla
was waiting to take them back to their mission. They promptly
came and warmly welcomed Father Pinilla and the soldiers with
a military salute and a dance, which, by the way, the Father
stopped. They expressed themselves as willing to return to
mission life, though not at San Xavier, because the Spaniards
there were angry at them. But they were willing to go to the
Guadalupe, the Comal, or any other place that Father Pinilla
might wish. However, it must be at a later date, after the cold
weather had passed, because he had brought them no blankets
or cottons to clothe them. The frankness with which the Indians
received the Father and the soldiers was taken as evidence of
their innocence of the charge of the murders.[3]

---

[2] Arricivita, 336.

[3] *Dilig⁸. a favor de los Cocos en los homicidios de Sⁿ. Xavʳ. 1753.* Arricivita's account on p. 336 is evidently based on the same document. He
gives no date, however, and omits to state that the Cocos stipulated that
if they were to return to a mission it must be elsewhere than at San
Xavier.

The mission of San Francisco Xavier continued in operation, and Arricivita states that in general its neophytes remained
constant. Some, however, were led off by the Texas, and others
roamed about in the woods; but the missionaries felt obliged to
dissimulate, for the stock was running wild for lack of herds-
men, and the fields remained uncultivated for lack of help from
the soldiers.[4]

Between the time of Father Pinilla's visit to the Coco and
the summer of 1754, Father Francisco Aparicio was stationed
at Mission Candelaria, where he did effective work. He gathered
there one hundred and twenty Bidai and Orcoquiza, the ones
who had deserted Mission San Ildefonso. Having remained
twelve days without formally entering the mission, they deserted
and returned to their rancherías. In the summer of 1754 the
same missionary had under instruction at Mission Candelaria
one hundred and twenty Cocos who had been induced to return.
But the success was shortlived, for at the end of July they fled,
stealing the soldiers' weapons. On August 14 they returned at
night, attacked the horseherd, wounded a soldier, and ran off a
drove of mares from Mission San Xavier. They were recovered
next day, however, by a squadron of twenty-five soldiers.[5]

2. *Removal to the Apache country proposed.*—In the summer of 1753 Father Mariano went to San Xavier to assist in the
investigation of the troubles there, and in the re-establishment of
the missions. As a result of his visit he was convinced that
success there was no longer possible, for a new difficulty had
arisen. To complete the ruin wrought by the murders, the river

---

[4] Arricivita, 336–337. The Prefecto de Misiones wrote in April, 1759:
"Se hicieron muchas instancias, y diligencias por los Pastor*. de aquellos
errantes ovejas para volververlas [*sic*] a su redil; pero no tubieron efecto
sus deseos, siendo mucha parte de la renuencia de los Yndios, el genio
aspero de dho Cap^n. a q^n tenian buen conocido" (C, leg. 1, no. 1). This
statement must refer, if to anything definite, to the period before Rábago
was returned from San Xavier.

[5] *Testimonio de los Autos fechos, á consulta de Don Pedro Rauago*, etc.,
1753–54.

had ceased to run, leaving stagnant pools. The phenomenon was mysterious because there was plentiful rainfall and other streams in the vicinity were full. The place had become unhealthful, and the country round about, which had once afforded good pasturage, was now covered with briers. In view of this situation Father Mariano suggested moving the missions to the San Marcos, or better, to the Guadalupe and the Comal Springs, then so-called. At the same time, he suggested transferring the San Xavier presidio to the Apache country and that of San Antonio to the Guadalupe. The removal of the San Xavier neophytes might require force, but this he recommended.[6]

Rábago's arrival on August 11, 1754, nearly a year after the date of his order, was the occasion for another glimpse of conditions at San Xavier, and for a new proposal for its suppression. On his way up he examined the principal rivers with a view to their advantages for settlement. Near the Guadalupe springs he found a site to which, he thought, fifty families might be moved from San Antonio. The San Marcos, even at the spring, he thought offered small advantages for irrigation. Immediately upon reaching San Xavier he took possession and reviewed the troops. The presidio had its full quota of fifty soldiers, of whom Joseph Joaquin Músquiz (Eca y Músquiz) was lieutenant, Diego Ramón *alférez*, and Asencio del Raso sergeant. A number of names are identical with those of soldiers there in 1752.[7] They were in a sorry condition. Amongst them they had one hundred

---

[6] *Testimonio de los Autos fechos sobre la Reduccion de los Yndios Gentiles de la Nacion Apache, y establecimiento de el Precidio de San Saba. Quadᵒ. 5ᵒ. A.*, fols. 81–82. (A. G. I. Méjico, 92–6–22).

[7] The names given in the *revista* are: (1) Don Joseph Joaquin de Ecaymusquis, *teniente;* (2) Don Diego Ramon, *alférez;* (3) Asencio del Raso, *sargento iterinerario;* (4) Antonio Flores, *cavo;* (5) Nicolas Carauajal, *cavo;* (6) Joachin Garcia, *cauo interino;* (7) Carlos de Uruega; (8) Phelipe Neri del Valle; (9) Gueronimo Rodriguez; (10) Joseph Antonio de Estrada; (11) Marcos Minchaca; (12) Euseuio Garcia; (13) Joseph Visente Guerrero; (14) Fran.ᶜᵒ Sanchez; (15) Joseph Xptobal Vela; (16) Joseph Juachin de Estrada; (17) Juan Fran.ᶜᵒ de Auila; (18) Joseph Antonio Charles; (19) Pedro del Rio; (20) Joseph de Sosa; (21) Joseph Antonio Rodriguez; (22) Vicente Ferrer Moncalvo [sic]; (23) Fran.ᶜᵒ

and six horses and a mule, but eight soldiers were entirely without mounts. Some were completely equipped with arms, offensive and defensive, powder and balls, but others lacked cloak, leather jacket, shield, musket, saber, ammunition, bridle, saddle, spurs, one or all. The garrison was equipped with four re-enforced *pedreros,* or swivel guns, but they were without *sigueñas,* and the quarters were mere huts of thatch.

On September 2 Rábago wrote to the viceroy describing the deplorable condition of the garrison, "expatriated, without quarters even for lodgings, and lacking supplies and other necessities." Fray Mariano's complaint against the site was confirmed by the captain. It seemed pleasant and attractive enough, said Rábago, but it would never be habitable. The climate was conducive to contagious diseases; the water left in the pools by the falling river was corrupt from rotting fish, so that not even cattle or horses would drink it. To the oft-repeated complaint that the lands were not adapted to irrigation Rábago subscribed. The condition of the missions was even worse than that of the presidio. The Indians could not be made to work and when urged would flee to their native woods. Indeed, San Ildefonso was without missionaries or Indians. In San Xavier there were seventy neophytes under the instruction of Father López. In Candelaria Father Fray Francisco Aparicio was stationed, but his charges had all fled.

In short, in Rábago's opinion, the presidio would always be useless where it was, and should be moved to a new frontier. And

---

Maldonado; (24) Santiago Garcia; (25) Joseph Flores; (26) Pedro Duran; (27) Pedro Martin; (28) Miguel de Sosa; (29) Jose de Torres; (30) Franᶜᵒ. de Iruegas; (31) Mario Martines; (32) Joseph Manuel Martin; (33) Joseph Joachin Perez; (34) Joseph Calletano de Ulivarri; (35) Gregorio Dominges de Renteria; (36) Thomas Barreda; (37) Antonio Clemente Flores; (38) Juan Antonio Ramires; (39) Ignacio de Raso; (40) Joseph Joachin del Valle; (41) Juan Diego de la Garza; (42) Fran.ᶜᵒ Xavier de Suniga; (43) Joseph Barroso; (44) Pablo Joseph Carmona; (45) Asencio Cadena; (46) Manuel de la Garza; (47) Joseph Marcos Mendez; (48) Mariano de Esquibal; (49) Joseph Maria Martinez; (50) Juan de Sosa (*Testimonio de los Autos fechos, á consulta de Don Pedro Rauago Terán,* etc., 1753–54).

for this he had a proposal. Let the neophytes there be moved to the San Antonio missions, which could easily serve three thousand. Then let the missionaries and soldiers at San Xavier, with their entire outfit and aided by fifty more soldiers, be sent to work among the Apache, on the San Sabá River, or on the Río Florido (the Concho), discovered by himself in 1748. Here were the finest of lands, water, pastures, and mineral prospects. Near by were the Comanche, who could likewise by Christianized. Through their country a direct route could be opened to New Mexico, and commerce established between that province, Texas, Coahuila, and Nuevo León. Finally, by these means French traders, of whom there were rumors current, would be kept out of New Mexico. A question of jurisdiction would arise, Rábago said, between New Mexico, Texas, and Coahuila, but he recommended that the new establishment be made dependent solely on the captaincy-general of the viceroy.[8]

This proposal of Rábago's fitted right in with the plan for Apache missions which for years had been on foot, and of which it may have been but an echo. At any rate, it ultimately became the solution of the San Xavier problem.

3. Nature conspires against the missions.—The order of events at San Xavier during 1754 and 1755 is as yet obscure, but we know with some precision the circumstances which led to the abandonment of the place in the year last named. The specific cause—or the principal one given, for this removal—was that nature had conspired to make the site untenable. In the foregoing report Rábago spoke emphatically of the unhealthfulness of the place. To this charge there were added tales of frightful supernatural phenomena. On this point, which became a disputed one, I venture no opinion, but merely give the statement of Father Mariano made some years later. He says:

---

[8] *Testimonio de los Autos fechos á consulta de Don Pedro Rauago Terán,* 1753–54.

"The sacrilegious homicides having been perpetrated, the elements at once conspired, declaring divine justice provoked; for in the sky appeared a ball of fire so horrible that all were terrified, and with so notable a circumstance that it circled from the presidio to the mission of the Occisos [Orcoquiza], and returned to the same presidio, when it exploded with a noise as loud as could be made by a heavily loaded cannon. The river ceased to run, and its waters became so corrupt that they were extremely noxious and intolerable to the smell. The air became so infected that all who went to the place, even though merely passing, became infected by the pest, which became so malicious that many of the inhabitants died, and we all found ourselves in the last extremes of life. Finally, the land became so accursed that what had been a beautiful plain became converted into a thicket, in which opened horrible crevices that caused terror. And the inhabitants became so put to it, in order to escape the complete extermination which threatened them, that they moved more than thirty leagues away, with no other permission than that granted them by the natural right to save their own lives."[9]

4. *The Removal to the San Marcos.*—As Father Mariano said, while his proposal and that of Rábago were being discussed in Mexico, the residents of the frontier took matters into their own hands. On July 15, 1755, the soldiers of the presidio presented a petition to Captain Rábago. It recited that the pest of

[9] Fray Mariano to the viceroy, *Ex. S. San Sabá*, 11–12, October 28, 1760. See also Bonilla, ''Breve Compendio,'' Texas Historical *Quarterly*, VIII, p. 50, and Morfi's repetition of some of Bonilla's statements; Morfi, *Memorias*, Bk. 9, paragraphs 29–35. See also *Informe de Misiones*, in *Memorias*, XXVIII, 179, for a statement of the natural phenomena.

On January 22, 1757, Fray Mariano made the following statement regarding the abandonment of San Xavier: ''The pueblo of San Xavier annihilated, the missions destitute, the Indians having deserted, terrified by the various general pests and epidemics which the Spaniards and Indians suffered, the missionaries not exempted, and from which many Indians were imperilled, for it was so severe that whoever passed through the place became ill, they abandoned it completely, returning to their ancient caverns, where, blind in the shadowy chaos of infidelity, they groan under the power of the common enemy, together with more than four hundred Christians who had been baptized'' (*Testimonio de los Autos fhos, sobre hauerse trasladado los Yndios . . .* 1757).

the three previous summers had recurred with increased vigor. The river had again ceased to run, the water was stagnant, and from its use some, especially Indians, had died. They begged the captain, therefore, to remove them to some habitable place, pledging their goods as a guarantee of the cost. Rábago replied that he had no authority to grant the request, and ordered them, like good subjects, to continue at their posts, even at the risk of their lives.

Eight days later a similar petition was presented by the friars, Joseph López, Francisco Aparicio, and Sebastián Flores. They recited that since early in May the missionaries, soldiers, and Indians had been suffering from the pest. The Indians had become terrified at the natural phenomena; some had fled to the San Marcos, and others were clamoring to go thither. They requested, therefore, that Rábago move them and the remaining neophytes to that stream. If the request were not granted, they declared that they would appeal to the viceroy. From Arricivita we learn that the missionaries had already addressed a petition to their President, Fray Mariano.

To this appeal Rábago yielded, even though he had no authority except that of necessity. He therefore ordered Alférez Diego Ramón, now a veteran of many years' service in Texas, to be ready within two days to go with ten soldiers, twenty picked Indians, and one missionary, to the San Marcos, to select a site and construct temporary *xacales,* while the captain himself followed with the remaining friars, neophytes, and movables. Another petition by the soldiers, dated the same day, was met with a rebuke, although the decision to move had already been made.

By August 23 the entire colony had been transported to San Marcos. Ever since their arrival the missionaries had been besieged by more than a thousand hungry Apaches, who were clamoring to have them move, with the presidio, to their country, on the San Sabá and the Florido. On September 6, Governor

Barrios wrote to the viceroy that the presidio of San Xavier had been moved to the San Marcos without his knowledge, although he supposed that Rábago had taken the step under the viceroy's orders. On February 6, 1756, the viceroy wrote to Rábago, rebuking him for having moved the garrison without authority, though he accepted the *fait accompli.*

In spite of the tenacity with which they had clung to the San Xavier site, the leading spirits in bringing about the removal seem to have been the friars. Arricivita states that the missionaries, in view of the peril involved in remaining at San Xavier, took pity on the soldiers, and appealed to their president, Fray Mariano, suggesting a removal; Fray Mariano in turn addressed the captain on the subject. The captain admitted the truth of the statements, but maintained that he had no authority to move without permission from the viceroy. The missionaries repeated the request, stating that the missions could no longer perform their duties, and that if they remained there both Spaniards and Indians would perish. "And proving the truth of their petitions, they were under necessity of agreeing to the decision which all, forced by such penuries, made to leave and encamp on the bank of the San Marcos, with no other license than that given them by the natural right, which prevails over every other right, to save their own lives. With this desertion of San Xavier the total desolation of that unfortunate land was completed.''

5. *San Xavier neophytes at San Antonio.*—When the soldiers and missionaries left San Xavier, most of the Indians who had remained at mission San Francisco went ''to their ancient selvas.'' For a time the missionaries stopped with the soldiers on the San Marcos, the step being spoken of as a transfer of the missions to that point, although they went with few neophytes. The removal, therefore, consisted mainly of a change of location

on the part of the missionaries, and of a transfer of bells, ornaments, and other movable mission property.[10]

But the missionaries did not leave their neophytes, many of
whom were baptized, to roam the forests unheeded. On the contrary, in the course of the succeeding months Fray Mariano
"several times" sent to seek them and "with flattery, gifts, and
urgent persuasion" succeeded in taking to the mission of San
Antonio de Valero numerous families belonging to the mission
of San Francisco Xavier, with the hope that their relatives would
follow them, "but with such bad results, on account of their
ancient repugnance to being congregated with these, that not
only did the rest . . . not come, but, deserting a few at a time,
there now [June 25, 1756] remain less than a fourth of those
who were here."[11] Meanwhile the Coco and other tribes belonging to Mission Candelaria were being gathered in considerable
numbers at Mission Valero.[12]

The plan for an Apache mission, which had been developing
for years, had now come to a head, and provision had been made
(May 18, 1756) for transferring to that new establishment the
missionaries and soldiers who had been employed at San Xavier.
The same despatch which ordered this transfer, provided also for
opening the San Antonio missions to the remnant of neophytes
who had been at the San Xavier missions.[13] When this provision

---

10 *Testimonio de los Autos fechos sobre la Reduccion de los Yndios Gentiles de la Nacion Apache*, fols. 177–186. Barrios to the viceroy, Sept.
6, 1755; the viceroy to Barrios, Feb. 14, 1756 (A. G. M. Historia, vol. 97,
Expediente 1). See also *Mem. de Nueva España*, XXVIII, 179–180, 183;
Arricivita, 335–336. The obvious source of Arricivita's account at this
point is Fray Mariano's statement.

11 Fray Mariano to Ortiz, Arch. Coll. Santa Cruz, K, leg. 6, no. 10;
Fray Mariano to Parrilla, January 22, 1757, Arch. Coll. Santa Cruz, K, leg.
6, no. 34.

12 Fray Mariano to Ortiz, Arch. Coll. Santa Cruz, K, leg. 6, no. 10,
June 25, 1756.

13 Fray Mariano to Parrilla, January 22, 1757. "Que en conse-
cuenzia de Su Ynstituto religiosa Christianidad, y acreditado Celo Rl
bien de las Almas, se apronten á rezibir los yndios de los tres suprimidas
misiones del Rio de San Javier."

was reported to Fray Mariano, he made it the occasion for an effort to gather the Mayeye and their kinsmen, that is, the neophytes of San Francisco Xavier, in a mission on the Guadalupe, without a presidial guard.

6. *The mission on the Guadalupe River.*—When the order came, Fray Francisco Ortiz was again at San Antonio as visitor of missions. He had been present at the birth of the unfortunate San Xavier missions, and he was now in at the death. His coming had already been made the occasion of a protest (May 6, 1756) against the evil influence of the Texas soldiery, and of a request by three of the missionaries of San Xavier, now at San Antonio, to be permitted to return to their missionary work unhampered by the control of presidial officers.[14] The petition was referred by Father Ortiz to all the other missionaries at the San Antonio missions, all of whom, by June 1, had expressed their approval of it. The reply of Fathers Mariano and Joseph de los Angeles, of Mission Valero, was a most instructive, if a partisan, disquisition upon the government of Texas.[15]

On June 25 Fray Mariano broached to Father Ortiz his plan regarding a mission on the Guadalupe River. He told of the destruction of the mission of San Xavier and of the efforts which have been made to assemble the neophytes at San Antonio. The tribes belonging to Candelaria, he said, were entering Mission Valero; the Orcoquiza and other tribes formerly at San Ildefonso could be gathered at the new mission just ordered established among the Orcoquiza tribe on the lower Trinity.[16] This left unprovided for only the Mayeye and their associates of Mission San Francisco Xavier. They could not be gathered at San Antonio,

---

[14] Petition of Fathers Francisco Aparicio, Benito Varela, and José López to Father Ortiz. *Mem. de Nueva España*, XXVIII, 76–79.

[15] *Memorias*, XXVIII, 86–88. The other missionaries approving were Fathers Aponte and Aranda, of Concepción; José Guadalupe and Sebastián Flores, of Capistrano; and Acisclos Valverde and Bartolomé García, of Espada.

[16] See Bolton, ''Spanish Activities on the Lower Trinity''; also pp. 327–374, below.

as had already been proved; they could not be established at San Marcos because, without more means, irrigating facilities could not be provided; moreover, since the garrison now at San Marcos was to go to San Sabá there would be no guard at the former place. Therefore, he proposed a site on the Guadalupe, twelve leagues from San Antonio—the site of modern New Braunfels—for a new mission. To care for them he proposed asking alms for two missionaries, and for the salaries of six soldiers. But instead of enlisting soldiers, let the fund be used to secure citizen Spaniards "who shall instruct the Indians in labor and serve as a protection to them." The missionaries would undertake to select the Spanish families. By this means many souls would be saved; the royal treasury would be relieved of a heavy burden; the missionaries would be exempt from the customary molestation by the presidial officers, while within a few years there would grow up a villa large enough to protect the place, when no guard would be necessary.[17]

On June 26 this memorial was submitted by Father Ortiz to all the missionaries near San Antonio, all of whom approved it. On July 2 Fray Sebastián Flores wrote his approval at "Mission San Francisco Xavier," and on the next day Fray Benito Varela wrote his approval at "Mission de la Candelaria." Neither one states where his mission was, but both imply that they were on the San Marcos.[18] On July 5 Father Ortiz approved the plan and ordered Fray Mariano "to carry out with all possible expedition whatever was in his part and whatever he might find conducive to the requested foundation and to the congregation of the said Indians."[19]

Having secured this license, Fray Mariano went to the garrison on the San Marcos, and asked its commander, who was now

---

[17] *Memorial,* on or before June 26, 1756.

[18] Varela, writing of the site on the Guadalupe, says: "I have been at said place."

[19] *Memorial,* on or before June 26, 1756. It will be noted that on May 31 Father Flores was missionary at Mission San Juan Capistrano, *Memorias* XXVIII, 88.

Diego Ramón, Rábago having died, to go to the Guadalupe to report on the suitability of the site proposed.[20] Ramón complied, and on the 15th was at the Guadalupe, accompanied by Gerónimo Rodríguez, Father Montalbo, Phelipe Neri del Valle, and Joseph Martínez. They described the site as unexceptionable. There were five springs close at hand, excellent opportunities for irrigation, fine arable fields, meadows, timber, "and other circumstances necessary to form a diversified settlement, with the advantage that the river is one of the best in this province." Ramón approved also Fray Mariano's plan for Spanish settlers instead of presidial soldiers.[21]

Having secured this support, Father Mariano now proposed to the Mayeye and their associates still at San Antonio that they should go to the Guadalupe to settle, "with the intention, of course, of going after the rest, the deserters." They embraced the proposal eagerly, and went to their new destination, promising to settle permanently, and expecting their friends to join them. With them the president sent Spanish families, Indian laborers, and two missionaries, Fathers Francisco Aparicio and Miguel de Aranda.[22]

In December Father Terreros and Captain Parrilla, who had been appointed respectively military and religious heads of the San Sabá enterprise, arrived with their outfits at San Antonio, where they spent some time in making preparations for their expedition. On January 14, 1757, at Mission San Antonio de Valero the property of the San Xavier missions was delivered by Fray Mariano, listed and appraised under the direction of Parrilla, and turned over to Fray Giraldo de Terreros. It was

---

[20] Fray Mariano to Ortiz, Arch. Coll. Santa Cruz, K, leg. 6, no. 10.

[21] *Ibid.*

[22] *Memorial del R. P. Fr. Mariano.* These two missionaries are not named in the document cited, but they are the ones on the Guadalupe in January, 1757.

valued at $1804.50.[23] This transaction had a bearing upon Fray Mariano's plan for a mission on the Guadalupe, for were it to be established an outfit must be forthcoming from somewhere. He therefore, on January 22, presented to Parrilla an *escrito* recounting what had been done with the Mayeye, and requesting that Parrilla go to the Guadalupe, examine the site and decide whether the missionaries should continue their work there or return to their college. He added that in case they were to remain they would need an outfit, of which they had just been deprived.[24] The petition was presented at an opportune time, because Parrilla was about to go to the San Marcos to attend to the removal to San Antonio of the garrison there under Ramón.[25]

Parrilla readily granted the request, and on January 25 he was "at the Congregation of San Francisco Jabier de el Rio de Guadalupe." With him were Fray Mariano, Fray Bartolomé García, of Mission Espada, Manuel Antonio de Bustillo y Zevallos, ex-lieutenant-general of Coahuila, Alférez Diego Ramón, and Antonio de Ribas. They reported a "settlement of several huts, in which live four families of Spaniards, servants of said congregation; some Indians; and the reverend father Fray Francisco Aparicio and Fray Miguel de Aranda . . . formerly missionaries of the abandoned Rio de San Jabier and now in charge of the establishment, care and administration of this." Parrilla examined the "governor" of the congregation, a Christian Mayeye Indian named Pablo, who spoke Spanish. The Indian settlement contained forty-one persons formerly at San Xavier, twenty-seven of whom had been baptized. Pablo stated that

---

[23] Among the notable items were six bells, weighing 252, 225, 223, 131, 128, and 125 pounds respectively, and valued at $542, or half a dollar per pound. *Testimonio de los Autos fechos sre la entrega*, etc.

[24] *Memorial del R. P. Fr. Mariano; Testimonio de los Autos fhos, sobre hauerse trasladado los Yndios*, 1751. Father Mariano stated that the bringing of the Mayeye to San Antonio had cost them about forty horses, besides endless hardships.

[25] Dunn, W. E., "The Apache Missions on the San Sabá River," 392.

though this region was not their native land, the Indians were content, since the missionaries supplied them with plenty to eat and wear and since the site was all that could be desired. Governor Pablo then called the rest of the Indians, who subscribed to what he had said.[26]

Next the site was examined. Note was taken of several springs flowing from the slope of a rocky hill near by; and of the advantages for an irrigation ditch on the west side of the river "a short distance from its source;" the excellent lands for crops; plentiful timber, pasture lands, and the ridge north of the stream, thought to contain mineral. Parrilla continued his exploration down stream ten leagues, "invited by its shadiness."

Having completed the examination, Parrilla stated in writing that the spirit of the viceroy's order would be kept by founding the desired mission, but preferred, before making a decision, to get the opinion of Father Terreros, president of the projected San Sabá missions. On February 13 Terreros recommended that Parrilla, after having made proper *diligencias* to test the desires of the Indians, report to the viceroy the need of one or more missions on the Guadalupe for the already Christianized neophytes of San Xavier; that meanwhile the missionaries should remain at their post, until the viceroy should decide the matter; and that the establishment should be under the San Antonio presidency, since the San Sabá enterprise was designed to convert heathen Apache north of Coahuila. According to one of the missionaries present at San Antonio at the time, Father Mariano was greatly offended that Father Terreros should have excluded the Guadalupe mission from participation in the endowment of the San Sabá mission, and a quarrel ensued between them.[27]

---

[26] The námes of the baptized Indians are given: Pablo, his wife Jertrudis, Reimundo, Feliz, Antonio, Diego, Maria, Rosa, Basilio, Bernardo, Ana, Joseph, Dorothea, Francisco, Thomas, Matías, Juana, Geronimo, Andrés, Matheo, Enrique, Margarita, Jabiela, Bárbara, another Margarita, Sebastiana, Josepha.

[27] Fray Francisco de la Santísima Trinidad, *Vindicta del Rio de Sⁿ. Saba.*

On February 18, Parrilla forwarded his *diligencias* to the viceroy, accompanied by a *consulta*. In his opinion the site on Guadalupe was beautifully adapted to two missions, and he believed that it would be a good thing to occupy a post between San Antonio and the San Sabá. In case this was done, four men would be necessary for a guard. For further information Parrilla referred the viceroy to Fray Miguel de Aranda, who was about to set out for Mexico in the interest of the new project.[28]

The matter being referred to Valcárcel, the *auditor*, and to the Marqués de Aranda, the fiscal, the latter gave an opinion on June 15. He agreed that the question at issue did not pertain to the San Sabá project. But he recommended that for the time being, until the question of a permanent mission should be determined, the Indians on the Guadalupe be provided with missionaries, and that Father Terreros be requested to return the necessary outfit. Valcárcel agreed, on June 30, and on August 2 the viceroy ordered the feeble mission continued and provided with two missionaries.[29]

At this point detailed knowledge of the mission on the Guadalupe fails us. But we have the statement of Father Mariano and his associates made in 1762 that, at the time of the destruction of the San Sabá mission, which was in March, 1758, the mission of Nuestra Señora de Guadalupe, which likewise by order of his Excellency had been founded on the river of this name, with the hope of congregating some of the dispersed nations of the Río de San Xavier, was abandoned, "since with insufficient garrison, it could not exist because of the multitude of enemies."[30]

---

[28] *Memorial del R. P. Fr. Mariano;* Parrilla, *Consulta* of February 18, in *Testimonio de los Autos fhos, sobre hauerse trasladado los Yndios,* etc.

[29] *Testimonio de los Autos fechos sre la entrega,* etc.

[30] *Informe de Misiones,* 1762, *Memorias,* XXVIII, 181. Bonilla says that the mission was allowed to continue "by special permission." *Breve Compendio,* p. 5.

III. THE REORGANIZATION OF THE LOWER GULF COAST

CHAPTER I

THE LOWER GULF COAST BEFORE 1746[1]

1. The Karankawan tribes about Matagorda Bay.—When, at the close of the seventeenth century, the French and the Spaniards first attempted to occupy the Gulf coast in the neighborhood of Matagorda Bay, that region was the home of a group of native tribes now called Karankawan, from their best known division. The principal tribes of the group, using the most common English forms of the names, were the Cujane, Karankawa, Guapite (or Coapite), Coco, and Copane. They were closely interrelated, and all apparently spoke dialects of the same language, which was different from that of their neighbors farther inland.[2] Though the Karankawa tribe has finally given its name to the group, it was not always the one best known to the Europeans or regarded by them as the leading one, for in the middle of the eighteenth century four tribes, at least, including the Karankawa, were frequently considered collectively under the name Cujane.[3]

---

[1] Unless otherwise indicated, the correspondence cited in this monograph is contained in a collection of manuscripts in the Archivo General de México (Sección de Historia, volume 287) entitled *Autos fhos. Apedimento . . . [de] Frai Benitto de Santa An[a] . . . que se le manden restitu[ir á la Mision de] Sn. Antonio que es á cargo de la Sta. Cruz de Querétaro los [con] Bersos Indios de la Nacion [Cujan] que se hallan agregados á [la Misión] de Santa Dorothea.* 1751–1758. Original. 108 Folios.

[2] The relation above asserted between these four tribes has not hitherto been established by ethnologists, nor do the scope and purpose of this study justify inserting here the evidence to prove it. Such evidence is not lacking, however, and will be published, it is hoped, in another place. The only essay in print on the Karankawan Indians is that by Dr. Gatschet, *The Karankawa Indians*, in *Archaeological and Ethnological Papers of the Peabody Museum, Harvard University*, Vol. I, no. 2 (1891) Recent work in the Mexican and the Texas archives has made accessible a great deal of material unused by him. [Since the above was written, some of the results of this work have been published].

[3] Captain Manuel Ramírez de la Piszina, of Bahía del Espíritu Santo, calls them "the four nations, who, under the name of Coxanes, have

Since these Indians did not occupy fixed localities, and since they mingled freely with each other, it is difficult to assign definite territorial limits to the different tribes; and yet in a general way the characteristic habitat of each can be designated with some certainty. The Karanwaka dwelt most commonly on the narrow fringe of islands extending along the coast to the east and the west of Matagorda Bay; the Coco on the mainland east of Matagorda Bay, about the lower Colorado River; the Cujane and Guapite on either side of the bay, particularly to the west of it; and the Copane west of the mouth of the San Antonio River about Copano Bay, to which the tribe has given its name.

Numerically the group was not large. A French writer of the seventeenth century estimates the "Quélancouchis," probably meaning the whole Karankawan group, at four hundred fighting men, and a Spaniard, upon the basis of a closer acquaintance, in 1751 put the number, excluding the Coco, at five hundred fighting men.[4]

These tribes represented perhaps the lowest grade of native society in Texas. Their tribal organization was loose, and their habits were extremely crude. With respect to clothing, they ordinarily went about in a state of nature. Being almost or entirely without agriculture, they lived largely on fish, eggs of sea-fowls, and sylvan roots and fruits, although to some extent they hunted buffalo and other game in the interior. They led a roving life, and therefore built only temporary habitations, consisting usually of poles covered or partly covered with reeds or skins. The Karankawa, in particular, as has been said, dwelt on the islands; but during the hunting season and the

been reduced. They are the Cujanes, Guapittes, Carancaguases, and Copanes.'' (Letter to the viceroy, December 26, 1751). This is only one of several instances of this usage of the word Cujanes that might be cited.

[4] A mémoire of 1699, in Margry, *Découvertes et Etablissements,* IV, 316; Captain Piszina, of Bahía, letter to the viceroy, December 26, 1751.

cold winter months they migrated to the mainland. For these migrations they used canoes, which they managed with great skill. Physically, the men were large and powerful, and they were correspondingly warlike. They were frequently in conflict with the interior tribes, and from their first contact with the whites they were regarded as particularly dangerous. Although their only weapons were the bow and the spear,[5] their island asylum and their skill with canoes made them unassailable in retreat, while horses, early secured from the Spaniards, increased their offensive strength. From very early times they were regarded as cannibals, and their religious superstitions were commensurate with their barbarity. Such Indians as these could hardly be called the most inviting material for the missionary.

2. *Early Spanish efforts among the Karakawan tribes.*—Although the Karankawan tribes were among the very earliest of the Texas natives to come to the notice of the Spaniards, and were visited by them again during the first attempts at actual occupation of the country, efforts to control them were for some time delayed. The Caoque, or Capoque, met by Cabeza de Vaca on the Texas coast (1528–1534) are thought to have been identical with the Coco of later times.[6] After this adventurer, their next white visitors to leave explicit records were the French. La Salle's unfortunate colony (1685–1689) on the Garcitas River had some of these tribes for neighbors, and was destroyed by them. It was among the Caocosi, the Coco, very probably, that De León in 1690 rescued some captive survivors of this French colony.[7] Again, in 1721, the hostility of what

---

[5] The "*dardo*" which they also used for catching fish (De Meziéres to Croix, October 7, 1779, in *Memorias de Nueva España*, XXVIII, 258).

[6] Bandelier, *The Journey of Alvar Nuñez Cabeza de Vaca* (Barnes & Co., 1905), 72; Gatschet, *The Karankawa Indians*, 34; *Handbook of American Indians* (Bureau of American Ethnology), I, 315.

[7] Velasco, *Dictamen Fiscal*, November 30, 1716, in *Memorias de Nueva España*, XXVIII, 182. This statement is made by Velasco on the basis of De León's own report. See "Carta de Damain Manzanet" (Texas State Hist. Assn. *Quarterly*, II, 301), and De León, *Derrotero*, 1690.

have been thought to be the same tribes caused La Harpe to abandon his project of occupying the Bay of St. Bernard for France, and thus put an end to serious French attempts to control this coast.[8] It may be, however, that La Harpe's landfall was farther east, among the Attacapa.

Up to this time the Spaniards had seen but little of the Karankawa Indians since the first *entradas* from Mexico more than a quarter of a century before, and had made no attempt to subdue them. But in 1722 the Marqués de Aguayo established on the very site of La Salle's fort the presidio of Nuestra Señora de Loreto, more commonly called Bahía, and aided the Zacatecan missionaries in founding nearby for the Cujane, Guapite, and Karankawa the mission of Espíritu Santo de Zúñiga. The presidio was left in charge of Captain Domingo Ramón, the man who had led the expedition to eastern Texas and Louisiana in 1716. Father Peña,[9] a member of Aguayo's expedition, recorded at the time in his diary that "it was seen that they [these three tribes] were very docile and would enter readily upon the work of cultivating the earth and their own souls, more especially because they live in greater misery than the other tribes, since they subsist altogether upon fish and go entirely without clothing."

In a short time forty or more families of Cujane, Karankawa, and Guapite established their ranchería near the presidio, and others may have entered the mission; but scarcely had they done so before trouble began. In the fall of 1723 a personal quarrel arose between them and the soldiers. An attempt to punish an offending Indian resulted in a fight, the death of Captain Ramón, and the flight of the natives.[10] In a few weeks

---

[8] Margry, *Découvertes et Etablissements*, VI, 354.

[9] Peña's diary of the Aguayo expedition calls him Jose Ramón, but authentic documents written at Loreto at the time of Ramón's death call him Domingo Ramón (*Autos fechos en la Bahía de el Espíritu Santo sobre . . . muertes*, 1723–1724.

[10] *Autos sobre muertes, etc.*, 1723–1724; Sotomayor, José Francisco, *Historia del Apostolico Colegio de Nuestra Señora de Guadalupe de Zacatecas* (Zacatecas, 1874), p. 195.

the Indians returned to make reprisals upon the lives and the goods of the soldiery—a practice which they kept up more or less continuously for the next twenty-five years.[11] Whether or not the garrison was to blame for bringing about the ill-feeling, as it was claimed they were, cannot be stated, but at any rate they showed little skill in dealing with this warlike people.[12]

Discouraged by the hostility between the Indians and the soldiery, the missionary at Espíritu Santo in 1726 removed his mission some ten leagues northwestward to the Guadalupe River, and labored among the Xaraname and the Tamique,[13] non-coast tribes, of a different language, hostile to, and having apparently a somewhat higher civilization than the Karankawa.[14] Shortly afterward the presidio was removed to the same site by Captain Ramón's successor.[15] The new location is now marked by the ruins in modern Mission Valley, west of the Guadalupe and near the northwestern line of Victoria County.[16]

[11] *Ibid.* In 1728 Rivera reported that the Cujanes, Cocos, Guapites, and Carancaguases were hostile to Bahía (*Proyecto*, Tercero Estado, par. 42). In 1730 Governor Bustillo y Zevallos wrote to the viceroy that a treaty had been made with Cujanes, Guapites, and Carancaguases, and that he hoped that the Copanes and Cocos would soon join them (Letter of November 29, 1720). Testimony given at Bahía November 20, 1749, states that Captain Orobio Bazterra had succeeded for some time in keeping the Cocos, Cujanes, and Orcoquizas quiet (Béxar Archives, Bahía, 1743–1778).

[12] *Ibid.*

[13] Bancroft, *North Mexican States and Texas*, edition of 1886, I, 631.

[14] Father Juan de Dios Maria Camberos, missionary at Bahía, wrote to the viceroy May 30, 1754, that "these Indians already mentioned [the Cujanes, Guapites, and Caranguases] do not wish to leave the neighborhood of la Bahía del Espíritu Santo, where their lands are, nor is it proper that they should be put with the Jaranames and Tamiques, who are in the mission called Espíritu Santo at said Bahía, since they are of different languages, incompatible dispositions, and do not like to be in their company." Solís, in his *Diario* (1768), reports that the Jaranames and their associates are "en mas politica" than the Karankawa (*Memorias de Nueva España*, XXVII, 265).

[15] Correspondence of Gov. Pérez de Almazán and Gov. Bustillo, with the viceroy, 1726, MSS. in A. G. M., Provincias Internas, vol. 236; Bancroft, *North Mexican States and Texas*, I, 631, on the authority of Morfi, *Mem. Hist. Tex.*, 195. The *presidio* was removed in 1726.

[16] This new site was later reported as fourteen leagues northwest from Bahía del Espíritu Santo (Report of Captain Orobio Bazterra, of Bahía, 1747) and about ten leagues northwest of the later site of Bahía,

Though the presidio and the mission had receded from their midst, the Karankawan tribes remained hostile, and, after Rivera's inspection in 1727, there was little prospect of subduing them. Rivera's reports made between 1728 and 1738 show that he regarded the Cujane, Coco, Guapite, Karankawa, and Copane tribes as all incapable of being reduced to mission life.[17] and that it was for this reason, mainly, that he considered projects for removing the presidio and the mission of Bahía, now to the San Marcos, now to the San Antonio, and now to the Medina. A missionary at San Antonio wrote in 1751 that "the Cujanes were for some thirty years considered unconquerable, and, according to various reports to be found in the Secretaría de Govierno, because unconquerable, they were the principal obstacle to the presidio of la Bahía." A little earlier he had written: "In truth, since the year 1733, when I came to this province, I have never heard that one of these Indians has attached himself to that mission [Espíritu Santo]."[18] In 1749 a number of Coco families entered the mission of Candelaria, at San Xavier. But with the exception of these and of a few families of Cujane and a few of Coco who had found their way into the San Antonio missions, by 1750 little progress had been made toward converting or even subduing these tribes. But now the problem of subduing the Karankawa was united with that of colonizing the whole Gulf coast lying to the southward.

3. Tamaulipas a center of disturbance.—No less in need of attention than the Karankawan district was the long stretch of coast to the southward, between the Nueces River and Pánuco.

---

or modern Goliad (Capt. Manuel Ramírez de la Piszina to the viceroy, February 18, 1750). Mr. H. J. Passmore, of Goliad, informs me that at the lower end of Mission Valley, and close to the Guadalupe River, and near what was known as the "De Leon Crossing," there were, within the memory of the old settlers, some fairly well preserved ruins of a mission, whose name none in his locality can tell him. The distances of this point from the original site of Bahía and from Goliad correspond very well with those given above.

[17] Santa Ana, president of the Querétaran Missions at San Antonio, to the viceroy, about May 22, 1752.

[18] Letters to the viceroy, June 17 and December 20, 1751.

This region, sheltered in its southern extremity behind the Sierra Madre and the Sierra Gorda, had long been the asylum of a multitude of native bands and broken-down tribes pushed in by the northward march of the Spanish conquest, or by their more powerful Indian neighbors on the west and north.

In the course of the centuries the region had become gradually narrowed by colonization on three sides, south, north, and west. In the sixteenth century Pánuco, Tampico, and Villa de Valles were founded as outposts of the Huasteca region on the coast, while north of the Valley of Mexico the conquest reached Querétaro, San Miguel el Grande, Celaya, Chamacuero, San Juan del Río, and Caderéyta, on the edge of the Sierra Gorda. But beyond this region colonization advanced but little further from the south and southwest until late in the eighteenth century. Missionary work in the region was for a long time scarcely more successful than colonization. In the last decade of the sixteenth century the Franciscans began work in the Sierra Gorda, and continued it intermittently during the course of the seventeenth, but without permanent success. In the latter part of the seventeenth century the Dominicans founded six missions in the district, but they were soon destroyed by the Indians, who fled to the fastnesses of the mountains, and from that vantage-ground preyed upon the frontier settlements of the Spaniards. The efforts of the local soldiery proving unequal to the situation, formal campaigns were made almost constantly between 1704 and 1715 by two military leaders named Zarza and Ardilla. Finally, in the year last mentioned, after a campaign with eight hundred soldiers, Ardilla secured peace, upon condition of leaving the Indians free and in possession of the Sierra Gorda. But the natives soon resumed their depredations, even to exacting tribute of the border towns and cities named above, which, till the second quarter of the eighteenth century were the outposts of settlement on the frontier of the Indian country.

On the western edge of the region settlements were planted before the end of the sixteenth century at San Luis Potosí, Saltillo, Monterey, and Cerralvo, and mining, ranching, and missionary work were begun. In the course of the seventeenth century, especially during the administration of Zavala in Nuevo León, settlements and missions were established in the north between Cerralvo and Monterey, and extended southeastward to the Sierra de Tamaulipas. But beyond this line the settlements were but little extended till the founding of Nuevo Santander, in the middle of the eighteenth century, the delay being chiefly due to Indian troubles.

During the whole of the seventeenth century the peace and prosperity of the province of Nuevo León were marred by the evils of the *encomienda* system and the hostility of the border tribes. The enslaved Indians frequently fled to the eastern mountains, or broke out in open revolt, in which they were joined by the eastern and northern border tribes. This bad condition led in 1715 to the sending of Francisco Barbadillo to Nuevo León as special commissioner to correct the evils. He organized a flying squadron (*compañia volante*) for the protection of the settlements, abolished *encomiendas*, quieted the fears of the Indians, brought back from the Sierra de Tamaulipas several thousand fugitives, settled them in the missions, assigned them lands, and distributed among them as teachers Tlascaltecos from Saltillo and Venado.

Barbadillo's work being undone as soon as he left, he was again sent to the province, where he remained as governor till 1723. But no sooner had he left the second time than the abuses again broke forth, and the Tamaulipas frontier, from Cerralvo to Sierra Gorda and Villa de Valles, became a menace to the Spanish border. It was seen by the government, therefore, that the coast lands north of Huasteca and east of Nuevo León, so long unoccupied, must be conquered and settled, as a means of ending the

Indian disturbances. Moreover, the region was understood to have valuable minerals, while the value of its extensive salines was well known. These general conditions in the Tamaulipas, combined with those farther north on the Karankawan coast, led to the founding of the new Colony of Nuevo Santander.[19]

4. *Escandón and the missionaries in Sierra Gorda.*—The first important step toward the definite subjugation of Tamaulipas was the reduction of the Sierra Gorda, in the years subsequent to 1738, by José de Escandón and the Franciscan missionaries. Escandón was a military officer of Querétaro who had already done good service in protecting that frontier. Now, in three campaigns, he entered the Sierra, subdued the natives, and assisted in the founding of missions. Crossing the Sierra to Rio Verde, Huasteca, and Tampico, he revised the government and corrected abuses in the administration.

Another important force in the subduing of this region was the Franciscan College of San Fernando. Its establishment in the eighteenth century had much the same relation to the colonization of the Sierra Gorda as had the founding of the College of the Holy Cross of Querétaro, in the later seventeenth century, to the development of Texas. The College of San Fernando, established at Mexico in 1735 as the third of the Colleges *de propaganda fide* in New Spain, took up as its first great task the conversion of the Sierra Gorda. The first mission of the college was founded in 1740 by the commissary, Fray José Cortés de Velasco. In 1744 work was extended to the very heart of the Sierra, among the Pames Indians, with Father Pedro Pérez de

---

[19] The foregoing summary is based largely on Prieto, Alexandro, *Historia, Geografía y Estadística del Estado de Tamaulipas* (Mexico, 1873), 70, 91; Mota Padilla, *Historia de la Conquista de la Provincia de la Nueva Galicia* (Mexico, 1870); González, *Lecciones Orales de Historia de Nuevo León* (Monterey, 1887); González, *Colección de Noticias y Documentos para la Historia del Estado de Nuevo León* (Monterey, 1885); Bancroft, *Mexico,* III, 340–347; *Instrucciones que los Vireyes de Nueva España Dejaron á Sus Sucesores,* 36–39.

Mezquía, a former missionary in Texas, as president. The central mission, founded with the personal assistance of Escandón, was that of Santiago de Jalpan. In 1750 Father Junípero Serra became president of the missions, and with his companion and biographer, Francisco Palou, lived for nine years at the mission of Santiago.[20]

---

[20] Palou, *Relación Histórica de la Vida y Apostólicas Tareas del Venerable Padre Junípero Serra,* 23–35.

CHAPTER II

THE COLONY OF NUEVO SANTANDER

1. The colonization of Tamaulipas entrusted to Escandón.—
Just at the time when Escandón began his work in the Sierra
Gorda, the demand for the subjugation and colonization of the
Seno Mexicano, lying farther north, came to a head, and resulted
in three simultaneous proposals for the undertaking, made by
three different men ambitious for honors. The first was made in
1738 by Antonio Ladrón de Guevara, a citizen of Nuevo León,
who based his claim to consideration on his acquaintance with
the geography of the region and his influence over its natives.
The essence of his plan was to colonize the Gulf Coast at royal
expense with colonies of Spaniards from Nuevo León, granting
them lands, and *fueros*, or privileges, of *conquistadores*, and re-
viving the system of *congregas*, or *encomiendas*. A second plan
was presented by Narciso de Montecuesta, *alcalde mayor* of Villa
de Valles, and looked to the colonization of the southern portion
of the region, as Guevara's had looked more particularly to the
occupation of the northern. The methods proposed were similar
in both cases; but as a personal reward Montecuesta asked for a
share in the profits of the salines which might be discovered in
the new region, suitable military rank, a salary of four thousand
pesos a year, and fourteen thousand dollars annually for the
support of a company of fifty cavalrymen. The third proposal,
similar to the others, came from José Fernández de Jáuregui,
governor of Nuevo León. One of his arguments for making haste
was the danger that some foreign nation might seize the stretch
of unoccupied coast.

All three proposals finally reached the king, and on July 10,
1739, a *cédula* was issued ordering them, especially that of

Guevara, with the portion relating to *congregas* left out, considered in a junta in Mexico. But the administration at Mexico had already opposed Guevara's plan, and it now delayed action until 1746, after the arrival of a new viceroy, the Conde de Revilla Gigedo.[1] Revilla Gigedo took up the matter at once, called a junta, and, on the advice of the Marqués de Altamira, the royal fiscal, committed the conquest of the Seno Mexicano to Escandón, in recognition of his masterly services in the Sierra Gorda. Escandón's commission was dated September 3, 1746. It made him lieutenant of the viceroy in the Seno Mexicano, or Gulf Coast, gave him ample powers, provided liberal appropriations, and ordered the frontier governors and other officials to lend him all possible aid. The viceroy's order provided for the conquest and settlement of a district more than one hundred leagues from north to south, and sixty or eighty leagues from east to west; it extended from Pánuco, Villa de Valles, and Sierra Gorda on the south, to the Medina and San Antonio rivers on the north; and from Guadalcázar, Las Charcas, Venado, Caderéyta, and Cerralvo, on the west, to the Gulf of Mexico on the east. The name given the new province was Colonia del Nuevo Santander.[2]

2. Escandón's plans.—Had the colonization of all New Spain been left to the care of men with the ability and the views of Escandón, the results of Spain's efforts would doubtless have been different. Soldier though he was, he was a firm believer in the superiority of civil settlements and missions as means of subduing the natives and of holding the country against foreign aggression; and an essential feature of his plan for Nuevo Santander was to colonize it with Spaniards and Christianized

---

[1] Prieto, *Historia de Tamaulipas*, 101–110; ''Instruccion del conde de Revillagigedo al Marqués de las Amarillas, sobre lo ocurrido en el Nuevo Santander y su Pacificacion por el Conde de Sierra Gorda,'' in *Instrucciones que los Vireyes Dejaron á Sus Sucesores* (Mexico, 1867), pp. 36–39. Important documents for the period are in the Saltillo Archives (see Bolton, *Guide to the Archives of Mexico*).

[2] Bancroft, *Mexico*, III, 332–342; *Reconocimiento del Seno Mexicano hecho por el Teniente de Capn. Gral. Dn. Joseph de Escandón*, 1746–1747.

Indians, in the hope of making it possible within a few years to withdraw the garrisons.[3]

In 1746 and 1747 Escandón personally inspected and explored the country to and along the Rio Grande, selecting suitable sites for settlements, while under his instructions Captain Joaquín de Orobio Bazterra, commander at La Bahía, in Texas, explored the region from the Guadalupe to the Rio Grande. Their reports contain the first detailed information that we have concerning the natives and the topography of many parts of this extended area. Hitherto, for example, it had been supposed that the Nueces River, known since 1689 and many times crossed higher up, emptied into the Rio Grande. Orobio discovered that such was not the case.

In consequence of these explorations, Escandón recommended founding in the region within his jurisdiction fourteen Spanish villas and a suitable number of missions. Twelve of the villas were to be established south of the Rio Grande, and two north of that stream. Of the last two, one was to be Villa de Vedoya, composed of fifty families, and situated on the left bank of the lower Nueces, that is, near the site of modern Corpus Christi. Adjacent to the town was to be the mission of Nuestra Señora del Soto, designed to minister to the Zuncal, Pajasequeis, or Carrizos, Apatines, Napuapes, Pantapareis and other tribes of the vicinity.

The other town in the northern district was to be Villa de Balmaceda, established with twenty-five families, at Santa Dorotea, a site on the lower San Antonio River.[4] To this site Escandón recommended moving the presidio and mission of La Bahía. The successful establishment of Balmaceda, he believed,

---

[3] Escandón's reports to the viceroy, October 26, 1747, and July 27, 1758.

[4] *Reconocimiento del Seno Mexicano*, folios 40–44, 85, 88, 110, 126; Valcárcel to the viceroy, February 1, 1758. The tribal names here given are those reported by Orobio Bazterra for the vicinity of the Nueces. I have not thus far attempted to identify the tribes with those of the region going under better known names.

would make possible the suppression of the presidio of La Bahía
in three or four years, and thus remove the chief ground for
hostility on the part of the coast Indians.[5]

The preparation for putting Escandón's colony into effect
was a work of more than two years. Before he set out with his
expedition he was made Conde de Sierra Gorda and given
new instructions. At Querétaro he raised seven hundred and
fifty soldiers and sent out invitations to the surrounding districts
to prospective settlers. Escandón's fame popularized the enterprise, and the response was hearty both about Querétaro and in
Huasteca and Nuevo León; "some offered to accompany him,
moved simply by the curiosity aroused by an expedition to lands
still unknown, and others bent on making their fortunes in the
pueblos which they went to found." Meanwhile the viceroy issued orders to the governors of Huasteca and Nuevo León to prepare auxillary companies and colonies of such Spaniards and
Christianized Indians as might wish to become settlers in the new
colony. The new missions were to be entrusted to the College of
Guadalupe de Zacatecas.

3. *The emigration of 1749.*—At the end of December, 1748,
Escandón left Querétaro with what was probably the largest
caravan that ever went to the interior provinces to found a colony.
In his train were the seven hundred and fifty soldiers, and more
than twenty-five hundred settlers, Spaniards and Christianized
Indians, while others joined him on the march. The families had
their household and agricultural equipments, and they drove before them many thousand head of horses, cattle, burros, sheep and
goats. In outward aspects the event was not unlike the Oregon
migration or the Mormon trek of a century later on the United
States frontier; the main difference was in the location of the
initiative and in the character of the colonists.

---

[5] Report of Escandón to the viceroy, October 26, 1747; Valcárcel to
the viceroy, February 1, 1758.

At the same time that Escandón left Querétaro, other parties of soldiers and settlers left Villa de Valles, Tampico, Linares, Cerralvo and San Juan Bautista, while missionaries from Zacatecas entered by way of Nuevo León, with small escorts, and explored Tamaulipas in pairs.

Escandón's route for some two hundred miles or more lay near the line of the present National Railway, through Los Pozos, San Luis de la Paz, Santa María del Río, and San Luis Potosí. At this point he turned northeastward, entering the Sierra at Tula. At Palmillas, the first site selected for a new colony, he left a garrison, and founded a mission for the neighborhood Indians; at Llera he founded a villa for sixty-seven of the families in his caravan, and a mission for the natives. Continuing northeastward, he repeated this process at Guëmes, Padilla, and Santander (modern Victoria), the last-named villa being made the capital.

From Santander Escandón hurried north across the Conchos, then west to the San Juan River, near the Rio Grande, to meet the families who had come under Captain Guevara from Nuevo León and Coahuila, by way of Cerralvo. On March 5 the villa of Santa Ana de Camargo was founded at the mouth of the San Juan and left in charge of Blas María de la Garza Falcón, a member of an old Coahuila family. Near by, the mission of San Agustín de Laredo was planted, and put in charge of Father García. Proceeding down the river twelve leagues, on March 14 Escandón founded Villa de Reynosa, of Nuevo León families led by Captain Cantú. Close by, the mission of San Joaquín del Monte was established.

Returning from Reynosa to the mouth of the Conchos, Escandón founded Villa de San Fernando; thence he went on to Santander and made a report to the viceroy; visited Padilla, Guëmes, and Llera in the west; went back to the coast and founded Altamira opposite Tampico; turned west again, and on May 19 founded the Ciudad de Horcasitas. From here he went by way of Tula to Querétaro, where he remained the rest of the year.[6]

4. *The settlements north of the Rio Grande.*—In accordance with Escandón's plan, in 1749 the presidio and mission of La Bahía were moved westward to the San Antonio, being planted at the present site of Goliad. The plans for the villas of Vedoya and Balmaceda, however, did not succeed. Villa de Balmaceda failed because at the fiscal's instance Escandón was refused the requisite funds. Villa de Vedoya failed for another reason. In 1749 a band of colonists and soldiers under Captain Diego González, with a double portion of supplies, crossed the Rio Grande at San Juan Bautista, marched down the north bank, then northeast toward the lower Nueces. While Escandón was at Reynosa in March 1749, he sent to Orobio orders to found Villa de Vedoya at the site already selected, east of the Nueces.[7] In the spring of 1750 Escandón returned to Nuevo Santander. While at Villa de Burgos, on his way north, he received messengers from the Nuevo León families who had been sent to the Nueces to settle, stating that their enterprise had failed. They had found that the site was unsuitable and the Indians hostile. Consequently, Captain González had established the families on the banks of Arroyo Salado, apparently the stream by that name running through northern Coahuila and Nuevo León, to await Escandón's orders. Here they had remained more than eight months, during which time González had died. Supplies becoming exhausted, suffering ensued, and part of the colonists deserted to their homes in Nuevo León. When the rest heard of Escandón's return, they sent the messengers, as stated, who found him at Burgos.

---

[6] Prieto, *Historia de Tamaulipas,* 140–159; *Instrucciones que los Vireyes de Nueva España Dejaron a sus sucesores,* 38–39. Original manuscript records of Escandón's work are in the Archivo General y Público, Mexico, *Historia,* vol. 29. See Bolton, *Guide to the Archives of Mexico,* 32, 38.

[7] Prieto, *Historia de Tamaulipas,* 154–155.

On hearing the report, Escandón ordered the families to go to Santander, there to await further orders. They did so, arriving there more than a year after they had left Nuevo León. Escandón equipped them anew with grain and stock, and sent them to the coast, where, on September 3, 1750, he founded for them the villa of Soto la Marina. Of this place Juan José Vázquez Borrego, a wealthy *hacendado,* was made captain, while Father Joaquín Saenz was put in charge of spiritual affairs.[8]

In 1750 two more settlements were made on the Rio Grande. one on the south and one on the north bank. The one on the south bank, named Revilla, was made by a colony from Coahuila. under Vicente Guerra. About the same time that Guerra was founding Revilla, Borrego went to see Escandón at Santander. asking permission to found a settlement opposite Revilla, where he already had ranches. Escandón accepted the proposal, named Borrego captain in charge of the north bank of the river, and granted him fifty *sitios de ganado mayor* for pasture, till permanent grants should be made.

Borrego's ranch became the nucleus of a little settlement named Rancho de Dolores. Four years later it had one hundred and twenty-three inhabitants, and nine thousand head of large stock. Several families of Borrado and Carrizo Indians joined the settlement as *Indios agregados,* but within three or four years they withdrew and began to steal stock. Borrego, thereupon, like a medieval lord, armed his servants and chastized the mauraders.

In 1753 Escandón founded the *lugar* of Mier with nineteen families enlisted in Camargo. The settlement was put under command of José Florencio de Chapa. This place was founded without expense to the royal treasury, and was defended by the settlers themselves.[9]

In 1755 Villa de Laredo was founded on the north side of the Rio Grande, ten leagues above Dolores. The founder of this town

---

8 Prieto, *Historia de Tamaulipas,* 168.
9 *Ibid.,* 174–175, 185–186, 189–190.

was Tomás Sánchez, owner of a stock ranch opposite Dolores. In 1754, while Escandón was at Revilla, Sánchez went to see him, proposing to cross over and settle on the other side, offering to take families at his own expense, in case sufficient lands were assigned them.

Escandón approved the proposal. But as he had not given up the idea of founding a town on the Nueces, he urged Don Tómas first to explore the Nueces to see if he could find a suitable site, and to report to Captain Borrego, of Dolores, in whose charge the establishment of the new settlement was left. Sánchez went to the Nueces, but returned, reporting to Borrego that there was no suitable site. He proposed, instead, settling farther up the river, ten leagues above Dolores, near the pass of Jacinto, so-called because it had been discovered nine years before by Jacinto de León. Borrego reported to Escandón, who gave Sánchez permission to establish at the proposed site the Villa de Laredo, making him captain and assigning to the inhabitants fifteen leagues of pasture land for *ganado mayor*. Sánchez moved his own family and other families and dependants, and on May 15, 1755, the villa was formally founded. The settlement, like Mier and Dolores, was made without expense to the Real Hacienda. Neither Dolores nor Laredo had a minister, but were visited by the priest of Revilla.

In October, 1755, Escandón made a report of the great work which he had accomplished in establishing the new colony, submitting with it a map. He had founded twenty-three settlements, including one city, seventeen villas, two *poblaciones,* one *lugar,* and two *reales de minas,* or mining camps. In them he had established one thousand three hundred and thirty-seven families of settlers and one hundred and forty-four soldiers, aggregating six thousand three hundred and eighty-five persons. In the fifteen missions there were two thousand eight hundred and thirty-seven Indians under instruction.

North of the lower Rio Grande there was the *población* de Dolores with twenty-five families, or one hundred and one settlers, governed by Captain Borrego; Villa de Laredo, with thirteen families, comprising sixty-two persons, and governed by Tomás Sánchez. Besides these the map shows ranching settlements north of the river opposite Revilla, Mier, Camargo, and Reynosa. In other words, ranching and settlements had been established on both sides of the river between Laredo and Reynosa.[10]

5. *Administrative arrangements.*—Among the conditions of settlement one had been that during ten years from the date of settlement the colonists should be subject to no tax; that they should be supplied with a military guard in each of their pueblos; and that the missionaries and priests should receive their stipends from the royal treasury. Villa de Escandón had these terms extended for five years because of the excessive Indian hostilities and of other misfortunes.

At the first foundation of the pueblos, the lands were not definitely assigned nor granted in severalty. A large grant was made in common, sufficient to satisfy the needs of the original settlers in the near future, estimating for each family two *sitios de ganado menor* and six *caballerías;* for the captains two *sitios de ganado mayor* and twelve *caballerías;* and for common use, four *sitios de ganado mayor* as *ejidos,* besides lands for the missions. Escandón was authorized on his first expedition to make these divisions, but he considered it unwise to do so, thinking that if the settlers held the lands in common they would stay closer together and be safer against Indian attacks. Hence the pueblos continued to hold their lands in common for fifteen years or more, it being 1764 when the first private grants were made.

---

[10] Bolton, H. E., ''Tienda de Cuervo's Ynspección of Laredo, 1757,'' in the Texas Historical Association *Quarterly*, January, 1903, pp. 187–203. Hierro, Fr. Simón, *Informe de las Misiones de Texas*, gives a sketch of the missions of Nuevo Santander.

The government in Nuevo Santander was special and essentially military and ecclesiastic. Each one of the pueblos or villas had a captain, named by Colonel Escandón, who was charged with both the military and the political control of the settlement. Beside them were the missionaries in charge of the missions and of the spiritual care of the Spanish settlements.

According to Cuervo, in 1757 the colony had cost the crown more than forty-three thousand pesos annually, although Hoyos, Santillana, Mier, Dolores, Laredo, Real de Infantes, Jaumave and Palmillas were established without cost to the treasury, and continued to bear their own expenses of protection and improvement.[11]

6. *The development of Nuevo Santander.*—Nuevo Santander fast became a stock-raising section and rapidly increased in population as is shown by the report of Tienda de Cuervo, who made a general visitation of the colony in 1757. His account shows that the settlements reported on by Escandón in 1755, now, two years later, with the addition of Jaumave, contained 8993 settlers, and 3473 Indians living in eighteen missions. The colony now possessed 58,000 horses, 25,000 cattle, 1874 burros, and 288,000 sheep and goats. Six irrigating ditches had been dug, eleven mines opened, and five salines exploited. The largest sheep and goat ranches were on the Rio Grande, at Camargo, Revilla, and Mier, whose stock pastured on both sides of the river. At Camargo there were 71,750 sheep and goats, at Revilla, 45,067, at Mier 38,659, and at Reynosa 13,050.

Dolores and Laredo, on the north side of the Rio Grande, had both prospered. At Dolores there were one hundred and twenty-three inhabitants, who pastured 5000 horses and 3000 cattle. At Laredo there were eleven families, comprising eighty-five persons, of whom twenty belonged to the family of the founder, Tomás Sánchez. He possessed five hundred range horses, seventy

---

[11] Prieto, *Historia de Tamaulipas*, 178–179, 194–195, 204–205.

saddle horses, one hundred and twenty-five mules, two yoke of oxen, fifty range cattle, two thousand sheep and goats, and thirty burros. The ten families settled under the protection of Sánchez possessed two hundred and twelve range horses, ninety-two saddle horses, 7080 sheep and goats, fifty-one cattle, and one burro. The superiority of Sánchez's position over that of his neighbors is manifest. He was a veritable medieval lord.[12]

Cuervo reported that Laredo had good prospects as a stock-raising center and that the place was important as being on the highway to Texas. There was as yet no priest or missionary, and the settlers, with those of Dolores, depended on the minister at Revilla.

In subsequent years ranching north of the Rio Grande gradually increased and extended northward, reaching the Nueces River. In 1761, Escandón spoke of Rancho de Dolores as "very large." At the same time he spoke of extending the ranches near the Rio Grande eastward to meet those established from Bahía as a center. In 1766 he was still promoting the same policy. He reported to the viceroy that "the settlement [of the country] between the Rio Del Norte and the Nueces, which you likewise charge me with, is making much progress, and I hope that it will be the most useful in the colony."[13] At this time Blas María de la Garza Falcón, founder and captain of Camargo, had his ranch of Santa Petronilla within five leagues of the mouth of the Nueces, "with a goodly number of the people, a stock of cattle, sheep and goats, and cornfields." Corpus Christi Bay had its present name. The name of Don Blas's ranch, some-

---

[12] Bolton, ''Tienda de Cuervo's Ynspección of Laredo, 1757,'' in the Texas Historical Association *Quarterly*, January, 1903, 187–203. The original reports of the inspection by Tienda de Cuervo are in the Archivo General y Público, Mexico, *Historia*, vols. 53–56.

[13] Escandón, *Informe*, December, 1761; Escandón to the viceroy, May 2, 1766; Escandón to viceroy, May 3, 1766. In 1776, when Colonel Parrilla explored the Gulf Coast he made Santa Petronilla his headquarters for a time (*Autos y diligᵃˢ. fhas. pʳ. el Coronel Dⁿ. Diego Ortiz Parrilla sre. las sircunstancias de la Isla de los Malaguitas q. comunmᵗᵉ. han llamado Isla Blanca. A. G. M., Historia, vol. 396*).

what corrupted, is still applied to the creek on which his ranch was located, the Petronita.

Having summarized briefly the general features of the founding of the colony of Nuevo Santander, a more detailed account will now be given of the efforts to reduce the Karankawa to mission life after the removal of the mission and presidio of Bahía to Santa Dorotea in 1749.

CHAPTER III

PLANS FOR A NEW KARANKAWA MISSION

1. The question of spiritual jurisdiction over the Cujane.—
On April 14, 1750, the viceroy exhorted the missionaries at the
new site to do all in their power to reduce, congregate, and
convert the Cujane, Karankawa, and Guapite. They were to
be treated with the utmost kindness, given presents, and promised, on behalf of the government, that if they would settle in
a pueblo they would be given new missions, protected, and supplied with all necessaries.[1] Similar instructions were written
to Captain Manuel Ramírez de la Piszina, the new commander of
the presidio of Bahía.

If we may trust the reports of the missionaries and the captain, they went zealously to work among these three tribes in
response to the viceroy's order. But little or nothing seems to
have been accomplished until the Querétaran friars at San
Antonio entered the same field.[2]

At this time the Querétaran missions at San Antonio were
short of neophytes, partly because of an epidemic which had
made ravages among the mission Indians.[3] On the other hand,
these missions were just now under the direction of Father Fr.
Francisco Mariano de los Dolores, one of the leaders of the missionary revival which we have mentioned. For these reasons,
and since the Karankawan tribes had long been without missionary influence, the Querétarans entertained the plan of gather-

[1] Summary by Camberos, missionary at this time in Bahía.

[2] Piszina to the viceroy, December 26, 1751; Camberos to the viceroy, May 30, 1754.

[3] Father Dolores, missionary at San Antonio, to Father González,
missionary at Espíritu Santo, June 17, 1751.

ing them, especially the Cujane,[4] into their particular fold. Whether the idea originated with Father Santa Ana, former president of the San Antonio missions, but now in Mexico, or with Father Mariano, his successor as president, does not appear; but it is through Father Santa Ana that we first learn of the project, while it was the former who put it into execution. Early in 1750, in a private communication to Altamira, the *auditor general*, Santa Ana made known the plan, intimating that he feared objections from the Zacatecan friars at Espíritu Santo, on the ground that the Karankawan tribes had once been assigned to that mission.[5] He doubtless knew, too, that the Zacatecans had recently been ordered to renew efforts on the coast. Altamira approved the project, saying that so long as these Indians remained in the forest they belonged only to the Devil, and that any one who wished was free to try his hand at winning them to the Lord.[6]

The actual work directed from San Antonio was undertaken by Fray Mariano with the aid of Fray Diego Martín García. Before entering the field Fray Mariano first asked the consent of the principal missionary at Espíritu Santo, Fray Juan Joseph González.[7] González replied that such a procedure would be satisfactory to him, and that he would waive whatever right his mission possessed to these Indians.[8]

The way was made easier for Fray Mariano by the presence of the few Cujane and Coco, previously mentioned as being at one of the missions.[9] Knowing by experience, as he said, ''that

---

[4] The plan evidently had in view the ''Puxanes and others clear to the Rio Grande del Norte'' (Santa Ana to the viceroy, January 31, 1752).

[5] Santa Ana to the viceroy, December 20, 1751.

[6] *Ibid.*

[7] His request was apparently made in 1750. Santa Ana to the viceroy, undated, but about March 22, 1752.

[8] Santa Ana to the viceroy, December 2, 1751; González to Dolores, April 13, 1751; Dolores to Santa Ana, October 26, 1751.

[9] Santa Ana to the viceroy, December 20, 1751.

presents were the most effective texts with which to open the conversion of savages,'' he began the revival by sending to the Cujane, early in 1751, a Coco mission Indian bearing gifts,[10] and a promise that a missionary would be sent to them.[11]

In spite of the assurance that had been given to Fray Mariano by González, this move of the former led very speedily to a politely worded, but none the less spirited dispute between the two. In the competition that attended the dispute Espíritu Santo had decidedly the advantage of geographical position.

The Cujane were pleased with the evidence of good will—or better, perhaps, with the prospects of more gifts—and, without awaiting the arrival of the promised minister, fifty-four adults[12] set out for San Antonio to confer with Father Mariano. When, on April 8, they reached the neighborhood of Santa Dorotea, or new Bahía, they were seen by some mission Indians. The latter warned Captain Piszina that hostile Cujane were nearby killing mission cattle. A squadron of soldiers and Indians was accordingly sent out, and the Cujane, after a slight show of fight, were taken to the presidio, and here they remained, notwithstanding their previous intention to go to San Antonio.[13] Father González and Captain Piszina claimed that the Cujane were told that they might continue their journey, that no force was used to keep them at Bahía, and that it was only with misgiving and after deliberation that their request to be allowed to remain

10 Dolores to González, June 17, 1751.

11 This promise is inferred from Santa Ana's letter of December 20, 1751.

12 In his letter to the viceroy, December 26, 1751, Captain Piszina calls them ''fifty-four Indians of the Coxan nation;'' but in the same letter he says that the four recently reduced tribes going under the name of Coxan are the ''Cojanes, Guapittes, Carancaguases, and Copanes.'' Hence we may infer that these fifty-four were not exclusively Cujanes, although they were called by this name.

13 González to Dolores, April 3, 1751; Dolores to Santa Ana, October 26, 1751; Santa Ana to the viceroy, December 20, 1756; Piszina to the viceroy, December 26, 1751. Piszina said that they were taken to Bahía at the end of March, but González's letter of April 13 is more reliable for the date, because nearer the event and more explicit.

at the mission was granted.[14] But Fray Mariano believed that if not force, then persuasion, had been used to rob him of the fruits of his efforts.

With a commendable forbearance, however, he held his peace, and made another attempt, which likewise resulted more to the advantage of the rival mission than of his own. Some of the Cujane had returned from Bahía to their own country and gathered ninety-five more Indians "of the Cujan, Copanes, Guapites, and Talancagues tribes." On their way they stopped at Bahía, left their women and children, and went back to gather a larger number of their people, with the intention, Fray Mariano understood, of going on with them to San Antonio. He thereupon sent a number of mules laden with such supplies as might be needed by the Indians on their way.[15] Shortly afterward a Coco arrived reporting that one hundred and five families were already collected near old Bahía and that more were gathering, but that, unless horses were sent at once to transport them, they would be diverted to new Bahía, just as the first band had been, there to remain. Fray Mariano now lost no time in dispatching Fray Diego Martín García with horses and a Coco guide to assist in bringing in the Cujane and their friends.[16]

In a note written soon after this, González claimed that these Indians desired to remain at Bahía.[17] Thereupon Fray Mariano entered a vigorous protest. He reminded González that he had once waived his right to the coast Indians, but was now enticing them to Espíritu Santo, that but for him (Father Mariano) the Cujane and the rest would still be in the woods and at war with the Spaniards, as they had always been; that if after many years

---

[14] González to Dolores, April 13, 1751; Piszina to the viceroy, December 26, 1751. This last assertion casts doubts upon any claim the Bahía authorities might make to have previously tried to take these Indians there.

[15] Dolores to González, June 17, 1751.

[16] *Ibid.*

[17] González to Dolores, May 22, 1751, referred to in *ibid.*

the Espíritu Santo mission had failed to subdue the Xaraname, whom they still claimed the right to monopolize, they could hardly expect to succeed with the additional task of subduing the Cujane. Disclaiming a wish to quarrel, he requested González to find out for certain, by whatever means he chose, whether these Indians preferred to be at Bahía or at San Antonio, and promised to abide by the result, with these conditions, that in case they wished to come to San Antonio they must not be hindered, and that if they remained at Bahía he would send a bill for the supplies he had given them.[18]

Fray Mariano was now called to the missions at San Xavier, and when he returned he found new cause for displeasure with the authorities at Bahía. In his absence Fray Diego had returned with twenty-four Indians of the four tribes and the report that he might have brought five hundred had it not been for their fear that they would be prevented, by the soldiers and missionaries at Bahía, from going to San Antonio. Meanwhile none of the families who had stopped at Bahía had appeared in San Antonio; consequently, again conceding the point, which was backed by the better argument of possession, Fray Mariano advised the twenty-four to go to their friends at Bahía. But, by no means giving up his claim, he appealed both to the *discretorio* of his college and to Father Santa Ana asking authority to bring the Cujane to his missions.[19]

Father Santa Ana took up the matter vigorously with the viceroy, with Andreu, the fiscal, and with Altamira, the *auditor*. He wrote letters, furnished documents, and sought personal interviews in defense of the rights of his college. He argued that until Fray Mariano had pacified them the Karankawa Indians had always been hostile; that the Querétaran friars had been robbed of the fruits of their efforts by the Zacatecans, who had done nothing except to spoil a good work well begun; that by thirty

---

[18] González to Dolores, May 22, 1751, *ibid*.
[19] Dolores to the *discretorio*, undated; to Santa Ana, October 26, 1751.

years of idleness the latter had forfeited all the rights they ever had to the Karankawan field; and that nothing could be expected of them in the future.[20]   In view of these considerations, he earnestly recommended that the work of converting these tribes be entrusted to the Querétarans.[21]

On the other hand, appeal was made to law 32, title 15, book I, of the *Recopilación de Indias,* which provided that when one religious order had begun the conversion of a tribe it should not be disturbed by another.   And thus the dispute went on until the end of 1752, when it was closed in effect by the fiscal's compromise decision that under the peculiar circumstances joint work among the tribes in question would be lawful and equitable, and by the viceroy's exhortation of all parties to co-operate in the work of saving Karankawan souls for the glory of "both majesties."

2. *Progress with the Cujane at Espíritu Santo.*—Meanwhile the possession of the Cujane and the others had proved a very temporary advantage to the Espíritu Santo mission, and even during that short time these "first fruits and hostages of all that heathen race" had added little to the mission's glory. While the Indians were there the missionaries succeeded in baptizing fifteen of them *in articulo mortis;* the rest deserted within a few weeks, so that at the end of 1751 none appear to have remained.   To make matters worse, relations between the tribes and the Spaniards again became strained through the unexplained killing of five Cujane by the soldiers of Bahía.[22]

Altamira had at first favored Father Santa Ana's proposal to take the Cujane to San Antonio.   But when conflicting re-

---

[20] Santa Ana to the viceroy, December 20, 1751; January 31, 1752; March 22.

[21] *Ibid.*

[22] Dolores to Santa Ana, October 26, 1751; Piszina to the viceroy, December 26, 1751 (Piszina, referring to the fifty-four, said they remained two and one-half months); Santa Ana to the viceroy, January 31, 1752.

ports and news of the desertion of the Indians reached him he lost his patience and delivered himself of a generous amount of ill-natured truth about frontier history, at the same time showing his hearty sympathy with Escandón's policy of settlement as a complement to the mission and as a substitute for the garrison. "All the foregoing," he said, "but illustrates how, in this as in all like affairs of places at such long and unpeopled distances, come inopportune and irregular letters, proposals, representations, and petitions, that only leave the questions unintelligible. Thus in his report the captain [Piszina] begins by saying 'In obedience to Your Excellency's superior order,' without saying what order, or without specifying what he considers necessary for the conversion of the Indians in question. This conversion he assumes as assured simply because a few of them have submitted, when he cannot be ignorant of their notorious inconstancy. And the Rev. Father Santa Ana, who had experienced this inconstancy, on December 20 plead the cause of these same Cujane, only to report forty days after, on January 31, of this year, that the occasion had passed because all of the Indians had deserted. This is what happens daily on those and all the other unsettled frontiers.

"The same will be true two hundred years hence unless there be established there settlements of Spaniards and civilized people to protect, restrain, and make respectable the barbarous Indians who may be newly congregated, assuring them before their eyes a living example of civilized life, application to labor, and to the faith. Without this they will always remain in the bonds of their native brutality, inherited for many centuries, as happens in the missions of the Rio Grande, of [Eastern] Texas, and all the rest where there are no Spanish settlements, for the Indians there, after having been congregated fifty years or more, return to the woods at will."[23]

---

23 Altamira to the viceroy, February 29, 1752.

Notwithstanding the unflattering outcome of the enterprise thus far, the missionaries and the captain at Bahía, roused into activity by their rivals, continued their efforts to cultivate friendship with their traditional enemies, and, although conversions were few, they were otherwise comparatively successful. During the next two years they spent considerable sums from their own pockets for presents and supplies, and Piszina made the occasion an excuse for asking the government for more soldiers, more money, and more missionaries. Writing in December, 1751, he said that the recent friendly attitude of the coast Indians, though favorable to missionary work, also increased the expenses and made more workers necessary, for the four tribes included under the name Coxanes would comprise five hundred warriors besides their families. Moreover, their conversion would make more soldiers necessary, since they were really more dangerous when at peace than when at war; for besides being treacherous themselves, the unfriendly Indians on the coast would visit their relatives at the mission and thus learn the weakness of the garrison. While, therefore, more missionaries and more supplies would be necessary before these tribes could be converted, their reduction would require an increase of soldiers to guard the Spaniards against the treachery of the neophytes and against their friends still upon the coast. Within two years Piszina made three such appeals to the viceroy.[24]

3. The plan to transfer the Ais mission to La Bahía.—By the end of this time the local authorities conceived the idea of founding a separate mission especially for the Cujane and their friends, as a substitute for trying to reduce them at Mission Espíritu Santo with Indians of another race. To effect this plan the best informed person, and probably the father of the project, Fray Juan de Dios Camberos, who was missionary at Espíritu Santo, went to Zacatecas, and was sent thence by the college to

---

[24] December 26, 1751; December 31, 1753, and another mentioned in this last.

Mexico. His appointment was dated February 26, 1754, and was signed by Fray Gaspar Joseph de Solís, guardian of the college, and later known in Texas by his tour of inspection among the missions.[25]

In his communications to the viceroy of April 29, May 6, 7 and 30, Father Camberos set forth the situation and his plan. The Cujane and their kindred, he said, were eagerly asking for a mission; so eagerly, indeed, that six of the chiefs of the Cujane, Karankawa, and Guapite were clamoring to be allowed to come to see the viceroy himself in reference to the matter. But it was inadvisable to put them into Mission Espíritu Santo together with the Xaraname and Tamique already there, for they were tribes of different languages, of different habits, and unfriendly. But to send them to San Antonio was equally impracticable, for they did not wish to leave the neighborhood of Bahía del Espíritu Santo, their native country. Even if the Indians were willing to be transplanted, experience had shown that this was bad policy, for the Pamaque and other tribes, when removed to San Antonio from their native soil on the Neuces, had speedily become almost extinguished. This very consideration had caused Colonel Escandón to order Captain Piszina not to allow the Indians of his district to be taken from their country. Moreover, if the mission were near the home of the Indians, fugitive neophytes could be easily recovered, whereas, if they were taken to San Antonio, the soldiers and missionaries would have to spend most of their time pursuing them.

Father Camberos advised, therefore, the establishment of a separate mission. But to save the expense of equipping a new one he recommended removing the mission which had served the Ais from near the Sabine River to the neighborhood of Bahía, and re-establishing it there for the Cujane. His arguments in favor of his plan are an interesting commentary, coming as they

---

[25] The original commission, with seal, is in the Archivo General de Mexico.

do from a zealous Zacatecan friar, upon the comparative failure of the missions of eastern Texas: missions San Miguel de los Adaes, Nuestra Señora de los Dolores de los Ais, and Nuestra Señora de Guadalupe de los Nacogdoches had been existing for more than thirty years, and yet, according to him, notwithstanding the untiring efforts of the missionaries to reduce the Indians to mission life, it was notorious that they had succeeded in little more than the baptizing of a few children and fewer adults upon the deathbed; and there was no hope that these tribes could ever be reduced to pueblos and induced to give up their tribal life. Under these circumstances four missionaries instead of five would suffice on that frontier. Since the Ais Indians consisted of only some forty families—perhaps two hundred persons—living within about fourteen leagues of Mission Nacogdoches,[26] their mission could be suppressed, one friar going to Nacogdoches to reside and from there ministering to the Ais, the other going to Bahía with the mission equipment, to work among the Karankawan tribes in question.[27]

At first Andreu, the fiscal, disapproved the plan on the ground that with the missionary so far away, travel so difficult, and the Ais Indians so indifferent, they would lose not only the wholesome example of the missionary in their daily life, but even the slight religious benefits which they were already receiving.[28] But Camberos suggested that the minister might incorporate the Ais with their kindred, the Little Ais (Aixittos),[29] who lived two leagues from the Nacogdoches mission. He concluded by reminding the fiscal that it was, after all, a question

---

[26] Father Vallejo, of Adaes, maintained that the distance was nearly twenty leagues. Letter to the *discretorio* of his college, December 1, 1754.

[27] Camberos to the viceroy, April 29, May 6, May 7, and May 31.

[28] Andreu to the viceroy, May 2, 1754.

[29] This name was sometimes written Aijitos, but it was intended for the diminutive of Ais, and when spelled with an *x* was pronounced, no doubt, ''Aisitos.''

of relative service. On the one hand, there were scarce forty families of Ais Indians, who for thirty years had shown themselves irreducible; on the other hand, there were five hundred or more families of Cujane, Guapite, and Karankawa, "as ready to be instructed in the mysteries of our faith as the Ayx are repugnant to living in Christian society"; for two years they had been and still were firm in their anxious desire to be reduced to a pueblo and instructed. Was it not a matter of duty to save the willing many rather than to struggle hopelessly with the unwilling few?[30]

These arguments convinced the fiscal and the *auditor*, whereupon the viceroy, on June 17 and 21, issued to the governor and the college the necessary decrees for effecting the transfer. The order to the college provided "that the mission of Nuestra Señora de los Dolores de los Ais, situated in the province of los Texas, should be totally abandoned; that of the two ministers there, one should remain at Mission Nacogdoches, it being the nearest at hand, in order that he might assist with the waters of holy baptism all the children and adults who might wish the benefit; and that the other should go to found the new mission of the Guapitte, Cujane, and Carancaguas in the territory of la Bahía del Espíritu Santo, for which purpose all the ornaments, furniture, and other goods of the mission of los Aix should be given to this minister and transferred to the new mission."[31]

But now a protest was heard from eastern Texas. Upon receiving the viceroy's order to extinguish the Ais mission, Father Vallejo, president of the Zacatecan establishments on the eastern frontier, and a veteran of thirty years' service, first sought the opinion of the governor. That official was hostile to

---

[30] Camberos to the viceroy, May 30, 1754.

[31] Summary contained in the communication of the *discretorio* to the viceroy, January 6, 1755.

the change.[32] Vallejo, with this backing, wrote to the guardian of his college that the Ais mission was by no means useless, and that until he should get further instructions he would defer the execution of the order. True, he said, the Ais Indians had not yet adopted mission life, in spite of the efforts of the fathers; yet they were being baptized *in articulo mortis*—the records showed one hundred and fifty-eight baptisms in thirty-six years; the missionary was useful as physician and nurse among them; and the friendly relations with the Indians, who assisted willingly in the domestic and agricultural duties about the mission, offered still a hope that they would settle down to pueblo life. Indeed, when Father Cypriano had been missionary he had had them congregated for a space of four years, and Father García had likewise kept them content about the mission till, because of a recent scarcity of mission supplies, one of the chiefs had persuaded them to return to their rancherías. But if the missionary were to retire to Nacogdoches, the distance and the difficulties of travel were so great that the Indians would be without aid, and would likely abandon their country, just as the Nazones had done when the missionaries had deserted them in 1729. The good father could not close his argument without appealing to the fear of the French, tactics which had stood many a special pleader in good stead within the last half century. So he added that, aside from the importance of the Ais mission to the Indians, it was necessary as a half-way station between Nacogdoches and Adaes to give succor in case of hostile invasion. He maintained therefore that the mission should be continued at all hazards, even if with only one minister.[33]

This letter put an end to the effort to suppress the Ais mission and set in motion a new plan. The *discretorio,* whence the

[32] Vallejo to Governor Barrios y Jáuregui, November 20, 1754; the governor to Vallejo, November 30, 1754. The president's name was sometimes spelled with a *B* and sometimes with a *V.*

[33] Fray Francisco Vallejo to the Guardian and the *discretorio* of the college, December 1, 1754.

idea of extinguishing the mission of Los Ais had come, reported to the viceroy and sustained Vallejo's objections, and suggested, instead, a new mission for the Cujane, maintaining, perhaps with truth, but with little regard for its former argument based on economy, that to equip a new mission would be little more expensive than to transfer the old one.[34] The matter again went, therefore, to the fiscal, and he, on March 6, 1755, without other discussion than a review of the question, approved the new plan, and recommended that the Ais mission be allowed to remain and that a new one be established for the coast tribes.[35] On March 22 the *auditor* approved the project, and on April 7 the viceroy issued the corresponding decree.[36]

---

[34] The *discretorio* of the college to the viceroy, January 6, 1755.

[35] Andreu to the viceroy, January 6, 1755.

[36] Valcárcel to the viceroy, March 22; viceroy's decree, April 7.

CHAPTER IV

THE MISSION OF ROSARIO

1. Founding Mission Nuestra Señora del Rosario de los Cujanes.—But matters at Bahía had not waited for the viceroy to change his mind. Some time before this, steps had already been taken, in consequence of the previous order (that looking to the transfer of the old establishment to a new site), toward the actual founding of a new mission for the Cujane and their friends.

The government was slower to supply means than to sanction projects, and the funds with which to begin the work were raised by private gifts to the college or advanced by Piszina and the missionaries at Bahía, while part of the mission furniture was borrowed from Mission Espíritu Santo.[1] Camberos was sent to supervise the founding,[2] which was begun in November, 1754. Piszina spared nine soldiers to act as a guard, to assist with their hands, and to direct the Indians, some of whom were induced to help in the building and in preparing the field. On January 15 Piszina thus wrote of the mission site and of progress in the work: "The place assigned for the congregation of these Indians, Excellent Sir, is four leagues from this presidio.[3] It has all the advantages known to be useful and necessary for the

---

[1] Letter to Camberos, May 26, 1758.

[2] It is not clear when the missionary from Los Ais went to Rosario to assist Camberos. But that he did go before May 27, 1757, appears from a letter of that date. Strangely, however, the correspondence in several instances speaks of the missionary in the singular, and while Camberos commends Captain Piszina for his co-operation, he mentions no ecclesiastical associate. (The *discretorio* to the viceroy, May 27, 1757; opinion of Valcárcel, February 1, 1758; report to the junta de guerra, April 17, 1758, Juan Martín de Astíz to the viceroy, on or before June 21, 1758).

[3] See page 318, below.

founding of a large settlement, and in my estimation, the country is the best yet discovered in these parts. It has spacious
plains, and very fine meadows skirted by the River San Antonio,
which appears to offer facilities for a canal to irrigate the crops.
In the short time of two months since the building of the material
part of the mission was begun, a decent [wooden] church for
divine worship has been finished. It is better made than that of
this presidio and the mission of Espíritu Santo. There have
been completed also the dwellings for the minister and the other
necessary houses and offices, all surrounded by a field large
enough to plant ten fanegas of maize."[4]

Two years later it was reported that irrigation facilities were
about to be completed; that a dam of lime and stone forty varas
long and four varas high had been built across an arroyo carrying enough water to fill it in four months, and that all that
was lacking was the canal, which would soon be finished.[5] But
this work seems not to have been completed. Within a few years
—how soon does not appear—a strong wooden stockade was built
around the mission.[6]

The name by which Camberos called the mission in his reports
was "Nuestra Señora del Rosario de los Cojanes."[7] Contemporary government documents sometimes call it by this name, and
sometimes simply "Nuestra Señora del Rosario;" while Father
Solís, official inspector for the college, in his diary of 1768, calls
it "Mision del Santíssimo Rosario," and "Mision del Rosario."[8]
The last is the more usual and popular form of the name. The
addition of "de los Cojanes" indicates in part the prominence
of the Cujane tribe in the mission, and also the prevalent usage
of their name as a generic term for the Karankawan tribes.

[4] Piszina to the viceroy, January 15.
[5] The *discretorio* of the college to the viceroy, May 27, 1757.
[6] Solís, *Diario*, 1767–1768. *Memorias*, XXVII, 258. See page 322, below.
[7] Camberos to the viceroy May 26, 1758.
[8] *Memorias* XXVII, 256, 266; Aranda to the viceroy, July 19, 1758.

The location of Mission Rosario was given by Piszina as four leagues from the presidio of Bahía[9]—in which direction he does not say, but it was clearly up stream. As will be seen, Piszina's estimate of the distance from Bahía was too great, unless the location of Rosario was subsequently changed. We learn from Solís's diary of 1768 that Mission Espíritu Santo was "in sight of the royal presidio [apparently almost on the site of modern Goliad], with nothing between them but the river, which is crossed by a canoe";[10] and in 1793 Revilla Gigedo reported Mission Rosario as two leagues nearer than Espíritu Santo to Béxar.[11] I am informed by Mr. J. H. Passmore, of Goliad, that the ruins today identified as those of Espíritu Santo are across the river from Goliad, and that four miles west of these, one-half a mile south of the San Antonio River, are the ruins identified, correctly, no doubt, as those of Mission Rosario.[12]

Lack of funds for current expenses and properly to establish agriculture and grazing greatly handicapped the missionaries and Captain Piszina, while, on the other hand, the Indians did not prove as eager to embrace the blessings of Christianity as the uninitiated might have been led to expect from the former reports of their anxiety to do so. They came to the mission from time to time, and helped more or less with the work, but when provisions gave out they were perforce allowed, or even advised, to return to the coast.[13]

The number who frequented the mission and availed themselves of these periodical supplies must have been considerable, for within less than a year of the founding of the mission Piszina reported that one thousand pesos in private funds had been spent

---

[9] See above, p. 316.

[10] *Memorias de Nueva España*, XXVII, 264.

[11] *Carta dirigida á la corte de España*, December 27, 1793.

[12] From what I can learn, it seems probable that the building at Goliad whose remains are now called "Mission Aranama" were connected with the *presidio* of Bahía rather than with a mission.

[13] Piszina to the viceroy, December 22, 1756; Camberos, May 26, 1758.

for maize, meat, cotton cloth, tobacco, etc.; a year later he said that the number of Indians at Mission Espíritu Santo—a number large enough to consume five or six bulls a week—was smaller than the number at Rosario,[14] and that in all six thousand pesos had been spent in supporting the latter.

But conversions were slow, and the total harvest after four years' work was twenty-one souls baptized *in articulo mortis*— twelve adults and nine children. In May. 1758, only one of the Indians living at the mission was baptized. This small showing of baptisms was partly due to the caution and conservatism of Father Camberos. "If I had been over-ready in baptizing Indians," he said, "at the end of these four years you would have found this coast nearly covered with the holy baptism; but experience has taught me that baptisms performed hastily make of Indians Christians who are so only in name, and who live in the woods undistinguishable from the heathen."[15] This caution on the part of Father Camberos was not only in conformity with the rules of the Church, but quite in keeping with the usual missionary practice as well.

The Indians of the new mission were hard to manage, gave the soldiers much difficulty,[16] and sustained their old reputation for being inconstant, unfaithful, and dissatisfied. The example of San Xavier, where a friar had recently been murdered, was fresh in the minds of the missionaries, and even when the Indians at Rosario were best disposed, it was feared that they might revolt and do violence to their benefactors. The Cujane in particular were feared, for, besides being the most numerous, they were regarded as especially bold and unmanageable.[17] This fear, together with danger from the Apache, was ground for some

---

[14] Piszina to the viceroy, November 10, 1755, and December 22, 1756.

[15] Letter dated May 23, 1758.

[16] Piszina to the viceroy, December 22, 1756.

[17] The *discretorio* to the viceroy, May 27, 1757.

of the numerous appeals made for an increase of soldiers at the presidio, and for the building of the stockade.

As soon as Captain Piszina finished the mission buildings, he renewed his former request for ten additional soldiers,[18] and asked the government to assist the new mission with the usual one year's supplies, in addition to the ornaments and furniture. Thereafter his appeal was frequently repeated,[19] and was seconded by the college, by Camberos, and by Governor Barrios y Jáuregui.[20] But for three years the government only discussed, procrastinated, and called for reports, until finally in a *junta de guerra y hacienda* held April 17, 1758, the various items asked for were granted.[21]

2. *Ten years after.*—With this belated aid the mission became more prosperous—as prosperous, indeed, as could be expected under the circumstances. In 1768 it was able to report a total of two hundred baptisms. This, so far as mere numbers go, was relatively as good a showing as had been made by its neighbor, Mission Espíritu Santo, among tribes somewhat more docile, and nearly as good as that made by Mission San José, once the finest mission in all New Spain. At this time there must have been from one hundred to two hundred Indians, at least, living intermittently in the mission. But residence or baptism did not of necessity signify any great change in the savage nature of the Indians. They were hard to control, and were with difficulty kept at the mission, made to work, and in-

---

[18] See above, p. 310.

[19] Letters to the viceroy, January 15, 1755, November 10, 1755; December 22, 1756.

[20] The *discretorio* to the viceroy, May 27, 1757. (At the end of 1755 the college sent an agent to the viceroy in person to urge haste in the matter); Barrios y Jáuregui to the viceroy, August 26, 1757; letter to Camberos, May 26, 1756.

[21] Report of the *junta*, in the Archivo General, original MS. The discussion of the question by the government may be found in communications of Aranda to the viceroy, January 24, 1758; Varcárcel to the viceroy, April 5, 1757; Valcárcel to the viceroy, February 1, 1758; report of the *junta de guerra*, April 17, 1758.

duced to give up their crude ways. If corporal punishment was used, which was sometimes the case,[22] the neophytes ran away; and if sometimes they complained of harsh treatment by the missionaries, they were likely to find willing listeners among the soldiers.

It is not the purpose of this paper to follow out the history of mission Rosario after its establishment. But it may vivify the reader's impression, and help him to secure a more correct idea of a frontier mission of the less substantial sort, and of the conditions surrounding it, to reproduce here some parts of the account of Mission Rosario given in his diary in 1768 by Father Solís, the official inspector of the Texas missions for his college. I therefore quote the following:

"(Feb.) 26. I passed through an opening called the Guardian, then through others, and arrived at Mission del Santissimo Rosario, where I was received by the minister with much attention. The Indians who had remained at the mission—for many were fugitive in the woods and on the coast—came out in gala array as an embassy to meet me on the way . . . The captain of La Bahía remained and posted a picket of soldiers to keep guard by day and by night. This mission is extremely well kept in all respects. It secures good water from Rio San Antonio de Vejar. The country is pleasant and luxuriant . . . The climate is very bad and unhealthful, hot, and humid, with southerly winds. Everything, including one's clothing, becomes damp, even within the houses, as if it were put in water. Even the inner walls reek with water as if it were raining.

"28. At the invitation of the captain I went to dine at the royal presidio of La Bahía del Espíritu Santo. I was accompanied by Fathers Ganuza and Lopez, and Brothers Francisco

---

[22] In 1768 an investigation was made at this mission as a result of the flight of some of the Karankawa, with the result that charges of harsh dealing with the neophytes were reported to the government at Mexico.

Sedano and Antonio Casas. . . . The captain received us with great respect and ceremony, welcoming us with a volley by the company, and four cannon shot, . . . serving us a very free, rich, and abundant table, and comporting himself in everything with the magnificence and opulence of a prince. . . .

"29. I said the mass of inspection and examined the church, the sacristy, and the entire mission. . . .

"(March) 3. . . . At night there returned thirty-three families of the Indians of this mission who had wandered, fugitives. I received them with suavity and affection. . . .

"4. . . . The opinion I have formed of this mission of Nuestra Señora del Rosario is as follows: As to material wealth it is in good condition. It has two droves of burros, about forty gentle horses, thirty gentle mules, twelve of them with harness, five thousand cattle, two hundred milch cows, and seven hundred sheep and goats. The buildings and the dwelling, both for the ministers and for the soldiers and the Indians, are good and adequate. The stockade of thick and strong stakes which protects the mission from its enemies is very well made. The church is very decent. It is substantially built of wood, plastered inside with mud, and whitewashed with lime; and its roof of good beams and shingles (*taxamanil*) looks like a dome (*parece arteson*). Its decoration is very bright and clean. It has sacred vessels, a bench for ornaments and utensils, a pulpit with confessional, altars, and all the things pertaining to the divine cult. Everything is properly arranged and kept in its place. There is a baptismal font, with a silver shell, and silver cruets for the holy oils. The mission has fields of crops, which depend upon the rainfall, for water cannot be got from the river, since it has very high and steep banks, nor from any where else, since there is no other place to get it from.

"This mission was founded in 1754. Its minister, who, as I have already said, is Fr. Joseph Escovar, labors hard for its welfare, growth, and improvement. He treats the Indians with much love, charity, and gentleness, employing methods soft, bland, and alluring. He makes them work, teaches them to pray, tries to teach them the catechism and to instruct them in the rudiments of our Holy Faith and in good manners. He aids and succors them as best he may in all their needs, corporal and spiritual, giving them food to eat and clothing to wear. In the afternoon, before evening prayers, with a stroke of the bell he assembles them, big and little, in the cemetery, has them say the prayers and the Christian doctrine, explains and tries to teach them the mysteries of our Holy Faith, exhorting them to keep the commandments of God and of Our Holy Mother Church, and setting forth what is necessary for salvation. On Saturday he collects them and has them repeat the rosary with its mysteries, and the *alavado cantado*. On Sundays and holidays, before mass, he has them repeat the prayers and the doctrine and afterward preaches to them, explaining the doctrine and whatever else they ought to understand. If he orders punishment given to those who need it, it is with due moderation, and not exceeding the limits of charity and paternal correction; looking only to the punishment of wrong and excess, it does not lean toward cruelty or tyranny.[23]

"The Indians with which this mission was founded are the Coxanes, Guapites, Carancaguases, and Coopanes, but of this last nation there are at present only a few, for most of them are in the woods or on the banks of some of the many rivers in these parts; or with another nation, their friends and confederates, on the shore of the sea, which is some thirteen or fourteen leagues distant to the east of the mission. They are all barbarous, idle, and lazy; and although they are so greedy and gluttonous that they eat meat almost raw, parboiled, or half roasted and dripping with blood, yet, rather than stay in the

---

[23] See above, p. 321.

mission where the father provides them everything needed to eat and wear, they prefer to suffer hunger, nakedness, and other necessities, in order to be at liberty and idle in the woods or on the beach, giving themselves up to all kinds of vice, especially lust, theft, and dancing.'"[24]

Such were the difficulties usually attending the labors of the frontier missionaries, increased somewhat in this instance, perhaps, by the exceptional crudeness of the tribes they were trying to subdue. And such were the first fruits of more than a decade's efforts on the part of several zealous missionaries. In after years the wooden church of the mission was replaced by one of stone, and the mission experienced varying degrees of prosperity. Escandón's project of establishing a Spanish pueblo near by was also realized, and, as we have seen, other settlements were founded near the Rio Grande.

---

[24] Solís, *Diario,* in *Memorias de Nueva España,* XXVII, 256–259.

IV. SPANISH ACTIVITIES ON THE LOWER TRINITY RIVER, 1746-1771

CHAPTER I

A NEW DANGER ON THE FRENCH BORDER[1]

1. French encroachments and Orobio Bazterra's exploring expedition, 1745-1746.—Spanish activities in Texas were from first to last inspired largely by fears of foreign aggression. When these fears slept, Texas was left pretty much to itself, so far as the government was concerned, but when serious rumors of encroaching strangers reached the official ears, there was likely to be vigorous proceedings for a time. The occupation of the lower Trinity River was no exception to this rule. Although settlements had been founded in eastern Texas as early as 1690, the authorities in Mexico, and even in the province of Texas itself, seem to have been almost entirely ignorant of the geography of the lower Trinity and the adjacent country until 1746, when they were called into it by tales of a French establishment somewhere

---

[1] This study is based entirely upon manuscript original sources. The older works in English which mention the subject are entirely valueless; the treatments given by modern writers in English are so brief as to be very unsatisfactory. The only printed account by an early Spanish historian is that of Bonilla, in his *Breve Compendio* (translated by West in the Texas State Hist. Ass'n. *Quarterly*, vol. VIII), which, although written by a contemporary who was in a position to know, contains numerous fundamental errors. At best Bonilla's account is very brief and incomplete, as he devotes only about a page to the matter. The manuscript materials on which my study is based are records in the Béxar Archives, the Lamar Papers, and the Nacogdoches Archives, and transcripts in the writer's personal collection from the archives of Mexico and Spain. What is presented here was practically completed several years ago. Subsequently the author's manuscripts were put at the disposal of Miss Elise Brown, a graduate student in the University of Texas, as material for a master's thesis. This was written, under the present writer's direction, with the title ''The History of the Spanish Settlements at Orcoquisac, 1746-1772.'' Though the two accounts are quite different in general, and at variance at some points, the writer has made some use of Miss Brown's valuable work, and hereby makes acknowledgment. In the citations which follow, B. A. stands for Béxar Archives, L. P. for Lamar Papers, N. A. for Nacogdoches Archives.

in that vicinity. One previous official expedition to the locality had been made in 1727,[2] but it led to no further steps toward occupation, and gave no permanent knowledge of the topography or of the natives of the region. As early as 1741, it is said, Governor Prudencio Orobio Bazterra, hearing of French incursions, urged the establishment of a presidio on the lower Trinity, but nothing came of the recommendation.

What stirred the authorities to action in 1745 was a letter reporting the rumors alluded to above, written in July[3] to the viceroy by Don Joaquín de Orobio Bazterra, captain of the presidio of Bahía del Espíritu Santo, but for the time being in Coahuila.

In reply to this communication the viceroy ordered Captain Orobio to proceed in all haste to learn the truth about the French settlement, where and when it had been established, if at all, and what and how many Indians there were in the vicinity. If he should find Frenchmen established or intending to settle, he was to order them to leave forthwith.[4]

The prevailing ignorance of and the lack of communication with the coast country between the Guadalupe and the Trinity rivers at this time are amply illustrated by Orobio's difficulties and uncertainty in getting from La Bahía to his destination. His first efforts were directed to ascertaining whether the investi-

---

[2] In 1727, when Rivera inspected the northern establishments of New Spain, he sent engineer Francisco Álvarez Barreyro from La Bahía eastward with a detachment of twenty soldiers to examine the coast country as far as the Neches. Barreyto spent thirty-five days on the expedition and travelled 363 leagues, but what he recorded in his reports I cannot say, as I have not seen them, though I do know of their whereabouts, and have taken steps toward securing them (See Rivera, *Diario*, 1727, leg. 2466).

[3] July 2.

[4] The viceroy's order was dated July 18 (*Diligencias Practicadas por Dn. Joaquin de Orobio Capn. de la Bahia Sobre establecimiento de Franceses.* B. A.). Orobio signed his name as above, but other Spanish officials frequently wrote it "Orobio y Basterra." The brief form of his name is usually given as Orobio.

gation could be made on *terra firma* by way of Matagorda Bay
and the coast. To determine this point he went in October with
a squad of men down the banks of the Guadalupe; but, because
of high water and the roughness of the country, he decided to
build a fleet of canoes and take thirty men on a two months'
expedition by water, down the river and along the coast. New
discouragements and difficulties led him finally to decide to take
the Adaes road to the crossing of the Trinity, a hundred miles
or more above its mouth, and descend to the coast from that
point.[5] Such an expedition made it necessary to send to San
Antonio and Presidio del Rio Grande for more soldiers, in order
that La Bahía might not be left unprotected. As a consequence
of this and other delays, it was late in December before Orobio
was ready to start.[6]

From Orobio's diary, which has not hitherto been used, we are
able to follow his movements in detail. Setting out on December
20 with twenty-one soldiers, he marched to the Trinity, where
he arrived on January 9th. Failing to learn from the Indians
of this locality what he wished to know regarding the country
below, he again changed his plan and continued northeast to
San Pedro, the Nabedache village near the Neches. Here he saw
in the firearms, clothing, and trinkets possessed by the natives—
the sight was no new one at San Pedro—abundant signs of
French influence. But these things, he was told, had all come
from the French of Natchitoches, by way of the Cadodacho, and
not from the coast. The rumors of the French settlement on the
Gulf near the Trinity, however, were confirmed and repeated
with exaggeration. But Orobio was informed that the place
could be reached only from Nacogdoches, by way of the Bidai

---

[5] Lieut. Miguel de Olivares investigated the possibilities of the proposed expedition by water, and reported that the river was obstructed,
and, besides, that suitable boats could not be built. (Report by Olivares
to Orobio, *ibid.*, 2).

[6] Order of Orobio, October 22, 1745; Orobio to Urrutia, December 7.
Ibid., 2, 4.

trail, "a path which the Vidais have made in going to Nacog-doches."

Acting on this suggestion, Orobio went on to Nacogdoches. Here a report by the veteran missionary, Father Joseph Cala-horra y Saenz, to the effect that fifteen shipwrecked Frenchmen had recently passed that way from the coast, caused him to go on to Los Adaes to consult with the governor, García Larios, before plunging into the unknown south country. The con-ference over, Orobio returned to Nacogdoches, where he arrived on February 4, and where he secured an Indian guide to conduct him over the Bidai trail to the coast.[7]

Since his diary gives us our first intimate account of a large stretch of country and of the earliest Spanish contact with a distinct group of natives in their own home, its contents have intrinsic and unique historical interest, and will, therefore, be still further drawn upon. Leaving Nacogdoches on February 7 and going southwest, on March 6 Orobio was near the Trinity at a place which he named Santa Rosa de Viterbo. Here he found a settlement of Bidai Indians living in seven rancherías[8] of bearskin tents, their regular winter habitations.

The presence of Spaniards here, which, we are informed, "had never occurred before," aroused much interest and com-ment among the natives, as can be well understood. With the chief Orobio held a long conference, but that over, his stay was brief. Taking a Bidai guide, he set out across the Trinity, and on March 15 was at Puesto de San Rafael, so named by himself, thirty leagues west-southwest from Santa Rosa de Viterbo. It will appear later on that San Rafael was in all probability on Spring Creek, west of the San Jacinto River. Here were two Orcoquiza villages, near which Orobio camped. The surprise of these Indians at seeing "Yegsa," as they called the Spaniards.

---

[7] *Diligencias Practicadas*, 4-9.

[8] It is sometimes difficult to determine whether a *ranchería* was a small village or a single dwelling. This is one of those cases.

and whom, we are told, they had only heard of and never seen, was even greater than that of the Bidai.

Among both the Bidai and the Orcoquiza the rumors of Frenchmen on the coast were confirmed with circumstantial detail. Orobio was informed that men who lived among the Pachina near the Mississippi had for six years been coming by land to the Orcoquiza, while others came annually by water, entering the Neches, Trinity, and Brazos rivers. The implication is that they regularly visited the Bidai as well as the Orcoquiza. As yet there was no regular settlement of Frenchmen, but one had been promised. In the past summer those coming by sea had even chosen a site, and had sent the Orcoquiza to notify the Bidai, Doxsas (Deadoses), and Texas to come next season to this place with their bearskins, buckskins, and buffalo hides, which the French were accustomed to buy.[9] The site designated for the settlement was described as some distance from the mouth of a river between the Trinity and the Brazos, but a tributary of neither. The stream was obviously the San Jacinto, an inference which is supported by positive evidence which will appear later.[10] Among the Orcoquiza Orobio learned that some Frenchmen had been lost among the Cujane, to the southwest, and that the shipwrecked Frenchmen who had passed through Nacogdoches were apparently a party who had been to rescue them.

Going toward the coast a distance of fifteen leagues, Orobio reached the place on the San Jacinto designated by the Orcoquiza as the site chosen by the French. The stream Orobio named Nuestra Señora de Aranzazu. Finding no signs of a habitation, and recording the opinion that there was little likelihood that one would be established,[11] since the site was ill fitted for settle-

---

[9] *Diligencias Practicadas*, 11–12.

[10] See below, p. 333, note 13.

[11] "I found no habitation whatever, but such a scarcity of lands that in case of wishing to establish a presidio, there are facilities for sup-

ment, he struck northwestward to the *camino real* leading from
Nacogdoches, and returned to La Bahía, where he arrived on
April 6. On June 25 he sent a report of his reconnoissance to
Governor Larios.

2. *The Orcoquiza tribe.*[12]—This visit of Orobio to the
Orcoquiza Indians was the beginning of a quarter of a century
of Spanish activity in their country. While among them Orobio
talked to them of missions. In a short while, apparently in the
same year, he made them another visit and went again to the San
Jacinto to look for Frenchmen, though we have not the details
of this second expedition. To counteract French influence, one
of the Orcoquiza chiefs was honored by being made a "captain,"
and during the next few years Spanish agents, in the guise of
traders, were regularly sent among both the Orcoquiza and the
Bidai. Finally, further encroachments of the French, as we shall
see, led to the occupation of the Orcoquiza country by a presidio
and a mission. In the course of this contact, a large fund of
information regarding the tribe, whose early history has been
strangely unknown, was acquired. It was not till 1755–1757 that
this information, precious to the ethnologist and the historian,
was extensively recorded in the documents at our command, but
it will facilitate the remainder of the narrative if these later
documents are drawn upon somewhat in advance for a general
sketch of the Orcoquiza tribe, who, with their territory, form
the chief center of interest in the story.

It was learned by these traders, explorers, soldiers, and missionaries, that the Orcoquiza lived in four (or five) rancherías,
or scattered villages, near the lower Trinity and the San Jacinto
rivers. The center of their population was a western branch

porting only five or six families for a short time, because of the small
amount of timber and the entire lack of stone on the margin of the
river." *Ibid.,* 12.

[12] The form of this word adopted by the Bureau of American Ethnology is "Arkokisa," but it seems better, historically considered, to
use in this study the spelling common in the contemporary sources.

of the San Jacinto, usually called in the eighteenth century the Arroyo de Santa Rosa de Alcázar (the ''San Rafael'' of Orobio), which, after a careful study of the evidence, is clearly the Spring Creek of today.[13] Near the junction of the San Jacinto and the Santa Rosa, and within a gunshot of the latter, was the village which became known as that of Chief Canos, so called because of his leaning toward the French. Farther up the Santa Rosa, some twenty miles, perhaps, at the junction of two small branches, was the village of El Gordo (the Fat), while ''above'' this point, perhaps northwest, was that of Mateo. East of the Trinity, and some ten or fifteen miles from its mouth was another village, known for a long time as that of Calzones Colorados (Red Breeches). There is some indication that there was another village under the authority of this chief, but just where it was located is not clear. These statements, which rest on unques-

---

[13] This conclusion was reached, after careful study of the documents, before the whereabouts of Miranda's map of April 18, 1757, was learned. The map bears it out. The following are some of the data on which the conclusion was reached independently. Miranda tells us that going ten leagues nearly eastward from the Springs of Santa Rosa, one comes to the San Jacinto; and that from the San Jacinto to the site of El Orcoquisac, just across the Trinity, it was not more than six leagues, by implication in the same general direction. Now, a direct line west from El Orcoquisac would fall between Buffalo Bayou and Spring Creek, while both of those streams run for a stretch of ten leagues almost east into the San Jacinto, leaving little to choose between them, as the claimant to being the Santa Rosa. (Miranda, Report of survey, April 26, 1757). According to the same authority the three western Orcoquiza villages were ranged along the Santa Rosa. But the southernmost village visited by Orobio in 1746 became a landmark in the later descriptions. Orobio tells us that after leaving the two Orcoquiza villages at San Rafael, which, we have positive evidence, was Santa Rosa (N. A., doc. 488, fol. 22), he went fifteen leagues southward to the place designated as that where the French were expected to settle, which was some distance from the mouth of a river called Aranzazu, the stream subsequently called San Jacinto (*Diligencias Practicadas*, 13–14). The two villages at San Rafael must, therefore, have been at least fifteen leagues or more northward from the mouth of the San Jacinto. In August, 1756, Joseph Valentín testified that he had gone ''down the bank of the San Jacinto River to the place reached by Dn. Joaquin de Orobio Basterra,'' and that ''from this place he returned up the said river to its crossing, near which it joins the Spring (or Arroyo) of Santa Rosa.'' (N. A., doc. 488, ff. 7–8). Marcos Ruiz gave almost the same testimony. Domingo del Rio, who a year before had passed from the Bidai on Bidai Creek to the western Orcoquiza village, now testified that this arroyo of Santa

tioned sources, make it appear that the Orcoquiza lived rather
more to the westward than has been supposed, as is true also of
the Attacapa.   On the east the Orcoquiza divided the country
between the Trinity and the Neches with the latter tribe, who
had two villages on opposite sides of the Neches near modern
Beaumont; on the north the neighbors of the Orcoquiza were
the Bidai, and, apparently, the Deadose (Agdocas, Doxsas); on
the west, the Coco; on the west and the southwest, the Karankawa and the Cujane.[14] With all of these tribes, except the
Karankawa, the Orcoquiza were generally on good terms, but
racially they seem to have been quite distinct from them, excepting the Attacapa, with whom they were considerably mixed.[15]

Although they went periodically back and forth, with the
changes of seasons, between the coast and the interior, the
Orcoquiza lived in relatively fixed villages.   If they were like

---

Rosa appeared to be the same as that which rose near the village of the
Bidai chief Tomás (*ibid.*, fol. 3).   This testimony, combined with that
of Orobio, seems to make it clear that Santa Rosa could not be Buffalo
Bayou.   One statement made by Miranda was puzzling until I saw his
map.   He states that he went west from El Orcoquisac for some twelve
leagues, till he reached the San Jacinto, thence south about fifteen
leagues to the point reached by Orobio, thence between south and west
along the bed of the San Jacinto to its junction with the Santa Rosa.
This testimony taken alone would point to Buffalo Bayou as the Santa
Rosa, but it directly contradicts the statement of Valentín and Orobio.
By changing Miranda's south to north, his statement would agree with
the others.   The difficulty is partly cleared up by the fact that on his
map his south is west and his west north (*ibid.*, 10).   The country
about the Santa Rosa was described as being marked by beautiful prairies,
forest of oak, walnut, pine and cedar, and many lakes.   In this season,
which was dry, the creek had two inches of water.   There was lack of
stone for a dam, and the bed of the stream was deep, but irrigation was
hardly necessary for the Indians had fine corn, although the season had
been dry (*ibid.*, 12).   Miranda's map does not unquestionably clear
up the difficulty of deciding between Buffalo Bayou and Spring Creek,
but it points in the same direction as the rest of the data.

[14] The Bidai told Orobio that the Orcoquiza occupied the country
from the Neches to a point half way between the Trinity and the Brazos.
See Miranda's report, N. A., doc. 488.

[15] The present writer has shown, in another study, that the Bidai,
Orcoquiza, and Deadose all belonged to the same linguistic group (*Handbook of American Indians*, II, under "San Francisco Xavier de Horcasitas.")   See also pp. 147, 197–198, above.

the Bidai, they remained inland during the winter. They practiced agriculture to some extent, raising what was called by Bernardo de Mirando "superfine maize." But this article seems to have been a minor element of their subsistence, for they lived to a large extent on a fish diet, supplemented by sylvan fruits and game, among which deer and bear were prominent. It was trade in the skins and the fat of these animals that chiefly attracted the French intruders.

An indication that the tribal organization of the Orcoquiza was loose is the fact that during the clash between the French and the Spaniards in the region, the tribe was divided in its allegiance, Canos, particularly, leaning toward the French. Another indication is the conflicting contemporary statements by different witnesses as to which of the chiefs was "Capitan Grande," or head chief of the group. Had there been a conspicuous tribal headship, such a conflict of opinion would not have been likely to occur. At first Canos appears as head chief, and is the one to whom Governor Barrios gave the title of captain sometime before October, 1754. Indeed, there are some reasons for thinking that he had the best claim to this distinction, but it was assigned also to Mateo and to Calzones Colorados.[16] The last-named chief became the one best known to the Spaniards.

Although our data on this point are conflicting, the tribe was evidently small in numbers, even at this early date. Orobio, after his second visit, reported that it was composed of five villages, containing three hundred families, or perhaps twelve hundred souls. It was later claimed that Captain Pacheco "reduced" two villages of four hundred persons each. But compared with subsequent estimates, these numbers appear to be too large. Bernardo de Miranda, for example, on being asked in 1756 what was their number, could not say definitely, but declared that he had seen at the village of Canos more than twenty warriors and

---

[16] *Diligencias Practicadas*, 1755, 3, 4, 7; N. A., doc. 488, fol. 3.

their families. If this was the entire village, and that one representative, the total of the tribe would not have exceeded one
hundred men, or five or six hundred persons. An official estimate
made in 1778, after a period of great general decrease in the
native population of Texas, it is true, put the Orcoquiza fighting
strength at only fifty men.[17] It was not, therefore, in any case,
a very large Indian population for which the French and the
Spaniards were contending. To either party, the territory involved was far more important.

3. *Spanish Trade with the Bidai and Orcoquiza Tribes.*—
Soon after the visit of Orobio, it has already been noted, Spanish
traders from Los Adaes began to operate in the Indian villages
of the lower Trinity. The exact circumstances under which this
trade was established are not clear, but it is evident that it
flourished after 1751, and that its chief beneficiary was Governor
Jacinto de Barrios y Jáuregui, who went to Texas in that year.

The evidence regarding this trade, which was regarded as
contraband, came out in a special investigation made in 1760,
after Barrios had departed, and it may well be that it is not
altogether trustworthy; but the main allegations seem well established. From the testimony given during the inquiry we learn
that between 1751 and 1759 Governor Barrios engaged pretty
regularly in commerce with the Bidai, Orcoquiza, and other
tribes. The trade was kept a strict monopoly in his hands and
carried on by his personal agents, among whom were Marcos
Ruiz, Domingo del Rio, Juan Antonio Maldonado and Jacinto de
León. Goods were carried to the tribes in pack-trains, convoyed
by small guards of soldiers. The merchandise was procured by
the government at Natchitoches, in open defiance of the law.
Among the articles taken to the Indians were French knives,
scissors, tobacco, combs, and even firearms, though it was a serious

---

[17] Orobio to the viceroy, Jan. 29, 1748, B. A., Miscellaneous, 1742–
1793; N. A., doc. 488, f. 11; estimate by the *junta de guerra*, December
5, 1778, in Cabello, *Informe*, 1784.

offense to furnish weapons or ammunition to the natives. In exchange the Indians gave horses (stolen usually from the Spanish settlements and missions), corn, and hides of deer and buffalo. The corn and horses were used by the governor at the presidio of Los Adaes; the skins were either sold at Natchitoches, likewise an unlawful proceeding, or were sent to Saltillo. This trade, conducted at first from Los Adaes, was later continued from the presidio of San Agustín, at the mouth of the Trinity.[18]

4. *The arrest of Blancpain, 1754.*—The interest in the lower Trinity aroused by Orobio's visit was crystallized by the arrest in October, 1754, of some Frenchmen, caught by Marcos Ruiz among the Orocoquiza Indians. The leader of the French party was Joseph Blancpain, whose name sometimes appears as Lanpen. With him were captured two other Frenchmen, Elias George and Antonio de la Fars, besides two negroes. Their goods were confiscated and divided among the captors, their huts given to Chief Calzones Colorados; their boat was left stranded on the river bank, and they, after being questioned as to their purposes, were sent to the City of Mexico and imprisoned. The connection between the arrest of Blancpain and French aggression on other parts of the Spanish frontier are set forth in an earlier part of this work.[19]

According to Blancpain's own statement he had long been an Indian interpreter in the employ of the government of Louisiana, and had a trading establishment at Natchitoches, but lived on his plantation near the Mississippi, twenty-two leagues from New Orleans. He claimed that, at the time of his arrest, which oc-

---

[18] The facts recorded above are drawn mainly from the records of the investigation entitled *Testimonio practicado sobre si D. Jasinto de Barrios tuvo comersio con Muniziones de Guerra con los Yndios Barbaros de Esta Prova. y fuera de ella*, etc. In the residencia of the governor held a few weeks before the investigation, the same witnesses testified solemly that Barrios had not engaged in illegal trade, but later explained the discrepancy on the ground of a technicality in the meaning of contraband trade. *Autos de la Residencia . . . de Barrios y Jauregui.*

[19] See above, pp. 66–73.

curred east of the Trinity at the village of Calzones Colorados, he had been trading for two months with the Attacapa, with whom he had dealt for more than a quarter of a century. The list of goods confiscated by his captors shows that, among other things, he was furnishing the Indians of the locality with a goodly supply of firearms, a proceeding which the Spanish government had always strenuously opposed. He had in his possession a license from the governor of Louisiana authorizing him to go among the Attacapa to trade for horses, as well as instructions to keep a diary, and, if he encountered any strange Indian villages, to make friends of the inhabitants and take the chiefs to see the governor at New Orleans. Until shortly before his arrest he had been accompanied by a considerable party.

These instructions the Spaniards regarded as evidence that Blancpain was acting as a government agent to extend French authority over the Indians living in Spanish territory. It was charged against him that he had taken away the Spanish commission of chief Canos and given him a French one. More than this, Barrios reported to the viceroy, on the testimony of the soldiers who made the arrest and who claimed to have the information from the Indians and Blancpain himself, that the Orcoquiza were expecting from New Orleans fifty families of settlers and a minister, to plant a colony and a mission at El Orcoquisac, as the site of the Orcoquiza village was called. But later, when his examination occurred at Mexico in February, 1755, Blancpain with great hardihood, it would seem, considering the circumstances, denied having had anything to do with the Orcoquiza or Bidai, and, with greater truthfulness, perhaps, claimed not to know of any plans for a mission or a settlement.

Blancpain died in prison at Mexico, and, after a year's incarceration, his companions, according to the then customary dealing with strangers in Mexico, were deported in "La América" to Spain, to be disposed of by the Casa de Contratación.

Their case brought forth a royal order requiring that if any more Frenchmen were caught on Spanish territory without license they should be sent to Acapulco and thence to South America, there to be kept on the Isle of San Fernández or at the presidio of Valdivia.[20]

[20] The account of the arrest of Blancpain is gathered mainly from an *expediente* called *Dilixensias sobre Lanpen*, dated February 19, 1755 (B. A., Provincias Internas, 1755–1793). See also a communication of the viceroy to the king, March 14, 1756; royal *cedula* directed to the viceroy, July 19, 1757; statement by Varcárcel, in *Testimonio del Dictamen dado por el Señor Don Domingo de Valcarcel del Consejo de Su Magd su oydor en la Rl Auda de esta Nueba Espana en los autos fechos a consulta de Don Jazinto de Barrios y Jauregui Governador de la Provincia de Texas de que dá quenta el comandante frances de el Presidio del Nachitos se prebino que los yndios de aquella Dominacion intentaban saltar el Presidio.* Dated October 11, 1755. The title is incorrect. The document is a recommendation of the auditor concerning the proposed garrisoning of the mouth of the Trinity. Report of the *junta de guerra* held at Los Adaes, October 23, 1754 (B. A., San Agustín de Ahumada). *Expediente sobre la aprehencion . . . de tres Franceses, y dos Negros, etc.* (A. G. I. Guadalajara, 103–106–123.)

CHAPTER II

THE DEFENSE OF THE BORDER

1. El Orcoquisac garrisoned, 1755.—As soon as Ruiz, the captor of Blancpain, returned to Los Adaes, Governor Barrios held a council, in which testimony was given to show that the French were clearly intending to establish a colony on the Trinity. In consequence, Barrios reported the danger to the viceroy, and at the same time took measures to provide temporary defence. In his account of the Blancpain affair, sent to the viceroy on November 30, 1754, Barrios proposed guarding El Orcoquisac against further intrusion by establishing a presidio and a mission as well as a civil settlement strong enough to exist after a few years without the protection of a garrison, suggesting that the families be recruited from Adaes and that they be given the government subsidy usually granted to new colonies.[1] This initiation by Barrios of a plan to colonize the lower Trinity country should be kept in mind for consideration in connection with the governor's later conduct.

With respect to the temporary defense of Orcoquisac, the junta recommended sending to the Trinity ten soldiers and ten armed settlers. Failing to find this number of men available at Los Adaes, Barrios at once corresponded with the captains at San Antonio, Bahía, and San Xavier, asking for eighteen men to add to the ten which he proposed to detach from his post; but he did not at first meet with success.[2] Meanwhile Domingo del Rio was sent among the Bidai and Orcoquiza to learn, as Barrios put it, how they reacted toward the arrest of Blancpain. He re-

---

[1] The viceroy to Barrios, February 12, 1756; *Test. del Dictamen*, October 11, 1755, fol. 7.

[2] *Dilijen* *Practicadas*, p. 19, L. P., doc. 25.

turned in April bearing a new rumor that the French had settled and fortified El Orcoquisac. Thereupon the governor dispatched him with a squad of soldiers to make another investigation and to bring back a careful report. To strengthen the Spanish hold upon the Indians, Del Rio's party were supplied with abundant merchandise for gifts and for "cambalache," or barter. In view of the defection of chief Canos to the French, they took for Mateo a commission as captain, a cane, symbol of authority, a jacket, a sombrero, and a shirt, while for Tomás, chief of the Bidai, who already had a commission as captain, they carried a like outfit. When they returned from this journey, which included a visit to the Nabedache, to the Bidai villages of Antonio and Tomás, and to the Orcoquiza village of El Gordo, they were accompanied by Mateo, Tomás, and a band of braves, who were duly entertained by the governor, and who repeated former requests for missions.[3]

Del Rio had found no French settlement, but he had heard from the Indians, who, as was to be expected, told a good story, that subsequent to the arrest of Blancpain some Frenchman had been among them, that Mateo and his people (loyal to the Spaniards, of course!) had withdrawn from the coast, but that Canos, Blancpain's proselyte, had been to New Orleans, and, on his return, all decked out in French garb and laden with presents, had tried to win the rest of his tribe to the French cause.

This report evidently caused Barrios to act. Del Rio's return was early in June. Sometime between this date and August 27—probably at least a month before this—the governor sent twenty-eight soldiers recruited from San Xavier, San Antonio, La Bahía, and Adaes, to garrison El Orcoquisac until permanent arrange-

---

[3] *Dilijens Practicadas*, 1755. L. P., no. 25. The details of this expedition are given in the declarations of the soldiers who accompanied Del Rio (*ibid.*) Miss Brown makes no mention of Del Rio's journey between October and April.

ments should be made by the superior government.[4] The posting
of this garrison marks the beginning of the Spanish occupation
of El Orcoquisac.

2. Presidio, mission and town authorized, 1756.—The examination of Blancpain in the royal hall of confessions had
occurred in February, 1755. For a year after this nothing was
done by the superior government in Mexico but to discuss and
refer, a process all too well known to the special student of
Spanish-American history. To follow the details of this correspondence would be profitless except as a study in Spanish
provincial administration. Viewed from this standpoint, however, it is interesting, as it furnishes a typical example of procedure in the matter of frontier defense, and a suggestion of the
baneful effect of long-distance legislation upon the missions and
colonies, as well as insight into Spanish governmental ideas.

According to the customary routine, Barrios' proposal concerning the defense of the Trinity went, during the spring and
summer of 1755, to the auditor, the fiscal, and a *junta de guerra
y hacienda*. But there was so little agreement of opinion that
the viceroy could reach no decision. Nominally, the difference
was upon the size of the garrison and the question as to whether
the proposed settlement should be subsidized or not. One gets
the impression, however, that the real reason for delay was lack
of interest. The fiscal recommended retaining at El Orcoquisac
twenty of the soldiers already placed there by Barrios, and
favored establishing one or more missions for the Orcoquiza. But
he opposed Barrios's proposal of a subsidized colony, recommending, instead, dependence upon settlers who should be attracted to the vicinity by lands alone. The six officials of the
junta which was called could agree neither with the fiscal nor

---

[4] *Test. del Dictamen*, October 11, 1755. The date, August 25, is fixed
by Varcárcel's statement that on this day the fiscal had suggested that
part of the temporary garrison sent by Barrios should remain. *Ibid.*
Miss Brown concluded that this garrison was not sent. My inference
is drawn from Varcárcel's *Dictamen*.

with each other. While all were of the opinion that El Orcoquisac should be garrisoned, two voted for twenty soldiers aided by the Indians of the locality, two for a larger number of soldiers, and two for ten soldiers and ten citizens.

After receiving Barrios's letter of September 6, 1755, which reported not only that Frenchmen had again been seen on the Trinity, but also that the governor of Louisiana had set up a claim to the territory which he had garrisoned, the viceroy asked for a new opinion of the auditor.

Valcárcel, coinciding with views that had been expressed by Altamira in his famous *dictamen* of 1744, and of Escandón, frequently voiced during his long struggle to people the country between the San Antonio River and Tampico, had in his mind the germs of a colonizing policy which might have been successful if really carried out. Reporting on October 11, he opposed the fiscal's plan for an unsubsidized settlement, on the ground that it would be more expensive to maintain a garrison for the long time that would be necessary under that plan, since there was little chance of a pueblo formed without special inducements to settlers, than to equip at once fifty families, withdrawing the garrison within a definite time. Citing Altamira's opinion, he argued with some logic that, in time of peace, on the one hand, good citizens would be more useful than soldiers as agents in winning the Indians, since presidial soldiers were proverbially low characters, and always making trouble; while, in time of war, on the other hand, twenty soldiers would be virtually useless. He advised, therefore, selecting fifty families of good character, attracting them not only with the lands, but also with the usual subsidy given to new colonists, putting them under a governor of their own number, and suppressing the presidio as soon as the civil settlement should be established.

He also made recommendations concerning the choice of a site. First a good location should be selected. He doubted the fitness of El Orcoquisac for the settlement, for lack of wood, and because of the marshiness of the country. Agreeing with the fiscal in this, he recommended ordering the garrison to take the president of the eastern Texas missions, go to the Trinity country, and select a site for a town and missions. The townsite must be so chosen that it would serve to protect the missions, control the Indians, and keep the French from among them. He advised, also, requiring Barrios to report the necessary supplies to be furnished the families at government expense.

But still the matter dragged on. Further delay was caused by a change of viceroys, and when the new one, the Marqués de las Amarillas, arrived in Mexico, he found the defence of the Trinity one of the questions first demanding attention. Accordingly, on February 4 he called a junta whose resolutions, supplemented by the viceroy's decree of February 12, brought the matter to a head. The provisions thus jointly made for the lower Trinity were as follows: (1) For the present a garrison of thirty soldiers and a mission were to be established precisely on the site of Blancpain's arrest. (2) As soon as a suitable permanent site could be selected—it being conceded that El Orcoquisac was unhealthful—a villa of fifty families was to be founded, and to this site the mission and presidio were to be removed. Of these families twenty-five were to be Spaniards and twenty-five Tlascaltecan Indians, both classes to be recruited mainly at Saltillo, and to be aided by a single government subsidy sufficient to transport them and to provide them with an outfit for agriculture, the sum to be determined by Barrios. (3) At the end of six years the presidio was to be suppressed, the soldiers becoming citizen colonists. For this reason, as well as for the immediate benefit of the Indians, married men and men of good character were to be preferred in the selection of the garrison. (4) The mission was to be conducted by two friars from the College of Guadalupe de Zacatecas, on a stipend of four hundred pesos each. (5) Barrios was ordered to report the funds necessary for the subsidy, to proceed at once to establish the presidio and mission on the temporary site, and, assisted by two friars and by men acquainted with the country, to choose the site for the villa.[5]

This provision regarding the sending of Tlascaltecan families to the Texas frontier is an illustration of the interesting part played by the Tlascaltecan tribe during the whole period of Spanish expansion in New Spain. After their spirited fight with Cortés, resulting in an alliance, they became the most trusted supporters of the Spaniards. After playing an important part in the conquest of the valley of Mexico, they became a regular factor in the extension of Spanish rule over the north country. Thus, when San Luis Potosí and Saltillo had been conquered, colonies of Tlascaltecans were sent to teach the more barbarous Indians of those places both loyalty to the Spaniards and the elements of civilization. In Saltillo a large colony of Tlascaltecans was establihed by Urdiñola at the end of the sixteenth century, and became the mother colony from which numerous off-shoots were planted at the new missions and villages further north. At one time one hundred families of Tlascaltecans were ordered sent to Pensacola; we see them figure now in the plans for a colony on the Trinity River; in 1757 a little colony of them was sent to San Sabá to assist in subduing the Apache; and twenty years later it was suggested that a settlement, with these people as a nucleus, be established far to the north, on the upper Red River, among the Taovayas Indians.

3. The presidio of San Agustín de Ahumada.—Barrios promptly set about establishing the presidio, which was evidently

---

[5] The proceedings in Mexico are recorded in a report of the *junta de guerra* of February 4, 1756 (B. A., San Agustín de Ahumada); *Testimonio del dictamen de Valcarcel*, October 11, 1755; the viceroy to Barrios, February 12, 1756; the viceroy to the king, March 14, 1756; royal cedula, August 20, 1756. The auditor, Valcárcel, gave his opinion on February 11, 1755, the fiscal on August 27. The date of the first *junta* has not been ascertained. Note Bancroft's error in saying that all the families were to be Tlascaltecans.

accomplished late in May or in June, 1756.[6]   It was certainly
established by July 14.   In compliment to the viceroy, the name
given it, San Agustín de Ahumada, like that of the presidio of
San Luis de las Amarillas, established a year later at San Sabá,
was borrowed from that official's generous title.[7]   The site was
fixed according to the instructions, at El Orcoquisac, the spot
where Blancpain had been arrested.   This was near a lagoon a
short distance east of the left bank of the Trinity some two
leagues from the head of the bay, or near the north line of present
Chambers County.[8]   It is easy to explain Bancroft's mistake of
supposing that El Orcoquisac and Los Horconsitos, which will
appear later in the narrative, were identical, but it is difficult
to understand how he came to place San Agustín de Ahumada on
his map more than one hundred miles up the river instead of
near its mouth.[9]   Marcos Ruiz was made recruiting officer for
the garrison; Domingo del Rio's skill as an Indian agent was
recognized by his appointment as lieutenant *ad interim* in command, while Cristóbal de Córdoba was made sergeant.   On June
12, 1757, it was reported that the presidio, church, granary and
corrals were all completed, and that fields and gardens had been
prepared.   We learn little about the structure of this presidio
except that it was good.   It was undoubtedly an unpretentious
affair, and perhaps not very different from that soon ordered
substituted for it when a change of site was being planned.   The

[6] On March 14 Barrios ordered Ruiz to enlist recruits.   On May 16
Cristóbal de Córdoba issued supplies to those who went to establish the
presidio.   This, probably, may be taken as the day when they set out
for the new establishment (Declaration of Córdoba, October 10, 1757;
Barrios to the viceroy, July 14.

[7] This was Don Agustín de Ahumada Villalón Mendoza y Narváez,
Marqués de las Amarillas.

[8] This conclusion, based upon an independent study of the sources,
is borne out by Miranda's map, which I did not see till long after the
above had been written.

[9] *North Mexican States and Texas*, I, 615, 643.   It may be noted, for
brevity's sake, that nearly every statement made by Bancroft with
reference to the presidio is erroneous in matters of detail.

latter was to be a wooden stockade, triangular in shape, with three bulwarks, six curtains, one gate near the barracks, and a *plaza de armas* in the center. As a temporary part of the equipment of the presidio, two swivel guns were sent from Adaes, to remain until other provisions could be made.[10]

The new establishment on the Trinity served to keep Barrios in Texas nearly three additional years. On August 21, 1756, by royal order, he was appointed governor of Coahuila and Don Angel Martos y Navarrete named in his place. But in view of the Orcoquisac enterprise just begun, the viceroy requested that Martos be sent temporarily to Coahuila in Barrios's stead. The request was granted, and Barrios continued in office until 1759.[11]

4. The mission of Nuestra Señora de la Luz.—The mission established in the neighborhood of San Agustín was called Nuestra Señora de la Luz (Our Lady of Light) with the addition, sometimes of "del Orcoquisac." Before the arrival of the regular missionaries, Father Romero, of the Ais mission, went among the Orcoquiza and secured promises that they would enter a pueblo, with the result that, in July, 1756, Barrios was able to report that even Canos, the French partisan, had become "reduced" to mission life, whatever this may have meant, in the absence of a mission. At this time Barrios talked hopefully of even three missions instead of one.[12]

The first missionaries sent were Fr. Bruno Chavira and Fr. Marcos Satereyn, the former old, and the latter youthful. Just when they arrived is not clear, but it was evidently after August,

---

[10] Order to survey the Trinity, N. A., doc. 488, f. 2; Barrios to the viceroy, July 14, 1756; Barrios to the viceroy, June 12, 1757; Appeal of the Father, N. A., doc. 487; the viceroy to Barrios, May 26, 1757. Miss Brown implies that Ruiz led the garrison to El Orcoquisac.

[11] Brown, "The History of the Spanish Settlements at Orcoquisac, 1746–1772," MS; the viceroy to the king, April 19, 1757, *autos* of the *residencia* of Barrios. B. A., Adaes, 1756–1766. Martos began his administration on February 6, 1759.

[12] The Viceroy to Arriaga, citing Barrios' opinion, April 18, 1757.

1756, and certainly before the end of January, 1757.[13] Barrios soon complained that these missionaries were unsuited for their task, one because he was very young, and the other, Fr. Chavira, because he was old and feeble in health. Moreover, he said, though the Indians were docile and anxious to live at the mission, the *padres* had brought nothing to support them. He carried his complaint to President Vallejo, who promised to have the college recall these two missionaries and send others.[14]

Chavira's removal, however, was by a more powerful hand, for on June 27 he succumbed to the unhealthfulness of the country and died. Fr. Chavira's companion remained for some time and was approved by the governor.[15]

In January, 1757, as we shall see, the viceroy ordered the missionaries to transfer their mission to Santa Rosa, and to "reduce" there, at El Gordo's village, all four of the Orcoquiza bands and the Bidai tribe as well. This plan does not exactly harmonize with the decision of the junta of March 3, that efforts should be made to keep the different bands hostile toward each other. The Indians, however, opposed the transfer, and, to meet this difficulty, Barrios suggested dividing the missionary forces, leaving one friar at El Orcoquisac, with a small guard of soldiers, the other going to Santa Rosa.[16]

As was usually the case in the initial stages of founding a mission, the Orcoquiza were at first very tractable and friendly. They professed anxiety to enter upon mission life, built a house

---

[13] They are not mentioned in the *Diligencias* of August, 1756, but Barrios wrote of their being there in January, 1757 (letter to the viceroy, June 12, 1757). From his statement it is inferred that January was the month of their arrival, although this is not certain. See the statement that the viceroy was sending letters by the missionaries, January 19, 1757. These might be new missionaries. (A. G. M., Historia, 91, *expediente* 2).

[14] The viceroy to Arriaga, April 18, 1757.

[15] *Ibid.*, postscript.

[16] Viceroy's decree, January 19, 1757; Barrios to the viceroy, June 12, 1757.

for the missionaries, and the first spring planted for them six *almuds* of corn, something "never before seen in these natives."[17]

The church, reported by Barrios as already completed in June, was evidently a very temporary structure which was substituted afterwards by a somewhat better one, itself miserable enough. A complaint made two years later by Fr. Abad de Jesús María, who was then head minister at the place, to the effect that he could not get help from the soldiers to complete the mission, reveals to us the site and the nature of the newer buildings. He writes: "Fearful of what might result, I had to set about the mentioned material establishment. . . . The two ministers having explored and examined the territory with all care and exactitude, we did not find any place more suitable or nearer the presidio than a hill, something less than a fourth of a league's distance to the east from the latter and on the same bank of the lagoon. This place, Excellent Sir, because of its elevation, commands a view of the whole site of the presidio and of a circumference to the west and south, where this River Trinity turns, as far as the eye can reach. Toward the east the land is a little less elevated. At a distance of a league enough corn might be planted to supply a large population. . . . All these advantages being seen, the mission was erected on this site. It is made of wood, all hewn (*labrada*), and beaten clay mixed with moss, and has four arched portals (*portales en círculo*). This building, because of its strength and arrangement, is the most pleasing in all those lands of the Spaniards and the French —or it would be if your Excellency should be pleased to have completed its construction, which for the present has been suspended."[18]

Such are some of the glimpses which we are able to get of the new mission and presidio.

---

[17] The viceroy to Arriaga, April 18, 1757.

[18] Father Abad to the viceroy, November 27, 1759.

5. *Plans for the villa, 1756–1757.*—To select the site for the colony, Barrios commissioned Lieutenant Del Rio and Don Bernardo de Miranda (the latter known for his recent explorations of the Los Almagres mineral vein), each to make an independent survey, which they did in the mid-summer of 1756. When, on August 26, 1756, they and their assistants gave their reports before Governor Barrios and Father Romero, all agreed as to the most desirable location. Above the presidio, within a space of six leagues, they reported three arroyos, on the middle one of which was the village of Calzones Colorados. These arroyos, they thought, would afford moderate facilities for a townsite. But much better was the country along the arroyo of Santa Rosa del Alcázar, mentioned before as in the center of the Orcoquiza tribe.[19]

Pleased with the glowing description of Santa Rosa, as it came to be called commonly, Barrios next had it surveyed by two surveyors named Morales[20] and Hernández. In October these men reported favorably upon three sites, but most favorably on that near El Gordo's village at the junction of two small branches joining the Santa Rosa, about ten leagues or perhaps twenty miles west of the San Jacinto—evidently Mill Creek and Spring Creek.[21] Barrios required the surveyors to prepare estimates of

---

[19] Order for the survey of the banks of the Trinity and select the townsite. N. A., doc. 488, 2, 8, 9.

[20] Miss Brown gives his name as Morelos.

[21] Order for the survey. N. A., doc. 488, 14–22. The survey was begun early in September, 1756, Barrios going with the party. He returned to Los Adaes on September 6, leaving Miranda in charge, and with orders to go up the Santa Rosa to three arroyos that had been mentioned before. On the 13th the survey was resumed, the first *ojo* examined being one about three leagues west of the San Jacinto; within three leagues of this two others were examined. Going up stream to the village of El Gordo they found a larger stream, carrying two hands of water (*bueyes*), and dividing at a short distance into two smaller streams, one coming from the northwest and one from the south. This was regarded as the best place for the site, and is the place marked on Miranda's map as Santa Rosa. It was apparently about where Dustin now is; if not, then at Houston.

the cost of building the necessary dams and *acequias,* and in November reported to the viceroy in favor of Santa Rosa (which Miranda had already done in October), recommending three missions instead of one. On January 7 this site was approved by a *junta de guerra y hacienda,* and shortly afterward the viceroy ordered the presidio moved thither, on condition that each week a squad of soldiers must be sent to reconnoiter El Orcoquisac for Frenchmen.

The missionaries were required likewise to transfer the mission with the people of Calzones Colorados and Canos (assumed by the authorities, from previous reports, to be in the mission) to El Gordo's village, and to strive to attract thither the people of Mateo and also those of the Bidai tribe. Thus was it planned to gather all of the Orcoquiza and Bidai into one settlement.[22]

In March and April the central government proceeded in good faith to provide 30,000 pesos, the sum asked for by Barrios, for equipping and transporting the settlers, and ordered three swivel guns to San Agustín, to take the place of the cannon brought from Los Adaes. The details of recruiting the families were left to Barrios, but he was ordered to take from Saltillo fifty saddle horses, fifty brood mares, twenty-five cows, nine thousand one hundred and twenty-five sheep, and six yoke of oxen. Other necessary stock was to be purchased in Los Adaes. Each family was to be supplied with a limited outfit for engaging in agriculture, and a gun and a sabre for defence, while, during the journey, each member of the Spanish families was to be allowed three reals a day, and each member of the Tlascaltecan families two reals. The actual work of recruiting, equipping and transporting the families was entrusted by Barrios sometime later to the merchant of Mexico, named Giraud, whom Miranda

---

22 Barrios to the viceroy, November 8, 1756; the viceroy to the governor, January 7, 1757; decree of the viceroy, January 19, 1757; the viceroy to the missionaries, March 23, 1757.

had made his representative in the matter of the Los Almagres mines.[23]

6. *Efforts to move the presidio and the mission; failure of the project for a villa.*—To this point prospects seemed good for the beginning in Texas of a new civil settlement, the element most lacking, and a lack which meant ultimate failure. But now' ensued a period of disheartening inactivity, flimsy excuse-making, and pernicious quarrelling, that shatters the reader's patience, and that resulted in killing the projected settlement.

The plan for a colony had originated with Barrios, and hitherto he had acted with reasonable promptitude in carrying it out. As late as June, 1757, his attitude was favorable, for then, when reporting that the Indians at El Orcoquisac might oppose moving to Santa Rosa, he had suggested that this difficulty might be overcome by leaving one missionary at El Orcoquisac, protected by a small garrison, and establishing the other at Santa Rosa.[24] But from now on he seems to have entirely changed his mind. It may have been sincere conviction that there was no suitable site—he could not foresee the building in the vicinity of a great city like Houston;—or it may have been some unexplained influence that caused him positively to oppose the town. A suggestion of jealousy of Miranda appears in the documents, but one is not warranted in accepting this suggestion as fact.

Whatever the cause, his subsequent conduct is most exasperating. In October he reported that he had been deceived by Miranda's report and that a personal examination made in October by himself and President Vallejo proved that Santa Rosa was unfit for a settlement,[25], but that a place called "El Atas-

---

[23] Action of the *junta* of March 3, and a supplementary decree of April 3; viceroy's decrees of March 3 and March 8; viceroy to the king, April 18, 1757. *Appeal of the Father*, 9.

[24] Barrios to the viceroy, June 12, 1757.

[25] This report is missing, but it seems from references to it that his objection was the difficulty of making an *acequia*. (See *Appeal of the Father;* viceroy to Barrios, March 3, 1758).

cosito'' or ''El Atascoso y Los Tranquillos'' on the Trinity; some nineteen leagues above the presidio, was a suitable location.[26]

While the viceroy was putting Barrios's suggestion through the usual attenuating legislative routine,[27] the governor was forced into temporary activity by the missionary then at Nuestra Señora de la Luz, Fray Joseph Francisco Caro. This friar wrote in February, 1758, to Father Vallejo, his superior at Adaes, a mournful tale about the physical miseries of life at his swampy, malarial, mosquito-infested post. Father Chavira had died, he said, from the unhealthfulness of the place; his companion, Fray Marcos Satereyn, and all the soldiers, were sick from dysentery, due to bad water, excessive humidity, and putrid lagoons near by. He requested, therefore, that the presidio and mission be moved at once to another site, preferably El Atascosito. If this could not be done, he begged leave either to move the mission with a small guard of soldiers to the place designated or to abandon his post. Vallejo reported the complaint to Barrios and requested that one of the alternatives be granted, preferably that looking to the transfer of the presidio as well as the mission to El Atascosito; he closed with a threat that unless something were done, he would order Father Caro to retire and, acting in the name of his college, would renounce the mission.[28]

In response to this threat Barrios went in April to San Agustín, selected a site within two gunshots of El Atascosito, ordered crops sown there, and instructed Lieutenant Del Río, as soon as the sowing should be completed, to build here a new triangular stockade, and to transfer the garrison and the mission.[29] To offset this apparent compliance, however, Barrios gave the idea of a colony a serious blow by declaring that neither

---

[26] *Dictamen fiscal*, February 5, 1758. With this report he seems to have sent *autos* of his examination of El Atascosito.

[27] On March 13, 1758, he ordered Barrios to make another report so that the government could decide whether or not to accept El Atascosito as a substitute for Santa Rosa. Barrios either ignored or failed to get this order (the viceroy to Barrios, March 13, 1758).

[28] *Appeal of the Father*, 4. N. A., doc. 487.

El Atascosito, the place he had himself proposed as a substitute for Santa Rosa, nor any of the several others that had been considered, would support a settlement of fifty families, and recommended accordingly that Giraud, his agent sent to Saltillo to recruit families, should be repaid for his trouble and expense, and, it is inferred, relieved of his commission.[30]

On March 4, 1758, and again on March 13, Barrios was ordered to make another search for a townsite, or at least one to which the mission might be removed. But after all the delays and failures recounted above, one will hardly be surprised that these renewed orders were not obeyed. The reason, if the reader were to require a specific one, does not appear, for it happens that in our sources there is a gap, so far as events on the Trinity go, between April, 1758, and October, 1759. Before that time Governor Barrios had gone to his new post in Coahuila, leaving half done the task to accomplish which, because of his supposed special fitness for it, his transfer had been indefinitely suspended. His successor proved to be no more efficient than he. so far as the defence of the Trinity is concerned.

7. *Los Horconsitos and Los Piélagos.*—When the curtain again rises after the year and a half of darkness the tables are turned. The mission and presidio are still at El Orcoquisac, but the new missionary, Fray Joseph Abad de Jesus María, is in dispute with the new governor, Don Angel Martos y Navarrete, over the question of removal to Los Horconsitos, a new site, three or four leagues up the river. But this time it is the missionary who opposes the transfer.

[29] Barrios replied on March 13 that as soon as the weather would permit he would attend to removing the presidio to El Atascosito. While at Nacogdoches, early in April, on his way to San Agustín, he received news of the destruction of the San Sabá Mission. Only high rivers prevented him from going to San Antonio and leaving the affairs of San Agustín to his lieutenants. *Appeal of the Father.* N. A., doc. 487.

[30] *Appeal of the Father,* 9. N. A., doc. 487. Barrios had denounced El Orcoquisac and the San Jacinto sites in August, 1756, Santa Rosa in October, 1757, and now he declared against El Atascosito and, by implication, against the whole plan.

Don Angel began his administration on February 6, 1759,[31] and after attending to matters of most pressing moment he took up the question of locating the proposed villa and transferring the mission and presidio from El Orcoquisac. In October he visited Santa Rosa and decided against it.[32] On November 4, in company with Del Rio and Father Abad, he visited El Atascosito, and decided against it also. But farther south he found a place called Los Horconsitos (Little Forks) three and one-half leagues above El Orcoquisac, and a league north of this, a juniper covered arroyo called Los Piélagos, either of which he regarded suitable for a town, as well as for the presidio and mission.[33]

But Father Abad opposed the governor's suggestion. He argued, and with reason, that the trouble with the presidio and the mission was one of laziness rather than one of faults of the site; that Del Rio, being a common soldier, was unfit to be a commander, that the Indians objected to leaving their native soil; that the buildings and crops, secured at the cost of great labor, should not be abandoned; and that new rumors of the French made removal unwise. In spite of Father Abad's opinion, on December 12 Martos reported favorably on Los Horconsitos, and on March 15 the viceroy ordered the removal made to that point. But instead of complying with the order, in May Martos took more testimony, which added a "Place on the Trinity," to Los Horconsitos and Los Piélagos, as sites suitable for a town and for the transfer in question, but he declared against El Atascosito and El Orcoquisac.[34] After recommending to the viceroy on May 30 the three places named, Martos inquired of Father Vallejo if the removal was imperative. The president, after re-

---

[31] *Autos de Residencia de Barrios*, B. A., Adaes, 1756–1766.

[32] Martos to the viceroy, December 6, 1759. B. A., San Agustín de Ahumada.

[33] Martos to the viceroy, December 6, 1759. B. A., San Agustín de Ahumada; *Informe* by Father Abad, November 27, 1759.

[34] Abad to the viceroy, November 27, 1759; *dictamen fiscal*, February 5, 1760; *Interrogatorio*, May 20, 1760. B. A., San Agustín de Ahumada.

ferring the matter to Father Romero, the missionary from Los Ais who had been at San Agustín, replied in the affirmative, with emphasis.[35] Thus Father Abad was now opposed by Fathers Vallejo and Romero, while the governor stood between them. Put another way, all parties at Los Adaes favored the transfer, but Father Abad, at El Orcoquisac, opposed it.

Meanwhile Martos had added his opposition to the project of a villa. On December 16, ten days after recommending Los Horconsitos and Los Piélagos as suitable for such a purpose, he asked the viceroy to relieve him of responsibility for founding the town. What his reason was is not clear, but it may have been his unwillingness to oppose Father Abad.[36] At any rate, on March 6, 1760, his request was granted, until the site should be determined. As this never occurred, the plan for the villa was never again taken up in Mexico, and the villa never was founded.

8. *The removal never made.*—If it were not for the fact that Bonilla and those who have followed him had made the fundamental error of saying that the presidio and mission were moved one or more times, finally to Los Horconsitos (which Bancroft confuses with Orcoquisac), the reader might be spared the pain of following further such frivolous excuse-making and disgusting inactivity. Since, however, such errors have been made, it is necessary to show that, excepting a probable removal to a site a quarter of a league away, the transfer had not been effected down to 1767, when steps for final abandonment of the place were begun, and after which, of course, no further effort was likely to be made.[37]

A year and a half passed after the events related above had occurred, when a *junta de guerra*, held December 9, 1762, again approved Los Horconsitos, and, on December 22, Martos was

---

[35] Martos to the viceroy, May 30, 1760, in Abad's *Informe;* Martos to Vallejo, June 10, *ibid.;* Romero to Vallejo, June 12, *ibid.;* Vallejo to Martos, June 13, *ibid.*

[36] Abad, *Informe*, B. A., San Agustín de Ahumada, ff. 9–10.

[37] Bonilla, *Breve Compendio*, Tex. Hist. Ass'n. *Quarterly*, VIII, 57.

again ordered to move the presidio and mission thither and to
do it at once. It is clear from what follows, however, that the
order was never carried out.

In November, 1763, the presidio was put under the command
of a captain, Don Rafael Martínez Pacheco, when Martos, resenting the change, became anxious to do what for five years he had
neglected. In June, 1764, therefore, he went to the presidio
in company with Father Calahorra to effect the transfer, but
the Indians, bribed by Pacheco, as it later appeared, opposed the
change, and, though the governor remained on the ground a
month, the object was not accomplished.[38] Martos reported his
failure to the viceroy, and on August 12, 1764, the command to
remove the establishment to Los Horconsitos was repeated.[39] In
the course of the ensuing trouble with Pacheco, the presidio
was partially burned. Subsequently, in the administration of
Afan de Rivera, temporary repairs were made on the partially
burned establishment, which indicates that no removal had been
made. In 1766 a storm damaged the presidio and mission, and
a new clamor was made for a transfer, there being some evidence
that the presidio was moved to a higher ground a quarter of a
league away.[40] Finally, in October, 1767, when the Marqués de
Rubí inspected the place he found the presidio still at El Orcoquisac, for in his diary describing his journey to the coast, La
Fora records passing El Atascosito and Los Horconsitos, and
proceeding south from this point to the Presidio of Orcoquisac.
His entry makes it clear that the presidio and mission were still
at El Orcoquisac. He says: "We traveled . . . four leagues to

---

[38] The viceroy to Martos, December 22, 1762; Martos to the viceroy,
December 14, 1763; the viceroy to Martos, August 12, 1764; Martos to
the viceroy, December 14, 1763. Testimony was given on January 2,
1765, to the effect that Pacheco had bribed the Indians. What his motives
were do not appear. Declaration of Calzones Colorados before Marcos
Ruiz, January 2, 1765, L. P., no. 25.

[39] The viceroy to Martos, August 12, 1764.

[40] The viceroy to Rivera, November 17, 1766; *dictamen fiscal*, November 17, 1766.

a small ranch at the place called El Atascoso, where we camped.''
On the next day ''We traveled ten leagues, generally south, although the road forms a semicircle, to escape the lagoon formed
by the Rio de la Trinidad, which during the whole day we kept
at our right and two leagues away. After going four leagues in
level country . . . we crossed the arroyo de Calzones, which runs
west and empties into the Trinidad, and leaving behind the Paraje
de los Horconsitos, we forded that of El Pielago, . . . which
flows in the same direction and like that of Calzones empties into
said river, both overflowing in rainy seasons and flooding the
six leagues between this place [evidently Los Horconsitos] and
the Presidio of San Luis de Ahumada, commonly called El Orcoquisac.''[41]

It is clear, then, that down to October, 1767, no material
change of site had been made. Rubí recommended that the
establishment, like the rest of those in eastern Texas, be abandoned. This suggestion was soon acted upon and, if any transfer
was ever effected, of which there is no evidence, it was between
1767 and 1770, a period when the affairs of the place were going
from bad to worse.

---

[41] *Relacion del Viaje que de orden del Excelentísimo Senor Virrey
Marquéz de Cruillas Hizo el Capitan de Ingenieros Dn. Nicolás de la Fora*,
entries for October 8 and 9.

CHAPTER III

AN INGLORIOUS COLONY

1. Relations with the French.—The arrest of Blancpain brought forth a protest from Kerlérec, the new governor of Louisiana, who claimed that the trader had been arrested on French territory.[1] He added that only with difficulty had he been able to restrain the Attacapa Indians from destroying the Spanish establishment, on account of their anger at the expulsion of the French. On September 11, 1756, he proposed to Barrios that a joint commission be appointed to examine the site of San Agustín to determine the question of ownership, and named Athanase de Mézières to serve as the French representative. Barrios refused the proffered aid and expressed the fear that Kerlérec intended to found a presidio near that of San Agustín.

In spite of the arrest and harsh treatment of Blancpain and his party, fear of the Spaniards was not so great as to keep away all Frenchmen. Domingo del Rio reported, in the summer of 1755, after his visit to El Orcoquisac, that since the arrest of Blancpain four Frenchmen had been there on horseback. Scarcely had the new presidio been established when a Frenchman presented a petition to the viceroy through Barrios asking permission to settle at Orcoquisac. The petitioner, M. Masse, a ranchman who lived in the Attacapa region, was evidently well known to Governor Barrios, for when the latter went to establish the presidio he asked permission to go by way of M. Masse's hacienda among the Attacapa, but his request was refused. In his petition Masse enlarged upon his distinguished birth and attainments, and explained that he was led to make

---

[1] Kerlérec protested on January 12, 1755, and again on April 7 (Report of the *junta de guerra* of February 6, 1756).

the request by his desire to emancipate his slaves, which was not possible in Louisiana. As arguments in his favor he referred to his large herds of stock, which would be at the disposal of the new establishment; the increase of population which would result from the settlement of his numerous slaves; and the important service he would be able to perform among the Indians. In this connection, he promised to secure the allegiance of the Attacapa, as well as the friendly help of the northern nations, the Taovayazes, the Letas (Comanche), the Patoca (Comanche), the Icara, and the Pares (Panis). He did not speak for himself alone, but for his partner, also, the Abbé Disdier, whose loyalty he was ready to guarantee. On July 22, Governor Barrios forwarded the petition, and added the information that Masse was a chancellor of Grenoble, of good standing among the French, absolute master of the Attacapa and the northern Indians, owner of twenty negroes, seven hundred head of cattle, and one hundred horses, all of which he was willing to contribute to the support of the town. When we learn that for many years after this date Monsieur Masse was a contraband trader on the Gulf Coast and know that Barrios was engaged in illicit trade, we are inclined to see something besides generosity in Masse's request.

The viceroy in Mexico regarded the petition as a part of a plan to establish a French settlement on soil claimed by Spain, and the answer was the only one which could be expected. Barrios was instructed to inform Masse and Disdier that it would be contrary to law for them even to enter the Spanish province, and that if they did so their goods would be confiscated and they sent prisoners to Spain. He was further instructed to ascertain why the Frenchmen had wished to settle in Texas; and to find out if the Abbé during his stay at Los Adaes had caused any desertions.

In the course of the correspondence which ensued it was stated that Disdier had come to New Orleans as chaplain of a vessel; had been made chaplain of a seminary in New Orleans;

had been ejected by Kerlérec because of trouble with the boys; had gone to the establishment of M. Masse, thence to Natchitoches, and thence to Los Adaes, where he served for two months as tutor of the governor's sons. Regarding Masse it was stated that he was a military officer who had been engaged in secret trade among the Attacapa. In June, 1757, Barrios reported that Disdier had left Texas on the pretext of going to Mexico to visit the shrine of the Virgin of Guadalupe; but instead had gone to Orcoquisac to persuade the missionaries there to desert to Louisiana and Europe. Barrios professed to believe that Disdier was not a priest, but a fraud, and mentioned a correspondence that he had carried on with De Mézières.[2]

Kerlérec did not confine his protests to those made to Barrios. but wrote to his home government on the matter, addressing his complaint to the Minister of Marine. This correspondence was reported to the viceroy of Mexico on March 9, 1757, by the governor of Havana. Reporting the incident to the king on April 18, the viceroy suggested the erection of a presidio on the bank of the Mississippi River opposite New Orleans "to protect the boundaries" and so that this establishment, the new presidio of San Agustín, and that of La Bahía, might protect the coast, "and in future prevent any introduction whatever." With the dispatch he sent a map made by Bernardo de Miranda, the surveyor of Santa Rosa, who happened to be in Mexico, and a report on the French border, by the same individual. The map, which, as the viceroy remarked, is not "subject to the rules of geography," shows Texas as extending to the Mississippi.[3]

Frenchmen continued to operate among the Indians in the neighborhood of San Agustín, and to cause trouble for the small

[2] Miranda to the viceroy, April 26, 1757; Petition of Masse, July 19, 1756; Barrios to the viceroy, July 22, 1756; the viceroy to the king, September 14, 1756; royal cédula, June 10, 1757; Barrios to the viceroy, June 16, 1757; the viceroy to Barrios, 1757, draft.

[3] The viceroy to Arriaga, April 18, 1757.

garrison. Sometime in 1759, for example, two Frenchmen entered the Orcoquiza country with a band of one hundred warriors and were expelled by Del Rio and ten soldiers, after some show of resistance. It later came out that they were connected with a plot to destroy the Spanish settlement. In November of the same year eight Spanish soldiers were sent to the Brazos, to reconnoiter a place where Frenchmen had encamped among the Karankawa, promising to return to build a town.[4]

Allusions have already been made to a French plot to destroy the settlement at San Agustín. Sometime in 1759, late in the year, we have seen, two Frenchmen entered the Orcoquiza country in company with a band of Attacapa, and were expelled by Del Rio, after some resistance in which Del Rio's life was endangered. In January, 1760, Del Rio wrote to Governor Martos that Louis de St. Denis (son of the famous Louis Juchereau de St. Denis so long commander of Natchitoches) had sent an Adaes Indian among the Orcoquiza and Bidai tribes to bribe them to destroy the presidio of San Agustín. Barrios at once protested to Governor Kerlérec, and added that he believed that the destruction of San Sabá had been accomplished by French weapons. Kerlérec replied on March 13, in great indignation, demanding that Martos produce evidence to support the charge against St. Denis, and threatening to complain to the Spanish king.[5] Martos sent his correspondence with Del Rio and Kerlérec to Mexico, whereupon a secret investigation of the charges was ordered, and special care enjoined to discover, whenever an Indian outbreak should occur, if it was due to French intrigue.[6]

The testimony presented in the investigation which followed was not altogether conclusive, but it was nevertheless significant.

---

[4] Declaration of Miguel Ramos and others, April 17–20, 1761.

[5] Kerlérec to Martos, March 13, 1760, in *Testimonio Practicado sobre si Dn. Jasinto de Barrios tuvo comersio*, etc. B. A., 1756–1766.

[6] *Dictamen fiscal*, August 26, 1760; viceroy's decree, August 27, 1760; *dictamen del auditor*, September 1, 1760; decree of the viceroy, September 3, 1760; the viceroy to Martos, September 8, 1760.

Calzones Colorados testified that early in 1760 two Bidai Indians had brought a message from St. Denis, inviting his tribe to go to Natchitoches to secure ammunition with which to return and kill all the Spaniards at Orcoquisac; he had refused to listen (of course); that the emissaries had gone to make the same proposal to Canos and Tomás; and that later one of them had returned saying that the offer had been made by St. Denis merely to test their loyalty to the Spaniards.

Canos, well known to be a partisan of the French (as his name implied), could not be secured as a witness, as he had escaped to the Attacapa; El Gordo denied having been offered bribes, but declared that during a visit to Calzones Colorados he had heard of the proposal. Tamoges, another chief, corroborated the story as told by Calzones; Boca Floja testified that the two Frenchmen who had been expelled by Del Rio had come with one hundred Attacapa to induce them to aid in killing all the Spaniards and running off the stock. The conference had been broken up by the opportune arrival of Del Rio and ten soldiers. The Bidai chief claimed that, so far as they were concerned, no bribes had been offered them.[7]

This testimony, considering the circumstances under which it was given, is not conclusive, but taken in connection with Kerlérec's avowed design of pushing through Texas into Coahuila, his protests against the settlement at San Agustín, his recent proposal of a joint commission, and the contemporary Indian attack of San Sabá, in which French influence was clearly seen, the evidence is not to be rejected altogether.

Again, in November, 1763, after the Louisiana cession, but

---

[7] The whole investigation is recorded in the documents called *Testimonio practicado sobre si Dn. Jasinto de Barrios tuvo comersio*. B. A., Adaes, 1756–1766. Martos sent the correspondence on March 16; on August 26 the fiscal gave his opinion; the auditor his on September 1; the viceroy approved this opinion on September 3, and on September 5 issued his instructions to Barrios. Martos received the instructions on January 17, 1761, and on the 22d began the investigation. The investigation at San Agustín was conducted by Del Rio and Juan Prieto.

before it was generally known in Texas and Louisiana, a lively dispute over boundaries arose between Governor Martos and Cavalier Macarty, commander at Natchitoches. The precise point at issue was not the ownership of the lower Trinity, but in the course of the correspondence Macarty laid claim, on the basis of La Salle's colony, to the Bay of Espíritu Santo, adding: "This being granted, you cannot fail to be convinced both of our rights to the Bay of San Luis [Espíritu Santo], and that if from there we draw a line running straight north, the lands lying to the east thereof belong to the Most Christian dominions."[8]

After the occupation of Louisiana by Spain the question of the boundary ceased to have political significance, and the troubles arising over the French contraband traders on the border were matters of internal administrative concern only.

2. Mission progress, 1759–1771.—Regarding progress and events at the mission of Nuestra Señora de la Luz, which had the misfortune to be placed amidst a multitude of discordant and hostile elements, natural, moral, and political, we have only incomplete data. Nevertheless, here and there we get glimpses of occurrences and personalities.

Father Chavira's place was filled by Fray Francisco Caro, formerly of the mission of Nuestra Señora de los Dolores de los Ais, who was at the Trinity mission in February, 1758. The most notable recorded event of his administration was his denunciation of the climate, swamps, and insect pests at the site, and his strenuous fight to have the mission removed to El Atascosito. As we have already seen, in 1759 and 1760 the superior of the mission was Father Abad de Jesús María. He opposed the removal of the mission as strenuously as Father Caro had favored it. It is from him that we get the description of the second church, which was being built in 1759.

---

8 Macarty to Martos, November 17, 1673.

The Indians of the place were not always docile, and there is no evidence that they actually entered the mission and submitted to its discipline. In 1759, during some trouble, the Attacapa joined the Orcoquiza in an outbreak, and in order to pacify them it was necessary to shoot a soldier. The trouble was evidently caused by one of the ever-recurring instances of misconduct on the part of the presidial soldiers.[9]

Slight as is our information before 1760, we are in possession of even less for the period between that date and the coming of Captain Pacheco, in 1764. But the occurrences at the time of his advent indicate that few Indians were living in the mission before that time, and that the mission building was in a state of decay when he arrived.

The coming of Captain Pacheco was followed by a temporary revival of missionary activity under Fathers Salvino and Aristorena, aided by the new captain. Pacheco arrived on May 13. 1764, and on the next day he began his reforms. He called an assembly of the one hundred and fifty Orcoquiza living about the place, passed them in review and addressed them in the presence of the missionaries, urging them to settle in the mission at once. A peace pipe was passed, dances were performed, and the Indians declared themselves eager to enter a mission, for which they had waited three years. Del Rio, the interpreter, informed them of the duties of neophytes, telling them that they must obey the king, his officers, and the missionaries, throw away their idols, attend prayers, work in the field for the fathers, remain always in the mission enclosure, and defend the place against the French or hostile tribes. In return Del Rio assured them of four rations of food a week and clothing when necessary.[10] The Orcoquiza agreed. Gifts and feasting followed, and next day the heathen

---

[9] Vallejo to Barrios, February 27, 1758; Father Abad to the governor, November 27, 1759; Hierro, *Informe de las Misiones de Texas.*

[10] Pacheco to Solís, May 26, 1764. *Papeles pertenecientes al Orcoquiza;* Hierro, *Informe.*

idols and ornaments were solemnly turned over to the missionaries.

The new zeal extended to other villages besides that of Calzones. On May 31, Chief Canos and his band, mainly of Attacapa, it seems, came, flying a French flag, to consider entering the mission. The same ceremony was performed, and after a day's deliberation Canos declared himself willing to part with the French flag and the native idols, and to enter a mission, providing it were separate from that of Calzones. On June 6 the Bidai chief Tomás came with forty-eight of his tribe, participated in the same ceremonies, and promised to enter a mission if it were established in his own country—his people had already tried one in foreign lands at San Xavier—and also to persuade the northern tribes to do likewise.

Captain Pacheco, on June 14, sent to Mexico an account of all that had been done, and requested funds to rebuild the mission and the presidio, both of which were in a state of decay, to furnish supplies for the Indians, and to found missions for the villages of Tomás and Canos. He asked, besides, for permission to go with Chief Tomás on a missionary and diplomatic trip among the northern tribes. Pacheco assisted further in the missionary work by furnishing supplies, and within a short time he was reported to have furnished the Indians with clothing to the value of 1079 pesos, and with tools and implements for agriculture. Calzones' village was supplied with two beeves and five fanegas of corn a week, and that of Canos half as much.[11]

This was, however, but a temporary wave of enthusiasm, lasting only a few months. The scandalous quarrel which ensued before the year was over between Pacheco and Governor Barrios, resulting in the flight of the former and his absence during the next five years, removed the best support of the missionaries, and

---

[11] *Papeles pertenecientes al Orcoquiza* (this collection gives an account of Pacheco's assistance to the missionaries); Pacheco to Cruillas, July 22, and July 29, 1764, *ibid.*

there was a recurrence of former conditions at Nuestra Señora de la Luz, which the Marqués de Rubí, after a visit in 1767, referred to as "an imaginary mission."[12]

Nevertheless, the missionaries continued their work and in the course of the next six years effected the "perfect conversion" of thirty Indians, mainly adults. The missionaries whose names appear are Fathers Luis Salvino and Bernardino Aristorena, in 1764–1766; Fray Bernardo de Silva, 1766; Fray Joseph Marenti, 1767; Fray Ignacio María Laba, 1768–1771; Fray Anselmo García, 1770; and Fray Joseph del Rosario Soto, 1770. Presidents Vallejo and Calahorra each visited the place once in the course of its existence, but Father Solís, who came all the way from Zacatecas in 1766 to visit the missions, slighted this one, and caused complaint thereby. Missionary supplies were continued with some regularity between 1765 and 1769, during the administration of Afan de Rivera at San Agustín, who spent for the Indians 2724 pesos; and during his stay of a year after he returned in the fall of 1769, Pacheco spent 2496 pesos for the Orcoquiza, Attacapa, Bidai, and "Asinaio" tribes "resident on this frontier." The Asinai had by this time acquired the hope of coming to the post for *regalos*.

In 1770 chiefs Tomás and Calzones were still living. At least one missionary expedition was made by a *padre* among the Bidai, and in all probability more than one. And even after the garrison of the presidio was removed in 1771, the missionaries, Fray Ignacio Laba and his companion, were the last to leave the place.[13]

3. Administration scandals.—Up to 1764 the presidio of San Agustín was commanded by Domingo del Rio, who was responsible to Governor Martos. But in 1763 Del Rio wrote to the viceroy complaining of the lack of flour and clothing, and even

---

[12] Rubí, *Dictamen*, paragraphs 24–25.
[13] *Testimonio del expediente*, 138.

of ammunition, charging Governor Martos with neglect, and recommending that the post be taken out of the governor's hands and put under the command of a captain directly responsible to the viceroy. On November 23 the viceroy acted upon this recommendation (though it seems that the change was already under contemplation) and appointed to the new office Rafael Martínez Pacheco.[14] The first result of the change was the promising wave of missionary activity and general prosperity which we have already recounted. But this was soon followed by one of the disgraceful quarrels which so often marred the success of frontier Spanish administration.

Pacheco was charged by his troops, on what ground we know not, with arrogance, ill temper, harshness, and avarice. By June 24 his soldiers had planned a general mutiny, but it was temporarily checked by a visit of Governor Martos and President Calahorra, who came to attend to moving the presidio and mission. The governor's stay of a month did not help matters— perhaps the contrary—and in a short time the plan to desert was carried out. One by one the garrison slipped away to Natchitoches, and before August 18 had sought French protection, while two took refuge at the Mission of San Miguel, only five, among whom was Domingo del Rio, remaining at the presidio.

Hearing of the event Governor Martos sent a squad of soldiers to the provincial boundary to overtake the deserters if possible. In this he failed, and a few days later Périère, commander at Natchitoches, forwarded to Martos a petition of the deserters, who told of their wrongs, but professed a willingness to return if they were put under another commander.[15]

Martos proceeded, in the usual way, to take depositions, and in consequence, on September 12, he formally suspended Pacheco

---

14 Order of the viceroy, November 23, 1763, *Papeles pertenecientes al Orcoquiza.*

15 *Testimonio de los Autos fhos por el Govor de la Provincia de Texas contra Rafael Martinez Pacheco, Año de 1764.* B. A., Adaes, 1756–1766. This *expediente* contains the evidence regarding the trouble at San Agustín.

and promised the deserters pardon. He then sent Marcos Ruiz at the head of the band of twenty deserters to arrest Pacheco and to restore peace and order, two entirely incompatible aims, it proved.

About noon of October 7 Ruiz reached San Agustín. He found the garrison deserted except for four soldiers, Lieutenant Del Rio being across the Trinity after cattle and Pacheco enjoying his siesta. Whether or not Ruiz's arrival had been heralded, his reception was anything but friendly. He marched his men to the plaza and halted before the captain's quarters. When he called for Pacheco, the latter appeared at the door, musket in hand. Undaunted, Ruiz proceeded to read aloud the orders for the captain's arrest and suspension, and called upon him to obey. Refusing to listen, Pacheco declared that he had no superiors save the viceroy and the king. Calling his servants to his aid, he ordered Ruiz and his soldiers back to Adaes, declared that he would not leave his house alive as a prisoner, and fired into Ruiz's band. One of Ruiz's men sprang forward to disarm the captain, and a free-for-all scramble ensued, at the end of which Pacheco recovered his gun. Thereupon Ruiz, seeing valor in discretion, withdrew with his men, and halted behind the mission, to await Del Rio, who had been sent for. When Del Rio appeared, Ruiz read to him the order for Pacheco's arrest and his own appointment to the command. Although this order in effect displaced Del Rio, he submitted without protest and promised to do his best to restore peace.

The next step in the strategy was to compete for the support of the Indians, who then, as so often, held the balance of power. Going to Chief Calzones, Del Rio found that Pacheco had distributed guns among the nearby Indians, and had secured a promise of support. Calzones, however, agreed to try for three days to induce Pacheco to submit to the governor's orders, and then, if the captain still held out, to obey any command of Ruiz.

For the next three days every effort was made to induce Pacheco to yield. All this while the captain, with a few adherents, remained defiant within his quarters, heavily barricaded, sheltered behind two cannons, and with loaded weapons stacked about him. Pacheco stood gun in hand, day and night, beside the cannons, while his half-sick brother, Don Leandro, guarded one window, and Ambrossio Brioso and Andrés Zambrano watched the other. Meanwhile Calzones Colorados and Del Rio made daily efforts to communicate with Pacheco, but in vain. Ruiz sent Juan Valdés with letters to warn the captain that his quarters would be fired, but they were returned unopened. Fray Luis Salvino also, and Rosa Guerra, one of the maidens of the settlement, tried their hand at diplomacy, but likewise in vain, for Pacheco was adamant.

On October 10 the three days asked by Calzones Colorados came to an end, and he again promised obedience. Ruiz now called a council of war, in which it was decided to try diplomacy once more, and then to fire the presidio. Another letter to Pacheco was returned, and a personal interview met by defiance. In a final council the details of firing the quarters were arranged, plans being made to protect property and to prevent the captain's escape.

Next morning Ruiz and his soldiers approached Pacheco's quarters. A message demanding his surrender was answered by a cannon shot, and an appeal to the Indians for help. The soldiers now proceeded to apply the torch, and a fight ensued. Joachín del Rio fell dead from a musket shot, and two more soldiers were wounded. When the blaze gained strength from the freshening wind, Ruiz and his men took shelter from the flying bullets in the presidial church and the nearby store. Inside the barracks Pacheco and his men conducted the defence. While Brioso fired his musket, he fought the flames with a wet flag. In the battle Zambrano was wounded. As the blaze mounted higher most of Pacheco's handful of retainers fled into the arms of the soldiers. Pacheco's sick brother, Don Leonardo, was carried from the burning buildings, but nothing was seen of Pacheco and his faithful adherent Brioso.

The fire was now checked by the soldiers, and it seems to have destroyed only the governor's quarters and some empty barracks adjoining. Though the fire was out, no sign was seen of Pacheco and Brioso. It was thought that they had perished in the flames, but a search of the ruins revealed no bodies. It was then learned from Pacheco's friends who had surrendered that their captain and Brioso had escaped through a secret door in the chimney.

Ruiz now issued a proclamation, requiring Pacheco's arrest. A search was ordered, but without avail. For two days nothing was heard of the fugitives. The fact is they had escaped across the river. On the thirteenth two teamsters returning with corn from San Antonio reached San Agustín and reported that the night before they had met Pacheco and Brioso at Caramanchel, twelve leagues away, trudging along the Bahia road, with their guns upon their shoulders.[15]

Reaching La Bahía, Pacheco hid for a day and two nights in the house of Captain Ramírez de la Piszina. Going thence to the mission of San José on a horse loaned him by Piszina and aided by Father Camberos, he took refuge at the mission but was arrested by Captain Menchaca in virtue of a proclamation issued by Ruiz. But in December he was freed, after an attack on one of his guards, and thereafter lived at liberty for several months at the mission of San José, going to San Antonio with entire freedom.[16] Later on he went to Mexico, where he was imprisoned and tried.

---

[15] For this incident I am greatly indebted to Miss Brown's ''History of the Spanish Settlements at Orcoquisac.'' The account is based on *Testimonio de autos fhos por el Thente D Marcos Ruiz contra el Cappitan D Raphael Martinez Pacheco* (B. A., San Agustín de Ahumada); *Testimonio de Dilixensias comenzadas en San Agustin de Aumada y continuadas en este Preso de los Adaes por el Govor de esta Prova de Texas contra el Capitan Don Rafael Martinez Pacheco. Año de 1765* (B. A. Béxar, 1751–1769).

[16] *Testimonio de los Autos; Testimonio de Diligencias comenzadas en San Agustin de Ahumada y continuadas en este Preso. de los Adaes por el*

After the escape of Pacheco, Ruiz, aided by Fray Salvino, managed affairs at the garrison on the Trinity for a time in peace, writing reports of the damage done to the presidio, and of Pacheco's misdeeds, and making new attempts to reduce the Indians to mission life. It now came out that Calzones had been bribed by Pacheco to oppose the attempts made by Martos in the preceding summer to remove the presidio and mission to Los Horconsitos. This disclosure involved Del Rio and hastened the appointment of Afan de Rivera as commander, who in May arrested Del Rio for his partisanship with Pacheco. In November of the same year Ruiz was arrested by Hugo Oconor to answer to the charge of burning the presidio. Another man of some prominence to become entangled was Manuel de Soto, who, to escape arrest, fled to Natchitoches, where he lived for some years as a refugee.

Finally in 1767 Martos himself fell under the charge of burning the presidio, and subsequently underwent a trial that lasted fourteen years and that ended with the imposition of a heavy fine upon him.[17] Truly an unfortunate establishment was that of San Agustín.

4. The abandonment of El Orcoquisac, 1771.—The remaining five years of the outpost's existence were less eventful. Afan de Rivera, successor to Ruiz, commanded the garrison till the fall of 1769. At that time Captain Pacheco, who had been tried, exonerated and reinstated by the government in Mexico, returned to his post, welcomed by both missionaries and Indians, with whom he was a favorite.

The monotony of mere existence at the forlorn place was broken on September 4, 1766, by one of those terrible storms

---

Govor de esta Prova de Texas contra el Capitan Don Rafael Martinez Pacheco. Año de 1765. B. A., Béxar, 1751–1769.

[17] *Testimonio de Autos fhos . . . contra . . . Pacheco,* B. A., San Agustín de Ahumada; *Testimonio de la Declaracion que hicieron los principales Indios de la Nacion Orcoquiza ante Don Marcos Ruiz . . .* 1765.

which since the dawn of history there in 1528 have periodically swept the Texas coast. It damaged the buildings, led to more talk of "moving" and, it appears, actually caused the transfer of the presidio to higher ground a quarter of a league away. In 1767 Marqués de Rubí, the distinguished officer from Spain, honored the place with an inspection, but not with his good opinion. In his diary of the inspection La Fora made the following comment on the establishment at Orcoquisac:

"The map which I made shows the size of this presidio, which is situated, according to my observation, in 30° 23' north latitude and in 283° 52' longitude, from the meridian of Tenerife. It is in the country of the Orcoquizaes nation of Indians, and is distant a league from the coast of the Gulf of Mexico toward the east and five toward the south, where said [Trinidad] River disembogues, passing a fourth of a league west of the presidio. The river is very wide and deep, and stands in pools, because of its low banks and a sand dune which, blocking its mouth, checks its course. For this reason all this country is full of lagoons which make it difficult to explore the coast. These there are to the east, and it is therefore necessary to make a detour of ten leagues to reach the sea, which is accomplished with great difficulties and the loss of many horses. Of the same nature is the whole coast to La Valise, in Luisiana, near the mouth of the Rio de Misisipi, and for this reason it is impassable.

"The garrison of this presidio consists of a company of cavalry of thirty-one men, including the captain, a lieutenant, and a sergeant, and its annual allowance amounts to $13,245.90, [besides] that of two religious of San Francisco who minister to the soldiers and the Mission of Nuestra Señora de la Luz, which is nearby, and wherein is accomplished what I have said of the others. I therefore consider this presidio useless, for it does not serve to support the missions, which are absolved by the slight inclination of those natives to embrace our sacred religion, a

fact which has been well experienced since the year 1758, when
the only one there is was founded, without accomplishing in all
this time the reduction of a single Indian. Much less can it
serve other purposes of state which were claimed for its establishment, sacrificing a M^r. Lampin who was trading for a few
skins on that uninhabitable coast, which is entirely proof against
any nation's trying to establish a colony on it, especially where
the presidio is, for it is a very unhealthful place, in the midst
of lagoons which make impossible communication with any other
of our settlements. Here, by a bad arrangement, those unfor-
tunates are obliged to sustain themselves the greater part of the
year on some roots called *camotes,* on *nisperos,* nuts, cherries,
some chestnuts smaller than those of Spain, and other equally
wild foods.'"[18]

For the reasons set forth above, and since Louisiana no longer
belonged to France, Rubí recommended that both the presidio
and the mission on the Trinity should be suppressed, a measure
which was ordered carried out in 1772.

But before that order came El Orcoquisac was already
abandoned. In June, 1770, the governor of Texas, the Baron
de Ripperdá, made a call for help against the Apache. In consequence Captain Pacheco responded in July with a part of his
garrison. In February, 1771, the rest of the soldiers, except
three, went to San Antonio in answer to another call. The three
had remained behind with Father Laba and his companion,
whose departure was opposed by their charges. But within a
few weeks the missionaries also left, and the mission and presidio passed out of existence.[19]

---

[18] La Fora, Nicolás, *Relación del Viaje.* In 1769 the monotony of existence was again relieved by the passage that way of a party of shipwrecked Acadians who had been rescued at La Bahía and sent, after
being harshly treated, to their compatriots in Louisiana.

[19] References to the events of the last days of the establishment are
made in *Test. del Expediente,* 132–134; Thobar to Pacheco, June 12, 1770;
certificate by Ripperdá, July 3, 1770, to the effect that Pacheco had aided
in an Indian campaign.

V. THE REMOVAL FROM AND THE RE-OCCUPATION OF EASTERN TEXAS, 1773-1779

CHAPTER I

RUBI'S INSPECTION AND THE NEW "REGLAMENTO"

In 1772 the Spanish government decided to give back to nature and the Indians, temporarily at least, all that portion of Texas lying northeast of San Antonio de Béxar and Bahía del Espíritu Santo, some parts of which had been occupied, continuously even if weakly, for more than half a century. That this plan failed was due primarily to the attachment of the settlers of the district to their homes, and to the temporizing and double policy of the viceroy. The story of the removal of the Spanish settlers from the eastern frontier in pursuance of this plan and of their early return regardless of the royal policy, is not without human interest as an episode in the history of the Franco-Spanish border, nor without importance as a study in actual administration on the frontiers of new Spain.

Spain's reasons for withdrawing the eastern settlements were connected primarily with the Louisiana cession of 1762, with the Indian troubles of the interior provinces, and with the general reorganization of the frontiers of New Spain by the aggressive Charles III in response to the outcome of the Seven Years' War. This reorganization involved not alone the strengthening of the old military frontier, but embraced as well the occupation of Louisiana and Alta California, and the opening of lines of connection between them.

1. *Rubí's inspection and recommendations.*—These changes were not all wrought immediately, or without much discussion and investigation. It was to secure information on which to base a reorganization that the Marqués de Rubí was sent to the

northern frontier. Leaving Mexico in March, 1766, accompanied by the engineer Nicolás de la Fora, he passed from one province to another, arriving in Texas in August, 1767. What he saw was recorded in the diary kept and the map made by La Fora, and in the *dictamen* which Rubí himself later presented to the government.[1] With respect to the frontier in general, Rubí reported in detail the bad condition of affairs which has been briefly indicated hereinbefore.[2] What he found in Texas, which is our chief concern here, was, when viewed as the results of three-quarters of a century's occupation, discouraging enough. Beyond San Antonio de Béxar toward the northeast the nearest Spanish establishment was the mission at Nacogdoches, across the Neches[3] River, administered by one missionary, but without a resident Indian either converted or under instruction. A few leagues further on was the mission at Los Ais, with a few ranches round about. Here lived two missionaries in the same inactivity as those at Nacogdoches, without a single Indian upon whom to "exercise their calling."[4]

---

[1] The version of the diary kept by La Fora which I have used is entitled *Relacion del Viaje que de orden del Excelentissimo Señor Virrey Marquéz de Cruillas Hizo el Capitan de Ingenieros Dn. Nicolás de la Fora, en Compañia del Mariscal de Campo Marq.z de Rubí, commissionado por su Magestad a la Revista de los Presidios internos, zituados en la Frontera de la parte de la America Septentrional perteneciente al Rey.* MS. What is apparently the original of the La Fora map is in the Secretaría de Fomento, Mexico, Sección de Cartografía, map n. 1138, size 64 x 128 inches. See Bolton, *Guide to Materials for the History of the United States in the Principal Archives of Mexico,* 365. Another copy is in the Archivo General de Indias (see above, p. 107). A copy of the map was once in volume V of Sección de Historia, Archivo General y Público, Mexico. I find a statement to this effect in some notes made by Father Talamantes, and the evidence of its having been torn out is still visible in the volume. Bancroft knew of the existence of this map, but was unable to find it (see his *Arizona and New Mexico,* 258, note). A copy of the part of Rubí's *Dictamen* bearing on Texas is contained in *Quaderno que Corresponde,* Vol. 51, Sección de Historia, Archivo General y Público, Mexico.

[2] See above, p. 107; see also Bancroft, *North Mexican States and Texas,* I, 585, 629–630.

[3] It may be a matter of interest to know that the favorite and almost invariable form of spelling the name of this river in the documents on which this study is based is Nechas.

[4] Reference to page 399 will show that a few baptisms were made at these missions as late as the time when Rubí made his inspection.

On the Louisiana frontier, seven leagues from Natchitoches, were the mission and presidio of Adaes. At this mission, like the others without neophytes, were two missionaries. The presidio was garrisoned by sixty soldiers, who, with the Indians in the neighborhood peaceful and Louisiana a Spanish province, had nothing to do. Round about the presidio, in a village and on ranches, was a declining population of some thirty families. Toward the south, on the eastern bank of the Trinity, ''amid a thousand misfortunes and inconveniences,'' was the presidio of Orcoquisac, or San Agustín, with a company of thirty-one soldiers and an imaginary mission with two friars. Though an attempt had been made to establish a colony there, the place had no citizen population. Finally, north of Béxar, at San Sabá, now regarded as outside the limits of Texas, was a small garrison of soldiers, at the mercy of the Comanche and their allies. as had recently been proved.

Here, then, said Rubí, was a stretch of country beyond Béxar several hundred miles wide over which Spain claimed dominion, but which was crossed by only two rude paths, and occupied by only three small garrisons, a handful of impoverished settlers, and four useless missions.[5]

As a general result of his inspection, which revealed to him some establishments stagnant and useless and others without defence, Rubí concluded—what ought to have been seen long before—that Spain was trying to spread over too much ground, and that a wise policy for her to pursue would be to distinguish between her true and her ''imaginary'' dominions, and to sacrifice the latter to the former.[6]

Consistent with this conclusion, he made some far-reaching recommendations. The central one was to rearrange the frontier presidios in such a way as to form a cordon of fifteen strongholds placed at regular intervals between Bahía del Espíritu Santo, in

---

[5] Rubí, *Dictamen*, section 25.

[6] *Ibid.*

Texas, and the head of the Gulf of California, with San Antonio de Béxar and Santa Fé as outposts. This line he considered the true frontier of New Spain, upon the defence of which all efforts should be concentrated.[7]

This central recommendation involved radical changes in Texas. Those parts of the province that lay beyond San Antonio de Béxar he regarded as only "imaginary possessions," and he believed that, considering the pressing need elsewhere, they should be abandoned. San Sabá, he said, was at the mercy of the Comanche and their allies, Orcoquisac was at best of little use, and Adaes was bringing to a close a career that had been unfortunate from the outset. His first recommendation immediately affecting Texas was, therefore, that San Sabá be abandoned; that the presidio and mission of Orcoquisac be either extinguished or removed to a place somewhere in the neighborhood of Béxar and Bahía del Espíritu Santo; and that Adaes either be annexed to the province of Louisiana, now a Spanish possession, or that it be extinguished and the settlers there brought near Béxar, or if they preferred, allowed to settle somewhere in Louisiana.[8]

Rubí's next proposal was to strengthen the defences of San Antonio de Béxar and to increase the population in its neighborhood. By abandoning the northeastern settlements, Béxar would be left, he said, the frontier establishment of all the interior provinces—distant, indeed, more than fifty leagues from the nearest of the presidios in the proposed cordon. Being thus isolated, it would still be in its present danger from the Apache-Comanche wars. The thieving Lipan Apache,[9] living between Béxar and the Rio Grande, would not only continue to be un-

---

[7] Bancroft, *North Mexican States and Texas*, I, 585; Rubí, *Dictamen*, section 17.

[8] *Dictamen*, sections 17, 20, 25. The proposals are not given here in the order of the document, but rather in an order determined by the viewpoint of this paper.

[9] The branch of the Apache who principally were infesting Texas were the Lipan, commonly called the Lipan Apache.

pleasant neighbors themselves, but they would still attract to the settlements their enemies, the Comanche and their allies. Moreover, if the Comanche, now dangerous only to San Sabá, regarded by them as a bulwark for the Apache, should ever invade the interior, a circumstance not to be expected,[10] Béxar would become the chief object of their attacks. These considerations led him even to suggest withdrawing the villa of San Fernando and the costly and imposing but decadent missions at Béxar to the Rio Grande, within the shelter of the projected line of presidios. Refraining, however, from so radical a proposal, he advised that a fortification be built adjacent to the presidio of Béxar, to protect the citizens of the villa of San Fernando, and that the garrison of the presidio should be increased from twenty-three to eighty men by bringing to Béxar the soldiers from San Sabá, Adaes, and Orcoquisac, unless the last should be needed at Bahía del Espíritu Santo. The governor, residing at Béxar, should, he thought, be made commander of the presidio of San Juan Bautista, on the Rio Grande, which might be moved nearer to Béxar if circumstances demanded it. Since fear of Indians had been the chief obstacle to the growth of population, he predicted that such a strengthening of the defences of Béxar would make it possible to colonize in its vicinity on a considerable scale.[11]

With regard to the Apache, who were troubling the frontiers from Chihuahua to Texas, and the settlements of Coahuila and Texas in particular, Rubí declared mercy to be ill-timed, and maintained that since the Comanche came to the settlements only in pursuit of the Apache, danger from the Comanche and their allies would cease as soon as the Apache should be exterminated. He recommended, therefore, that Apache should no longer be

---

[10] Rubí reflected the fears of many when he said that he could not subscribe to the opinion that the Indians might be incited by the European neighbors of Spain toward the northeast to invade the interior Spanish provinces (*Dictamen*, section 17).

[11] *Dictamen*, section 17.

admitted to the shelter of the missions and presidios, where they would only prove their treachery, but that a vigorous war should be waged against them, and that, when conquered, the tribe should be dissolved and the captives taken to the interior of Mexico.[12]

Turning his attention to the Gulf coast policy, he said, contrary to the opinions of some, that it was impossible, even if necessary, to occupy the Texas part of that coast by land, because of its inaccessibility from the Gulf and of its bad climatic conditions. He advised, therefore, that the presidio of Bahía del Espíritu Santo should remain where it was, on the San Antonio River, for these reasons as well as to protect the well-stocked ranches already established there and the people whom it was proposed to remove thither from the eastern frontier.[13]

Rubí realized that there would be no lack of persons to call him unpatriotic in suggesting so enormous a diminution of the king's dominion; but he reminded such that the Spanish hold upon eastern Texas was so slight as to be only nominal; that relinquishing this shadowy grasp would be offset by a saving of forty-four thousand pesos a year; and that the spiritual and the political losses would be slight. On these points he said: "With respect to the conversion of the unfaithful, not a Christian or a neophyte . . . will be lost on the day when the four missions are suppressed; and with respect to the protection of our real dominions, by retiring this figurative frontier of two hundred leagues and more, we shall substitute for this weak barrier one that is being more respectably constituted on the Colorado [Red] and Missouri rivers, since the present governor of that colony [Louisiana] . . . much more according to the

---

[12] *Dictamen*, section 26; Bonilla, *Breve Compendio*, 61; Garrison, *Texas*, 91. A few years after this time, Governor Ripperdá recommended using the northern nations as allies in the war against the Apache (Bonilla, *Breve Compendio*, 66). See also Bolton, *Athanase de Mézières and the Louisiana-Texas Frontier, 1768–1780, passim.*

[13] *Dictamen*, section 19.

intentions of the king, impedes communication and traffic between it and the dominions of this realm.'"[14]

We should not, of course, regard these proposals of the Marqués de Rubí as a recommendation that Spain should relinquish her title to the territory in question, or that she should never undertake to occupy it, for they were conditioned by the fact that beyond Texas lay another Spanish possession, which, in effect, made Texas an interior province. But they did mean that Rubí was of the opinion that for some time to come, at least, it would be useless for Spain to try to colonize or to exercise any real control in the country between Louisiana and San Antonio de Béxar; and the adoption of these recommendations was, on the part of the central government, a confession of the same sort.

2. *The royal order of 1772.*—Rubí's report passed to the hands of the king, and, after the usual deliberate course of Spanish legislation, the monarch issued, on September 10, 1772, an order popularly known as the "New Regulation of Presidios."[15] This was practically an adoption of Rubí's proposals, with the supplementary legislation requisite to carry them into effect.[16]

We have seen that the central point of Rubí's plan was to concentrate effort upon the defence of what he considered the real possessions of New Spain. To do this it was necessary to place the fortifications in such relations that one could support

---

[14] *Dictamen*, section 25.

[15] *Reglamento é instruccion para los presidios que han de formar en la linea de frontera de la Nueva España. Resuelto por el Rey en cédula de 10 de Setiembre de 1772.* First printed in Madrid, 1772. The copy of the document which I have used is in Arrillaga, *Recopilación de Leyes, decretos Bandos, Reglamentos, Circulares y Providencias de los Supremos Poderes de los Estados-Unidos Mexicanos,* etc. (Mexico, 1835), IX, 139-189.

[16] On the changes made on the northern frontier in consequence of this royal order, see, besides, the authorities already cited, Revillagigedo's *Informe de Abril, 1793* (in Cavo, *Tres Siglos,* III, 112), and his *Carta de 27 de Deciembre,* in *Diccionario Universal de Historia y de Geografía,* V, 426 (Mexico, 1853–1856, 4°, 10 Vols., and Madrid, 1846–1850, 4°, 8 Vols.); Velasco, *Sonora, Its Extent,* etc. (San Francisco, 1861); Escudero, *Noticias Estadísticas de Sonora y Sinaloa* (Mexico, 1849).

another, and near enough together to prevent hostile Indians breaking through the intervening spaces. Accordingly, the royal order provided that the fifteen frontier presidios should be placed forty leagues apart in an irregular line extending from Altar, near the head of the Gulf of California, as the westernmost, to Bahía del Espíritu Santo, on the San Antonio River in Texas, as the easternmost. The intermediate presidios of the line, named in order from west to east, were to be Tubác, Terrenate, Fronteras, Janos, San Buenaventura, Paso del Norte, Guajoquilla, Julimes, Cerrogordo, San Sabá, Monclova, and San Juan Bautista. Of these only three, Janos, San Juan Bautista, and Bahía del Espíritu Santo, were to remain unmoved.[17]

From the outposts, Santa Fé and San Antonio de Béxar, respectively, Robledo, twenty leagues above El Paso, and Arroyo del Cíbolo, between San Antonio de Béxar and Bahía del Espíritu Santo, were to be garrisoned.[18] The force at San Antonio de Béxar was to be increased to the size recommended by Rubí, by bringing the requisite number of soldiers from Adaes and Orcoquisac; Santa Fé was likewise to have eighty soldiers, Bahía del Espíritu Santo fifty-one, and the rest of the presidios of the line forty-six each.[19] The presidio of San Sabá, instead of being extinguished, as Rubí had suggested, was to be removed to the banks of the Rio Grande, while those of Adaes and Orcoquisac, with their missions, were to be suppressed. The families at Adaes and Los Ais were to be brought to the vicinity of Béxar and given lands.

---

[17] The map made by La Fora (see p. 378) was the one by which the king's advisers were guided in drawing up the "New Regulation" (Arrillaga, *Recopilación*, IX, 172). For the location of most of these presidios before they were changed, see maps in Bancroft, *North Mexican States and Texas*, 1, 251, 310, 377, 381.

[18] *Reglamento é instrucción*, title "Instruccion para la nueva colocacion de presidios," Sec. 1.

[19] At each of the other presidios there were to be kept ten Indian scouts, but as it was thought that there were no Indians near Bahía suitable for this purpose, that place was to have five additional soldiers (*Reglamento é instrucción*, Titulo Segundo, in Arrillaga, *Recopilación*, IX, 142).

To secure a more uniform and efficient military service on the frontier, the order provided for a new general officer, the *inspector comandante* of the interior provinces of New Spain. He must be a person of the rank of colonel or higher, and might not, while inspector, be a provincial governor or a presidial captain. He was put directly under orders from the viceroy, but in case a *comandante general* of the interior provinces should ever be appointed, he was to be directly subject to that officer. To aid him in the discharge of his duties two assistant inspectors were provided. These duties were primarily to keep the viceroy informed of presidial and military affairs, direct frontier campaigns, and supervise the presidios and presidial officers. Either he or his assistants must make an annual inspection of each of the presidios and report to the viceroy.

The office of *inspector comandante* was filled by the appointment of Don Hugo Oconor, who had recently served as governor of Texas *ad interim*. Of his career there Bonilla, author of the *Breve Compendio*, wrote: ''Oconor attained the glorious distinction of leaving an immortal name in the province. He attested his valor, disinterested conduct, and military policy, he preserved peace in the land, and he made himself an object of fear to the savages, who know him by the name of el Capitan Colorado [the Red Captain].''[20]   Oconor had for his assistants Antonio Bonilla, just quoted, and Don Roque Medina.[21]

3. *Oconor's instructions to Ripperdá.*—The viceroy's instructions to Oconor for carrying the new policy into effect were issued March 10, 1773, and on May 6, Oconor, from camp at Nuestra Señora del Carmen, despatched to Baron de Ripperdá, then governor of Texas, orders for putting in force so much of the new plan as concerned his province.[22]   Immediately upon

---

[20] *Breve Compendio*, 62.

[21] The *Breve Compendio* was written before Bonilla became Oconor's assistant.

[22] *Ynstruccion Reservada que han de tener presente el Colonel de Cavallería Baron de Riperda Governador de la Prova. de texas para la practica

receiving the orders the governor was to go to the frontier and extinguish the two presidios and the four missions[23] condemned by Rubí, taking in charge the ornaments that had been given to the mission churches by the crown,[24] and removing to Béxar the garrisons, artillery, and munitions, and whatever settlers might be found at any of the four places.   The settlers were to be brought to the villa of San Fernando, given lands within the villa for building spots, and outside the villa for pasture and for fields, and the privilege of making at their own expense an irrigating ditch from the San Antonio River.[25]   On returning to Béxar, he was to reorganize the garrison, choosing for the prescribed eighty men the best in all three of the companies at Adaes, Orcoquisac, and Béxar.   Ripperdá was to remain captain; Córdova and Oranday, lieutenants of the garrisons of Orcoquisac and Béxar, were to be lieutenants of the reformed company; while the aged lieutenant of Adaes, José González, a veteran of some forty years' service at the same place, was to be retired with other superannuated and useless soldiers.   The company at Béxar having been reorganized, a detachment of twenty men was to be sent at once to Arroyo del Cíbolo.[26]   The purpose of garrisoning this place was to protect a number of ranches in the neighborhood, and to cover the long distance between Béxar and Bahía del Espíritu Santo.[27]

---

en los dos Presidios de alla del neubo Reglamto. qe. su Magd. se há servido expedir en Diez de Septre. del Año proximo pasado y demas puntos que contiene, para el Govno. Politica de dha. Provincia dispuesta por mi Dn. Hugo Oconor, Coronel de Infanteria Comandte. Ynspector de las Provincias de este Reyno de Nueva España de Orden del Exmo. Sor Fr. Dn. Antonio Maria Bucareli y Ursua, Virrey Governor, y Capitan General de ella (in *Expediente sobre proposiciones,* 79–90).

[23] The official names of these missions were Nuestra Señora de Guadalupe de Nacogdoches, Nuestra Señora del Pilar de los Adaes, Nuestra Señora de los Dolores de los Ais, and Nuestra Señora de la Luz.

[24] The rest of the movables of the missions were to go to the College of Guadalupe de Zacatecas, which administered the missions (*Ynstruccion Reservada,* Sec. 2).

[25] *Ynstruccion Reservada,* Secs. 5–9.

[26] *Ibid.,* Secs. 10–15.

[27] See note on Arroyo del Cíbolo, p. 392, below.

CHAPTER II

THE REMOVAL OF THE SETTLERS FROM THE EASTERN FRONTIER

1. Ripperdá on the frontier.—These instructions reached the hands of Ripperdá on May 18. He apparently did not favor the step about to. be taken, but within a week, nevertheless, he set out for the frontier, going first to Adaes and returning by way of Nacogdoches.[1] It seems that the garrison of Orcoquisac was already at Béxar, and that, therefore, Ripperdá did not go to the lower Trinity.[2] As affairs at Béxar demanded his attention, he remained only eight days in the settlements, leaving the execution of his mission to Lieutenant González, of the Adaes garrison.

At Mission Nacogdoches, where a large concourse of Indians was assembled, the governor was visited by Sauto, or Bigotes, the head chief of the Texas, who had suspended hostilities with the Osages in order to entreat the Spaniards not to leave the frontier. Bigotes seems to have been moved to this solicitude in part by the fact that the Lipan were just then threatening hostilities.[3] He undoubtedly feared, too, that the withdrawal of the Spaniards meant a decrease in the number of presents and in the available supply of firearms and other articles of trade.

---

[1] Ripperdá to the viceroy, May 28, 1773, and July 11, 1773, in Vol. 100, Provincias Internas, Archivo General y Público, Mexico.

[2] On his return from the frontier the governor mentioned finding Captain Pacheco, of the Orcoquisac garrison, at Béxar. A report made on December 15, 1771, shows that at that time all of the garrison belonging to Orcoquisac, as well as fifty of the soldiers from Adaes, were in Béxar. Whether the Orcoquisac garrison had remained there all this time I can not say. Ripperdá may have gone to Adaes by way of Orcoquisac, which would account for the garrison reaching Béxar in advance of the governor (Ripperdá to the viceroy, December 15, 1771, and July 11, 1773, in Vol. 100, Provincias Internas, Archivo General y Público, Mexico).

[3] Ripperdá to the viceroy, July 11, 1773 (Letter No. 30, Vol. 100, Provincias Internas, Archivo General y Público, Mexico).

Contrary to Rubí's prediction that Adaes was bringing to a close its unfortunate career, since his visit six years before the place seems to have prospered, at least in so far as numbers are a sign of prosperity; for whereas in 1767 Rubí was able to report only about thirty families, perhaps two hundred persons, Ripperdá estimated a population of more than five hundred, living near the presidio and on ranches round about Adaes and Los Ais.[4] These figures are fairly substantiated by other evidence.[5] The population was a mixture of Spanish, French, Indians, and, perhaps, Negroes. Part of the recent growth seems to have been due to an influx, after Louisiana became a Spanish province, of French and half-breeds from Natchitoches, some of them being Indian traders.

2. Antonio Gil Ybarbo.—The most prominent citizen of the vicinity was Antonio Gil Ybarbo, who becomes the central character of the remainder of this sketch. The few facts that we can gather of his previous career shed light upon conditions on the eastern frontier, and, viewed in connection with Ybarbo's subsequent influence, upon the attitude of the government towards these conditions. Ybarbo was a native of Adaes, and at the time when this story opens he was about forty-four years old.[6] By his enemies he was reputed to be a mulatto.[7] Though his headquarters seem to have been at Adaes, he was the owner of and lived part of the time upon a large ranch, called El Lobanillo (the Mole, or Wart), situated between the mission of Los Ais and the Sabine River. The documents represent this ranch as "al-

---

[4] Ripperdá to the viceroy, July 11, 1773.

[5] See p. 394, below.

[6] According to a statement made by Ybarbo in 1792, he was then sixty-three years old. This would have made him about forty-four years old in 1773. See a census of Nacogdoches, dated at Béxar, December 31, 1792, and signed by Ybarbo (Béxar Archives).

[7] This statement is based on the assertion of Juan Ugalde, *comandante general* of the Eastern Interior Provinces, who was hostile to Ybarbo, and who, at the time he made the assertion, was trying to secure Ybarbo's removal from the office (Ugalde to the viceroy, October 30, 1788, in *Consulta del Sr. Comandante Gral.*, etc., 9–11).

ready a pueblo,'' and tell us that Ybarbo possessed there a large amount of stock. In addition to his ranching interests, he was also a trader, having for several years maintained commercial relations, both at Adaes and El Lobanillo, with a wealthy French merchant, Nicholás de la Mathe, from Point Coupée,[8] Louisiana.[9]

In view of the hostility of the Spanish government toward French trade among the Indians and of the chronic complaint about French smuggling on the border, Ybarbo's position might be regarded as a questionable one did we not have good reason to suspect that, in spite of a multitude of laws, such things were customarily winked at by the local officials and lightly regarded as a question of private morals. Once at least, however, Ybarbo's trading activities had got him into trouble. It was during the administration of Hugo Oconor, who, in some circles, had the unusual reputation of having entirely put an end to contraband trade in Texas.[10] This official tells us that at one time Ybarbo had been imprisoned several months, in handcuffs, for complicity in the sale at Natchitoches and New Orleans of various droves of mules and horses stolen by the Indians from San Sabá, Béxar, and Bahía.[11] Just what form the complicity took is not stated.

Notwithstanding his illegal pursuits, he was prominent in the affairs of the locality, and was held in favor by Oconor's successor, the Baron de Ripperdá. Because of his prominence, he was intrusted by Governor Ripperdá, who had never seen him, with the administration of the funds for purchasing the presidial

---

[8] The Spanish documents render this name Punta Cortada or Puente Cortada.

[9] *Quaderno que Corresponde*, 9; testimony of Fr. Josef Francisco Mariano de la Garza, November 14, 1787, Béxar Archives. Garza was for several years in charge of spiritual affairs at Bucareli and Nacogdoches, and he knew Ybarbo well. His testimony was that of a warm supporter of Ybarbo, and was, therefore, not intended to be damaging in any way. For more about Father Garza, see p. 419, below; and about La Mathe, p. 415, below.

[10] See *Expediente sobre la dolosa y fingida paz.*

[11] Oconor to the viceroy, December 31, 1775, in *Quaderno que Corresponde*, 41.

supplies, a responsibility which he is said to have discharged wisely and honestly.[12] Other indications of his good standing with the governor and of his influence in the affairs of Texas will appear as the story proceeds.

3. *Consternation among the settlers.*—As soon as he had arrived at Adaes, Ripperdá had issued an order that within five days every one must be ready for the march to Béxar.[13] To the inhabitants this meant no less than expatriation. The love of home is deeply rooted in the human breast, more deeply the simpler the people. Many of these frontier folk had been born and had spent all their lives at Adaes; some had personal ties across Arroyo Hondo in the French settlement or in the Indian villages; and some had material interest in ranches and in Indian trade. It can not cause surprise, therefore, that the governor's order created a commotion. An extension of the time was asked and a few days were granted.[14] A number of persons, thirty-five according to the reports, refusing to be thus evicted, fled to the woods. Most of the inhabitants, however, prepared to obey the command, though apparently with bad grace in some cases, for complaint was made against González that "when the day for leaving arrived he mounted a horse and went from house to house, driving the people from them."[15] This, no doubt, reflects the unwillingness of the people to leave rather than any harshness on the part of the old officer.

---

[12] Testimony of Father Garza, November 14, 1787 (Béxar Archives).

[13] Ybarbo to Oconor, January 2, 1774, in *Quaderno que Corresponde*, 6.

[14] Ybarbo does not mention the request for or the granting of the extension of time in his complaints about the hardships of the Adaesans. But Ripperdá (letter to the viceroy, July 11, 1773), says that such a request was made and conceded, a statement that is borne out by other evidence. Ripperdá left Béxar for Adaes on May 25th. He says he was twelve days going, eight days there, and twelve days returning. He must have arrived in Adaes, therefore, on June 6th, and left on the 14th. His final order required that Adaes be abandoned on June 26th (Letter No. 30, Vol. 100, Provincias Internas, Archivo General y Público, Mexico.

[15] Ybarbo to Oconor, January 8, 1774, in *Quaderno que Corresponde*, 6.

The sudden removal involved, of course, the abandonment of whatever permanent improvements the settlers had made, small in general though these doubtless were. The urgency of the order did not allow time for suitable preparation for the march. The people were without supplies sufficient for so long a journey. Their stock, of which they seem to have had considerable, was scattered, and much of it could not be collected. Corn was nearly ready for harvesting, but it had to be abandoned. Some things which could not be carried, including the gun carriages, some of the cannons, and the greater part of the ammunition, were buried within the presidio.[16]

4. *The journey to San Antonio de Béxar.*—On June 25, the day appointed, the weary journey from Adaes to San Antonio de Béxar was begun. When the company reached Ybarbo's ranch at El Lobanillo, twenty-four persons dropped behind, some being too ill to travel, others remaining to care for the sick. Several of those who remained were of Ybarbo's family. His mother, sister, and sister-in-law were, it was represented, all unable to make the trip, and Ybarbo had secured from the governor a written permission to leave them, and with them his son and another family.[17] These facts, considered in connection with subsequent events, lead one to suspect that Ybarbo was not at this time intending to abandon his home for good and all. At the Nacogdoches mission nine persons, comprising two families, dropped out, at the request, so the story goes, of the Texas chief, Bigotes, who declared his intention of going to Béxar with his people to beg the governor to allow the Spaniards to return with a missionary. At this place the aged González and two women died. In González's stead, the sergeant took charge of the march.

According to the reports, after leaving Nacogdoches the suf-

---

[16] Ripperdá to the viceroy, September 28, 1773, in *Autos*, 21–22; Ybarbo to Oconor, January 8, 1774, in *Quaderno que Corresponde*, 6.

[17] Ybarbo to Oconor, January 8, 1774, in *Quaderno que Corresponde*, 7.

fering of the emigrants was severe.[18]   They were poorly supplied
with riding animals, and many of them, women as well as men,
had to go on foot till they reached Brazos.   In order to obtain
food some were forced to sell not only their clothing, but even
their rosaries and other sacred treasures.   Owing to this scarcity
of food, the drought experienced during the first half of the
way, and the heavy floods encountered on the latter portion,
there was much sickness among both people and animals, as a
result of which ten children died, and some of the cattle were
lost.   At the Brazos, however, the party was met by supplies
and mules sent out by the governor, and the suffering was relieved.   At Arroyo del Cíbolo, where, in pursuance of the royal
order, a garrison of twenty men had just been stationed by the
governor,[19] a few more persons dropped out of the weary company.   Finally, on September 26, the residue straggled into
Béxar, foot-sore, and so broken in health that within some three
months more than thirty others died.   With the party had come
the four missionaries[20] from Adaes, Los Ais, and Nacogdoches.
The soldiers brought with them, drawn by the oxen of the settlers, twelve four-pound cannons, fifteen boxes of ammunition
and eight *tercios* of gun-carriage iron.[21]

---

[18] González died on July 30; hence more than a month was consumed
in getting past Nacogdoches.   This does not indicate any great haste
(*Autos*, 22).

[19] Arroyo del Cíbolo was identical with modern Cíbolo Creek, which
joins the San Antonio River about half way between San Antonio and
Goliad, or old Bahía del Espíritu Santo.   According to Governor Ripperdá,
the settlement on this *arroyo* was located ''at the crossing of the Texas
and Tuacanes'' (Ripperdá to the viceroy, November 25, 1773.   Letter
No. 52, Vol. 100, Provincias Internas, Archivo General y Público
Mexico).   According to a representation made by the government of
the villa of San Fernando to Croix, January 12, 1778 (*Los Vecinos*, etc.,
10) it was about eighteen leagues eastward from San Antonio de Béxar.
In 1782 the *ranchos* here were six in number, with a population of 85.
Some twenty-five *ranchos* had been abandoned (see Bancroft, *North Mexican States and Texas*, I, 632).   For additional information concerning
this settlement, see *Los Vecinos*, etc., *passim*.

[20] According to Rubí (see ante, p. 379) there had been five in 1767.

[21] Ripperdá to the viceroy, September 28, 1773; petition of Ybarbo
and others to the governor, October 4, 1773 (both in *Autos*, 21–22, 4).

5. The aftermath.—No sooner had the Spaniards left Adaes than the neighboring Indians raided the place, scattered things about, and unearthed and carried away part of the ammunition and other effects buried within the presidio.[22] But the Indians did not get all the spoils, for the families left at El Lobanillo appeared upon the scene and saved what they could.[23] The runaways from Adaes shortly transferred their headquarters to El Lobanillo. On September 13, Périer, in command at Natchitoches, wrote to Ripperdá that "many fugitives who escaped from the convoy going from Los Adaes have taken refuge at Lobanillo. They come surreptiously to my post in search of liquor (*aguardiente*) with the purpose of introducing it into the tribes."[24] With the Spanish garrison removed, the French from Natchitoches apparently flocked in to trade and live among the Indians in greater numbers than before.[25]

So far as I have been able to ascertain, some of these people never left El Lobanillo, although orders were given to remove them, and although Ybarbo did remove some of them. Thus it is possible, and even probable, that in spite of government commands the frontier was never wholly abandoned.

Ybarbo to Oconor, January 8, 1774, in *Quaderno que Corresponde*, 7. Four of the cannons brought to Béxar were ordered sent to Monclova (the viceroy to Ripperdá, February 9, 1774, in Vol. 99, Provincias Internas).

22 Testimony of a Spaniard who returned to Adaes for a sick man who had been left behind (Ripperdá to the viceroy, September 28, 1773, in *Autos*, 21–22).

23 Oconor to Ripperdá, February 17, 1774, reviewing a letter which he had received from Ripperdá.

24 Volume 100, Provincias Internas, Archivo General y Público, Mexico. The original letter is in French. It is accompanied by a translation into Spanish.

25 Ybarbo, in writing to Oconor, January 8, 1774, said: "Scarcely had we left when Frenchmen settled in all the nations. This report we got from a Spaniard who remained behind sick, as well as from one of the French traders who came with some Indians and reported the fact" (*Quaderno que Corresponde*, 8).

CHAPTER III

THE ATTEMPT TO SETTLE AT LOS AIS

1. The petition of the Exiles.—As soon as the "Adaesaños" arrived at Béxar, Ripperdá, in accordance with his instructions, promulgated among them an order to choose anywhere within the villa of San Fernando such lands as they desired for their building spots, fields, and pastures, provided that by the choice they should not interfere with the rights of settlers or of the Indians at the missions. Thinking that the families who had stopped at Arroyo del Cíbolo could do no better than to settle there, he sent a lieutenant to that place to lay out lands for them in case they chose to remain there.[1]

But the exiles, both those at Arroyo del Cíbolo and those at Béxar, promptly refused to choose lands or to accept them, for they wished to return to the eastern frontier;[2] and eight days after arriving they presented to the governor a petition to that effect signed by seventy-five men. It stated that the locality at San Fernando offered little or no opportunity to form a settlement without encroaching upon the rights of

---

[1] Ripperdá to the viceroy, September 28, and December 10, 1773, in *Autos*, 8, 21; Ybarbo to Oconor, January 8, 1774, in *Quaderno que Corresponde*, 8.

[2] Only seventy-five names appear on the copy of the petition in my possession, but Ripperdá says there were seventy-six (Reply to the petitioners, in *Autos*, 5). It may be that the original petition contained seventy-six. Ripperdá stated that the families of these petitioners included 126 persons, which would make 202 individuals represented by the petition. In a letter of December 11, 1773, the governor says the petition represented the majority of the Adaesans. If this be true, his estimate of the number of persons on the frontiers (see p. 388) was too large, even if he meant to include the soldiers who were there. According to Lieutenant Pacheco there were in Béxar in April, 1774, 140 men from Adaes capable of bearing arms (*Expediente sobre la dolosa y fingida paz*, 13).

others;[3] that, because of the loss of all their property through the removal from the frontier, the petitioners were bankrupt and could not make the proposed aqueduct; that they wished permission to form a new pueblo at the old mission of Nuestra Señora de los Dolores de los Ais, where, because of its nearness to Adaes, they might be able to recover some of the property they had left scattered at their former homes; and that they hoped that, because of their known loyalty, their sufferings on the way from Adaes, and their present need, their prayer would be granted. In this event they agreed to bear, themselves, all the expense of the return, except for the support of a chaplain, whom they wished provided at government expense for ten years.[4]

There is no reason to doubt the sincerity of these petitioners so far as their request to be allowed to return to the frontier is concerned. But the claim that there was no room for them at Béxar seems absurd, while the choice of the particular location asked for is suggestive of the part played by Gil Ybarbo in the matter. Mission Los Ais was close by his ranch, El Lobanillo. He was the person who had the most to lose by being driven from the frontier. He was the most influential man among the emigrants, and was spokesman for the rest, and, naturally enough, his interests were not forgotten in the choice of a site for a new settlement. At El Lobanillo he had left his family; there he hoped to recover his lost stock and other property; there he had a well established ranch; and it may be supposed that, as was afterwards charged, he was loath to abandon the interests he had developed in contraband trade. Other persons who signed the petition were, no doubt, for similar reasons genuinely anxious to return, but the impression remains, never-

---

[3] In a letter to Oconor, Ybarbo said that the country from the Béxar to the Guadalupe was "overrun (*infestado*) with stock, missions, and men" (*Quaderno que Corresponde*, 7).

[4] Petition of Gil Ybarbo and others, October 4, 1773, in *Autos*, 1–5.

theless, that, although he represented the sincere wishes of his neighbors, Ybarbo was the moving spirit in the attempt to undo the policy of the government. It was Spain's misfortune that she had not more men like Ybarbo on the frontiers of her colonies.

2. *The petition favored by Ripperdá.*—The petitioners probably expected support from Ripperdá; indeed he may have encouraged them to present their request, for it was known that withdrawal from the frontier was not in accord with his desires. Ever since he had become governor he had taken, under the influence of Captain Athanase de Mézières y Clugny, of Natchitoches, a definite position regarding relations with the northeastern tribes. Of first importance was to keep them under Spanish influence so that they not only would remain friendly themselves, but also might be used against the enemies of the Spaniards, particularly the Apache and the Comanche. This was the key-note of his dealings with the northeastern Indians, and it seems to have been a foremost consideration in his relations with Ybarbo.

Through the aid of De Mézières, and of Father Ramírez, president of the Texas missions, Ripperdá had in 1771 and 1772 ratified treaties of friendship with several of the northernmost tribes,[5] who had formerly been considered as enemies, and, at De Mézières's suggestion, he had advocated enlisting these new friends in a campaign against the Apache.[6] He maintained,

---

[5] The principal ones of these tribes were the Quitseis (Kichai), west or a little northwest of Nacogdoches; the Yscanis, a short distance west of the Quitseis; the Tawakoni on the Trinity and the Brazos rivers west of the Yscanis; the Tonkawa, who lived a wandering life between the middle courses of the Brazos and the Trinity; the Xaraname, apostates from the mission at Bahía, at the time living among or near the Tawakoni; the Ovedsitas (Wichita), living on the Salt Fork of the Brazos; and the Taovayas, living northeast of the Ovedsitas on the Red River west of one of the Cross Timbers (De Mézières, *Informe, passim*). See map in Bolton, *De Mézières*, I, frontispiece.

[6] De Mézières to Ripperdá, July 4, 1772, in *Expediente sobre proposi ciones*, 24–61. Bonilla, *Breve Compendio*, 66.

moreover, that they could not be kept friendly unless, like the French, the Spaniards would supply them with firearms and ammunition. Otherwise, he said, they would prefer war to peace, for the sake of an excuse for engaging in their favorite pursuit of stealing horses from the Spaniards and selling them to the French. As an additional means of cementing their friendship he recommended establishing among them a new presidio, with a colony of citizens and a mission near it.

With foreign enemies as well as the Indians in view, he advocated extending a line of presidios all the way from New Mexico to the Mississippi.[7] A new argument for more strongly defending the eastern frontier was now available and was made use of by Ripperdá to support this proposal. It was not long after the cession of the country east of the Mississippi to the English before there began to be talk of danger from that quarter, much as formerly there has been talk of danger from the French. Rubí had said that he did not entertain any such fears[8] even though others did. Later on, rumors floated in from the north that gave some ground for such apprehensions. De Mézières claimed that when he was on his extended tour among the northern Indians in 1772, carrying to them the sword and the olive branch, he found among the Taovayas a certain Indian, named José, who was engaged in bringing from the Panis-mahas firearms of foreign—that is, neither French nor Spanish—make. He found there also two Panis-mahas advertising the advantages of trading with the English. These he brought to Béxar to be questioned on the subject.[9] In addition, De Mézières declared

---

[7] Ripperdá to the viceroy, April 28, 1772, and July 5, 1772, in *Expediente sobre proposiciones*, 2–3, 19–20; Bonilla, *Breve Compendio*, 65–66. Ripperdá had earlier than this expressed similar opinions. See the *informe* of Barrios to the viceroy, November 6, 1771, in Vol. 99, Provincias Internas, Archivo General y Público, Mexico.

[8] *Dictamen*, paragraph 1*i*.

[9] *Informe del Capn. infanta. Dn. Athanacio de Mézières al Sr. Coronel Baron de Ripperdá*, July 4, 1772, in *Expediente sobre proposiciones*, 37–39.

the Osage Indians to be hostile to the Spaniards and friendly toward the English.[10]

The report made by De Mézières convinced Ripperdá that, to keep them from contamination, the Toavayas and Ovedsita should be brought from their remote homes on the upper Brazos and the upper Red rivers to the interior, and the new presidio established among them; and he saw in the situation of the Osage and the threatened English trade an additional argument for keeping an influence over all the northern Indians, namely, that they might be used eventually in driving the Osage and their allies across the Missouri River, or even in repelling an invasion by the English themselves.

The eastern tribes, living between Adaes and the middle Trinity, were generally friendly toward the Spaniards, but recently suspicion had arisen that the Bidai and the Texas were becoming too friendly toward the Apache, the worst enemy of the Spaniards. Ripperdá accordingly favored establishing a closer surveillance over these tribes.[11]

It is not surprising, therefore, that the governor, entertaining for the frontier such plans as these, should use his influence in behalf of the exiles, whose wish accorded so well with his own. He replied to the petitioners that he could not grant their request without the infraction of a royal command, that is, the king's order of 1772, but that he sympathized with their cause, and that if they could not find suitable lands at San Fernando, at Arroyo del Cíbolo, or in any of the old ranches in the neighborhood, they might carry their petition to the viceroy.[12]

3. *Ybarbo and Flores sent to Mexico.*—After some delays, during which an attempt may have been made to find lands to their liking, although this is doubtful, the exiles acted upon

---

[10] *Informe del Capn.*

[11] *Expediente sobre proposiciones,* 1–3, 11–17; Ripperdá to the viceroy, July 5, 1775, in *Expediente sobre proposiciones,* 19–21.

[12] *Autos,* 5.

the governor's suggestion. On December 10, Ybarbo and Gil Flores, the two most prominent of their number,[13] were formally made the authorized agents of the citizens to carry the petition to the viceroy.[14] When they left Béxar they carried with them letters from the governor to the viceroy and Hugo Oconor. To prove the need of a minister on the frontier they carried a certificate taken from the records just brought to Béxar of the number of baptisms performed at the missions at Adaes and at Nacogdoches during their existence. This statement could hardly be considered the most convincing evidence, for it showed that in over half a century the aggregate number of baptisms at the two missions had been only three hundred and forty.[15]

In these letters to the viceroy and the inspector general, Ripperdá made it clear that an adverse royal order had not served to change his mind with respect to the frontier. On the contrary, he restated his views with emphasis.

He said that he was not fully informed of the reason for having abandoned eastern Texas, but that he believed it would be advantageous to Béxar and the other interior settlements to establish Spaniards among the northern Indians, particularly the Tawakoni and Taovayas, the northernmost and at the same time the most numerous and powerful of all the nations in the province. Since these tribes were new friends, such settlements would be valuable as serving to cement and retain their alliance. By forming a militia of the settlers, a line of defence would be established from Béxar to Natchitoches. The only objection to such a plan that he could see would be the encouragement that might be given by the presence of the settlers to trade with the

---

13 "We who have most to lose" (Petition of Ybarbo and Flores, May 10, 1774, in *Quaderno que Corresponde*, 30).

14 The certificate of authority is signed by fifty-two persons (*Autos*, 6). The agents were elected by majority vote (*Los Vecinos*, etc., 7).

15 The report for the mission at Nacogdoches extended from June 24, 1717, to April 17, 1768, and for that at Los Adaes from August 6, 1716, to February 12, 1773 (*Autos*, 17, 18).

French at Natchitoches. But that, he said, was going on briskly even now, not only with the Taovayas, Tawakoni and other tribes hitherto supplied from Louisiana, but also with those supposedly supplied from the interior of Texas, as was proved by the fact that these Indians were so well provided with goods that when they came to Béxar they even had guns to sell to the Spaniards. He thought, moreover, that an attempt to close the trade with Natchitoches might have even worse results, in driving the Indians to trade with the English, which they could easily do. These considerations induced him to recommend the petition carried by Ybarbo and Flores as one worthy of careful consideration. In his letter to Oconor Ripperdá referred to a private request which Ybarbo had to make, and bespoke for him Oconor's assistance, so that in case the main petition should not be granted, "ultimately his ranch, El Lobanillo, might come to form a pueblo of more than sixty persons." From this it seems probable that at this time Ybarbo intended to ask permission to return to his ranch, without the remainder of the petitioners, to collect and form a settlement of the sixty or more persons left on the frontier.[16] It will be seen further on that the private request actually made of the viceroy was slightly different in form from what Ripperdá apparently understood it to be, although it was not essentially different in effect.

The commissioners left for Mexico sometime in December or early in January. On the 8th of January they were at Santa Rosa María. From this place Ybarbo dispatched a letter to Oconor, who was at Chihuahua.[17] In it he set forth in great detail the hardship incident to the eviction from Adaes and the sad plight of the exiles at Béxar. He said that more than thirty of his compatriots had died at Béxar previous to his leaving, and only God knew how many since; that subsequent to arriving

---

[16] Ripperdá to the viceroy, December 10, 1773 (*Autos*, 8) and to Oconor, December 11, 1773 (*Quaderno que Corresponde*, 10–11).

[17] The letter was sent by Roque Medina, assistant inspector (*Quaderno que Corresponde*, 16).

there some of the families had been forced to go about the.presidio and missions begging, and some had even been forced to steal, in consequence of which trouble had arisen with the citizens; and that within two days after reaching Béxar the Indians had carried off the few animals they had brought. In conclusion, he said that he thought a settlement ought to be established on the frontier to keep out the French who were flocking in, and asked Oconor to support his demands.

4. *The petition granted.*—Having arrived in Mexico, the agents presented their petition, together with an address, on the 28th of February. The readiness with which the viceroy's government now proceeded to reverse a definite policy of the king is, to say the least, surprising. In his action in the matter Bucareli, the viceroy, was guided almost entirely by the advice of Areche, the royal fiscal, who, in his turn, was dependent upon conflicting reports from Béxar, Bahía, and Chihuahua. Areche, to whom the petition and Ripperdá's letter were referred,[18] reported[19] that in his opinion the proposal to establish a settlement at Los Ais was commendable, as a means of checking Indian assaults; that the king's reason for extinguishing the mission at Los Ais had been that it was without Indians and useless; and that the viceroy would do well to grant the request and to order the governor to put the measure into effect.[20] He does not seem to have been impressed with the argument predicated upon danger from the English, for he did not refer to it in his report. He advised proceeding through the governor on the ground that Oconor's many duties and his distance from Texas would entail delay.[21]

The matter next went before a *junta de guerra y hacienda* called by the viceroy for the purpose. This body resolved that,

---

[18] On February 28.
[19] On March 7.
[20] *Autos*, 13.
[21] *Ibid.*, 13–14.

in view of the situation of the exiles, and, more particularly, of
the advantage that would, according to the governor, result from
a settlement on the eastern frontier, the petition should be
granted; that the exiles should be settled in Los Ais in conformity
with the laws for the settlement of new pueblos and *lugares;*[22]
that the viceroy should instruct the president of the Texas missions to appoint a minister for the proposed settlement, provide
for his equipment and maintenance, and make plans for bringing
near the new pueblo as many of the surrounding tribes as possible, as a means of keeping them quiet and of preventing their
communication with the English and other foreigners.   This
decision of the junta the viceroy ordered carried out.[23]

5.   *Oconor interferes.*—Thus far Ybarbo's mission had prospered without adverse circumstances.   But a communication received by the viceroy suddenly changed the situation.   In reply
to Ripperdá's letter of December 11, Oconor had written saying
that he could not support Ybarbo's petition, and ordering the
governor to bring to Béxar the people and the ammunition left
on the frontier.[24]   To the viceroy he wrote in terms of strongest
disapproval of the whole plan.   He said that he was convinced
that private interest, ignorance, mistaken piety, and malice had
combined to defeat royal plans favorable to peace.   Citing Rubí's
report as authority, he maintained that Adaes had long been the
seat of contraband trade in fire-arms and ammunition, carried
on among the northern Indians in spite of numerous royal orders,
and that the reason why Gil Ybarbo and his co-petitioners
wished to return to Los Ais was that they might engage in this
illicit trade.   Referring to an Indian who had accompanied
Ybarbo and Flores to Mexico, he said that it was sad indeed

[22] See *Recopilación de Leyes de las Indias,* Lib. IV, Titulo VII.

[23] The junta was held March 17, and on March 23 the viceroy gave
the order to put its resolution into effect (*Quaderno que Corresponde,*
12–13).

[24] Oconor to Ripperdá, February 17, 1774, in *Autos,* 19–20.

that in addition to supporting so preposterous a petition, diametrically opposed to a royal order, Ripperdá should give to northern Indians a passport clear to the capital, thus enabling them to learn the routes into Coahuila and the state of its defences. Finally, he requested that Ripperdá should be required to carry out his previous orders with respect to the exiles from Adaes, and to put a stop to contraband trade in Texas carried on from Natchitoches.[25]

Just when this letter reached the viceroy does not appear, but four days after the junta had granted Ybarbo's petition it was referred to Areche.[26] A week later he advised that the recent action be rescinded and that a new junta be called to reconsider the matter in the light of Oconor's letter and of the reports of Rubí and Rivera, to which Oconor had referred. This plan was adopted, and on May 5 the new junta decided to refer the matter, with full testimony, to Oconor, with authority to grant or refuse the request, as he thought best.[27] What his decision would be could hardly have been doubtful in the light of his previous expressions relative to the subject.

6. *The matter referred to Ripperdá.*—Upon learning of the decision of the junta, Ybarbo and Flores decided to present the private petition to which Ripperdá had referred,[28] and to return to Texas without waiting for the settlement of their main business. Accordingly, on May 10, they asked permission to remove their families temporarily to Natchitoches, as a base of operations from which to recover their abandoned property.[29] This request was refused by the viceroy, and on the same day that he referred

---

[25] Oconor to the viceroy, February 21, in *Quaderno que Corresponde,* 14–17.

[26] March 21.

[27] Areche to the viceroy, March 28, in *Quaderno que Corresponde,* 17–18; decision of the junta, *ibid.,* 28–29.

[28] See p. 399.

[29] To enable them to make the journey home, they asked for financial aid from the government, which was granted them in the form of a loan. During their stay in Mexico the government had supplied them each with a stipend of two *reals* a day (*Quaderno que Corresponde,* 30–32).

the decision to Oconor he instructed Ripperdá not to permit Ybarbo and Flores to go to Natchitoches under any consideration. But the force of this prohibition was greatly weakened by adding to it the very elastic instruction that he should give Ybarbo and Flores aid in locating the exiles "in a suitable place."[30] It seems that the viceroy verbally told Ybarbo that the new settlement must be one hundred leagues from Natchitoches, meaning, doubtless, that it should be no nearer than this.[31]

Thus, on one and the same day the viceroy had left the matter in the hands of two different persons whose policies were at variance. While Bucareli doubtless intended Ripperdá to make only a temporary arrangement pending Oconor's decision, this vacillating and double policy left open the way for misunderstanding and for the eventual defeat of the royal plans, a result which was fostered also by Oconor's preoccupation and his procrastination. After a lapse of six weeks Oconor asked to be relieved of the responsibility imposed upon him, on the ground that it was an affair of Ripperdá's, and that he was too far away and too busy to perform the duty.

The viceroy insisted, however; but long before Oconor was ready to turn his attention to the affair, Ripperdá had made arrangements difficult to set aside.[32] When Oconor took the matter up with Ripperdá, the latter replied that he had already established the exiles in a new settlement. Apparently in ignorance of the viceroy's order of May 17 to Ripperdá, Oconor now reprimanded the governor for exceeding his authority, since the decision had been left to himself.

---

[30] "Donde corresponde, segun lo que está prevenido" (the viceroy to Ripperdá, May 17, 1774, in the Béxar Archives.) See also Oconor to the viceroy, December 31, 1775, in *Quaderno que Corresponde*, 42.

[31] Ripperdá to the viceroy, September 10, 1774, in *Quaderno que Corresponde*, 34.

[32] Oconor to the viceroy, July 5, 1775, and December 31, 1775; the viceroy to Oconor, August 30, 1775; Oconor to Ripperdá, November 20, 1775; and Ripperdá to Oconor, February 5, 1775 (all in *Quaderno que Corresponde*, 40–54).

CHAPTER IV

THE SETTLEMENT AT PILAR DE BUCARELI, 1774–1779[1]

1. The selection of a site for the exiles.—The location of the exiles from Adaes was thus left temporarily, until Oconor should interfere, to Ripperdá, with only the restriction that the place chosen must be at least one hundred leagues from Natchitoches. In the performance of this commission he again showed his sympathy with the desires of Ybarbo and his opposition to the royal policy, by sending the exiles to a place as far from Béxar and as near to the northeastern frontier as the terms of his instructions would permit.

The site designated by him was on the right bank of the Trinity River, at Paso Tomás, a place which was apparently at the crossing of the San Antonio Road and the La Bahía Road over that stream. This conclusion as to location of Paso Tomás is based upon the following data: Ripperdá said that it was the place where "the lower Adaes road," or, as he otherwise described it, "the road leading [from Béxar] to . . . Adaes and Orcoquisac" crossed the Trinity.[2] We are told, too, that it was above Orcoquisac, and considerably nearer to Nacogdoches than to the coast, the distances to these places being roughly in the proportion of two to three.[3] It must, therefore, have been at

---

[1] The fullest printed account of this settlement, so far as I know, is the one by Bancroft (*North Mexican States and Texas*, I, 630), which occupies only a page, and that much marred by errors and half truths.

[2] Ripperdá, writing from Béxar; to the viceroy, September 1, 1774, and November 15, 1774, in *Quaderno que Corresponde*, 34–36.

[3] Ripperdá said that Paso Tomás was "three regular days' [march] from the coast" (Letter to the viceroy, November 15, 1774, in *Quaderno que Corresponde*, 36). Ybarbo reported that it was only a two days' march from the Texas village at Nacogdoches (Letter to Croix, May 13, 1779).

least as far up the river as the upper portion of Walker County. It was, moreover, at a point in a pretty direct line between Nacogdoches and Béxar,[4] and could not, therefore, have been very far from the San Antonio Road which, it has usually been supposed, passed very directly between these places. Finally, it was near the country of the Bidai, their main village being within two leagues.[5] The location of this tribe in the later Spanish period of Texas history is marked in modern geography by Bidais Creek, which flows into Trinity River between Walker and Madison counties.

These data, taken all together, make it seem probable, as has been said, that Paso Tomás was at the crossing of the San Antonio Road and the La Bahía Road over the Trinity. The La Bahía Road could with propriety have been referred to as the lower Adaes road and, at the same time, as the road leading from Béxar to Adaes and Orcoquisac. Moreover, according to most of the old maps, the San Antonio Road and the La Bahía Road crossed the Trinity together at a point above the mouth of Bidais Creek.[6] This place has in modern times been identified with the crossing known as Robbin's Ferry, at the old village of Randolph, in Madison County.

---

[4] Francisco Xavier Fragoso, in company with Pedro Vial, made, in 1788, a careful survey of the distances from Santa Fé to Natchitoches, from Natchitoches to Béxar, and from Béxar to Santa Fé. As he had been sent out expressly to survey these routes, we should be able to place dependence upon what he says about directions and distances. According to his diary practically no change was made from a southwesterly direction in passing from Nacogdoches to Béxar. He was on one of the well known routes across Texas, which was in all likelihood the San Antonio Road. On the way between these two places he passed through the abandoned site of Bucareli, as the settlement made at Paso Tomás was called (Fragoso, *Derrotero, Diario, y Calculacion de Leguas*).

[5] Ripperdá to the viceroy, November 15, 1774, in *Quaderno que Corresponde*, 36, and to Croix, April 27, 1777, in *Documentos para la Historia . . . de Texas*, XXVIII, 224.

[6] See Austin's map, made in 1835, in Bancroft, *North Mexican States and Texas*, II, 75; another map made in 1835, given in Wooten, *A Comprehensive History of Texas*, I, 784; E. E. Lee's map of Texas, made in 1836, in McMaster, *History of the People of the United States*, V, 12; John Arrowsmith's map, made in 1840, in Kennedy, *Texas* (ed. 2, 1841), I.

2. *The reasons for the selection.*—The reasons given by Ripperdá in his correspondence, either directly or by implication, for the selection of this site, were: (1) that Paso Tomás was on the highway from Béxar to Natchitoches, somewhere near midway, and that a settlement there would facilitate communication between the two places; (2) that it was sheltered from the Comanche through having between it and this dread foe the friendly Tawakoni and Tonkawa; (3) that it was in an agricultural region of extreme richness, which might be expected later on to provide the presidios of Béxar and Bahía with horses and certain other products that then came from outside; (4) that it would be a good place from which to watch and cut off French contraband trade; (5) that it lay in the midst of a number of friendly Indian tribes, some to the north and some to the south, a fact which gave it special advantages as a base of operations for keeping them amicable and for conducting missionary work among them; and finally (6) that it was a vantage point from which to guard the Gulf coast from the inroads of the English,[7] who were now beginning to be feared in that direction as well as toward the northeast.

The last two reasons were the ones most emphasized by the governor. His desire to establish and maintain an influence over the northeastern tribes has already been set forth. His emphasis of danger from the English may be accounted for by the fact that rumors of English traders on the Gulf coast were becoming numerous. An example of these rumors may be of interest. In the fall of 1772 it was reported that Englishmen were in the

[7] See letters of Ripperdá to the viceroy, September 1, and November 15, 1774, and January 15, 1776, in *Quaderno que Corresponde*, 34–36, 68–70; Ripperdá to Croix, October 28, 1777, in *Representacion del Justicia*, 3. When De Mézières visited Bucareli in 1778 he gave essentially the above reasons why the place should be fostered, adding the argument that the Trinity would offer a good outlet to New Orleans for the abundant products certain to be raised in the new settlement. This argument was based on the assumption that trade between Texas and Louisiana would be allowed. De Mézières to Croix, March 18, 1778, in *Expediente sobre el abandono . . . y establecer Comercio con los Yndios Gentiles*, 2.

neighborhood of the mouth of the Trinity cutting wood for houses and giving presents to the Indians.   Captain Cazorla, commander of the garrison at Bahía, was sent out to investigate the grounds for such a tale.   He spent about a month on the expedition, heard in the neighborhood of the Trinity reports of English traders, and found what he thought to be English guns.   The Indians at a ranchería above Orcoquisac, reputed to be a center for French trade, told him that some Frenchmen living across the Neches in Louisiana were procuring these guns from Englishmen and bringing them to the Trinity, but that the French would not allow the English traders to come to the Indian villages in person.   Other reports of this kind were not lacking, and taken all together they may have caused the governor genuine uneasiness.   He hoped, perhaps, in a settlement of the exiles on the Trinity, for a partial restoration of the coast protection that had recently been withdrawn by the removal of the garrison from Orcoquisac.[8]   That this was a genuine consideration with Ripperdá is borne out by Ybarbo's activities on the coast, under the governor's direction, after settling on the Trinity.   But the fact that Paso Tomás, in the midst of a large number of northeastern tribes, was chosen instead of a point near the coast, is a good indication that Ripperdá's desire to maintain an influence among these northeastern tribes and Ybarbo's desire to return to the neighborhood which he had left, together outweighed Ripperdá's fear of the English on the south.

The reasons given by Ripperdá for the choice of Paso Tomás as the site for the new settlement all sound unselfish and patriotic enough.   Other persons maintained, however, that the selection was determined by the personal interest of the governor and Ybarbo in the forbidden Indian trade.   Ripperdá had for

---

[8] The place which I have designated as the probable site of Paso Tomás corresponds very closely with the one erroneously indicated by Bancroft (*North Mexican States and Texas*, I, 612) as the site of San Agustín de Ahumada before the removals which finally placed it at Orcoquisac.

some time been suspected of encouraging, if not of direct complicity with, French smuggling.[9] He was well known to favor its continuance rather than leave the Indians unsupplied with what they desired, or to run the risk of having it furnished by the English, for he had distinctly said so.[10] In spite of numerous orders from the viceroy and of repeated promises from Ripperdá that the French traders should be driven from the province,[11] it was patent that they still frequented or lived among most of the tribes of eastern Texas. Their presence there is proved by evidence from all sources—the testimony of the friars, of Cazorla, Oconor, Medina, Ybarbo, De Mézières, and of the governor himself. Though the viceroy's orders that they should be expelled were answered with promises of compliance, local protests Ripperdá met, if not with threats, with the assertion that it was not an opportune time to stop the trade.[12] Suspicion of Ripperdá was increased by the fact that his principal representative among the Indians, De Mézières, had the reputation of being a veteran Indian trader,[13] while the most prominent of the French mer-

---

[9] Father Josef Abad, missionary at Bahía, who went with De Mézières in 1771 to make the treaties with the northern Indians, in reporting the "scandalous trade" that he witnessed on the frontier, said, "I thought (I do not know for certain) that the governor was implicated in the trade, through his communication with de Mecieres" (Report to the viceroy, July 15, 1774, in *Expediente sobre la dolosa y fingida paz*, 149–150).

[10] See pp. 396–398.

[11] In communications dated December 9 and December 19, 1772, and January 6, March 5, May 25, and June 30, 1773, the viceroy issued orders to the governor to cut off this trade. Ripperdá as frequently promised that the commands should be complied with (See a letter from the viceroy to Ripperdá, April 23, 1774, in *Expediente sobré la dolosa y fingida paz*, 138. Some of these orders are in Doc. 1, Vol. 51, Sección de Historia, Archivo General y Público, Mexico).

[12] When Father Abad, in 1771, asked permission to go to the governor of Louisiana to report the contraband trade that he had seen, Ripperdá replied, according to Abad, that "an immediate prevention of the trade would be undesirable" (Abad to the viceroy, July 15, 1774, in *Expediente sobre la dolosa y fingida paz*, 149–150). Cazorla complained that any one who remonstrated with Ripperdá about the contraband trade was threatened with arrest. See also the charge made by Medina, below, p. 410.

[13] Father Abad said that it was "notorious" that De Mézières was one of the principal promoters of the French trade with the Indians

chants, Nicholas de la Mathe, stood in high favor with the governor.

Ripperdá was charged even with sheltering contraband traders in Béxar. Don Roque Medina, one of Oconor's assistant inspectors, who was in that place early in 1774 inquiring into Ripperdá's administration, reported that some Frenchmen were there under various pretexts, but apparently engaged in trade. "These," he added, "are not the only ones who have come to the interior of this province with the Indians. There have been various others, who have stopped at the house of the governor and then returned to the northern nations, serving as couriers to fetch and carry letters from Natchitoches.

"The French continue to trade in guns, powder, and balls, which they exchange for . . . beasts of burden. They do not raise horses and mules, hence, in order to supply the need it is necessary to obtain them from the Indians in trade. To supply these it is the custom for the Indians to come and rob our lands, as in fact they are now doing. Indeed they have no other occupation. They never enter this presidio as friends without carrying off horses and mules when they depart, and there is no human being who can control this governor, or make him believe that they [the thieves] are the northern tribes. Any one who says so is imprisoned. Only a serious measure can remedy this situation."[14] Medina no doubt got his information in part from the citizens of Béxar, who as a rule were just then hostile to Ripperdá, but his statement is a fair sample of the general feeling in regard to the governor's relations with the French and the northern Indians.[15] Ripperdá maintained, of course, that

(Letter to the viceroy, July 15, 1774, in *Expediente sobre la dolosa y fingida paz*, 150). Raphael Pacheco, lieutenant at Béxar, wrote on April 20, 1774, that De Mézières was a person "who had always lived among the said nations, since the time of Dn. Jacinto de Barrios, trading in guns and ammunition." (*Ibid.*, 133).

[14] Oconor to the viceroy, May 13, 1774, in *Expediente sobre la dolosa y fingida paz*, 141; Medina to Oconor, March 8, 1774, *ibid.*, 129.

[15] Upon receiving Medina's report through Oconor, the viceroy severely reprimanded Ripperdá for not having put a stop to the French

all these charges were gross calumnies, and it is difficult to determine where the truth lay.[16]

Added to these grounds for distrust were Ybarbo's previous record on the frontier and the fact that the Bidai Indians, who lived near Paso Tomás, were the chief intermediaries between the French and the Apache in the trade of fire-arms. It is not altogether surprising, therefore, that selfish motives were attributed to Ripperdá and Ybarbo in the selection of a site for the Adaes exiles.

As soon as Oconor gave the governor's choice any attention, he reported what he knew of Ybarbo's previous career and of smuggling at Adaes before its abandonment, and proceeded to say that the exiles had been located by Ripperdá in "the place which better than any other enables them to engage in illicit trade and to encourage the northern Indians in stealing droves of horses from the presidios of San Antonio de Bèjar, Bahía del Espíritu Santo, and even as far as Laredo, as lately has been done. Moreover, the Trinity River facilitates navigation to the Opelusas and the neighborhood of New Orleans itself. Hence, it is concluded that the citizens established on the Trinity have better facilities than formerly for their contraband trade."[17] That Cazorla and others made similar charges will appear farther on.

In concluding this subject one comment may be made. For Ripperdá to have been tolerant with French traders would have been quite consistent with his desire to keep the Indians friendly and quiet, to say nothing of any desire for private gain, considering, on the one hand, the great influence of the French

---

trade and for being deceived by the Indians of the north, and forbade him henceforth to allow a single Frenchman in Texas or even to communicate with De Mézières (The viceroy to Ripperdá; May 8, 1774).

[16] Ripperdá to the viceroy, June 24, 1774, in *Expediente sobre la dolosa y fingida paz*, 163.

[17] Oconor to the viceroy, December 31, 1775, in *Quaderno que Corresponde*, 41–42.

over the Indians, and, on the other, the insistent demand of the
Indians that French traders be allowed to go to them. Moreover, the complaint that Ripperdá's administration was marked
by French influence seems to have some foundation. Hence, if
all these charges made against him were true, the chief causes for
surprise would be that he so persistently denied them, and that
Ybarbo, while on the Trinity, seems to have made some show of
cutting off illicit trade.

   3. The removal to Bucareli.—Preparations for removal of
the exiles to the Trinity were made in August, 1774. Before
leaving Béxar the emigrants chose[18] for their prospective settlement the name of Nuestra Señora del Pilar de Bucareli, thus
perpetuating the memory of their former home,[19] and at the
same time invoking the patronage of the viceroy, Antonio María
de Bucareli y Ursua. The governor, in view of the distance of
Paso Tomás from any settlement and of the fact that the new
pueblo was to have no regular garrison, organized from their
number a company of fifty militia, and named officers "for
greater stimulation among them." Gil Ybarbo was made captain of the company and *justicia mayor*[20] of the prospective
pueblo since he was, as Ripperdá said, "the best fitted and the
most acceptable to his compatriots." Gil Flores was appointed
lieutenant and Juan de la Mora *alférez*. These appointments
were made, of course, subject to the viceroy's approval.[21] Of

---

   [18] Ripperdá to the viceroy, September 1, 1774, in *Quaderno que Corresponde*, 35. Ybarbo said that he was made captain on August 7 (Letter
to the viceroy, March 22, 1791, Béxar Archives).

   [19] Pilar de los Adaes.

   [20] Bancroft is apparently wrong in calling Ybarbo alcalde of Bucareli
(see his *North Mexican States and Texas*, I, 656).

   [21] There is some evidence that the appointment of Ybarbo was approved on January 1, 1775, although this is not certain. An official statement dated at Béxar, January 17, 1784, says that Ybarbo began exercising the office of lieutenant-governor of the pueblo of Nuestra Señora del
Pilar de Bucareli on the date named. Since, however, this is not the
title which he was given by Ripperdá, and by which he was known,
namely, captain of militia and *justicia mayor* of the pueblo, it seems
probable that the statement referred to is unreliable.

guns and ammunition most of these "militia men" had none, but the governor interceded with the viceroy to have this lack supplied, asking at the same time that a parish priest be provided for ten years at government expense.[22]

Because of the poverty of the exiles from Adaes, only a part of the families, including at the most not more than seventy full-grown men,[23] could get together an outfit for the exodus, and even these had to be aided by the missions with a supply of corn. Nearly all the rest, however, declared their intention to follow as soon as they could manage to get horses and a site should be selected.

Before September 1 the start for Paso Tomás was made,[24] the party being conducted by Lieutenant Simón de Arocha and four soldiers, who were charged with the duty of founding the new pueblo.[25]

Thus the little band of ignorant, poverty-stricken colonists had been able, through the aid of the governor, the vacillation of the viceroy, the delays of Oconor, and the personal force of Ybarbo, their leader, to circumvent the royal policy. They were now starting upon the first stage of a journey that was, when finished, to signalize a complete victory over the home government, and to take them back to the neighborhood of the place which they had been so reluctant to leave a year before.

---

[22] Ripperdá to the viceroy, September 1, 1774, and November 15, 1774, in *Quaderno que Corresponde,* 34–36.

[23] On September 1 Ripperdá wrote that only a few families had been able to go, yet there were enough, it seems, to form a company of fifty militia. On November 15 he wrote that Pilar de Bucareli had seventy men capable of bearing arms. There is some indication that others besides the first emigrants had gone by that time, hence I conclude that the first party included less than seventy adult men (*Quaderno que Corresponde,* 34–36). Ybarbo stated that a "large portion" of the Adaes people remained at Béxar (*Expediente Sobre . . . Parroco,* 2).

[24] This was the date upon which the governor reported to the departure. Ripperdá said, several years after, that the settlement was begun in August (Letter to Croix, April 27, 1777, in *Documentos para la Historia . . . de Texas,* XXVIII, 223).

[25] *Expediente sobre el abandono,* 16.

4. The growth of the settlement.—As soon as the emigrants reached Paso Tomás, Ybarbo took the lead in forming the material beginnings of a settlement. Of his energy and efficiency as head of the community, Ripperdá always gave good report, which was sustained by his successor, Domingo Cabello, and by the religious who were put in charge of the spiritual affairs at Bucareli. Ripperdá declared that Ybarbo set the citizens a worthy example of thrift, aided them with his own tools, oxen, and mules, gave them good advice, and kept them in due subjection.

Soon after arriving at the Trinity, Ybarbo brought from Adaes the nails and other iron work of the houses that had been left there, powder, shot, six cracked cannons, and some gun-carriage iron, to be utilized in the buildings and for the defense of the new pueblo. There were also brought to Bucareli two cannons from the deserted presidio at Orcoquisac and two that had been left at the Taovayas village by Colonel Parrilla in his flight before the Indians in 1759.[26]

In the buildings erected at Bucareli apparently neither stone nor adobe was used. The town was laid out with a plaza, with the houses surrounding it, as required by law. The cannons Ybarbo had mended and mounted, and round the place he built a wooden stockade.[27]   The first church structure was a ''decent

---

[26] See a statement in the Béxar Archives concerning the whereabouts in 1792 of the soldiers and the cannon that had been at Los Adaes. One of the terms of the treaty made in 1771 between the Taovayas and the Spaniards was that the latter should be allowed to remove the cannons (*Expediente sobre proposiciones*, 4). In 1772, when De Mézières was at the Ovedsita village on the upper Brazos, he organized a party to send for them, but later gave up the plan (*ibid.*, 34). The cannons were brought to Bucareli by De Mézières about May 1, 1778. In April of that year he made a visit to the Taovayas village, while there he expressed his intention to remove them, and on his return he went direct to Bucareli (De Mézières to Croix, May 2, 1778, in *Documentos para la Historia . . . de Texas*, XXVIII, 280, 283–284). On September 23, 1778, Croix wrote to the home government that De Mézières had recovered the cannon. (Bolton, *De Mézières*, II, 228).

[27] Ripperdá to the viceroy, January 25, 1776, in *Quaderno que Corresponde*, 69–70; Botello to Cabello, December 23, 1778, in *Expediente sobre el abandono*, 2–3.

chapel," built by the settlers shortly after their arrival, although at that time they had no minister. This chapel was soon replaced by a more pretentious church supplied by Nicholas de la Mathe, the French trader with whom Ybarbo had so long sustained relations, and who was not tardy in visiting the new settlement and establishing himself in its good will. The motive assigned to La Mathe by the governor for this benevolence was extreme piety and special fondness for the patron saint of the pueblo, the Lady of Pilar. Be the truth as it may, early in 1776 he sent to Bucareli two carpenters, who built a wooden church twenty-five *varas* (yards) long, the timber used being brought from the forest by the inhabitants. When the removal had been made from Adaes, the ornaments of the mission had been placed in charge of the governor. Some of them were taken to Bucareli early in 1775, and Ybarbo later on asked for the rest, but part of them, at least, remained in the governor's hands until after Bucareli had passed out of existence.[28]

Something more than a year after its beginning, Ripperdá was able to report that Bucareli contained, besides numerous *jacales*, or huts, twenty houses of hewn wood, grouped round the plaza, a wooden church, and a guard-house and stocks, the last two items having been provided at the personal expense of Ybarbo. And in June, 1777, Ybarbo reported that there were at the place more than fifty houses of hewn wood, corrals, fields, roads cut open, and an improved river crossing.[29]

The little settlement grew slowly in numbers by the addition of various odds and ends of humanity. Ybarbo brought some, but I suspect not all, of the people who had been left at El

---

[28] Ybarbo to Ripperdá, November 23, 1775, and to the viceroy, January 15, 1776, in *Expediente sobre . . . Parroco*, 3–4; Croix to Cabello, January 5, 1780, in the Béxar Archives.

[29] Ripperdá to the viceroy, January 25, 1776, in *Quaderno que Corresponde*, 69–70; Ybarbo to Ripperdá, June 30, 1777, in *Representacion del Justicia*, 2.

Lobanillo and Nacogdoches; some of the families from Adaes who had remained at Béxar followed, as they had intended; an occasional slave, escaped from Louisiana, drifted into the place; though Ripperdá professed to allow no settlers other than Adaesans to go to Bucareli, he made exceptions in case of ''useless vagabonds'' who might be at Béxar; and finally, French traders made their way to Bucareli from Louisiana. During the winter of 1776–1777 the pueblo was visited by an epidemic that made an inroad into its population by causing the death of seventeen persons. Among these, apparently, was Lieutenant Gil Flores. At the same time the nearby Bidai Indian tribe was reduced by nearly one-half of its entire number.[30] What the nature of the malady was I do not know, but it was attributed to the excessive amount of water in the river valley. Before this epidemic there had been in Bucareli, according to report, ninety-nine *vecinos,* or, as I understood the term, adult male residents.[31] A census taken some time in 1777 showed the population of the place to consist of three hundred and forty-seven persons, comprising one hundred and twenty-five men, eighty-seven women, one hundred and twenty-eight children, and five slaves.[32] Round about lived the Bidai and other Indian bands. Small though it was, this was a growth that compared very favorably with that of the Spanish settlements that had grown up in Texas less irregularly and more under the paternal care of the government.

    5. *Economic conditions.*—Bucareli was granted the usual favor accorded to new pueblos of exemption for ten years from

---

[30] De Mézières to Croix, March 18, 1778, in *Expediente sobre el abandono,* 2; Ripperdá to Croix, October 30, 1777, in *Expediente sobre . . . Parroco,* 12.

[31] Ripperdá to Croix, January 11, 1778, in *Los Vecinos, etc.,* 7.

[32] Ripperdá to the viceroy, January 25, 1776, in *Quaderno que Corresponde,* 67–70; Ybarbo to the viceroy, November 25, 1775, in *Expediente sobre . . . Parroco,* 2; Cabello to Croix, May 31, 1779, *Expediente sobre el abandono,* 16.

all forms of royal taxation.[33] As we have seen, one of the special
advantages at first claimed for the place was its agricultural
possibilities. True to the traditions of Spanish farming, Ripperdá had instructed Arocha to choose for the pueblo a site
affording facilities for irrigation. The location selected failing
in these facilities, which were little needed, as the event
proved,[34] the settlers sowed their first grain east of the Trinity,
where there were some permanent lagoons. This crop was
spoiled by a flood. The second summer they succeeded in raising
a crop of corn west of the river, in a place pointed out by the
Bidai Indians. Thereafter a number of families settled on
ranchos, or farms, some distance in this direction from the pueblo.
Here they raised at least one good crop of wheat before the settlement was abandoned.

Hoping to enable the place to supply its own blankets and
coarse cloth, Ybarbo took from Béxar cotton seed, sheep, and a
Negro weaver, who was expected to teach his craft to the settlers.
With a Béxar merchant, one Don Juan Ysurrieta, Ybarbo made
a contract to have Bucareli furnished with merchandise in exchange for the prospective agricultural products of the place.
Ripperdá professed to hope that Bucareli would in time prove
especially productive of horses, cattle, sheep and goats, tallow,
soap, corn, wheat, and rice, and that it would not only furnish
the presidios of Béxar and Bahía with horses, but also put an
end to frontier smuggling by furnishing the Indians with a
substitute for French goods. De Mézières, who visited Bucareli
in March, 1778, reported that the place was well capable of becoming the basis of a rich trade with New Orleans, by way of
the Trinity River and Opelousas, if such a boon should be allowed by the government.[35]

---

[33] *Representacion del Justica*, 6.

[34] Ybarbo told De Mézières that good irrigation could be had at a
distance of twelve leagues (De Mézières to Croix, in *Expediente sobre el
abandono . . . y establacer Comercio*, 2).

[35] Ripperdá to the viceroy, January 25, 1776, in *Quaderno que Corresponde*, 69–71; Botello to Cabello, December 23, 1778, in *Expediente sobre*

Such dreams as these could have come true only on condition that the settlement had enjoyed a longer existence, that its population had been more intelligent and enterprising, and that the government had changed its blind policy of discouraging the trade best calculated to induce the colonists to effort. As it was, the settlers were poor and shiftless, and during their short stay there they eked out an existence not far above that of their Indian neighbors, supplementing the scanty products of their fields and herds by hunting the buffalo and wild cattle that abounded between the Trinity and the Brazos.[36] From the testimony in the documents we are led to think that they spent a large part of their time in this primitive pursuit. As the French who traded among the Indians in the vicinity were interested in fur dealing as well as in procuring horses, it is reasonable to suppose that the Spanish colonists who engaged in hunting took advantage of the market for their peltries, exchanging them for the goods in which the French dealt. Of course, all trade between them and the French was contraband, for the Spanish government strictly forbade trade with Louisiana in any form.

6. Spiritual affairs.—Notwithstanding due efforts on the part of Ybarbo and the governor to secure a priest for Bucareli, there seemed to be some danger of the realization of the prophecy made by the friars of the mission at Bahía that the place would become a resort famed for "liberty of conscience" and "an asylum for apostates."[37] The little flock went to their new pasture unaccompanied by a shepherd, and for more than two

---

el abandono, 2; De Mézières to Croix, March 18, 1778, in *Expediente sobre el abandono . . . y establacer Comercio,* 2.

[36] *Expediente sobre el abandono,* 2, 8; *Representacion del Justica,* 7, 9; *Quaderno que Corresponde,* 67–70.

[37] Cazorla wrote to the viceroy that the friars at the Bahía mission anticipated "the loss of many souls" at Bucareli. "Many wish to go to that settlement," he said, "because it is notorious that in it the Indians keep peace for the sake of the barter or trade which is carried on with them, as well as because they live there, as it is understood, with liberty of conscience" (Letter of May 15, 1775, in *Quaderno que Corresponde,* 38).

years remained without one. During that time they enjoyed no other spiritual aid than that afforded by two short visits made by some priests from Béxar.

It has been seen that when the Adaes exiles first requested permission to return to Los Ais, they asked also that a minister might be provided for them ten years at government expense.[38] As soon as they left Béxar Ripperdá repeated the request, and asked of the bishop of Guadalajara, to whose jurisdiction Béxar now belonged, that the settlers be allowed to build a church. The latter petition was promptly granted.[39] In February, 1775, temporary spiritual aid was furnished by the chaplain of the presidio at Béxar, who went to Bucareli, placed in the chapel which the settlers had built the image of the patron saint, the Lady of Pilar, and performed religious offices. A year later two missionaries from San Antonio spent a few days at Bucareli.[40] Who they were I have not learned, but there is some indication that one of them was Fr. Josef Francisco Mariano de la Garza, a Franciscian friar from Mission San Antonio de Valero, who eventually became regularly installed at Bucareli.[41]

---

[38] See above, p. 395.

[39] Ripperdá to the viceroy, September 1, 1774, in *Quaderno que Corresponde*, 34; the bishop of Guadalaxara to Ripperdá, December 19, 1775, in the Béxar Archives. Some five years later a bishopric of Nuevo León, including Texas, was erected.

[40] Ybarbo to the viceroy, November 25, 1775, and Arrellano to Croix, April 27, 1777, both in *Expediente sobre . . . Parroco*, 2, 8. The bishop of Guadalaxara to Ripperdá, December 13, 1775, in the Béxar Archives; Ripperdá to the viceroy, January 25, 1776, in *Quaderno qué Corresponde*, 69.

[41] Ybarbo to the viceroy, November 25, 1775; Ripperdá to the viceroy, January 15, 1776; Oconor to the viceroy, June 15, 1776; opinion of the fiscal, August 8, 1776—all in *Expediente sobre . . . Parroco*, 3–5; the viceroy to Ripperdá, August 21, 1776, in the Béxar Archives. The viceroy carelessly took Oconor's statement that there were five missions near the presidio of San Antonio to mean that they were near Bucareli. Arrellano caught him up on this point, as the text below shows. Arrellano said that he promptly sent to Bucareli a friar, whose name he did not mention, and asked him to have him relieved. Croix (June 24, 1777), recommended relieving him, without mentioning his name; and Ripperdá (August 30, 1777) mentioned Father Garza as the priest at Bucareli whom he had seen fit to relieve. As no other religious is mentioned in this connection, and as Father Garza's presence at Bucareli from this

Before this time Ybarbo had again addressed the viceroy on the subject of a regular pastor supported by the government, and again Ripperdá had seconded the request. In response, the viceroy, on the advice of Oconor, wrote Ripperdá, in August, 1776, that, since there were already ten religious on royal pay at the five missions near by, as a temporary measure the governor should require the president of the mission to send one of them to Bucareli until the disposal of that place should be decided. Ripperdá served the order on September 27, and the president, Fr. Pedro Ramírez de Arrellano promptly complied by sending Father Garza, mentioned above.

It now became a question whether Father Garza should remain at Bucareli or be relieved by one of the presidial chaplains of Bahía and Béxar. Though the president had obeyed, he resented the loss of his missionary, and ere long he appealed to Caballero de Croix, who was now *comandante general* of the Interior Provinces. To him he wrote that the viceroy's order was obviously based on an error, namely, the supposition that Bucareli was near the missions, when in fact it was one hundred and forty leagues away; that since one missionary must always be present at each mission to minister to the neophytes, if one were sent to Bucareli there would be no one to go into the forests to bring back absconded apostates or to seek new converts; and that, since the stipend of the friars was often the

---

time on can be established, I conclude that he was the one sent in consequence of Ripperdá's order of September 27, 1776 (see *Expediente sobre . . . Parroco*, 12; *Representacion del Justicia*, 4; and *Expediente sobre el abandono*, 14, 38). Father Garza stated in his deposition made at Zacatecas in November, 1787 (see note 9, p. 389) that he had known and dealt with Gil Ybarbo ''almost without intermission, except for a few days, from February, 1776, to September, 1783. This would indicate that he was, perhaps, one of the two missionaries sent to Bucareli in the spring of 1776. But it seems that these missionaries returned in a short time, and that during the summer of 1776 the place was without a spiritual adviser. Hence his statement is puzzling. It appears that Ybarbo was in Béxar in February, 1776. This might account for the beginning of their acquaintance at this time, without supposing Garza to have been in Bucareli. In either case, I can not explain Father Garza's almost continuous dealings with Ybarbo after February, 1776.

sole support of these Indians, the latter might suffer if one of
the missionaries, with his stipend, were removed. He concluded
by suggesting that, since the bishop of Guadalajara had entertained such a plan, one of the presidial chaplains should be sent
occasionally to Bucareli, as had been done in the spring of 1775,
and the missionary fathers required to take his place while
absent.[42]

Croix now yielded, conditionally, and ordered the governor to
relieve Father Garza by sending one of the presidial chaplains,
unless he had good reasons for not doing so. But Ripperdá,
instead of relieving Father Garza, wrote to Croix that the objections to doing so were strong; that the presidios would suffer
more than the missions by the absence of their ministers; and
finally, that he was hoping to establish a mission at Bucareli, in
which case the services of a trained missionary would be indispensable. In this tilt with the president of the missions, the
governor apparently won, for Father Garza remained the minister in charge at Bucareli to the end of its history.[43]

If we may judge of Father Garza's personality from his subsequent preferment, we would conclude that Bucareli was for-
tunate in securing for its pastor a man of more than ordinary
ability. After leaving Nacogdoches, in 1783, whither he went
from Bucareli, he became president of the Zacatecan missions of
the province of Texas, and later was reader in sacred theology,
then member of the council (*discretorio*) of the Franciscan college at Zacatecas.[44] About 1790 he became one of the founders
of the mission of Refugio.

---

[42] Arrellano to Croix, April 27, 1777, in *Expediente sobre* . . .
Parroco, 6–9.

[43] Croix to Ripperdá, June 24, 1777; Croix to Arrellano, June 25, 1777,
and Ripperdá to Croix, August 30, 1777 (all in *Expediente sobre* . . .
Parroco, 9–11).

[44] Testimony of Father Garza, November 14, 1787; Schmidt, Rev.
Edmond, J. P., *A Catalogue of Franciscan Missionaries in Texas,* 1528–
1859 (Austin, 1901), 10–11.

A short time before Bucareli was abandoned another missionary, Fr. Juan García Botello, was there. When or under what circumstances he went I have not been able to determine.[45]

Having secured a minister at government expense, the pueblo of Bucareli next applied for exemption from church tithes. In the summer of 1777 it was announced in the church that tithes would be collected, and two years' dues were gathered; but Ybarbo made this the occasion of an appeal to Ripperdá, in the name of the citizens, asking relief from this burden, on the ground of the poverty and misfortunes of the community and of the public services which it had rendered. The petition was passed by the governor, with his approval, to Croix, who referred it to Pedro Galindo Navarro, the *asesor* of the commandancy general. Navarro recommended granting the request on two grounds, first, because Bucareli was exempt from all civil dues, and, second, because the tithes could not legally be collected, since tithes were intended for the support of ministers of the altar, and since no religious of this class was serving there. Acting on this advice, Croix requested the church authorities at Guadalajara to exempt Bucareli for ten years, and the petition was soon granted.[46]

It has been seen that Ripperdá informed Croix in August, 1777, that he had hoped to establish a mission at Bucareli.[47] This was not the first indication that he entertained such a plan. It was clearly his desire from the first to gather around Bucareli as many Indian tribes as possible. His mission project, however, seems to have looked primarily to collecting there the apos-

---

[45] In his letter of August 30, 1777, Ripperdá seems to say that Arrellano had been forced to send a second padre to Bucareli, although his meaning is not clear. This may have referred to Botello's going (*Expediente Sobre . . . Parroco.* See also *Quaderno que Corresponde,* 72).

[46] Croix presented the request to the bishop, the dean, and the cabildo of the church of Guadalajara, by way of command and entreaty (*ruego y encargo*). For the facts involved in this paragraph, see *Representacion del Justicia, passim.*

[47] See above, p. 421.

tate Indians who had in times past deserted the various missions of the province, a prospect which he knew could not lack attractiveness to persons who had had experience with mission Indians. In January, 1776, he informed the viceroy that one purpose of sending the two missionaries just then about to depart for Bucareli was to minister to the neighboring heathen and to found a mission to attract apostates, and his subsequent requests for a minister for Bucareli were based in part upon the same ground.

Often Ripperdá wrote hopefully about prospects for the fulfillment of his desires in this particular. Now he reported that many of the Indians living near Bucareli were being baptized and that the Karankawa were beginning to come to the pueblo to live; and that there were good indications that many apostates from the old missions of San Xavier would gather there; and, again, that Texas, Quitseis, and Tonkawa were in the habit of coming for presents; that the Mayeses had failed to settle near the place only through groundlessly having taken offence at the Spaniards; that he hoped, by gentle means, to retain the friendship of the Tawakoni with whom lived the desired apostate Xaraname; and that the Orcoquiza, who years before had deserted their mission, were likely to come to settle near Bucareli, since they were imploring Ybarbo for a mission and were sending presents to Father Garza. In spite of these hopeful expressions, however, which, doubtless were as strong as the facts would justify, nothing came of the plan for a mission at Bucareli except the baptism of numerous Bidai and a few other Indians, and the restoration of some of the Xaraname to Bahía, unless, perhaps, it is this plan for a mission that explains the presence of Fray Botéllo at Bucareli in the fall of 1778.[48]

---

[48] Ripperdá to the viceroy, January 25, 1776, in *Quaderno que Cor responde*, 69, 71; to Croix, August 30, 1777, in *Expediente sobre . . . Parroco*, 11–12; and to Croix, October 28, 1777, in *Representacion del Justicia*, 4.

7. Ybarbo among the Indians and his search for the English.—Ybarbo's activities were by no means confined to establishing the pueblo of Bucareli and administering its internal affairs. He was equally active, as Ripperdá had predicted that he would be, in promoting good relations with the Indians and in watching the coast. Indeed, it was at Bucareli that Ybarbo received his best training for a more conspicuous career later on. His life at Adaes and El Lobanillo had given him some knowledge of Indian character, and now, by his four years in a position of responsibility, and at the same time of semi-independence, at Bucareli, he so extended his acquaintance with the natives and his knowledge of Indian affairs that he became very influential among the tribes of eastern Texas.

During those four years, he made, according to his own statement, in addition to hostile campaigns against the Comanche, no less than three friendly tours among the northern Indians and as many to the coast for the double purpose of conducting Indian relations and of looking for Englishmen.[49] The governor ordered Lieutenant Arocha, when he founded Bucareli, to go with Ybarbo to invite the Bidai, Texas, Quitseis, Yscanis, and, if possible, the more distant tribes, to come and live near the new establishment. Before Arocha returned to Béxar he and Ybarbo were unable, through lack of horses, to visit more than the Texas and the Bidai.[50] But later, through friendly visits, presents, and other inducements, Ybarbo gradually attracted various bands to the vicinity of Bucareli to live or to trade and receive presents. In March, 1778, he went with De Mézières and helped to make a treaty with the Tonkawa, one of the conditions of which was that this tribe should regularly be visited by a trader.[51] On the same expedition he, Father Garza, and De

---

[49] Ybarbo to Ripperdá, June 30, 1777, in *Representacion del Justicia*, 2.

[50] Ripperdá to the viceroy, November 15, 1774, in *Quaderno que Corresponde*, 36.

[51] Ybarbo to Cabello, December 7, 1778, in *Expediente sobre el abandono*, 5.

Mézières persuaded part of the Xaraname living among the Tawakoni to return to their mission at Bahía.[52]

The most noteworthy of these expeditions of Ybarbo was that made in 1777 to the mouth of the Sabine River. In the summer of that year a trader stationed among the Orcoquiza Indians reported to Ybarbo that in the mouth of the Neches River there was a stranded English vessel laden with bricks; that the bricks had been given to the Opelousa and the Attacapa Indians near by; and that there was another vessel in the mouth of the Trinity. Ybarbo at once enlisted thirty men and started for the coast, going first to the Orcoquiza town. The Indians here told him that the Englishmen had entered the Neches with small vessels to trade with the natives; that in the summer of 1774 they had remained long enough to sow a crop; and that the vessel now lying in the Neches had arrived in the previous May (1777), had missed the channel, and stranded, the occupants withdrawing, but promising to return. Ybarbo scolded the Indians for not reporting the matter promptly, and then, with ten men and two paid Indian guides, he reconnoitered the coast. He passed eastward along the shore and came upon the vessel, apparently in Sabine Lake. It still contained some bricks but nothing else. Such other things as had been on board were seen in the possession of the nearby Attacapa. These Indians told Ybarbo that the English had left three men to guard the vessel until the main party should return, but nothing was seen of them by the Spaniards.

Ybarbo now returned to reconnoiter the mouth of the Trinity, but he did not find the vessel reported to have been there. Near the shore some distance farther west, however, he found an Englishman, lost and nearly naked. Ybarbo understood him to say that his name was Bautista Miler, that he had come from Jamaica bound for the Mississippi with a captain named José

---

[52] De Mézières to Croix, April 5, 7, and 8, 1778, in *Documentos para la Historia . . . Texas*, XXVIII, 273–278.

David, who in order to rob him of some coffee, whiskey, and five Negroes, had cast him adrift in a canoe, and that he had been lost for seven months. This story told by Miler gives no further hint as to who the English were that the Spaniards had been hearing of and dreading in the direction of the coast.

Before returning to Bucareli, Ybarbo made a map of the coast from Sabine Pass to a point some distance west of the Trinity River. The sketch has historical value, particularly as it helps us to locate with some accuracy the Spanish presidio of San Agustín, or Orcoquisac.[53] After an absence of twenty-two days, Ybarbo returned with Miler in custody, and reported his exploit to Croix.

Wishing to ascertain the truth regarding the other English vessel, Ripperdá dispatched a second expedition, composed of fifty men, including Ybarbo and thirty of his militia, to reconnoiter the coast from where Ybarbo had left off to the Colorado. The party set out from Bucareli July 11, 1777, but what it accomplished does not appear.[54]

8. Contraband trade, and the question of suppressing Bucareli.—To what extent the establishment of Bucareli actually increased or decreased smuggling in its vicinity it is hard to determine. It had previously existed among the Indians thereabouts, and it continued to flourish, but the exact part taken in it by Ybarbo and his colonists is a difficult matter to decide, for the evidence is conflicting. If we were to accept, unquestioned, the reports of Ybarbo and Ripperdá, we would conclude that the latter made special efforts to prevent it.

Ybarbo found French traders from Adaes and Natchitoches

---

[53] It is in volume 51, Sección de Historia, Archivo General y Público, Mexico.

[54] The story given here is based on Ripperdá's letter to Croix, dated August 30, 1777, accompanying which is the map referred to. I have not seen Ybarbo's original report to the governor. Navarro's report to Croix, dated June 8, 1779, has aided me in reading Ripperdá's letter (see *Expediente sobre . . . Parroco,* 13–19).

among the Bidai Indians when he first went to establish Bucareli. Some of them, whose Spanish wives went to live at Bucareli, applied for residence there, which, according to Ripperdá, was granted only upon condition of their giving up Indian trade.[55] Bucareli had scarcely been founded when La Mathe, apparently prince of the Indian traders at this time, arrived at the place, with a passport from the government authorizing him to "collect some debts," a subterfuge, perhaps, to enable him to continue his traffic.[56] As we have seen, he put himself into the good graces of the community by building a church for it, but one is inclined to be skeptical when told that he did this through extreme piety alone, particularly when informed by one of Ybarbo's admirers that La Mathe and Ybarbo kept up former relations during the whole existence of Bucareli, buying and selling of each other just as before.[57]

A few instances of actual smuggling at Bucareli came to light, and, we may assume that, in the nature of the case, for each one that was reported numerous others escaped notice. The reports of these cases suggest much more than they actually say in regard to what was going on. In the spring of 1775 some men from Bahía, who had been across the Guadalupe River, met a party of Béxar men coming from Bucareli with French tobacco in their possession, some of which the men from Bahía obtained. The Béxar men reported that the article was plentiful at Bucareli, whither it was being brought by Frenchmen, who also traded with the Indians. The matter reaching the ears of Captain Cazorla, he, by strategem, verified the report, identified one of the culprits at Béxar, and notified Ripperdá. The governor replied that he had ascertained that the amount of tobacco smuggled had been small. Cazorla afterward intimated, how-

---

[55] Ripperdá to the viceroy, January 25, 1776, in *Quaderno que Corresponde*, 67.

[56] See above, p. 388.

[57] See Garza's disposition of November 14, 1787, in the Béxar Archives.

ever, that the governor may not have taken due pains to find
out. Cazorla reported the affair to the viceroy, with the comment that "it appears that the sole motive of the subjects who
go to Bucareli to live is to smuggle and to be free from the yoke
of justice." He added that, since so many were desirous of
going to that place where license reigned, and where the Indians
were more friendly than elsewhere, there was danger of depopu-
lating and weakening the defenses of the other settlements.[58]

Not long after this, Ybarbo seized contraband goods from
one Marcos Vidal, of Béxar, who was on the way from Natchitoches. Vidal was sent in custody to Béxar, was convicted of
smuggling, and imprisoned, but escaped. These two cases show
that the Spaniards as well as the French and Indians engaged
in the forbidden trade.[59]

On another occasion Ybarbo confiscated a large quantity of
merchandise from Agustín de Grevenverge,[60] captain of militia
at Attacapa, in Louisiana, while on his way to Béxar to trade
for horses and mules, ignorant, he claimed, of the law forbidding
trade between the provinces. How this could be when these
prohibitions were so oft repeated is a matter to cause wonder,
but when the trifling affair finally reached clear to the royal
throne this excuse was accepted by His Majesty.[61]

Cazorla's report to the viceroy established at once in Mexico
a bad reputation for Bucareli, and set on foot an attempt to
remove it from the frontier. On the advice of Areche,[62] Rip-

---

[58] Cazorla to the viceroy, May 14, 1775, in *Quaderno que Corresponde,* 37.

[59] Ripperdá to the viceroy, in *Quaderno que Corresponde,* 68. A report
of the case is in Béxar Archives.

[60] Variously spelled in the documents.

[61] In *Expediente sobre comercio reciproco entre las Provincias de la
Luisiana y Texas,* 4–6 (Vol. 43, Sección de Historia, Archivo General y
Público, Mexico), is a copy of the memorandum of the goods confiscated
by Ybarbo.

[62] Areche to the viceroy, July 13, 1775, in *Quaderno que Corresponde,*
38–39. Areche said in his note, "It appears that this settlement pre-

perdá was instructed, in July, 1775, to report upon the reputed disorders at Bucareli, and, if necessary, without further notice to remove its inhabitants nearer to the center of the province.[63] Cazorla was complimented for his vigilance and enjoined to continue it, while Oconor, to whom was sent a copy of Cazorla's letter, was requested to hurry up and decide the final disposition to be made of the exiles from Adaes. He was even to send them to Los Ais if he saw fit, the royal order to the contrary notwithstanding.[64] Oconor did not reply until December 31, but on that date he expressed to the viceroy the strongest condemnation of the settlement at Bucareli. He repeated the objections that he had made to allowing Adaes exiles to go to Los Ais; indulged in more or less "I told you so;" gave Ybarbo a bad name; and declared his disappointment that the governor should establish the settlers in the very place best calculated to cause trouble. To permit them to remain, he said, was certain to entail evil consequences. He recommended, therefore, that the matter be taken out of Ripperdá's hands and put into Cazorla's, giving him authority to distribute the Bucareli settlers at Béxar, Bahía, and Arroyo del Cíbolo, as the royal order had required.[65] On hearing from Oconor, the government again, in February, 1776, referred the matter to him, and decided that no further step should be taken in Mexico until Ripperdá should be heard from. His report. when it came,[66] containing only contradictory testimony. the government concluded to try to get at the truth of

---

sents some dangers that, lest they increase, ought to be remedied, and at the opportune moment cut off at the roots.''

[63] The viceroy to Ripperdá, July 26, 1775, in the Béxar Archives.

[64] Areche to the viceroy, July 13, 1775, and Cazorla to the viceroy, February 27, 1776, both in *Quaderno que Corresponde*, 39, 65; Oconor to the viceroy, December 31, 1775, *Ibid.*, 40–45. The date of the order to Oconor was July 26, 1775.

[65] Oconor to the viceroy, December 31, 1775, in *Quaderno que Corresponde*, 40–45.

[66] It was dated January 25, 1776.

the situation by having the president of the Texas missions make a report based on the testimony of the religious at Bucareli. Oconor, not to be outdone in the matter of procrastination, decided in April to suspend action until he could go in person to Béxar, and there, in conference with the cabildo, to consider the whole matter. This, he said, was the only way to avoid the endless importunities which "some persons might make, with the sole purpose of succeeding in their caprice of not obeying the viceroy's and his [Oconor's] repeated orders."[67] Thus, so far as any immediate action on the part of Oconor or the viceroy was concerned, the Frenchmen, Spaniards, and Indians on the frontier were left to carry on illicit trade at will. But Ripperdá consistently denied that it was openly allowed by the Texas authorities. Although he admitted that it existed, he claimed that Ybarbo was active in trying to prevent it, that the citizens of Bucareli were law-abiding, and that positive public advantage would be realized by fostering the settlement which was under such general suspicion.[68] He defended the place to the last. Shortly before he retired from the office of governor he urged that it be reinforced by sending to it the Adaes families still remaining in Béxar, instead of trying to form of them a new pueblo at Béxar, Arroyo del Cíbolo, or on the Guadalupe or the San Marcos River, as was then being talked of.[69]

Had Oconor remained in power, it is not at all improbable that, with his wonted vigor, as soon as his hands had become really free he would have carried out the royal order to the letter and suppressed the place. But Bucareli now profited by another year's delay due to Oconor's preoccupation, and then by a

---

[67] Areche to the viceroy, February 21, 1776, and May 2, 1776; Oconor to the viceroy, April 5, 1776—all in *Quaderno que Corresponde*, 54, 72, 66.

[68] Ripperdá to the viceroy, January 25, 1775, in *Quaderno que Corresponde*, 67–71.

[69] Ripperdá to Croix, January 11, 1778, in *Los Vecinos*, etc., 7, Croix was at this time in Béxar.

change in the government. Early in 1777 the affairs of the Interior Provinces were put into the hands of a *comandante general*, independent of the viceroy. The person appointed to this office was the Caballero de Croix. The mere change of administration gave the pueblo of Bucareli an additional term of grace, and, of more importance, it transferred the supervision of the interests of Texas from Oconor, the main opponent of Bucareli, to Croix, who was not only opposed to the royal policy of withdrawing from eastern Texas,[70] but who also enjoyed a high degree of independence in his office.

It was more than a year after Croix took charge of affairs before he reopened the question of Bucareli's continuance or suppression. Then, in July, 1778, he ordered that Domingo Cabello, the new governor of Texas, should be requested, as soon as he should take charge of his office, to report upon the advantages and disadvantages of Bucareli.[71] But before Cabello replied the fate of Bucareli had been decided independently of governmental authority. The frontier community, as is characteristic of frontier communities, had settled the matter for itself.

---

[70] On May 18, 1779, he wrote to De Mézières stating that Texas was, of all the Spanish provinces, one of those most worthy of attention, because of its size, fertility, good climate, and location (De Mézières to Croix, October 7, 1779, reviewing the letter to Croix referred to, in *Expediente sobre el abandono . . . y establecer Comercio*, 7–8). In 1778 he tried hard to secure permission to open up trade between the provinces of Texas and Louisiana (*Expediente sobre Comercio Reciproco*).

[71] Croix to Navarro, July 24, 1778, in *Representacion del Justicia*, 7. Croix to Cabello, July 30, 1778, cited in Cabello to Croix, May 31, 1779, in *Expediente sobre el abandono*, 13.

CHAPTER V

THE REMOVAL TO NACOGDOCHES

1. Comanche troubles at Bucareli, May and October, 1778.—
One of the advantages that had been claimed for Bucareli was
that it was protected by the powerful Tonkawa[1] and Tawakoni
from the dreaded Comanche. And this claim may have been
well founded, for it was more than three years before the peace
of the settlement was disturbed by the Comanche's unwelcome
presence. But at last it became the object of their attention.

One day in May, 1778, the inhabitants of Bucareli were
frightened half out of their wits by the arrival in the neighborhood of about thirty warriors of this tribe, led by the son of
the head chief, Evea. Ybarbo sallied out with his men, however, pursued the Indians, overtook them at the Brazos, killed
three, and put the rest to flight. The story of this occurrence rests upon the testimony of Ybarbo, Garza, Botello, and
De Mézières, who agree upon the points thus far stated. But
as to the objects of the Comanche's visit to the pueblo there is
conflicting testimony. Ybarbo, Garza and Botello represented
the occurrence as an attack, and Father Garza even claimed that
the Indians stole some of the horses of the settlers. De Mézières,
however, who happened to be in the neighborhood at the time,
and who doubtless got his information from the Comanche, told
and professed to believe a different story. According to his
version, the Indians were on the way to make a friendly visit
to himself, had camped near the ranches at Bucareli, had turned

---

[1] The Tonkawa tribe was at this time one of the most numerous of
those in Texas. It was estimated in 1778 that it comprised 300 warriors
(*Informe del Governador de Texas*, in Vol. 64, Provincias Internas, Archivo General y Público, Mexico).

their horses loose, and were resting—anything but hostile actions —when they were frightened off by the boisterous commotion raised by the terrified Spaniards in their haste to corral their stock and raise an attacking party. When he heard this story from Croix, Governor Cabello flatly rejected it, on the ground that in the first place it was absurd to assume, as did De Mézières, that a Comanche Indian would approach a Spanish settlement with friendly intent, and secondly, that he had full confidence in the testimony of the three eye-witnesses of the event, particularly that of Botello, whom he had closely questioned on the matter, and that all of them had represented the Comanche visit as an attack.[2]

Whatever may have been the purpose of this first visit of the Comanche, the object of the second was not doubtful. In October of the same year, Bucareli was raided by a much larger party than the one which had approached before. Driving off two hundred and seventy-six horses, mainly the property of Nicholas de la Mathe, the Comanche crossed the Brazos. Here, at the point where on the former occasion they had been overtaken, they left an ambush to cover their retreat. The Spaniards apparently followed, but hearing of the ambush, they gave up the pursuit, and the Indians escaped with their rich booty.[3] Near a Taovayas village they left the stock in charge of seven braves. Shortly afterward this guard was attacked by a party of Quitseis and Texas, both of which tribes were friendly toward the Spaniards. In the fight three Comanche were killed and the

---

[2] See Botello to Cabello, December 23, 1778; Garza to Cabello, January 8, 1779; Ybarbo to Cabello, January 12 and October 19, 1779; Cabello to Croix, August 31, 1779, all in *Expediente sobre el abandono,* 2, 5, 7, 8, 17, 38; De Mézières to Croix, November 15, 1778, in *Expediente sobre el abandono . . . y establecer Comercio,* 4.

Ybarbo (letter of January 12) reported the date of the Comanche visit as May 3 (*tres*). According to De Mézières (letter cited above) it was after May 6. This leads me to suspect that *tres* in my copy of Ybarbo's letter should be *trese* (13).

[3] See references cited above, note 2, p. 433. The different accounts vary somewhat as to the number of horses stolen on this occasion.

horses were recovered. But the triumph was short, for the escaping Comanche returned with friends, overtook their enemies, killed three Texas warriors, and recaptured horses.[4]

This raid on the Bucareli ranches was followed by rumors in the settlement that something worse was to be expected at the hands of the Comanche. Traces were found indicating that· Indian spies had effected a night entrance into the stockade and learned the weakness of its defence. Rumors were brought in by French traders and friendly Indians, now to the effect that the Indians were planning the total destruction of the place by burning the town, killing the men, and carrying off the women and children; now that traces of Comanche had been seen in the neighborhood of the Nabasat; and again that their attack was delayed only to secure the alliance, or at least the neutrality, of the Bidai and other Indians friendly to the Spaniards.[5]

Such rumors as these were usually very disturbing to Spanish settlements stronger and less isolated than Bucareli, and we need not be surprised that they terrorized this weak village. Ybarbo could muster only a handful of men, and these poorly equipped. The cannon were useless to resist a surprise attack. The houses were of wood and easily combustible, and the stockade was in a bad state of repair. Ybarbo feared, moreover, the disaffection of the Tonkawa, one of the tribes on which Bucareli relied for protection. In the March preceding he and De Mézières had promised to send them a trader, for whom they had asked. But the promise had not been kept, and the Indians were complaining. To pacify them Ybarbo was compelled to make them presents at his own expense.[6]

---

[4] Ybarbo to Cabello, December 7, 1778, in *Expediente sobre el abandono*, 4.

[5] Ybarbo to Cabello, December 7, 1778, and January 12, 1779; Botello to Cabello, January 8, 1779, all in *Expediente sobre el abandono*, 2–6.

[6] Ybarbo to Cabello, December 7, 1778, in *Expediente sobre el abandono*, 5.

To strengthen the means of defense, Ybarbo appealed to the governor for arms and ammunition, but without practical avail. Once more he collected a handful of men and went out to reconnoiter, but, after one day's march, upon being overtaken by a messenger and informed that a large party of Comanche and Taovayas were between the San Xavier and the Brazos, on the way to attack the Spaniards and the Bidai, he turned back.[7]

Of this situation in Bucareli Father Garza, who was there at the time, now wrote: "These miserable inhabitants are left in such deplorable state that they have no way even to hunt for food . . . for they cannot go out to hunt except in large numbers and well armed, nor yet can they go out together and with their weapons, lest they should leave the settlement helpless. . . . Hence they can follow no other occupation than to be continually on guard of the horses and the settlement, relieving each other morning and night. The time left free from this fatiguing work they spend in witnessing the need and miseries of their families, without being able to furnish them daily food by the ordinary work of hunting, fishing, or other similar means, and, moreover, without hope of remedy in the future, since the best time for sowing wheat has passed without a grain being sown up to the present."[8]

2. *The flight from Bucareli, January–February, 1779.*—The settlers now began to appeal either for protection or for permission to remove to the neighborhood of the Texas villages to the eastward.[9] It is a matter for comment that they did not request permission to go to Béxar, where the defences of the province were strongest and where the king had ordered that

---

[7] This event happened some time before December 7, 1778, when Ybarbo reported it to Cabello (*Expediente sobre el abandono*, 4–5. See also his letter of January 12, 1779, *ibid.*, 9).

[8] Garza to Cabello, January 8, 1778, in *Expediente sobre el abandono*, 6.

[9] Ybarbo to Cabello, January 12, and January 27, 1779, in *Expediente sobre el abandono*. 8.

they should establish themselves, but that, instead, they asked
to be allowed to return a step nearer to the place whence they
had been removed in 1773.   Whether the suggestion of a removal came from Ybarbo or from some one else I cannot say.
The first mention of such a plan in the correspondence is found
in a letter written in December,[10] 1778, by Father Botello, who
had recently returned from Bucareli.   In response to an inquiry
made by Governor Cabello about the condition of affairs at
Bucareli, Father Botello said that, in his opinion, the place
should be abandoned; that, besides being threatened with destruction by the Comanche, it was incapable of irrigation, and
had proved unhealthful because of heavy rains; that these short-
comings could be remedied and all of the advantages of Bucareli
with respect to fertility and location[11] secured at a little additional
cost by establishing the settlers ''on the Neches River among the
pueblos of the Téxas; on the Angelina River among the pueblos of
the same tribe; with even greater security in the place where
the mission of Nacogdoches formerly was; with still much more
on the Atoyaque River; and with advantages and security beyond comparison at the site of the mission of Los Ais, on the
road from Natchitoches, thirty-nine leagues from the post.''[12]
It is not at all unlikely that this preference of Father Botello's
for Los Ais was simply his reflection of the desires of the settlers at Bucareli learned by him during his residence there.

About two weeks after the date of this letter,[13] Ybarbo wrote
the governor that the people had twice come to him in a body
begging that they might either be supplied with a suitable military guard, or be allowed to go with their families to the neigh-

---

[10] December 23.

[11] The advantages of Bucareli's location he conceived to be its position midway between Natchitoches and Béxar, and its importance as a
place from which to watch the coast and to keep up friendly relations
with the Indians.

[12] Botello to Cabello, December 23, 1778, in *Expediente sobre el
abandono*, 2–3.

[13] On January 8, 1779.

borhood of the Texas villages. In the name of the settlers, Ybarbo forwarded the petition to the governor.[14] Cabello replied that he could not send men and arms to aid the place, but that he could furnish ammunition if Ybarbo would come after it, though he dared not send it for fear it would fall into the hands of the Indians[15]

But before help was received, Ybarbo, compelled, as he claimed, by the straits and the supplications of his people, granted their request to be allowed to remove to the Texas country. On January 25 the larger part of the families, including Ybarbo's own, began to leave. Two days later Father Garza set off on foot with the sick and the church treasures in his care, Ybarbo remaining behind with twenty men to protect the families and to guard the stock and goods left in the flight until the owners might return for them.[16] Incident to the departure of these families, either by accident or design, half of the houses of the place were destroyed by fire.[17]

Now an additional reason for deserting Bucareli presented itself in the form of a flood. On the night of February 14, according to the story, the Trinity River overflowed its banks, rose to half the height of the houses of the pueblo, and drowned part of the remaining stock. The women and children and some of the stock were saved on improvised boats and rafts and removed to higher land some distance from the river. Here the people remained a few days, when they were again molested by Comanche, who, after what was reported to be an all-night siege, ran off thirty-eight head of horses which had been saved from the deluge,

---

[14] *Expediente sobre el abandono*, 9–10.

[15] Cabello to Croix, February 11, 1779, in *Expediente sobre el abandono*, 11.

[16] Ybarbo to Cabello, January 27, 1779, in *Expediente sobre el abandono*, 10.

[17] This fact was not reported by Ybarbo, but Cabello said that he learned it "extrajudicially" (Letter to Croix, February 11, 1779, in *Expediente sobre el abandono*, 11).

and then killed, nearby, half a dozen Indians friendly to the Spaniards. After this raid, haste was made to remove the people in boats to the east bank of the river, but here they were again disturbed by the Indians.[18] The settlers being now thoroughly frightened by the Indians and evicted by fire and flood, Ybarbo at once set out with them for the Texas country.[19]

3. The beginnings of modern Nacogdoches.—On the way Ybarbo apparently picked up the people who had gone on before and who were now living scattered among the Indians. The journey was continued toward the northeast "until," to use the words of Ybarbo in his report to Croix, "there were seen the site of the Téxas Indians and, three leagues beyond, the old mission of Nacogdoches, where there was a small chapel, in which the reverend father may perform the holy sacraments and a house where he may live,[20] as well as plenty of water, lands, and materials for houses." He does not mention the "Old Stone Fort,"[21] which it has been supposed had been built before this

[18] Ybarbo to Croix, May 13, 1779, in *Expediente sobre el abandono*, 22; Cabello to Croix, August 31, 1779, *ibid.*, 37; Garza to Croix, April 30, 1779, *ibid.*, 23.

[19] When the settlers departed from Bucareli they left six cannon, four of which were sooner or later taken to Nacogdoches. Those remaining at Bucareli were ordered sent to Béxar, and in 1793 steps were taken to remove them thither, but that they ever reached there I can not say (see a document entitled *Provincia de Téxas, Año de 1792*, and a letter from Revilla Gigedo to Governor Muñoz, April 10, 1793, both in Béxar Archives).

[20] De Mézières, in his letter of August 23, 1779, testifies to the fact that the mission buildings were still standing when the Spaniards returned. He says "It [the mission] is situated at the foot of a knoll, where its buildings still remain" (*Expediente sobre el abandono . . . y estableer Comercio*, 6).

[21] It is quite possible, and even probable, that one of the mission buildings mentioned by Ybarbo and De Mézières was identical with what has been known as the Old Stone Fort. I can not assert with certainty that Ybarbo did not build the Old Stone Fort for defense against the Indians soon after going to Nacogdoches, as has been supposed was the case. Indeed, in one communication he refers indefinitely to "fortifying" the place, but this probably meant the building of a wooden stockade. A strong indication that no stone fortification had been built before September 4, 1788, is the testimony of Francisco Xavier Fragoso in his *Derrotero* (see p. 467). He notes that at Nacogdoches, where

time.[22] "I approached," he continues, "in order that we might sow grain to support ourselves and to await the decision of your Grace, whom I humbly beg to approve this my action, since it is impossible to return to the same place or to the banks [of the river] below or above, because the lands are low, or farther away [from the river], because of even greater risk. There is not to be found in this vicinity another place better than this one or the one which was granted to us by his Excellency, the viceroy,[23] and this one facilitates watching the movements and operations of the friendly Indian nations and keeping in touch with the doings of the traders, as well as getting news from the coast, a matter with which I am charged by the governor.[24]

Unless some of the Bucareli families who had set out in January reached Nacogdoches in advance of Ybarbo, and it would appear that they did not, this entry of Ybarbo into the abandoned mission was the beginning of the modern city of Nacogdoches, for the continuous existence of a settlement there from this time forward can be traced.

There would be some satisfaction in being able to give the exact date when this event took place, but from the available records I am unable to do so. The best I can do is to say that it was certainly as early as April 30, 1779, the date of the first communication from Nacogdoches known to me. On that day Father Garza wrote from there to Croix recounting the story of the Bucareli flood, stating that Ybarbo had already given a report of the situation at Nacogdoches, and using terms that imply that all or nearly all of the settlers from Bucareli had already arrived.[25] Ybarbo's first report of his arrival at Nacog-

---

he arrived on that date, the houses were of wood and eighty or ninety in number. If a stone fort had been there, he in all probability would have mentioned it as a noteworthy object.

22 See *The American Magazine* for April, 1888, pp. 721–728.

23 That is, Los Ais (see above, p. 402).

24 Ybarbo to Croix, May 13, 1779, in *Expediente sobre el abandono*, 23.

25 *Expediente sobre el abandono*, 23–24.

doches I have not been able to find. The earliest communication of his from there that I have seen is dated May 9. It is a letter to Governor Cabello, and contains language implying that he had been at Nacogdoches some time and that Cabello already knew about the removal from Bucareli.[26]. In relating to Croix on May 13 the story of the desertion of Bucareli he says that more than a hundred days were spent in getting to Nacogdoches. To have been true this could not have referred to the party he conducted, for he did not leave Bucareli till some days after February 14. Neither could it have referred to the whole party led by Father Garza, because one hundred days from January 25, when he set out, was May 5; but, as we have seen, some, if not most, of the settlers had arrived at Nacogdoches as early as April 30. If Ybarbo's statement was true, therefore, he probably meant that it was one hundred days from the time when Father Garza started before all the stragglers who had stopped by the way arrived at the new settlement.

It is necessary here to correct an error that crept into the story of the abandonment of Bucareli as it was told in the Spanish correspondence, namely, the assertion that the cause of leaving the place was the flood. It is clear from the above account that the Comanche raid was the external cause of the removal of the people to the east, and that the flood did not occur till three weeks after most of them had left. Yet, through an increasing emphasis of what was in reality a secondary matter, it soon became current in the governmental accounts that the change of location had been primarily due to the overflow of the Trinity.[27]

---

[26] *Expediente sobre el abandono*, 32–33.

[27] It is true, however, that a previous flood had destroyed the crops at the place, and that the recurrence of the disaster had been a strong reason for not returning to Bucareli (Botello to Cabello, December 23, 1778, in *Expediente sobre el abandono*, 2–3). Interesting examples of the way the story became distorted are the following: In reviewing Cabello's first report Croix wrote, "The governor of the province of Texas says . . . that because an inundation occurred at that pueblo and the Comanches stole the greater part of their horses, they were so

4. Nacogdoches recognized by the government.—Since it is
not my aim here to pursue the history of eastern Texas beyond the
founding of Nacogdoches, it only remains to show how this place,
settled without authority, secured recognition from the government, and to indicate briefly the importance it soon attained.

The main purpose of Ybarbo and Garza in their first reports
to Croix of the desertion of Bucareli was to show their unwillingness to return thither, and to secure permission to remain at
Nacogdoches. By this time Ybarbo had changed his mind as to
the relative desirability of Los Ais as a location, for he concluded
the letter of May 13 to Croix with the opinion that of the two
available places, Los Ais and Nacogdoches, the advantages were
with the latter.[28] At the same time that he was asking Croix for
permission to remain at Nacogdoches, he was making recom-

---

frightened that they have deserted the settlement'' (Croix to Cabello,
May 21, 1779, in *Expediente sobre el abandono*, 12). Croix's *asessor general*, Navarro, in reviewing the history of Bucareli in 1780, wrote that
''the flood which the river caused, and the fire which followed it, reduced to ashes the buildings that had been made, and obliged the settlers
to disperse and seek shelter and asylum among the friendly nations near
by'' (*Expediente sobre el abandono . . . y establecer Comercio*, 45–46).

[28] With respect to returning to Bucareli, Father Garza had written
two weeks before (Letter to Croix, April 30, 1779, in *Expediente sobre el
abandono*, 23–24): ''It is now wholly impossible to restore this population to the same unprotected place whence they fled, without exposing
them to greater and more evident perils than those which they have
already experienced, because—not to mention this hostility [of the
Comanches], which was the cause of their flight and which may be
greater in the future—that district has been proved uninhabitable by
the inundation which it suffered on the 14th of February.'' To possible
locations elsewhere on the Trinity or nearer to San Antonio he was
even less favorable: ''Since this is the place formerly considered the
best,'' he wrote, ''I judge that such other as there may be on the river
to the north or to the south are as bad if not worse. And not less unsuitable are the places which might offer some advantages toward the
west between the Brazos, San Marcos, and Guadalupe rivers, since these
places, because of their large *encenades*, are the paths of ingress and
egress for the Comanches, and are much more dangerous [than the
others] in proportion as they are more frequented by these Indians,
nearer their lands, and distant from the friendly tribes, circumstances
which, having been weighed by these settlers, led them to flee to this
vicinity.'' His opinion of Nacogdoches, on the contrary though based
mainly on hearsay, as he frankly admitted, was highly favorable and
he intimated a preference for it over Los Ais. ''Under these circumstances,'' he continued, ''there is no doubt that your Grace's generous

mendations to Cabello which implied an expectation that his request would not be refused. These recommendations were of a kind that he knew would appeal to the government, since they concerned the control of the Indian tribes about him. In May he reported[29] that the Tonkawa Indians who had been promised traders and had been disappointed were becoming insolent; and as a remedy he suggested that a trading post be established at Nacogdoches and that a commissary be stationed there. A month later he reported new difficulties with the Indians, and said that Nacogdoches should be supplied with a good garrison.[30]

Croix and Cabello discussed the new situation without any reference to the royal order in response to which the inhabitants of Adaes had been removed from the frontier, further than to indicate that they were aware that it was not being complied with. They both showed plainly that they desired that Ybarbo be allowed to remain wherever he could be most useful as an Indian agent, the only question being what was the most desirable location. When Croix learned of the break-up of Bucareli

---

piety will deign to approve this temporary withdrawal, and, if it be your superior wish, concede them permission to attempt to establish their settlement in another place,—even if it be in (*hasta la*) the old mission of Los Ais, which the excellent viceroy, Dn. Fr. Antonio Bucareli granted them—where, free from hostile invasions, they may in some measure retrieve what they have lost in all these removals. . . . And I believe that the advantages which, they assure me, this depopulated mission of Nacogdoches possesses, will contribute to this end. Although the site for the settlement is not the best nor the most beautiful, it is yet the most suitable, judging from what I have heard and the little which I have seen, for it is on firm land, commanding, entirely free from inundation, and between two arroyos abundantly supplied with good water. Besides having a healthful climate, it enjoys the advantage of having near by many spacious plains of proved fertility, some more and others less watered, for the plain and open commons, good pastures, and numerous springs of water for raising horses and cattle, and affords all other conveniences that these people could wish for their relief. The advantage to the province resulting from their settlement in this place would not be slight, through their being able to visit the friendly Indians frequently, having them near by, and to report promptly everything that they may attempt anew contrary to the peace promised to your excellency.''

[29] In his letter of May 9, cited before.

[30] Letter to Cabello, June 13, 1779, in *Expediente sobre el abandono*.

he left the temporary disposition of the inhabitants to Cabello, giving him permission to bring them back to Trinity River, or, better, as he thought, to establish them in any one of the places to the northeast that had been suggested by Father Botello. Far from recommending that they be brought back to Béxar, to do which now was the opportune time if it was to be done at all, he distinctly said that such a procedure "would be prejudicial to the plans which are being meditated, by interfering with the cultivation of the friendship of the Texas and other allied tribes."[31] Cabello, who had already given his opinion that Bucareli could not be held against the Comanche without a garrison,[32] soon expressed a preference for Nacogdoches over any other place, approved Ybarbo's request for a garrison on regular pay, and recommended that it be formed of the settlers already there.[33]

While Croix and Cabello thus favored Nacogdoches, De Mézières advocated re-occupying Bucareli. We have already noted the good opinion entertained by him of the site of Bucareli, and his charge that the Comanche attack which caused its desertion had been brought on by the foolish fears of the Spaniards. Now, in August, 1779, while on his way to northern Texas, he stopped at Nacogdoches to assist the settlers during the absence of Ybarbo in pursuit of Comanche, and while there he wrote to Croix a gloomy account of the situation of the inhabitants. He criticised their location, said that plenty of places safe from flood could be found near Bucareli, insisted, as before, on the importance of a settlement there to maintain Indian relations and with a view to opening up trade with New Orleans, and suggested that the people be sent back there and reinforced by a regular

---

[31] Croix to Cabello, May 21, 1779, in *Expediente sobre el abandono,* 12–13.

[32] Cabello to Croix, February 11, 1779, in *Expediente sobre el abandono,* 12.

[33] Cabello to Croix, May 31, 1779, April 30, 1779, and August 31, 1779 (all in *Expediente sobre el abandono,* 13, 19, 31). In his letter of May 31, Cabello said that he was hardly decided as to the respective merits of the two places, but by the time of his next letter he had no doubts.

garrison and by the Adaes exiles who had remained at Béxar.[34]
But De Mézières died soon after the expression of this opinion,[35]
and the only effective opposition to the occupation of Nacogdoches
was removed.

Only to Navarro, in Chihuahua, did it occur that perhaps, in
order to fulfill the king's command made seven years before,
Ybarbo and his people should be brought to the neighborhood
of Béxar. But even to him this was but a passing thought, and
he recommended, instead, that choice be made between Bucareli
and Nacogdoches, and that the decision be left to an impartial
observer after a careful examination of the two sites.[36]   Croix
appointed as this impartial observer Governor Cabello, whose
preference was already known. But Cabello found excuses for
not performing the commission himself or delegating it to any
one else, while Croix claimed that he knew of no one outside of
Texas available to fill the place.[37]   And thus the matter appears
to have been dropped by a tacit understanding, and the pueblo
of Nacogdoches remained undisturbed.

Not only did Croix and Cabello refrain from breaking up the
settlement, but in effect they legalized its existence by assigning
Ybarbo a salary and conferring on him a new and more dignified
title.   At Bucareli Ybarbo and his men had served without pay,
and had furnished their own arms and ammunition.   Ybarbo
claimed, besides, that making presents to the Indians and aiding
the settlers had cost him a goodly sum from his own private

---

[34] He said that the first crop sown at Nacogdoches had failed and
that the people were "scattered among the gentile Indians, carrying
what they possessed, offering clothing for food, bartering hunger for
nakedness" (*Expediente sobre el abandono . . . y establecer Comercio,*
6–8).

[35] Some time before January 18, 1870 (*Expediente sobre el abandono,* 46).

[36] Navarro to Croix, January 17, 1780, in *Expediente sobre el abandono,* 46–48.

[37] Croix to Cabello, January 29, 1780; Cabello to Croix, April 1, 1780;
Croix to Cabello, January 19, 1780 (all in *Expediente sobre el abandono,*
50–53).

means. He asked, therefore, shortly before leaving the place, that arms and ammunition be furnished him and his men, and that they be paid for time spent in actual service. Ripperdá, and after him his successor, Governor Cabello, supported his request before Croix. Failing to secure his demands, Ybarbo now threatened to leave his post. The effect of this threat discloses the real attitude of Cabello and Croix toward Ybarbo's presence on the frontier. Cabello wrote to the *comandante general* that it would be unwise to let Ybarbo retire, since there was no one else in the province who could wield such an influence among the Indians and do so much towards keeping them quiet. In consequence of this opinion, Croix, in October, 1779, assigned Ybarbo a salary of five hundred pesos a year.[38] At the same time the government conferred on him the title of Lieutenant-Governor of the Pueblo of Nacogdoches.[39] It is plain, therefore, that Ybarbo was no longer remaining on the frontier by mere sufferance; on the contrary, he was kept there through the positive desire of Cabello and Croix to maintain an influence over the Indians of the northeast.

With the occupation of Nacogdoches begins a new and important epoch in the history of the Texas-Louisiana frontier,

[38] Ybarbo to Croix, October 19, 1778; Ripperdá to Croix, October 31, 1778; Croix to Cabello, January 12, 1779; Cabello to Croix, April 3, 1779 (all in *Expediente sobre el abandono*, 16–18). Croix to Cabello, January 16, 1779; Cabello to Croix, March 30, 1779; Croix to Cabello, October 15, 1779; and Cabello to Croix, December 17, 1779 (all in the Béxar Archives).

[39] The first use of this title that I have found was by Cabello in a letter to Croix, dated December 17, 1779 (Béxar Archives). He then calls him captain of the militia and lieutenant-governor of the pueblo of Nuestra Señora del Pilar de Nacogdoches. Cabello's letter notifying Ybarbo that he had been assigned a salary was dated March 11, 1780. It would seem that this letter was considered by Ybarbo as the source of his authority and the title to his pay, for in after years, when an attempt was being made to remove him, he furnished a copy of the letter as evidence of his official standing. That the government also considered this letter as his commission would appear from the fact that Governor Pacheco in 1788 furnished a copy of it as evidence of one of the offices that had been created in Texas between 1775 and 1787 (Pacheco to Ugalde, May 29, 1788, in the Béxar Archives).

and of the developments there Nacogdoches, instead of Adaes, became the chief center. The trading house asked for by Ybarbo was established and the Indian trade was reorganized. Nacogdoches, through being made headquarters for the trade and the distribution of presents among the dozen or more tribes in whose midst it lay, became the most important Indian agency in the province, while Ybarbo, as head of the community, became among the Indians of the northeast the most influential Spaniard of his day. To Nacogdoches the government now looked for the maintenance of influence among the Indians as a makeweight against the Anglo-Americans, who made their way to the borders of the country; and when, in 1803, the American frontier was carried across Louisiana to Texas, Nacogdoches became for a time equal if not superior in importance to Béxar, through being at once the outpost for aggressive movements by the Americans and for resistance by the Spaniards.

BIBLIOGRAPHY

BIBLIOGRAPHY

LIST OF PRINTED WORKS CITED

ADDISON, JOSEPH.
 Charles the Third of Spain. Oxford, 1900.
ALTAMIRA, EL MARQUÉS DE.
 Testimo de un Parecer dado en los Auttos fechos en Virtud de Real Cedula en qe S. M. manda se le Imforme [sic] *sobre surttos* [sic] *Abusos Commettidos en la Provincia de Texas en el Tiempo que se expressa; y Tambien de un Parrapho de ottro Paracer dado en los proprios Auttos, uno y ottro del Sor Audittor Grâl de la Guerra,* in Yoakum, *History of Texas,* I, 381–402.
ARRICIVITA, FR. JUAN DOMINGO.
 Crónica Seráfica y Apostólica del Colegio de Propaganda Fide de la Santa Cruz de Querétaro en la Nueva España, Dedicada al Santísimo Patriarca el Señor San Joseph. Segunda Parte. Mexico, 1792.
ARRILLAGA, BASILIO JOSÉ.
 Recopilación de Leyes, decretos, Bandos, Reglamentos, Circulares y Providencias de los Supremos Poderes de los Estados-Unidos Mexicanos, y Otras Autoridades de la Union, Formada de Orden del Supremo Gobierno. 15 vols. Mexico, 1834–1850. (The titles of the different volumes vary somewhat).
AUSTIN, MATTIE ALICE.
 The Municipal Government of San Fernando de Béxar, 1730–1800, in Texas State Historical Association, *Quarterly,* VII, 277–352.
BANCROFT, HUBERT HOWE.
 History of Arizona and New Mexico. San Francisco, 1886.
 History of Mexico. 6 vols. San Francisco, 1883.
 History of the North Mexican States and Texas. 2 vols. San Francisco, 1883–1889.
BOLTON, HERBERT EUGENE.
 Athanase de Mézières and the Louisiana-Texas Frontier, 1768–1780. 2 vols. Cleveland, 1914.
 Guide to Materials for the History of the United States in the Principal Archives of Mexico. Washington, 1913.
 Spanish Activities on the lower Trinity River, 1746–1771, in *The Southwestern Historical Quarterly,* XVI, 339–377.
 Spanish Mission Records at San Antonio, in Texas State Historical Association *Quarterly,* X, 397–307.

The Founding of the Missions on the San Gabriel River, 1745–1749, in *The Southwestern Historical Quarterly*, XVII, 322–378.

The Spanish Abandonment and Reoccupation of East Texas, 1773–1779, in Texas State Historical Association *Quarterly*, IX, 67–137.

The Founding of Mission Rosario: A Chapter in the History of the Gulf Coast, In Texas State Historical Association, *Quarterly*, X, 113–139.

Tienda de Cuervo's Ynspección of Laredo, 1757, in Texas State Historical Association, *Quarterly*, VI, 187–203.

BONILLA, ANTONIO.

Brief Compendium of the Events which have Occurred in the Province of Texas from its Conquest, or Reduction, to the Present Date. Written in 1772. Translated by Elizabeth Howard West, in Texas State Historical Association, *Quarterly*, VIII, 9–22.

BUCKLEY, ELEANOR CLAIRE.

The Aguayo Expedition into Texas and Louisiana, 1719–1722, in Texas State Historical Association, *Quarterly*, XV, 1–65.

CAVO, ANDRÉS.

Los Tres Siglos de México, Durante el Gobierno Español Hasta la Entrada del Ejército trigarante. 4 vols. Mexico, 1836–1838. Carlos María Bustamente, ed.

COX, ISAAC JOSLIN.

The Early Exploration of Louisiana. Cincinnati, 1905.

The Early Settlers of San Fernando, in Texas State Historical Association, *Quarterly*, V, 142–160.

The Founding of the First Texas Municipality, in Texas State Historical Association, *Quarterly*, II, 217–226.

The Louisiana-Texas Frontier, in Texas State Historical Association, *Quarterly*, X, 1–76; XVII, 1–43.

The significance of the Texas-Louisiana Frontier, in Mississippi Valley Historical Association, *Proceedings*, III, 198–213.

The Southwest Boundary of Texas, in Texas State Historical Association, *Quarterly*, VI, 81–102.

COXE, WILLIAM.

Memoirs of the Kings of Spain of the House of Bourbon. 5 vols., London, 1815.

DANVILA Y COLLADO, MANUEL.

Historia del Reinado de Carlos III. 6 vols, 1891–96.

Diccionario Universal de Historia y de Geografía. Mexico, 1853–1856, 10 vols.; Madrid, 1846–1850, 8 vols.

DUNN, WILLIAM EDWARD.

Apache Relations in Texas, 1717–1750, in Texas State Historical Association, *Quarterly*, XIV, 198–274.

Missionary Activities Among the Eastern Apaches Previous to the Founding of the San Sabá Missions, in Texas State Historical Association, *Quarterly*, XV, 186–200.

The Apache Mission on the San Sabá River, its Founding and its Failure, in *Southwestern Historical Quarterly* XVI, 379–414.

ENGELHARDT, FR. ZEPHYRIN.
The Missions and Missionaries of California. 4 vols. San Francisco, 1908–1915.

ESCUDERO, JOSÉ A.
Noticias Estadísticas de Sonora y Sinaloa. Mexico, 1849.

ESPINOSA, FRAY ISIDRO FELIX.
Chrónica Apostólica y Seráfica de Todos los Colegios de Propaganda Fide de Esta Nueva-España. Mexico, 1746.

FICKLEN, JOHN R.
Was Texas Included in the Louisiana Purchase?, in Southern History Association, *Publications*, V, 351–387.

GARCÍA, FR. BARTHOLOMÉ.
Manual para Administrar los Santos Sacramentos de Penitencia, Eucharistía, Extremaunción, y Matrimonio, dar Gracias Despues de Comulgar, y Ayudar a Bien Morir, etc. Mexico, 1760.

GARRISON, GEORGE P.
Texas, a Contest of Civilizations. Boston, 1903.

GATSCHET, ALBERT.
The Karankawa Indians, in *Archaeological and Ethnological Papers of the Peabody Museum, Harvard University*, Vol. I, no. 2. (1891).

GONZÁLEZ, JOSÉ ELEUTERIO.
Colección de Noticias y Documentos para la Historia del Estado de Nuevo León. Monterey, 1885.
Lecciones Orales de Historia de Nuevo León. Monterey, Mexico, 1877.

HODGE, FREDERICK WEBB, ED.
Handbook of American Indians North of Mexico. Bureau of American Ethnology, Bulletin no. 30. 2 vols. Washington, 1907–1910.

HUME, MARTIN A. S.
Spain, Its Greatness and Decay, 1479–1788; with an Introduction by Edward Armstrong. Cambridge, 1905.

Instrucciones que los Vireyes de Nueva España Dejaron a Sus Sucesores. Añadense Algunas que los Mismos Trajeron de la Corte y Otros Documentos Semejantes a las Instrucciones. Mexico, 1867.

KENNEDY, WILLIAM.
Texas: the Rise, Progress and Prospects of the Republic of Texas. 2 vols. London, 1841.

MANZANET [MASSANET], FRAY DAMIÁN.

Carta de Damian Manzanet, in Texas State Historical Association, *Quarterly,* II. Austin, 1899. Reprinted, 1911. Lilia M. Casís, ed.

MARGRY, PIERRE.

Découvertes et Etablissements des Français dans l'ouest et dans le Sud de l'Amérique Septentrionale (1614–1754). 6 vols. Paris, 1876–86.

MARSHALL, THOMAS MAITLAND.

A History of the Western Boundary of the Louisana Purchase, 1819–1841. Berkeley, 1914.

The Southwestern Boundary of Texas, 1821–1840, in Texas State Historical Association, *Quarterly,* XIV, 277–293.

MCCALEB, WALTER FLAVIUS.

Some Obscure Points in the Mission Period, in Texas State Historical Association, *Quarterly,* I, 216–225.

MCMASTER, JOHN BACH.

History of the People of the United States from the Revolution to the Civil War. 8 vols. New York, 1888–1913.

MOTA PADILLA, MATÍAS DE LA.

Historia de la Conquista de la Provincia de la Nueva Galicia. Mexico, 1870–72.

NUÑEZ CABEZA DE VACA, ALVAR.

The Journey of Alvar Nuñez Cabeza de Vaca and his Companions from Florida to the Pacific, 1528–1536. New York, 1905. Ad. F. Bandelier, ed.

PALOU, FRAY FRANCISCO.

Relación Histórica de la Vida y Apostólicas Tareas del Venerable Padre Fray Junípero Serra, etc. Mexico, 1787.

PEÑA, EL BR. D. JUAN ANTONIO DE LA.

Derrotero de la Expedición en la Provincia de los Texas, Nuevo Reyno de Philipinas, que de orden del Excmo. Señor Marquès de Valero, Vi-Rey, y Capitan General de esta Nueva-España passa à executar el Muy Illustre Señor D. Joseph de Azlor, Cavallero Mesnadero de el Reyno de Aragō, Marqués de S. Miguel de Aguayo, Governador, y Capitan General de dichas Provincias de Texas, Nuevas Philipinas, y de esta de Coaguila, Nuevo Reyno de Estremadura, por el Rey N. S. (que Dios Guarde). Mexico, 1722.

PORTILLO, ESTÉBAN L.

Apuntes para la Historia Antigua de Coahuila y Texas. Saltillo, 1888.

PRIETO, ALEJANDRO.

Historia, Geográfica, y Estadística del Estado de Tamaulipas. Mexico, 1873.

Recopilación de Leyes de los Reynos de las Indias, etc. Tercera Edición. Madrid, 1774.

Reglamento e instruccion para los presidios que han de formar en la linea de frontera de la Nueva España. Resuelto por el Rey en cédula de 10 de Setiembre de 1772. Madrid, 1772.

SCHMITT, REV. EDMOND J. P.
  A Catalogue of Franciscan Missionaries in Texas (1528–1859). Austin, Texas, 1901.

SHEA, JOHN GILMARY.
  The Catholic Church in Colonial Days. 4 vols., New York, 1886–92.

SHEPHERD, WILLIAM R.
  The Cession of Louisiana to Spain, in *Political Science Quarterly,* XIX, 439–458.

SOTOMAYOR, JOSÉ FRANCISCO.
  Historia del Apostólico Colegio de Nuestra Señora de Guadalupe de Zacatecas. Zacatecas, 1889.

VELASCO, JOSÉ FRANCISCO.
  Sonora: its extent, population, natural productions, Indian tribes, mines, mineral lands, etc. Translated from the Spanish of Francisco Velasco by *Wm. F. Nye.* San Francisco, 1861.

WOOTEN, DUDLEY.
  A Comprehensive History of Texas, 1685–1897. 2 vols. Dallas, 1898.

LIST OF MANUSCRIPTS CITED

The following is a list, approximately chronological, of the principal manuscript materials cited in this work. In the citations A. G. M. means Archivo General y Público, Mexico; A. C. S. means Archivo del Colegio de la Santa Cruz, Querétaro (K, leg. 6, no. 1 means division K, legajo 6, document no. 1); A. C. G. means Archivo del Colegio de Guadalupe, Zacatecas; A. G. I. means Archivo General de Indias, Sevilla; B. A. means Béxar Archives; L. P. means Lamar Papers; N. A. means Nacogdoches Archives. The Béxar Archives are at the University of Texas, Austin. They are a part of the provincial archives of the Spanish province of Texas, having been transferred to Austin from San Antonio (Béxar). The Lamar Papers and Nacogdoches Archives cited are in the Texas State Library at Austin. The Spanish documents in these collections are also parts of the Béxar Archives which have become separated. The documents in the following list vary in length from a few pages to several hundred pages each, and aggregate many thousand sheets. Transcripts of most of them are in the author's private collection. *Expedientes* are listed according to the period covered (as indicated by the inclusive dates) rather than according to the dates of filing.

1691-1730

Casañas, Fray Francisco de Jesús María, Relación. August 15, 1691. Autograph copy owned by the Agricultural and Mechanical College of Texas. A copy is in A. G. M., Historia, vol. 395.

Ramón, Diego, Diario de la Jornada que executo el Sargento m^r. Diego Ramon Cavo Caudillo de la Compania de Campaña esquadra volante que esta Assiento en la Mission Principal de San Juan Baptista del Rio del Norte . . . a la parte del norte y lebante, etc., 1707. A. G. M., Provincias Internas, vol. 28, ff. 362–368.

Olivares, Fr. Antonio de San Buenaventura y, Diary of expedition to Texas, 1709. A. C. S., Ḱ, leg. 11, no. 1.

Espinosa, Fray Isidro Felix, Diario derrotero de la nueva entrada a la Prov^a. de los Tejas. Año de 1716. A. G. M., Provincias Internas, vol. 181.

Auttos fechos en la Bahia de el espiritu santo sobre dos muertos que ejecutaron los Yndios en los Soldados que guardavan la Cavallada de dho Presidio el dia 13 de en.° de este Año de 1724, por D.ⁿ Fern.ᵈᵒ Perez de Almasan Gov.ᵒʳ y Cap.ⁿ Gen.ˡ de esta Prov.ᵃ de tejas Nuebas Philipinas. A. G. M., Provincias Internas, vol. 181.

Autos hechos, Texas, no. 11, 1724. A. G. M., Provincias Internas, vol. 183.

Autos á consulta hecha del Pᵉ. Fr. Joseph Gonzˢ. contra Don Nicolas Flores, 1724. A. G. M., Provincias Internas, vol. 32.

Autos Sre diferentes puntos consultados por el Govr. de la Provincia de los tejas; Muerte de un Correo y otros materias, 1724. A. G. M., Provincias Internas, vol. 183.

Proyecto Mandado hacer por el Ex.ᵐᵒ S.ᵒʳ Marques de casafuerte Virey Governador y Capitan General de esta Nueba España y Presidente de la Real Audiencia de Ella, Reducido de la Visita hecha por el Brigadier Don Pedro de Rivera, que contiene tres puntos, etc., 1728. A. G. M., Provincias Internas, vol. 29.

Diligˢˢ. qᵉ hiso el Colegio año de 1729, para la mudanza de las Mis.ᵉˢ de Texas. A. C. S., K, leg. 19, no. 19.

Transsumpto de vn. Memorial que por parte de este collegio se remitio al Rey en el Consejo Real de Indias estaño de 1729. A. C. S., K, leg. 3, no. 3.

Tantos de Memoriales y carta del R. P. Sevillano al exmo. Sor. Virrey, para qᵉ. se den las providencias al resguarda de las misiones y misioneros, y a esto se erija el Presidio de Texas. Año de 1729. A. C. S., K, leg. 4, no. 7.

Tanto del Despacho del Exmo. Señor Virrey Marqˢ. de Casafuerte, mandando se ponga en cada Missᵒⁿ. del Rio grande, y Sn. Antonio Vn. soldado. Fecha 23 de Febrero de 1730. A. C. S., K, leg. 3, no. 4.

Ynforme al R Discreᵒ. de los PPˢ. Preᵉ. y Missˢ. de Tejas en que piden salir al Rio de S. Xavier, March 18, 1730. A. C. G., M, leg. 5.

Royal decree for extinguishing illicit trade in Spanish America, June 19, 1730. B. A. Cédulas and Orders, 1730–1779.

Escrito del P. Sevillano pidiendo dos soldados en cada mision; despacho en que se concede uno. Yt. una carta del assumpto, 1730. A. C. S., K, leg. 19, no. 20.

1731–1740

Testimonio de Asiento de Misiones, 1731. General Land Office of Texas, Spanish Archives, vol. 50, folios 13–28.

Autos sobre las providencias dadas pr. su exa. al Governador de la Provincia de Texas pa. la pazificazn. de los Yndios Apaches y sus aliados. Año de 1731. A. G. M., Provincias Internas, vol. 32.

Despacho librado pr. el Virrey Marques de Casafuerte pa. que no se obliguen á los Yndios de la frontera de N. S. de Guadalupe á servicios involuntarios. Año de 1732. N. 89. Arch. de Gob. Saltillo.

Del s^{or}. Casafuerte sobre el repartimt°. de los Aguas a los Ysleños, 1733. A. C. S., K, leg. 4, no. 6.

Oficio, Para que el Governador de la Provincia de Tejas mantenga por ahora el Presidio de los Adayis en el Parage, en q se halla, y execute todas las demas providencias que se previenen en este Dpacho; en la forma q se expresa Mexico, Dec. 17, 1733. L. P., no. 49.

Vergara, Fray Gabriel de, Padron de Baptismo, etc., de las misiones de Texas trasladadas al Rio de Sn. Antonio, Jan. 30, 1734. A. C. S., K, leg. 1, no. 8.

Oficio, Para que el Governador de la Provincia de Texas observe y execute la Real Cédula inserta conforme á lo resuelto por su Majestad, y ultimamente determinado por Vex^a. en razon de la pretencion del P^e. Fray Miguel Sevillano de Paredes, sobre q. se le asista con la escolta de soldados. Feb. 15, 1734. L. P., no. 42.

Real Cedula que inserta el Brebe de Su Santidad p^a. que en los Dominios de Yndias no puedan los Religiosos ni clerigos Seculares tratar, ni contratar, aun p^r. interposita persona. El Brebe de S. S. es de 22, de Feb°. de 1633. Año de 1735. Arch. de Gob., Saltillo, leg. 1, expediente 105.

Testimonio de Diligencias sobre Ynfidelidad de los Apaches, 1738. B. A., Province of Texas, 1754–1776.

Auttos fechos por el Govr. de Texas Sobre la Remision de el Capn. Cabellos Colorados y otros treze Yndios e Yndias de Nacion Apaches, a la Rl. carcel de Cortte, etta. 1738. A. G. M., Provincias Internas, vol. 32.

Expediente sobre la Campaña q a su costa ha de hacer en la Prov^a. de Texas Nuevas Philipinas p^r. el mes de Abril del sig^{te}. año D^n. Joseph de Urrutia Cap^n. del Presidio de S^n. Antonio de Bexar, etc., 1739. A. G. M., Provincias Internas, vol. 32, expediente no. 12.

Santa Ana to Fray Pedro del Barco, March 26, 1740, in Carta del P. Muñoz [Santa Ana] Del estado de las cosas de adentro. A. C. S., K, leg. 6, no. 4.

Santa Ana, Fray Benito Fernández de, Descripción de las Misiones del Colegio de la Santa Cruz en el Rio de San Antonio, Año de 1740. Memorias de Nueva España, XXVIII, 200–207.

Patente del R. P. Barco p^a. q°. no se vendan los generos de los habios, 1740 as. A. C. S., K, leg. 3, no. 30.

Varias Noticias por lo q mira a franzeses—dadas el año de 1740. A. C. S., K, leg. 19, no. 38.

1741–1745

Autos a consulta de D^n. Thoribio de Vrrutia Cap^n. del Presidio de S^n. Antonio de Vejar en la Provincia de Texas, sobre aumento de Soldados, y ottras providencias que pide para contener los Ynsultos que hazen los

Yndios Apaches; sobre que tambien insto Dⁿ. Joseph de Vrrutia Su Pᵉ. difunto. 1741. Num. 5. A. G. M., Provincias Internas, vol. 32.

Diligencias practicadas por Dn. Joaquin de Orobio Capn de la Bahía sobre establecimto de Franceses. B. A., Bahía, 1743–1778. The papers included cover the years, 1745–1746.

Tanto y testimonio de Vna escritura de Concordia Entre Los Señores Ysleños y las Misiones, 1745. A. C. S., K, leg. 4, no. 9.

Visita de las Missiones hecha, de orden de N. M. R. P. Comm.º Gral. Fr. Fogueras, por el P. Fr. Fran.ᶜº Xavier Ortiz, en el año de 1745. A. C. S., K, leg. 4, no. 11.

García, Fr. Diego Martín, Breve y Legal Noticia de las Calidades y Costvmbres de los Indios, que han de observar con ellos, y consigo mismos, los Obreros Evangelicos que quieren ganar sus almas para Dios. Escrita por el P. F. Diego Martin Garcia, Predicador Apostolico, Hijo del Seminario de propaganda fide de la SSma. Cruz de Queretaro. Año de MDCCXLV. Original in author's collection.

1746

Despacho q sin provecho se saco el año de 1746 el qual no se presento, ni aprobecha. Sobre los Indios de S. Xavier, pretendientes de mission. N. 1.º February 18, 1746. A. C. S., K, leg. 6, no. 5.

Oficio para que el gobernador de la Provincia de Texas practique lo que se expresa, en quanto a coadiubar a la pacificacion del Seno Mexicano que se ha encomendado al coronel d.ⁿ Joseph de Escandon, como se previene, 1746. B. A., Province of Texas, 1754–76.

Dos testimonios de Diligencias, sobre los Yndios Cocos q.ᵉ mató el Cap.ⁿ de la Bahia año de 1746 [April]. A. C. S., K, leg. 19, no. 27.

Memorial del Gov.ʳ Bustillos en contra de la fundacion de S.ⁿ Xavier, presentado al exmo. Sor. Virrey, año de 1746 [May 28]. A. C. S., K, leg. 6, no. 20.

Copia de Carta del R. P. Guard.ⁿ Fr. Alonso Giraldo de Terreros; del Gen.ˡ D.ⁿ Melchor de Mediavilla, y Anchona [sic]; del R. P. Presid.ᵗᵉ fr. Mariano de los Dolores, sobre la fundacion de S.ⁿ Xavier. Año de 1746 [June]. A. C. S., K, leg. 6, no. 15.

Satisfaccion de los Missioneros á las objecciones hechas por el Gov.ʳ Bustillos contra las fundaciones de S.ⁿ Xavier. Evidently before July 30, 1746. A. C. S., K, leg. 6, no. 21.

Memorial del R. P. Ortiz al Exmo. Sor. Virrey exponiendo las razones para fundar en S.ⁿ Xavier, año de 1746 [July 30]. A. C. S., K, leg. 6, no. 25.

Instancia, y razones representadas al exmo. Sor. Virrey para la fundacion de S.ⁿ Xavier. October 10, 1746. A. C. S., K, leg. 6, no. 24.

Father Francisco Ortiz to the viceroy. October 10, 1746. A. C. S., K, leg. 19, no. 62.

Satisfacción del R. P. Lector Prado al exmo. sobre la quexa De la Villa de Sⁿ. Fernᵈᵒ. De que los Padres se extendian fuera de la jurisdicción de las tierras de las Misiones, 1746. A. C. S., K, leg. 4, no. 16.

Copia de Autos seguidos en el Superior govierno para la fundacion de las Nuevas Misiones de S.ⁿ Javier. Año de 1746 [February–July]. A. C. S., K, leg. 6, no. 17.

Reconocimiento del Seno Mexicano hecho por el Theniente de Cappn. Gral. Dn. Joseph de Escandon, 1746–1747. A. G. M. Historia.

1747

Testimonio de los Despachos del e. m.° S.ᵒʳ Virrey D.ⁿ Juan Antonio Guëmes, y Horcasitas, acerca de la fundacion de las Missiones del Rio de S.ⁿ Xavier. February 14, 1747. A. C. S., K, leg. 6, no. 6.

Tanto de un Despacho y diligenc.ˢ de S.ⁿ Xav.ʳ pᵃ qᵉ se den 12 Soldados de S.ⁿ Antt.° año de 1747 [February 14]. A. C. S., K, leg. 19, no. 68.

Oficio. VE ordena el Governador de la Provincia de Tejas, que luego que reciba esta Despacho providencie pasen por lo tocantte a su presidio de los Adays diez soldados al parage de San Xavier, etc. Mexico, February 14, 1747. A. C. S., K, leg. 19, no. 67.

Petition of Fray Francisco Xavier Ortiz to the king. After February 14, 1747. A. C. S., K, leg. 6, no. 5.

2 peticiones del P. Fr. Mariano sobre los Yndios de S.ⁿ Xav.ʳ año de 1747 qᵈᵒ se fueron del puesto (*Diligencias* relative to the declaration of Eusebio García de Prurᵣda, May 4, and May 9, 1747). A. C. S., K, leg. 19, no. 69.

Escrito sobre los 12 soldados, qᵉ avian de hir a Sⁿ. Xavʳ. del Presidio de S.ⁿ Ant.° 1747 a.ˢ [May 9]. ⅄. C. S., K, leg. 19, no. 70.

Memorial, en q.ᵉ insiste pidiendo la licencia para fundar en S.ⁿ Xavier. Evidently between May 19 and June 28, 1747. A. C. S., K, leg. 6, no. 22.

Second order of viceroy to send thirty soldiers to San Xavier. July 27, 1747. A. C. S., K, leg. 19, no. 71.

Memorial del P.ᵉ Anda al Exmo. Sor. Virrey sobre S.ⁿ Xavier. *Circa,* August, 1747. A. C. S., K, leg. 6, no. 29.

1748

Order by the viceroy to the governor of Texas concerning the protection of the missions of San Xavier and the bringing in of Spanish settlers. Mexico, January 23, 1748. B. A., Miscellaneous, 1742–1793.

The viceroy, Juan Francisco de Guëmes y Horcasitas, to Governor Francisco García Larios. Mexico, February 24, 1748. L. P.

Memorial del P.ᵉ Ganzabal, pidiendo fuerzas para el resguardo de las missiones de S.ⁿ Xavier. After March 18, 1748. A. C. S., K, leg. 6, no. 16.

Fr. Franco Xavier Castellanos to President Fr. Benito de Santa Ana. March 31, 1748. A. C. S., K, leg. 19, no. 74.

Real Cédula. Al Virrey de la Nueva España participandole lo representado por Fray Francisco Xavier Ortiz del Orden de S.ⁿ Francisco en quanto aver pedido diferentes Naciones de Indios de la Provincia de los Texas se les fundasen Misiones; y ordenandole las Provincias necesarias, en la forma que se expresa. April 16, 1748. A. G. M., Reales Cédulas, vol. 68.

Patente del R.º P. Guard.ⁿ y V. Discretorio expedida en el año de 1748 para el govierno de las Missiones. April 19, 1748. A. C. S., K, leg. 3, no. 30.

Memorial del R. P. Presid.ᵗᵉ al Cap.ⁿ de S.ᵃ Antonio pidiendo fuerzas para la defensa del Presidio, y Missiones de S. Xavier. 1748 [May 7]. A. C. S., K, leg. 6, no. 28.

Carta Ynforme q.ᵉ hizo a Su Ex.ⁿ el R.ᵈº P.ᵉ Pres.ᵗᵉ Fr. Benitto. June 24, 1748. A. C. S., K, leg. 19, no. 76.

1749

Carta del P. Galzaval, sobre el Ynforme del Gov.ʳ Varrio, año de 1749 [January 22]. A. C. S., K, leg. 19, no. 80.

Dictamen del Auditor de Guerra, para qᵉ Ynforme el Presidᵗᵉ de S.ⁿ Javier el estado de aquellas Missiones: copia de la carta qᵉ a este fin escrivieron el Presidᵗᵉ y el Pᵉ Fr. Mariano de los Dolores. March 10, 1749. A. C. S., K, leg. 6, no. 18.

Copia de Car.ᵗᵃ del P. Fr. Mariano para S. Ex.ᵃ March 13, 1749. A. C. S., K, leg. 6, no. 18.

Copia de una Carta del P. Guard.ⁿ al S. Aud.ʳ año de 1749 [March]. A. C. S., K, leg. 19, no. 81.

Parecer de el S.ºʳ Auditor para la fundacion de S.ⁿ Xavier. April 23, July 7, 1749. A. C. S., K, leg. 19, no. 82.

Escrito presentado al Gov.ʳ D.ⁿ Pedro del Varrio sobre S.ⁿ Xavier, 1749 [May]. A. C. S., K, leg. 19, no. 79.

Ynforme del R. P. Presidᵗᵉ Fr. Mariano de los Dolores, y copias de Cartas sobre fundacion del Presidio, y Missiones de S.ⁿ Javier. July 9, 1749. A. C. S., K, leg. 6, no. 23.

Cédula Real para fundar las Missiones de S.ⁿ Javier y un Hospicio para que moren Religiosos q.ᵉ remplacen las vacantes de los q.ᵉ faltan en las Missiones, y se curen los Enfermos. July–August, 1749. A. C. S., K, leg. 6, no. 5.

Ynforme q.ᵉ hizo D.ⁿ Pedro del Varrio Gov.ʳ el año de 1749 [September 11]. A. C. S., K, leg. 19, no. 85.

Varios papeles, de Tejas que parece son posteriores al año 1746. After September 11, 1749. A. C. S., K, leg. 19, no. 65.

Escritos presentados al Gov.ʳ D.ⁿ Pedro del Varrio sobre S.ᵃ Xav.ʳ 1749 [October 23]. A. C. S., K, leg. 19, no. 86.

1750

Dr. Andreu, Dictamen fiscal. Mexico, January 7, 1750, *in* Morfi, Memorias para la Historia de Texas escritas por el R. P. F. Juan Agustín Morfi, libro 8, paragraphs 50–59 (MS in the Bancroft Collection, University of California).

Copia de las Clausulas una del S.ʳ Fiscal, y otra Del S.ʳ Auditor sobre consulta del S.ʳ Virrey en los Despachos de diligencias cometidos á D.ⁿ Joseph Ecai y Muzquiz, en orden al intentado Presidio de las Miss.ˢ del Rio de S.ⁿ Xavier. January 7 and 30, 1750. A. C. S., K, leg 6, no. 33.

El Marqués de Altamira, Parecer. Mexico, January 30, 1750, *in* Morfi, *Memorias*, libro 8, paragraphs 61–70.

Despacho para q.ᵉ no se continuaran las dilig.ˢ del Rio de S.ⁿ Xav.ʳ el q.ᵉ no tuvo efecto, año de 175ʋ [April 8]. A. C. S., K, leg. 19, no. 91.

Carta del R. P. Guard.ⁿ Castellanos suplicando se favorescan las Miss.ˢ de S.ⁿ Xav.ʳ, 1750 [April 12]. A. C. S., K, leg. 19, no. 89.

Ynforme del th.ᵉ Galvan sobre S.ⁿ Xavier y carta escrito al dho el año de 1750 [April 12]. A. C. S., K, leg. 19, no. 90.

Testimonio de diligencias, Executadas sobre los dos Rios de S.ⁿ Fran.ᶜᵒ Xavier y San Andres, y demas que dellas Conste, prozesadas por mi Dⁿ Jph Joaquin de Ecay Muzquiz, por Comision del Exmo Senor Virrey de esta nueba españa. Comprenden a la Provincia de Texas. June–August, 1750. A. C. S., K, leg. 6, no. 12.

Carta del P.ᵉ Ganzabal al R. P. Presidente dando razon de haber desamparado los Yndios la mission, y la causa de ello. August 20, 1750. A. C. S., K, leg. 6, no. 9.

Memorial presentado por el R. P. Presid.ᵗᵉ Fr. Mariano de los Dolores al Cap.ⁿ D.ⁿ Thorivio de Urrutia, para qᵉ este haga juridica informacion de varios puntos tocantes a la fundacion de mission para los Apaches; va junta dha informacion: Año de 1750 [September 17]. A. C. S., K, leg. 7, no. 7.

Diligencias practicadas por R. P. Presid.ᵗᵉ Fr. Mariano de los Dolores para la establidad de las Missiones de S.ⁿ Xavier. October, 1750. A. C. S., K, leg. 6, no. 26.

Autos concerning removal of San Xavier missions, 1750–1751. A. C. S., K, leg. 19, no. 65.

Testimonio de los Autos hechos sobre la Reduccion de los Yndios Gentiles de la Nacion Apache, y establecimiento de el Presidio de San Saba, 1750–1763. A. G. I., Audiencia de Mexico, 92–6–22.

1751

Despacho de la fundacion de el Pres.° en S.ⁿ Xavier y administrac.ⁿ del año de 1751 [February–November]. A. C. S., K, leg. 6, no. 8.

Erecion de la Mision de Sn. Xavier (see next item).

Oficio Para que el Govenador de Texas se halle entterado de la erección que en los margenes del Rio de San Xavier se ha de haser de un Precidio con el tittulo de estto nombre, y en Intteligencia de haver de ser de su Jurisdiccion executte lo que se le previene. March 30, 1751. L. P. Labelled and cited as "Erecion de la Mision de Sn. Xavier."

Escrito presentado en S.ⁿ Xav.ʳ a D.ⁿ Jacinto Gov.ʳ y nada respondio, 1751 a.ˢ [*circa* June]. A. C. S., K, leg. 6, no. 27.

Testimo. de Autos de Pesquiza sobre comercio Ylicito y Demas que expresa el superior Despacho que esta por cavesa de ellos. Adaes, 1751. B. A., Adaes, 1739–1755.

Testimonio de los autos sre. la erecion del Precidio de S.ⁿ Xavier en las margenes del Rio, y Consulta hecha por D.ⁿ Ph.° de Ravago y Teran Cap.ⁿ de dho Precidio en que da quenta al Exmo Senor Virrey de este Reyno con las diligencias que executó, y sobre el caudal de agua de dho Rio en que le concidera falto de ella, como tambien de tierra para siembras, y Materiales para el reedificio, 1751. A. G. I., Mexico, 92–6–22.

Autos fhos Apedimento . . . [de] Frai Benitto de Santa An[a] . . . que se le Manden restitu[ir á la misión de] Sn. Antonio que es á cargo de la Sta. Cruz de Queréttaro los [con] Bersos Indios de la Nacion [Cujan] que se hallan agregados a [la Misión] de Santa Dorothea, 1751–1758. A. G. M., Historia, vol. 287

Testimo. De Autos de Pesquiza sobre comercio Ylicito y Demas que expresa el superior Despacho que está por caveza de ellos. Adais, 1751. B. A., Adaes, 1739–1755.

1752–1755

Memorial del R. P. Viana al exmo Sor. Virrey, pidiendo resguardo mayor para San Xavier, 1752 [January 12]. A. C. S., K, leg. 6, no. 19.

Carta de los Pad.ᵉˢ de S.ⁿ Javier al Discret.° dando razon de las cosas de Rabago, 1752 [January 12]. A. C. S., K, leg. 12, unnumbered.

Instructions to President Terreros. February 8, 1752. A. C. S., K, leg. 8, no. 2.

Pinilla, Fray Miguel, decree of censure. February 19, 1752. A. C. S., K, leg. 12, unnumbered.

Petiz.ⁿ Al Cap.ⁿ de S.ⁿ X.ʳ. February 22, 1752. A. C. S., K, leg. 6, no. 31.

Fray Miguel Pinilla to Fray Francisco Mariano de los Dolores. Mission Candelaria, March 1, 1752. A. C. S., K, leg. 12, unnumbered.

2.ª Consulta remitida a su Ex.ª en 13 de Junio de 1752 a.ˢ [June 13]. A. C. S., K, leg. 19, no. 99.

Testimonio de Autos fechos en virtud de Superior Decreto Expedido por el ex.^mo Señor Dn. Juan Franco. de Guëmes y Horcasitas Conde de Revillagigedo Gentil hom[br]e de la Camara de S. M. . . . los 26 de Sepre. de 1752, para los fines que en el se expresen. B. A., Adaes, 1739–1755.

Informe del R. P. fr. Benito de Sta Ana al Exmo. sobre la fundacion de Sn Xavier, 1752. A. C. S., K, leg. 6, no. 32.

Tantto de lo que se presento en los Auttos de los Apaches. *Circa* 1752. A. C. S., leg. 6, no. 32.

Dilig.^s a favor de los Cocos en los Homicidios de Sn Xav.^r, 1753 [May]. A. C. S., K., leg. 12, no. 5.

Testimonio de los Autos fechos, á consulta de Don Pedro Rauago Teran, en horden á hauerse aposesionado del Empleo de Capitan del Presidio de San Xavier, hauer pasado reuista de el, y otras prouidencias en orden á el estado en que se halla &. 1753–1754. A. G. I. Mexico, 92–6–22.

Proceedings of the junta held at Los Adaes October 23, 1754, in consequence of the arrest of Blancpain. B. A., San Agustín de Ahumada.

Diligencias sobre Lanpen su Declaracion, Ynbentario. 19 de Febrero de 1755. B. A., Provincias Internas, 1755–1793.

Dilijen.^s Practicadas de Horden del Señor D. Jasinto de Barrios y Jauregui en asumpto del reconozimto. del desemboque del Rio de la Trinidad y Descubrir si avian poblado en el como se avia dicho los franceses. Año de 1755. L. P., no. 25.

Testimonio del Dictamen dado por el Senor Don Domingo de Valcarzel del Consejo de Su Magd. su oydor en la Rl Auda. de esta Nueba Espana en los autos fechos a consulta de Don Jazinto de Jauregui Governador de la Provincia de Texas de que dá quenta el comandante Frances de el Presidio del Nachitos se prebino que los yndios de aquella Dominacion intentaban saltar el Presidio. October 11, 1755. A. G. M., Provincias Internas, vol. 249. The title is incorrect. The document is a recommendation of the auditor concerning the proposed garrisoning of the mouth of the Trinity.

1756

Proceedings of the junta de guerra y hacienda of February 4, 1756. B. A., San Agustín de Ahumada.

The viceroy to the king, March 14, 1756. A. G. M., Correspondencia de los Virreyes, second series, vol. 1, Amarillas, 1, 1755–1756, f. 166, no. 72.

Memorial del R. P. Fr. Mariano al R. P. Comisario Visitador Fr. Fran^co. Ortiz, pidiendo se traslade el Presidio de Sn Xavier a el Rio de Guadalupe: juridico Dictamen de los Padres, y del Alferez Dn Diego Ramon sobre el particular, 1756 [June 25]. A. C. S., K, leg. 6, no. 10.

Petition of Monsieur Masse to settle at San Agustín de Ahumada, July 19, 1756. A. G. M., Correspondencia de los Virreyes, vol. 1, Amarillas, 1, 1755–1756.

Governor Barrios to the viceroy, July 22, 1756. A. G. M., Correspondencia de los Virreyes, second series, vol. 1, Amarillas, 1, 1755–1756, f. 264.

Royal cédula, August 20, 1756. A. G. M., Reales Cédulas, 1756–1776. f. 163, no. 61.

Royal cédula, August 31, 1756. A. G. M., Reales Cédulas, 1756–1766, f. 195, no. 80.

The viceroy to the king, September 2. 1756. A. G. M., Correspondencia de los Virreyes, second series, vol. 1, Amarillas 1, 1755–1756, f. 267.

The viceroy to Governor Barrios, September 12, 1756. A. G. M., Correspondencia de los Virreyes, second series, vol. 1, Amarillas 1, 1755–1756, f. 269.

The viceroy to the king, September 14, 1756. A. G. M., Correspondencia de los Virreyes, second series, vol. 1, Amarillas 1, 1755–1756, f. 259, no. 119.

Order to survey the banks of the Trinity and select a place for a mission and settlement of fifty families, 1756. N. A., Nacogdoches, vol. 1, doc. 488. (The document is an account of surveys on the San Jacinto and of the selection of a site for a villa).

Tejas. Minutas de la Correspondencia seguida con el Governador de la Provincia y varios capitanes de los presidios, 1756. A. G. M., Historia, vol. 91, expediente 2.

Puntos que se concideraron pudieron servir, para que la verdad, no padeciera si en algun tiempo se intentara confundirla con aparente difraz; y no se exponen todos los acaecidos en la empresa de la fundasion de Missiones de Apaches, p.ʳ que solo se llebó la mira a dar a conocer, en parte, la clara oposicion, que los mismos hechos, y dichos manifiestan. Ano de 56 (1756–1758). This document contains the "Vindicta del Rio de S.ⁿ Saba," listed below, p. 464. A. C. S., K, leg. 8, no. 14.

Autos Fechos a consulta de Don Jacinto de Barrios y Jauregui, Gobernador de la Provincia de Tejas, sobre Haber Descubierto en el Paraje Nombrado Los Almagres unos Minerales, 1756. A. G. M., Provincias Internas, vol. 181.

1757

Testimonio de los Autos fhos a pedimento de Don Pedro Romero de Terreros sre que se le admita la obligacion, que haze de mantener de todo lo necessario las Missiones, que se fundaren en los Confines, y terminos de la Governazion de Coahuila siguiendo el rumbo del Norte Vajo de las condiziones, que expressa, 1757. A. G. I., Mexico, 92–6–22.

Memorial del R. P. Fr. Mariano al Cap.ⁿ D.ⁿ Diego Ortiz Parrilla, pidiendo declare, como los Indios de Sⁿ. Xavier (qᵉ fueron) no quieren salir de el Rio de Guadalupe: el Informe de dho. cap.ⁿ y del R. P. Fr. Alonso Terreros, 1757 [Jan. 22]. A. C. S., K, leg. 6, no. 34.

El P.ᵉ Fr. Mno pidio a Parrilla Mis.ⁿ en Guadalupe con los yndios de las Mis.ˢ de San Xavier, 1756 [Jan. 22, 1757]. A. C. S., K, leg. 19, no. 107; K, leg. 6, no. 34.

Decreto puesto en los Autos sobre la translacion del Presidio de Sn. Agustín de Ahumada establecido en el dia en las margenes del Rio de la Trinidad a parage mas ventajoso. January 19, 1757. A. G. M., Historia, vol. 91, exp. 2.

The viceroy to Arriaga. April 18, 1757. A. G. M., Correspondencia de los Virreyes, second series, vol. 2, Amarillas 2, 1757, f. 52, no. 196.

The viceroy to the king, April 18, 1757. A. G. M., Correspondencia de los Virreyes, second series, vol. 2, Amarillas 2, 1757, f. 53, no. 197. (Transmitting Miranda's map).

The viceroy to the king, April 19, 1757. A. G. M., Correspondencia de los Virreyes, second series, vol. 2, Amarillas 2, 1757, f. 54, no. 198.

Royal cédula, June 10, 1757. A. G. M., Reales Cédulas, 1757, vol. 77, ff. 161, no. 66.

Royal cédula, June 19, 1757. A. G. M., Reales Cédulas, 1757–1777, f. 196, no. 81.

Tejas. Minutas de la correspondencia que siguió el Gobernador, Don Jacinto de Barrios, 1757. A. G. M., Historia, vol. 91, expediente 3.

Vindicta del Rio de S.ⁿ Saba, 1757. Contained in "Puntos que se consideraron pudieron servir" (cited on p. 463), A. C. S., K, leg. 8, no. 14.

Testimonio de los Autos fhos, sobre hauerse trasladado los Indios que se hallauan en las Misiones establecidas en el Rio de S.ⁿ Xavier, a las de San Antonio de Bejar: estos Yndios se Trasladaron al parajue nombrado de Guadalupe, no a las Miciones de San Antonio. 1757. A. G. I., Mexico, 92–6–22.

Testimonio de los Autos fechos sre la entrega, que se hizo al R. P. Misionero Fray Alonso Giraldo de Terreros de las alajas ornamentos, y demas utencilios, con que se hallaban las Missiones establecidas en el Rio de San Xavier. 1757. A. G. I., Mexico, 92–6–22.

López de la Cámara Alta, Agustín, Descripcion General de la Nueva Colonia de Santander, y Relaciones Individuales, etc., 1757. A. G. M., Historia, vol. 53.

Tienda de Cuervo, Informe del Reconocimiento e Ynspeccion de la Colonia del Seno Mexicano, etc. A. G. M., Historia, vol. 54. This consists of an autograph report by Tienda de Cuervo of his inspection of Colonia del Nuevo Santander in 1757. It comprises the whole volume.

Expedientes relativos á Ynspeccion y Estadistica de la Colonia de Santander. A. G. M., Historia, vols. 55 and 56. These are the *autos* of Tienda de Cuervo's inspection of Nuevo Santander made in 1757. Vols. 55 and 56 contain the primary results of Tienda de Cuervo's operations in 1757. Vol. 54 is Cuervo's autograph report summarizing his work, together with recommendations; vol. 53 is López de la Cámara Alta's description of Santander, based on the documents in vols. 55 and 56. See Bolton, in Texas State Historical Association *Quarterly*, January, 1903, pp. 187–188.

1758–1760

The viceroy to Governor Barrios, March 3, 1758. B. A., San Agustín de Ahumada.

Oficio. Al Virrey de la Nueva España: aprobandole la providencia que tomo de trasladar el Presidio de Sᵃ Xavier de la Provincia de los Texas al Parage nombrado Sᵃ Sabá, y participandole, lo demas que se expresa. October 15, 1758. A. G. M., Reales Cédulas, vol. 22, 1752, no. 26.

"Appeal of the father at the Mission of Nuestra Señora de la Luz de Orcoquisa for permission to abandon that mission on account of the insufferable plague of mosquitoes and ants and of the unhealthfulness of the locality." 1758. N. A., no. 487, Nacogdoches, vol. 1.

Report on missions of the College of Santa Cruz, Querétaro, April, 1759; directed to "Emin.ᵐᵒ y R.ᵐᵒ S.ᵒʳ Prefecto de la Sag.ᵃ Congreg.ᵒⁿ de Prop.ᵈᵃ fide." A. C. S., C, leg. 1, no. 1.

Presidio de San Saba. Minutas de la Correspondencia seguida con el Gobernador de dicho Presidio, 1759. A. G. M., Historia, vol. 91, expediente 4.

Martos y Navarette, governor of Texas, report to the viceroy. December 6, 1759. B. A., San Agustín de Ahumada.

Power of attorney granted by the soldiers of San Agustín to Diego Giraud for the collection of salaries, December 31, 1759. B. A., San Agustín de Ahumada.

Testimonio de los Auttos fhos á consulta del Coronel Dⁿ. Diego Orttiz Parrilla . . . en qᵉ. dá cuentta de los sucessos de la Campaña, que de orn de estta Capittania General executtó contra los Genttiles qᵉ. insulttaron el Puesto de la Mision del Rio de San Zavá, 1759. A. G. I., Mejico, 93–6–22.

Testimonio practicado sobre si Dn. Jasinto de Barrios tuvo comersio con Muniziones de Guerra con los Yndios Barbaros de Esta Prova. y fuera de ella de Orn del Exmo.Señor Dn. Franco Caxigal virrey Govr. y Cappn Genl de Esta Nueba España. January to March, 1760. B. A., Adaes, 1756–1766.

Santa María, Fr. Vicente, Relación historica de la colonia del Nuevo Santander y costa del Seno Mexicano. Ca. 1760. Museo Nacional, Mexico.

Testimonio de los Auttos fechos a consultta del Governador de la Provincia de Texas en que da cuentta de haverle presentado, y pedido los Yndios, que ynsultaron la Mision de Sansaba se yntteresarà, e intercediese por ellos, a fin de que se les concediese paz, vaxo de varias condiciones, Quad[no]. 10 A. 1760–1763. A. G. I., Mexico, 92–6–22.

Testimonio de las Diligencias practicadas de Orn del Exmo. Sor. Marqs. de Cruillas ViRey Govor. y capitan Gral de la Nueva Esp[a]. por Dn. Ang[l]. de Martos y Navarrete (a quien se remitieron los orijinales) Gov[or]. y capit[n]. de esta Nueva Esp[a]., digo esta Prov[a]. de Tejas, sobre la reduccion de los Yndios Tehuacanas e yscanis a Mission, 1760–1763. Béxar Archives, Province of Texas, 1754–1776.

Autos de la Residencia Pública y Secreta que se le ha tomado a el theniente coronel Dn. Jazinto de Barrios y Jauregui de el tiempo que goberno esta provinzia. February and March, 1760. B. A., Adaes, 1756–1766.

1761–1765

Hierro, Fray Simón, Informe de las Misiones de Texas, January 8, 1762. A. C. G., M, no. 9.

Testimonio de lo determinado en Junta de Guerra y Hacienda celebrada sobre la translacion del Presidio de Sn. Agustín de Ahumada dho de la Trinidad, al parage de los Horconsitos despues de explorados los Yndios de aquellos Missiones y el reconocimiento de las costas de essa Provincia, etc. A. G. M., Mexico, Historia, vol. 91, expediente 6, 1762–1763.

Testimonio de los Autos fhos a Consulta del Capitan del Precidio de San Saba sobre el planteo de dos Missiones en el Valle de San Joseph, y que se la augmente la Tropa a dho Prezidio Q[no]. 24 A., 1763. A. G. I., Mexico, 92–6–22.

Testimonio de los Autos fechos á consulta de Don Lorenzo Cancio, y Don Phelipe de Rabago: El primero Capitan del Prezidio de Santa Rosa, y el segunda del de San Saba sre. assegurarse que los Comanches meditaban el sitado Prezidio de San Saba, 1763. A. G. I., Mexico, 92–6–22.

Testimonio de los Autos á Conz[ta]. de Don Lorenzo Cansio Capitan del Real Precidio de Santiago de la Monclova, en que dá quenta de haver aprehendido dos Indios del Nuebo Mex[co]. que aquel Gobernador embió á descubrir la comunicacion de aquellas Provincias con el Presidio de San Savá, 1763. A. G. I., Mexico, 92–6–22.

Expediente, Sobre establecimiento de Misiones en la inmediacion del Presidio de Sn Savas. En 122 fs. Texas. Año de 1763. Sn Saba: Gov.[or] D.[n] Ph.[e] Ravago. N. 2, Dup[do]. A. G. M.

Rafael Martínez Pacheco to Guardian Fr. Gaspar de Solis. Presidio de San Agustín de Ahumada, May 26, 1764. A. C. G., M, leg. 5.

Rafael Martínez Pacheco to the viceroy. San Agustín de Ahumada, July 22, 1764. A. C. G., M, leg. 5.

Testimonio de los Autos fhos por el Govnor de la Provincia de Texas contra Rafael Martinez Pacheco, Año de 1764. B. A., Adaes, 1756–1766.

Papeles pertenecientes al Orcoquiza, 1764. A. C. G., M, leg. 5. Gives account of work done at the missions by Pacheco, Fray Bernardino, Fr. Luis Joseph Dolores Salvino, and Fray Antonio Álvarez.

Testimonio de la Declaracion Que hizieron los principales Yndios de la Nacion Orcoquiza ante Dn. Marcos Ruiz sobre lo qe en ella refiere. Año de 1765. L. P., no. 192.

Testimonio de Diligencias comenzadas en San Agustín de Ahumada y continualas en este preso. de los Adaes por el Govor de esta Prova. de Texas contra el capitan Don Rafael Martínez Pacheco, Año de 1765. B. A., Béxar, 1751–1769.

Testimonio de dilixᵃˢ. practicadas sobre la debolucion que hizo de Antº. treviño el capitan principal de la nacion tagui, 1765. B. A. Province of Texas.

1766–1770

Autos y diligᵃˢ. fhas pʳ. el Coronel Dn. Diego Ortiz Parrilla Sre. las sircunstancias de la Isla de los Malaguitas q. communᵗᵉ. han llamado Isla Blanca, 1766. A. G. M. Historia, 396.

Diligencias practicadas por el Coronel Don Diego Orttiz Parrilla en que da punttual notticia de la Isla de los Malaguitas [Culebra], 1766. A. G. M. Historia, 396.

La Fora, Nicolás, Relación del Viaje que de orden del excelentissimo Señor Virrey Marqués de Cruillas Hizo el Capitan de Ingenieros. Dn. Nicolas de la Fora en Compañia del Mariscal de Campo Marqz. de Rubi, 1766–1767. Biblioteca Nacional, Mexico.

Oficio Al Virrey de Nueva España, ordenandole determine con la brevedad posible la causa pendiente en su Govierno sobre lo ocurrido en el Presidio de Ahumada entre el Capitan de él, y el Governador de la Provincia de los Texas con el motivo que se expresa; y que dé cuenta de sus resultas. December 15, 1766. A. G. M., Reales Cédulas, vol. 236, 1766.

Cargos, que en Vistta de las Declaraziones Juradas, rezividas a la Compañia del Presidio de los Adaes, September 23, 1767, and related documents pertaining to the inspection made by the Marqués de Rubí. A. G. I., Guadalajara, 104–6–13.

Solís, Gaspar José, Diario qᵉ. hizo el Padre Fr. Gaspar Jose de Solis en la Visita que fué a hacer de las Misiones de la Provincia de Texas, por orden y mandato del M. R. P. Guardian Fr. Tomas Cortez, y del Santo Venerable, Discretorio del Colegio de Ntra Señora de Guadalupe de la ciudad de Zacatecas el Año de 1767. A. G. M., Memorias de Nueva España, vol. XXVII, 248–297.

Oficio Al Virrey de Nueva España, ordenandole substancie, y determine con la mayor brevedad, y asesorandose con el Visitador Dn. Joseph de Galvez, la causa pendiente en su Tribunal sobre los exesos que se atribuyen á Dn. Angel Martos de Navarrete, Governador de la Provincia de Texas, y que actue el Proceso en la forma que se expresa. April 21, 1768. A. G. M., Reales Cédulas, vol. 92, p. 221, 1768, no. 128.

1771–1780

Expediente sobre proposiciones del Governador de Texas Baron de Ripperdá, para ereccion de un Nuevo Precidio, y Emprender una cruda Guerra contra los Apaches Lipanes, hacienda Alianza con las Naciones del Nortte. 107 folios. The papers included cover the years 1771–1773. A. G. M., Historia, vol. 51.

Testimonio del expediente formado á instancia de la parte del Capitan Don Raphael Marttin.ᵉ Pacheco, Capitan del Presidio de Sn. Agustín de Ahumada sobre los merittos, que se expresan haver adquirido en dho. Presidio. A. G. M., Correspondencia de los Virreyes, second series, Bucareli, vol. 7, 1772, f. 123, del 368.

Expediente sobre la dolosa y fingida paz de las Naciones del Norte; y comercio ilicito de los Franceses de la Nueba Orleans. 1772–1775, A. G. M., Historia, vol. 93.

Autos que se han introducido por los Vecinos del Presidio de los Adaes, Sobre que les deje ávecindar en el de la Mision de los Ais, y establecimto. del Pueblo de Nuestra Señora del Pilar de Bucareli. 22 folios. The papers fall within the years 1773–1774. A. G. M., Historia, vol. 51.

Quaderno que Corresponde para el completto del Expediente señalado con el Numo. 1 remetido con fecha 31 del proximo pasado Marzo del corriente año. 53 folios. The papers fall within the years 1773–1774. A. G. M., Historia, vol. 51.

Expediente Sobre que al Vecindario del Pueblo de Ntra. Señora del Pilar de Bucareli se le destine Parroco, por cuenta de la Real Hacienda. 21 folios. The papers are dated 1775–1779. A. G. M., Historia, vol. 51.

Expediente Sobre Comercio Reciproco entre las Provᵃˢ de la Louisiana y Texas: havilitacion de un Puerto en la costa de esta: ampliacion de limites de la primera estendiendolos hasta el Rio de Sabinas y otros puntos incidentes, 1776–1790. A. G. M., Provincias Internas, vol. 182.

Representacion del Justica de la Poblacion de Nuestra Señora de Pilar de Bucareli; Sobre livertad de Diezmos para aquellos Moradores. 10 folios. The correspondence falls within the period 1777–1778. A. G. M., Historia, vol. 51.

Los Vecinos del extinguido Presidio, y Poblacion de los Adais, hasta el Numero de Sesenta y tres, que sin establecimiento alguno se hayan agregados al de San Antonio de Bèxar, y Villa de San Fernando; Sobre que atendiendo al infeliz estado, en que han quedado, por haber abandonado sus Casas y Tierras; y á [la] fidelidad, con que han servido, y estan, prontas, á continuar sirviendo a S. M. en aquella Fronttera, se les conceda por el Señor Governador en Gefe, Comandante General algun establecimiento para que puedan Subsistir con sus Familias. 32 folios. The papers fall within the period 1778–1779. A G. M., Historia, vol. 51.

1780–1792

Expediente sobre el abandono del Pueblo de Nuestra Señora del Pilar de Bucareli: Quaderno 5º. 53 folios. Period covered, 1778–1780. A. G. M., Historia, vol. 51.

Expediente sobre el abandono del Pueblo de Bucarely, y establecer Comercio con los Yndios Gentiles del Nortte. Quaderno 6º. 46 folios. Period covered, 1780–1782. A. G. M., Historia, vol. 51.

Morfi, Fray Juan Agustín de, Memorias para la Historia de Texas Escritas por el R. P. F. Juan Agustin de Morfi, Lector Jubilado de la Provincia del Sto. Evangº. de Mexico (*ca.* 1781). Bancroft Collection, University of California. The references in the footnotes are to the translation of this MS which I am editing for publication.

Vial, Pedro, Diario que por la gracia de Dios, comienso á hacer desde este Presidio de San Antonio de Bejar hasta arrivar al de la capital Villa de Santa Fe por Comision de mi Governador Don. Domingo Cavello, Governador de la Provincia de los Texas, con expression de las Jornadas desde el dia 4 de Octubre de 1787 [1786]. Santa Fé, July 5, 1787, A. G. M. Historia, vol. 62.

Mares, José. Viaje ó descubrimiento de Camino desde la Capital del Nvo. Mexico a la de la Provincia de Texas, hecho pr. el Cavo de Ymbalidos Jose Mares. San Antonio, October 19, 1787. A. G. M. Historia, vol. 62.

Mares, Jose, Derrotero y Diario que comprende el numero de Leguas que hay desde la Capital de San Antonio de Bejar Provincia de los Texas hasta la de Santa Fe del Nuevo Mexico, que hago Yo Jose Mares Cabo Ymbalido de la Compañia de ella pr. los terrenos que conducen los Yndios Amigos Cumanches, para descubrir camino en derechura. Santa Fé, April 21, 1788. A. G. M. Historia, vol. 43.

Fernández, Santiago, Derrotero diario y Calculacion de leguas que hago Yo el abajo firmado (Santiago Fernandez) en descubrimiento desde esta Santa Fé a los Pueblos de humanes por orden superior del Sor Gouernador Dn. Fernando de la Concha, á conducion y guia de Pedro Vial. Santa Fé, December 16, 1788. A. G. M., Historia, vol. 43.

Consulta del Sor. Commandante Gral. de las Provas. de Oriente sobre solicitud que han hecho los Yndios Horcoquisac, Atacapaces, Vidais, y Cocos, pidiendole se establesca la Mision de. Orcoquisac: sobre que se separe del empleo de Tente. de Governador á Don Antonio Gil Ybarbo, etc. 1788, A. G. M., Historia, vol. 93.

Fragoso, Francisco Xavier, Derrotero, Diario y Calculacion de Leguas, que en descubrimiento por derecho desde esta Provincia del Nuevo Mexico hasta el Fuerte de Nachitoches y la de los Texas, de orden Superior voy á practicar en Compañia de Dn. Pedro Vial comisionado á este proposito, yo el abajo y á lo ultimo firmado (Francisco Xavier Fragoso). Villa de Santa Fé veinte y quatro de Junio de mil setecientos Ochenta y ocho. Santa Fé, August 20, 1789. A. G. M., Historia, vol. 43.

Memorias de Nueva España. Compiled in 1792 by Father Francisco Figueroa. 32 vols. A. G. M., Historia, vols. 1–32. Vols. XXVII and XXVIII are entitled ''Documentos para la Historia Eclesiástica y Civil de la Provincia de Texas,'' libros I and II.

INDEX

Cemetery Hill, site of Candelaria, 228.

Cerda, Francisco de la, soldier at San Xavier, 236–237.

Cerralvo, Nuevo León, question of moving garrison, 163, 166, 169, 171; settled, 287; aid asked from, 170; colonists from, 295.

Cerrogordo, presidio, 384.

Chamacuero, 287.

Chambers County, settlement in, 346.

Chanas River. *See* Llano.

Chapa, José Florencio, commander at Mier, 297.

Chapuis, French trader in New Mexico, 67, 68; sent to Spain, 71.

Charcas, Las, sends soldiers for Parrilla's campaign, 89.

Charles, Joseph Antonio, soldier at San Xavier, 266.

Chartres, Fort. *See* Fort Chartres.

Chavira, Father Bruno, at N. S. de la Luz, 74; death of, 75, 348, 353, 364.

Chayopines, Rancho de, 131.

Chihuahua, 126.

Chitimacha, Indians, 36.

Church, policy regarding baptism, 319; administration at Bucareli, 418–423. *See* Missions.

Cíbolo, Arroyo del, ranch, garrison, and settlement on, 29, 108, 111, 114–115, 384, 392, 430.

Coahuila, 2, 30, 58, 89, 107, 109, 110, 171, 268, 347, 354.

Coahuiltecan, tribes, 3; language, 96.

Coapite, tribe, 3, 281–283.

Cocay, Yatasí chief, 121.

Coco, tribe, 3, 45, 49, 54, 55, 60, 148, 154, 156–158, 166, 199–200, 202, 213, 216, 232, 234, 260, 261, 264, 272, 281, 283, 286. *See* Caocosi, Caoque.

Colleges *de Propaganda Fide*, administration of, 12. *See* Guadalupe, Santa Cruz.

Colonies, civil, asked or planned for, 43, 129, 171, 179, 207, 247, 274, 275, 342; urged by Altamira, 309; lack of, 352; founded in Nuevo Santander, 57–59, 294. *See* Families, Settlers, Colonization.

Colonization, methods, 299, 342, 344, 351.

Colorado River, 3, 63, 72, 81, 130, 382.

Comal Springs, mission for suggested, 264, 266; founded, 273–278. *See* New Braunfels, Guadalupe River.

Comanche, tribes, 3, 4; relation to French advance, 66, 67, 68; hostility to Apache, 79, 93, 121, 127, 379, 381; minerals in country of, 81, 82; troubles with, 87, 88–91, 107, 109, 117, 119, 396, 424, 432–438; alliance and trade with Taovayas, 90, 121; proposal to Christianize, 268; mentioned, 31, 126, 132, 407; De Mézières among, 123. *See* Evéa.

Comandante general, of the Provincias Internas, 385.

Commerce, 329, 331, 336, 417, 418, 426. *See* trade.

Concepción. *See* Nuestra Señora de la Concepción.

Index

Gálvez, Bernardo de, governor of Louisiana, 124, 127.

Gálvez, José de, *visitador general*, 103.

Ganuza, Father, with Father Solís at Rosario, 321.

Ganzábal, Fray José, missionary in Texas, 15; sent to Mexico to promote San Xavier missions, 48, 49, 185, 187, 195–196, 200, 204; murder of, 54, 260–262; at San Xavier missions, 223, 231, 233, 235, 248, 259.

Garcés, Fray Francisco Hermenegildo, 127.

García, Fray Anselmo, missionary at N. S. de la Luz, 367.

García, Fray Bartolomé, at S. F. de la Espada, author of *Manual*, 3, 96, 232, 235, 257, 273; aids in founding Guadalupe mission, 276.

García, Fray Diego Martín, writings of, 15, 96; career of, 15, 191; work at missions, 60, 80, 260, 304, 306.

García, Father, at Los Ais, 295.

García, Father, at Camargo, 314.

García Larios, Francisco. *See* Larios.

Garabito (Garavito), Joseph, testimony regarding English, 105.

Garcitas River, mission on, 5; site of La Salle's colony, 283.

Garza, Father José Francisco de la, missionary at Bucareli, 118, 419–423, 432, 435, 439, 441; at Nacogdoches, 119; among Xaraname, 424–425; founds mission Refugio, 421.

Garza, Juan Diego de la, at San Xavier, 224, 267.

Garza, Manuel de la, soldier at San Xavier, 267.

Garza Falcón, Blas María de la, founds Camargo, 295; ranch at Corpus Christi, 301.

Garza Falcón, Joseph de la, expedition to coast, 105.

Garza Falcón, Miguel de la, sent to San Xavier, 261.

George, Elias, French trader, arrested, 337.

Geotes, tribe, 154.

Gil y Barbo, Antonio. *See* Ybarbo.

Giraud, Diego, merchant in Mexico, agent for Miranda, 83; for Barrios, 75, 351, 354.

Goliad, founded, 58, 296; mission remains at, 318. *See* Bahía del Espíritu Santo.

González, Capt. Diego, leads colony to Nueces River, 58, 296; death of, 296.

González, Ensign José (later Lieut.), commander at Adaes, 33, 114; retirement proposed, 386; removes Adaes settlers, 387; death of, 114, 391.

González, Fray Joseph, at San Antonio, 15.

González, Fray Juan Joseph, missionary at Espíritu Santo de Zúñiga, 304, 305–306.

Gordo, El, Orcoquiza chief, 333, 341, 348, 350, 351, 363.

Government, policy regarding commerce, 418; of Nuevo Santander, 300. *See* Administration.

[483]

Index

Languages, Indian, 285.
Laredo, San Agustín de, mission, at Camargo, 295.
Laredo, Villa, founded, 59, 297, 300, 301; population, 299, 300; importance of, 301; horses stolen, 411.
Larios, Governor Francisco Garcia, 8, 64, 180–182.
La Salle, Robert Cavelier, Sieur de, 283, 364.
Lavaca Bay, 5, 56.
Layssards, the, French traders, 123.
Leal, sent to Mexico, 25.
Legros, Jean, arrested, 37.
León. See De León.
Letas, tribe, 360.
Linares, colonists from, 295.
Lipan, tribe, 3, 27–32, 127; trouble with, 29, 79; treaty with, 79; at missions, 86, 93–94, 95; Rubí recommends exterminating, 108. See Apache, San Sabá, Comanche.
List, of governors, 8; of missionaries, 15, 367; of soldiers at San Xavier, 247–248, 266–267.
Little River. See San Andrés River.
Llano (Chanas) River, 130; Apache on, 3; battle on, 110; minerals on, 31, 79–83; explorations near, 80–82. See Los Almagres.
Llera, villa, 295.
Lobanillo, El, ranch of Ybarbo, 113–114, 131, 388, 424; settlers remain at, 114; fugitives return to, 393; plan to reoccupy, 400; settlers go to Bucareli, 415–416.

Loco, El, creek, mission on suggested, 167, 169.
López, Father Joseph, at San Xavier missions, 54, 238, 248, 256–257, 260, 263, 267, 270; explores in San Sabá country, 80–81.
López, Father, with Solís, 321.
Loreto, Nuestra Señora de (See Bahía) presidio, moved, 58, 59, 285.
Los Almagres, mines, discovered, 80–83. See Llano River.
Losoya, Sergt. Antonio, arrests Legros, 37.
Louisiana, boundary, 32–41; cession of, 102–133, 364, 377; trade with cut off, 38–40; occupation by Spain, 102–103, 120; traders from in Santa Fé, 67; forces strengthened, 69, 70; communication with New Spain, 127–128. See Border, Boundary, French.
Lugar, founded by Escandón, 298.
Lugo. See Franquis de Lugo.
Macarty, Chevalier, claims part of Texas for France, 364.
Madison County, 406.
Maize, 335, 337.
Malaguitas, tribe, 97.
Malaguitas Island, explored, 104–106.
Maldonado, Francisco, at San Xavier, 267.
Maldonado, Juan Antonio, among Bidai, 336.
Mallet Brothers, expedition to New Mexico, 66–67.
Manos de Perro, tribe, visited by Father Molina, 15.
Manufactures, 417.

Marenti, Fray Joseph, at N. S. de
la Luz, 367.

Mares, Corporal José, exploration
of, 129–130.

Mariano, Father Fray. *See* Dolores y Viana.

Martín, Alejando, accompanies
Mares exploring party, 129.

Martín, Joseph Manuel, at San
Xavier, 267. *See* Martínez.

Martín, Pedro, at San Xavier,
267.

Martínez, Joseph Manuel, at San
Xavier, 248, 275.

Martínez, Joseph María, at San
Xavier, 267.

Martínez, Mario, at San Xavier,
267.

Martínez Pacheco. *See* Pacheco.

Martos y Navarrete, Angel de,
Governor, 8, 74; activities on
lower Trinity, 76, 112, 354–357;
quarrel with Pacheco, 368–372;
policy regarding Apache, 88–91;
reports French plot, 362; boundary dispute, 364; becomes governor of Coahuila, 347; trial of,
372.

Masse, M., petition to settle in
Texas, 359–360.

Matagorda Bay, tribes near, 281–
283. *See* Bahía del Espíritu
Santo.

Mateo, Orcoquiza chief, 333, 335,
341, 351.

Mathe, Nicolas de la. *See* La
Mathe.

Mayeye, tribe, 3, 44, 142, 145–
149, 165, 183, 248, 423; at San
Xavier missions, 50, 150, 186,

190, 198, 213, 230; in mission
on Guadalupe River, 273–276.
See Pablo.

Mazapil, 82, 83.

Mazo Calderón, Ignacio Joseph de,
treasurer of *Caxas Reales*, 244.

Mediavilla y Azcona, Melchor de,
defends mission plan, 46, 147,
167–169.

Medina River, boundary at, 1,
292; plan to move settlement
to, 286.

Medina, Roque de, *ayudante inspector*, 108, 385, 400, 409, 410.

Meghty, tribe, 145.

Melenudos, tribe, 147.

Menardville, site of San Sabá
settlement, 86, 93. *See* San
Sabá.

Menchaca, Capt. Louis Antonio,
at San Antonio, 271.

Menchaca, Marcos, at San Xavier,
248, 266.

Méndez, Joseph Marcos, at San
Xavier, 267.

Mescalero, tribe, 27, 127.

Mesquite, tribe, at San José, 99.

Mexico, archives of, 281. *See*
New Spain.

Mezquía, Fray Pedro Pérez de, in
Sierra Gorda, 289–290.

Mier, *Lugar* de, founded, 58, 297;
ranching opposite, 299, 300.

Miera y Pacheco, Bernardo, explorations of, 127.

Miler, Bautista, English castaway,
425, 426.

Militia, of Bucareli, 412, 413.

Mill Creek, site of Santa Rosa,
350.

Minchaca (Menchaca), Marcos.
See Menchaca.

Index

Mines, reports of and search for in Llano River country, 31, 42, 43, 79–83; discovery of Los Almagres, 80–83, French interest in mines of Coahuila, 68–69; in Nuevo Santander, 300.

Miranda, Bernardo, exploration on San Jacinto River, 75, 333–335, 350; explores Los Almagres mines, 81–82; map and report of, 334, 346, 350, 361.

Missionaries, work among Indians, 3, 14–21, 27, 44, 47, 49, 52–53, 191, 287, 295, 310, 324, 367, 419; difficulties with secular authorities, 13, 20–27; prominent missionaries, 14–15; expeditions by, 14–16; martyrs among, 15; list of, 15; duties of, 62; writings of, 96, 142; hospital for, 174–175; pay of, 299. *See* names of individual missionaries, as follows: Abad, Alaña, Amaya, Anda, Andrés, Angeles, Aparicio, Aponte, Aranda, Arquellos, Aristorena, Arricivita, Baños, Botello, Calahorra, Camberos, Caro, Casañas, Casos, Castellanos, Chavira, Cypriano, Dolores, Domínguez, Escalante, Escovar, Espinosa, Flores, Frías, Ganzábal, Ganuza, Garcés, García, González, Hernández, Hierro, Hurtado, Laba, López, Marenti, Mezquía, Molina, Morfi, Montalbo, Náxera, Olivares, Ortiz, Palou, Parras, Peredes, Peña, Pinilla, Pita, Prado, Ramírez, Romero, Santa Ana, Santiesteban, Satereyn, Sáenz, Silva, Solís, Soto, Terreros, Thoribio, Trinidad, Vallejo, Valverde, Varaona, Varela, Velasco, Vergara, Ximínez, Ysasmendi.

Missions, purposes, methods, and administration, 10–13, 84, 109, 310, 311, 316, 323, 348, 365, 366; as industrial schools, 10–11; political functions, 10–11; secularization, 12; described, 5, 10, 21, 95, 97–100, 303; industrial life, 19–21, 98–100; guards, 22–24; difficulties with Indians, 10–11, 16–17, 21, 24, 44; Indian attacks on, 49, 94, 87; discords with secular authorities, 20–27; work of in general, 16, 19, 50, 95–96, 97, 100; work at different missions, 43–45, 49, 50, 53, 62, 74, 78–80, 84, 86, 94, 109, 111, 113–119, 303–315, 332, 421–423; success at San Antonio, 18–21; failure in eastern Texas, 100–102, 107; criticised by Altamira, 309; gift to by Terreros, 84. *See* Missionaries, and names of individual missions, as follows: Adaes, Ais, Alamo, Aranama, Bahía, Espíritu Santo, Guadalupe, Laredo, Nacogdoches, N. S. de la Candelaria, N. S. de la Concepción, N. S. de Guadalupe, N. S. de la Luz, N. S. de Loreto, N. S. de los Dolores, N. S. del Refugio, N. S. del Rosario, N. S. del Soto, San Antonio, S. Antonio de Valero, S. Bernardo, S. Francisco, S. Ildefonso, S. Joaquín, S. José, S. J. Bautista, S. J. Capistrano, S. Lorenzo, S. Sabá, S. Xavier.